MARKETING
STRATEGY AND STRUCTURE

DAVID J. RACHMAN

Bernard M. Baruch College
City University of New York

PRENTICE-HALL, INC., Englewood Cliffs, New Jersey

Library of Congress Cataloging in Publication Data

Rachman, David J
  Marketing strategy and structure.

  Includes bibliographical references.
  1. Marketing. I. Title.
HF5415.R235   658.8   74-689
ISBN 0-13-558338-1

Printed in the United States of America

10 9 8 7 6 5 4 3 2

Prentice-Hall International, Inc., *London*
Prentice-Hall of Australia, Pty. Ltd., *Sydney*
Prentice-Hall of Canada, Ltd., *Toronto*
Prentice-Hall of India Private Limited, *New Delhi*
Prentice-Hall of Japan, Inc., *Tokyo*

Contents

iii

Preface

As a person interested in the practice of marketing, I have attempted to direct this book to a segment of the market. The market, as I visualize it, is made up of those who are interested in a relatively compact book for a one-semester or one-quarter course. In these eighteen chapters I have attempted to condense marketing by leaving out the endless details that appear in other books. In this manner I was able to cover pricing in one chapter, selling in part of another, and products in only one. Since whole books have been published on each of these chapter topics one can easily imagine that a great deal of editorial prerogative was exercised. Nevertheless I believe that a student interested in an introductory explanation of the marketing field will find the coverage sufficient.

Though the book follows what is considered to be the traditional approach, the compactness of the text still allowed me to treat some developing areas separately, the chapter on *Marketing Planning* being one and the section on *Consumerism* another. In addition, to supplement the chapters I have included twenty brief cases to allow the student to practice his marketing knowledge. To further reinforce the knowledge so gained, this text can be used in conjunction with a specially prepared workbook.

As in my previous book, *Retail Strategy and Structure,* I have elected to take the management approach in my presentation and choice of material. The decision to include or exclude material was made on the basis of whether it would be of importance to those involved in making top level marketing decisions.

I would like to thank the many people who have contributed their time and talents, especially Professor George Frey of C. W. Post for the forecasting material; Stan Hoff of Abraham and Straus for the material on consumer behavior; and I. Harold Kellar, Chairman of the Marketing Department of Baruch School of

Business Administration, for his supplying many of the aids and in particular, for establishing a pleasant working environment. Professor Barry Berman, Hofstra University; Professor John Sullivan, North Shore Community College; and Professor David T. Wilson, Pennsylvania State University, deserve acknowledgment for their help in reviewing the manuscript. In conclusion, I would also like to thank my secretary, Thelma Weil, for many hours of work on the manuscript.

DAVID J. RACHMAN
Great Neck, New York

MARKETING AND
DECISION MAKING

I

In this first section one is introduced to marketing as an activity concerned with the movement of goods from the producer to the consumer. Aside from an enumeration of these activities, one is presented with our major concern — how managers make decisions and the procedure they must perform in order to make profitable decisions.

The following chapters cover this aspect of their job, starting with an introduction in Chapter 1, and followed by an introduction to management decision making in Chapter 2 and marketing planning in Chapter 3. The latter chapter is particularly important, since management must plan all activities if they are to be successful. Chapter 2 outlines all the considerations that are discussed in the chapters throughout this book.

Chapter 4 is concerned with the various restraints on decision making, mostly consumerism, but including competitive and legal barriers.

Marketing:
An Introduction

1

SUMMARY KEY

Marketing is the function that involves itself with the management of the flow of goods and services from producer to the ultimate consumer.

Implied in this definition are certain functions being performed by management. These functions are collecting marketing information, developing marketing plans, determining the product mix, communication activities, and the management of physical distribution activities.

Although firms have been performing marketing functions for many years, their attitudes toward the performance of these functions have changed, and, in fact, one can divide marketing history into three distinct periods – the product-oriented period, with its emphasis on lowering the costs of production; the sales-oriented period, when scarcity was no longer a problem and products were sold through a strong sales effort; and the marketing concept period, when the firm was organized in such a manner so as to know the needs of the consumer before the product was produced.

Several reasons brought about the development of the marketing-concept approach aside from the growing abundance of products. These were population shifts, a changing income distribution pattern, and growing technological abilities that create new products and new ways of doing things.

In summary, the marketing concept calls on the company to make only what it can sell. Two views prevail: (1) all product planning and line operations should be oriented toward the consumer, and (2) the firm should attempt to attain a profitable sales volume, which indicates that the firm will only produce products that can be sold at a profit.

The marketing sequence that illustrates the activities a firm engages in when marketing a product includes developing research information concerning a needed product, developing the product, developing a marketing plan, a distribution plan, and a promotional plan, and, finally, coordinating the product for sale to the consumer.

Marketing costs from 35 to 59 cents of each dollar the consumer spends. In spite of these high costs, the United States has attained the highest standard of living in the world.

Yet marketing has been severely criticized for being unproductive, for being excessively costly, and for creating products that people do not desire.

As a consumer, you are well aware of the attempts of manufacturers of products to sell you merchandise. Television programming, as you are sometimes painfully aware, seems to consist of an endless presentation of commercials with the programs "sandwiched in between." During an average day, the potential consumer must be exposed to hundreds of messages received through reading billboards, transit and newspaper ads, plus radio and television commercials.

Although to the viewer of the ads, they seem to represent a kaleidoscope of messages, the receiver should be aware that all these messages represent a part of a carefully thought out strategy of the marketing department of a firm. In other words, the firm advertising a product has put a great deal of effort and thought into presenting or communicating the virtues of its product to the public.

It is the purpose of this book to examine the efforts of the marketing department of a firm to determine how they make those decisions.

Specific Product

In offering an initial example of the depth of the planning and decision making that goes into the marketing of a product, one could choose hundreds of examples. One interesting marketing program that can give us great insight into the many decisions and alternatives marketing management can select from is that of the Magnavox Company, a major manufacturer of television sets and other radio and electronic products.

Magnavox sets are sold in most cities in America. As a general rule, they are only found in one store in small cities, and limited to just a few retail outlets in larger metropolitan areas. In any case, Magnavox sets are not found in every store that sells television sets. They are only sold in what one calls franchised outlets. Magnavox has maintained an image of a quality product — and thus commands a premium price.

Magnavox sells its products directly to retailers, and does not use the services of a wholesaler. Retailers who carry the Magnavox line must maintain prices and are not allowed to engage in discounting. During specified periods of the year, Magnavox retailers are allowed to run sales, but only at prearranged prices. In a most recent year, Magnavox accounted for 7 percent of television set sales.

In direct contrast to Magnavox is Radio Corporation of America (RCA), another major producer of television sets. This firm sells to practically all retailers, and, as a result, their product can be found in most any type of retail outlet. RCA makes no attempt to franchise dealers exclusively, as does Magnavox.

RCA as a matter of policy sells its sets through wholesalers who carry a full line of all RCA products. No attempt is made to maintain retail selling prices by RCA, and sales and discounts can be offered by the retailers at any time. RCA, although attempting to maintain an image of quality, cannot maintain the retail price of its product. However, RCA accounts for the sale of 37 percent of all television sets in the country.

An interesting aspect about both of these companies is that RCA has been the major supplier of tubes for the Magnavox television set. In fact, therefore, an important part of the Magnavox set is produced by a competitor.

Why do two competitive firms marketing a product aimed at the same market, the user of a television set, use totally different approaches to reaching this market? It is the goal of this book to give the reader insight into the reasons behind the varying decisions made by the manufacturer of a product.[1] The choice of alternatives represents decision making in American business at its highest level.

Before proceeding, one should define marketing and consider the functions it performs.

Marketing is the function that involves itself with the management of the flow of goods and services from the producer to the ultimate consumer.

Implied in the definition is knowledge of what the *consumer wants* and certain *tasks* that are varied and directed. In Chapter 2 we discuss the tasks of marketing and what marketing management is and what it does. Right now one should become acquainted with the functions marketing involves and the current marketing philosophy, referred to as the *marketing concept.*

Marketing Defined

Marketing, as noted in the definition, is concerned with all the functions that are engaged in producing and selling a product that fills a need of the ultimate consumer. To accomplish this, marketing breaks down more or less into several activities. These activities include:

Functions of Marketing

1. *Collecting marketing information.* In the performance of this activity, management collects information on both a formal and informal basis concerning the consumer's needs. The goal of this function is to determine the needs of the consumer, assessing his ability to pay and his behavior related to the purchase of the product or service.

2. *Developing marketing plans.* Establish a detailed plan of what is to be sold, forecast its potential sale, determine to whom it is to be sold, and state steps to accomplish these goals. The plan must be in complete agreement with the objectives specified by the firm.

3. *Determining the product mix.* This includes the initiation of new products, a review of the older products, and deciding on the need for accompanying services. Included in this function is the determining of a proper price for the product.

4. *Communication activities.* Included here one finds the sales-force management, advertising, displays, and all efforts to communicate the product's attributes to the consumer. Advertising includes the management of all media (television, newspaper, radio, billboards, etc.) and all sales promotion activities, which may include costs of promotion, public relations, and all other forms of direct-to-consumer activities.

5. *Engaging in the management of physical distribution activities.* Here one is concerned with two major activities. The first is the choice of ways of marketing the firm's products through institutions, such as retailers, wholesalers, or direct to the consumer. The other major management activity involves the actual movement of

---

[1]Cases 6 and 15 in the Appendix deal specifically with Magnavox.

goods through a handling process that includes the choice of transportation (carrier) and a determination of warehousing and storage needs.

Although some firms may place greater stress on one aspect over another, it is likely that practically all manufacturers involved in marketing a product engage in performing all these functions. More will be said on the sequence of these functions later.

Broad Role of Marketing

In the past 10 years there has developed a growing awareness that marketing as a field of study is also applicable to fields other than business problems. For instance, government bodies have become aware of the use of marketing techniques in putting across their message to the public. Nonprofit institutions have begun to understand that marketing tactics can help them promote their missions. One of the most dramatic is the role that advertising has been playing in the growth and awareness of cigarettes as a cause of cancer and pulmonary problems, sponsored by many of the associations in the cancer, heart, and tuberculosis fields.

An excellent example of the use of marketing in government is the recent move on the part of the states of New Jersey and New York to promote state lotteries to pay for the high cost of government. It is known that by 1971 the state lottery in New Jersey was much more successful in reaching its dollar goal than the state of New York. The reasons offered were many; however, it is becoming obvious that New Jersey had established a better marketing plan through superior outlets (such as using computers to sell tickets in major stores) and a superior pricing policy by selling tickets in smaller denominations than in New York. It is the opinion of some experts that New Jersey was able to reach a larger market by using this plan. In recent years New York has started to adjust its marketing approach.

Candidates for public office have been relying more on developing what can be called a marketing strategy to bring to the voters their platform in the most favorable manner. Most campaigns use some of the tools of marketing, such as advertising and promotion. In addition, candidates at all levels are concerned with the voter (consumer) and gain much of their knowledge about the voters through commissioned polls. Polls have been playing a major role in campaign planning, and actually influence the decision of many potential candidates to run.

In a book entitled *The Selling of the President*[2] the author indicated that the then candidate Nixon was merchandised and promoted much like one would a product. He pointed out that the Nixon strategy included many staged in-studio interview shows, which consisted of partisan audiences. Throughout the campaign the candidate held very few press conferences, and relied mainly on television as a means of getting his message across to the public.

It is apparent to most that marketing is becoming an important subject of study and understanding in areas other than business.

Market Organization and the Marketing Concept

For the past 50 years, American firms have been performing all the previously mentioned functions to some extent. However, the whole attitude toward the overall management of the marketing functions has changed. The history of marketing is divided into distinct periods of time — the production-oriented, the sales-oriented, and the marketing-concept periods.

---

[2] J. McGinniss, *The Selling of the President* (New York: Trident Press, 1969).

The production-oriented period involves a time span beginning with the growth of major industry in the United States, at approximately the beginning of this century, to about 1940.

The production-oriented period placed great emphasis on unit costs and the firm's ability to produce such products at a lower cost. Great stress was placed on increasing efficiency through application of techniques that would result in increasing productivity, and thereby reduce the cost of production. Famous names were associated with this movement, the most notable being Frederick W. Taylor, Henry L. Gantt, and Frank and Lillian Gilbreth.

Their work became so well accepted in the 1920s and 1930s that the "efficiency experts" using their methods were criticized because of their alleged treatment of workers as automatons.[3] In a sense this period was characterized as a time of product scarcity.

Beyond 1940 and following World War II the economy entered a period where products were less scarce. Firms were faced with finding markets for their output. During this period of time, the firm usually made a decision to produce a product. Then an attempt was made to sell the product. The sales force was charged with the task, and the whole organization's emphasis was on the ability of the sales force to produce sales. As a matter of philosophy, the firm was sales oriented. Figure 1-1 demonstrates the typical organization chart for the product- and sales-oriented firm. Note, for instance, that manufacturing handles all product planning and servicing. Finance and accounting are charged with making forecasts and controlling costs.

With the continued emphasis on selling, many firms found that what was produced was not always what was needed or wanted by the consumer. Well into the end of the 1950s it became apparent to many firms that an organizational

Organization Chart of Product- and Sales-Oriented Firm   FIGURE 1-1

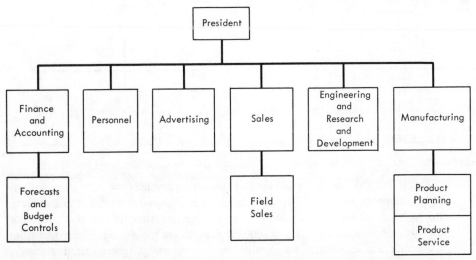

Source: G. F. Mackenzie, "How to Make the Marketing Concept Make Sense," *Industrial Marketing,* March 1960, p. 58.

---

[3]W. W. Haynes and J. L. Massie, *Management: Analysis, Concepts and Cases,* 2nd ed. (Englewood Cliffs, N.J.: Prentice-Hall, Inc., 1969), p. 7.

change had to take place. The reasons were many. Perhaps the most important reason was that consumers were rapidly reaching a point where their basic needs were being fulfilled by our mass-production capacity. Moreover, the typical family had more discretionary income available and a wider choice of places to spend it. Thus a family may buy different products, or may choose to spend money for services (nongoods) such as travel, education, insurance, and medical care.

This development brought about the third period, which was concerned with the finding of new markets and the development of an organization that could deal with these new economic conditions. In effect, it was recognized that the firm must organize in such a way so as to be aware at all times of the consumer's needs. This view, particularly the reorganization of the marketing department, became known as the *marketing concept.* It is best understood in terms of its overall focus on the consumer and his needs. With this emphasis, the firm has taken more interest in marketing information, product development, and planning. As a matter of fact, marketing planning has become one of the central points in the largest corporations, and almost all other activities are built around it.

FIGURE 1-2   Modern Organization Chart with an Integrative Marketing Approach

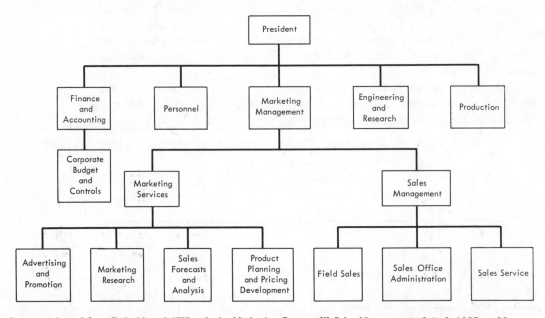

Source: Adapted from E. B. Marpel, "What Is the Marketing Concept?" *Sales Management,* July 5, 1957, p. 35.

Figure 1-2 indicates a typical *present* marketing organization with its approach. When compared to Figure 1-1, one can see the changing role of marketing. Note should be made of the location of the various departments. All the marketing activities are located under the marketing department's direction. Under this title, one now finds product planning, sales service, plus sales forecasting. Previously, they were under the control of the accounting or manufacturing divisions. Also, one finds the marketing research department, whose function will be detailed later.

Finally, advertising and promotion are also included under the marketing manager. The people charged with performing these functions no longer report directly to the firm's president.

With the marketing activities coordinated under one manager, all other supporting activities, such as finance, personnel, engineering, and manufacturing, can be coordinated.

The various periods of development of the marketing function can be seen in The Pillsbury Company. During the first period of its development the company was production oriented. As noted by one observer, the formation of the company came about because of the availability of wheat and the proximity of water power and not from the proximity of growing major markets or demand for less-expensive and more convenient flour products.[4] Although the latter was a consideration, the founder of the company placed great emphasis on production, as seen in the following statement:

> We are professional flour millers. Blessed with a supply of the finest North American wheat, plenty of water power, and excellent milling machinery, we produce flour of the highest quality, our basic function is to mill high-quality flour, and, of course (and almost incidentally), we must hire salesmen to sell it, just as we hire accountants to keep our books.[5]

In the second era of the firm the company, although still strongly production oriented, became what has been described in Figure 1-1 as sales oriented. Here the firm became aware of the thousands of grocers and wholesalers who moved their products. In essence, the company became aware of the fact that the dealer was a vital link in getting the product into the consumer's home.

Here again the philosophy can be summed up in a quote:

> We are a flour-milling company, manufacturing a number of products for the consumer market. We must have a first-rate sales organization which can dispose of all the products we can make at a favorable price. We must back up this sales force with consumer advertising and market intelligence. We want our salesmen and our dealers to have all the tools they need for moving the output of our plants to the consumer.[6]

Pressures for Change

The pressure to reorganize the marketing department, and thereby create a greater emphasis on the marketing concept as a way of conducting the firm's business, is caused by several major considerations. All these considerations can be characterized as changes that our society is constantly undergoing. For it is *change* that causes most of the problems that business must face. Change as such is not bad, but it does threaten the very existence of products that firms have developed

---

[4]R. J. Keith, "The Marketing Revolution," *Journal of Marketing,* Jan. 1960, p. 36.

[5]*Ibid.,* p. 36.

[6]*Ibid.,* p. 36.

and rely on. For instance, if people suddenly prefer to shop by car, this could create several distribution problems for a manufacturer of apparel, since his outlets would have to be in areas where parking was available. Even services such as banks and cleaning establishments would have to consider drive-in operations in order to cultivate these markets. Some of the major changes and considerations that have

TABLE 1-1   Center of Population[a]: 1790 to 1970

Year	North Latitude			West Longitude			Approximate Location
	°	'	"	°	'	"	
1790	39	16	30	76	11	12	23 miles east of Baltimore, Md.
1850	38	59	0	81	19	0	23 miles southeast of Parkersburg, W. Va.
1900	39	9	36	85	48	54	6 miles southeast of Columbus, Ind.
1950	38	50	21	88	9	33	8 miles north-northwest of Olney, Richland County, Ill.
1960	38	35	58	89	12	35	In Clinton County about 6½ miles northwest of Centralia, Ill.
1970	38	27	47	89	42	22	5.3 miles east southeast of the Mascoutah City Hall in St. Clair County, Ill.

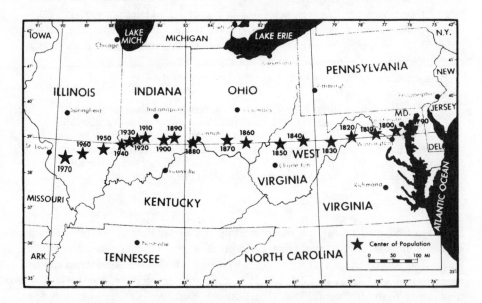

[a]"Center of population" is that point which may be considered as center of population gravity of the United States or that point upon which the United States would balance if it were a rigid plane without weight and the population distributed thereon with each individual being assumed to have equal weight and to exert an influence on a central point proportional to his distance from that point.

Source: *Statistical Abstract of the United States* (Washington, D.C.: Government Printing Office, 1971), p. 7.

forced companies to constantly adjust through the process of greater consumer orientation are:

1. Population shifts and growth. In Table 1-1 one sees the shift of the total U.S. population in a westward direction. Presently, the population center of the United States is in western Illinois not far from the border of Missouri. The shift of population has caused companies to move their outlets and promotional activities in this same direction. In addition, this same population has increased substantially by an average of somewhere around 2.5 million annually. This change has caused the development of markets for products that never existed before.

As the population grows, it is possible to find very narrow markets for goods with enough people to support them. For instance, one firm found enough of an interest among this huge population in the game of chess to support a magazine devoted to this market.

Pillsbury was faced with a similar challenge with the development of new cake mixes and the sudden realization that the firm through research and development could produce literally thousands of new products. The firm for the first time was faced with the necessity of selecting the best new products.

To accomplish this, the firm soon realized that they needed an organization that would establish company criteria for selecting which new products would be made and distributed. The basic criterion it was soon learned had to be the housewife. As a result, the firm was one of the first to establish the brand manager, whose major responsibility was to see that products were developed that appealed to this housewife. Marketing under his direction begins and ends with the consumer. Marketing under this system plans and executes the sale, all the way from the product idea through its development and distribution. All new product ideas develop only after careful study of the consumers' wants and needs.[7]

2. Changing income distribution. The income changes of the population have also affected the need for the typical firm to stay close to changes in markets throughout the country. The past two decades have witnessed substantial increases in family income. These income increases have been brought about by several factors, the major one perhaps being the increase in the number of working housewives.

Along with the increase in income has been the growth of discretionary income, that is, income that can be spent for luxury items. This has allowed the family to make choices among the growing variety of products without affecting expenditures for necessities. The increase in these expenditures has widened considerably the variety of choices the consumer can make.

Closely related to changing income patterns has been a change of the typical family's attitude toward going into debt. The family today is more prone to go into debt to obtain some good that cannot be purchased out of present income. The gradual increase in installment credit as a percentage of disposable personal income can be seen in Figure 1-3. This figure indicates clearly that the ratio of credit to income has increased substantially from early post World War II to the present.

Here again one can identify a pattern that increases the consumers' choices of goods and services.

---

[7]*Ibid.,* p. 37.

FIGURE 1-3 Credit as Percentage of Income

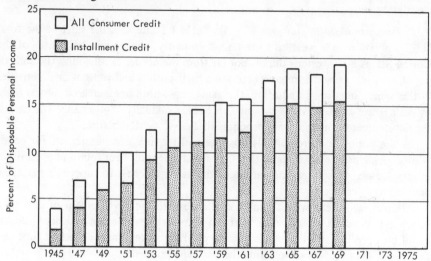

Source: *The Guide to Consumer Marketing, 1970* (New York: The Conference Board, Inc., 1970), p. 108.

3. Technological changes. Technological changes that occur in our economy have several effects on marketing. First, they can result in the development of new products that may increase the potential market of a firm. Second, they serve as a disruptive factor, in that research and development expenditures tend to reduce the monopolistic tendency of a firm's product position.

The size of research and development expenditures in various industries can be seen in Table 1-2. One should note that approximately 4 percent of all sales are spent on research and development. In some industries this figure may be exceeded substantially. In all cases these expenditures result in the marketing of an endless flow of new products, which may force a company to constantly monitor the consumer.

Simply spending money on research and development does not guarantee that a company will be successful. This is best illustrated by the experience of the Bristol-Myers Company, where between 1964 and 1971 10 new products failed. The list includes Fact and Vote toothpastes; Resolve (a competitor of Alka-Seltzer); Adulton cough medicine; Trig deodorant; Score hair preparation; That Look shampoo; First, hand lotion; Dynalife, a men's hair preparation; and Duramex, an analgesic.[8]

Marketing Concept Defined   The marketing concept in essence calls on the company to make only what it can sell. It reverses the previous logic that the task of marketing is to sell what the company makes.[9] In a sense, therefore, the marketing concept is a managerial philosophy and organizational structure that centers on the desires of the consumers.

---

[8]Fred Danzigs, "Bristol-Myers Turns Out Parade of Clinkers," *Advertising Age,* Aug. 2, 1971, p. 1.

[9]Philip Kotler, "Diagnosing the Marketing Takeover," *Harvard Business Review,* Nov.–Dec. 1965, p. 70.

12

The marketing concept, therefore, provides a direction to the total system of action by the manufacturer by integrating all the various departments of the business to accomplish the firm's objectives. Since the marketing manager is closest

Research and Development Patterns in American Industry, 1965   TABLE 1-2

Expenditures

	As Percentage of Total Sales	Total Amounts ($ million)	Federal Funds ($ million)	Federal as % of Total
Food and kindred products	0.4	150	1	1
Textiles and apparel	0.4	34	a	a
Lumber and allied products	0.5	13	0	a
Paper and allied products	0.7	70	0	0
Chemicals and allied products	4.2	1,377	190	14
Industrial chemicals	4.6	928	147	16
Drugs and medicines	5.9	268	a	a
Other chemicals	2.3	181	a	a
Petroleum products	1.2	435	69	16
Rubber products	1.9	166	25	15
Stone, clay, and glass products	1.6	119	4	3
Primary metals	0.8	216	8	4
Fabricated metals	1.4	145	17	11
Machinery	4.1	1,129	258	23
Electrical and communication equipment	9.4	3,167	1,978	62
Communication and components	12.2	1,912	1,253	66
Other electrical	7.0	1,255	725	58
Motor vehicles and equipment	3.1	1,238	326	26
Aircraft and missiles	28.0	5,120	4,500	88
Instruments	6.2	387	125	32
Other manufacturing	0.7	67	1	2
Nonmanufacturing	a	359	255	71
All industries	4.3	14,197	7,759	55

[a]Not shown separately but included in the total.
Source: Adapted from W. G. Shepherd, *Market Power and Economic Welfare* (New York: Random House, Inc., 1970), p. 205.

to the consumer, much of this internal coordination and planning must necessarily fall upon his shoulders.

The marketing concept is based on two fundamental views. The first is that all product planning and line operations should be line oriented toward the consumer. This means that not only should marketing be deeply committed to producing goods that are aimed at meeting consumer needs, but other departments within the firm, such as finance, production, and engineering, must accept this philosophy.

The second basic view is that the firm will engage in attempting to attain a profitable sales volume. By definition, this means that the firm will only try to produce products that can be sold at a profit, since they meet a consumer need.

To accomplish this, the firm must integrate all the above departments, since all are vital in developing these products.

Acceptance of this philosophy means that all personnel in the firm must become more marketing oriented. It means, for instance, that the accountant, the production manager, the engineer, the shop foreman, and the advertising executive must take into consideration the consumer in making most of their decisions.

For instance, a decision by the production department to reduce the cost of a product by reducing the package size must be made on the basis of its impact on the consumer rather than internal cost requirements, as a first step.

The overall differences between the marketing-oriented and the production-oriented viewpoints are spelled out in summary form in Table 1-3. Perhaps the clearest distinctions between these two views can be seen in the area of *packaging*. Here the production view is one of seeing packaging as a shipping and protection device, a rather common approach. Conversely, the marketing-oriented view thinks of packaging as a sales tool. That is, the package helps sell the product by enhancing its appearance and making it more attractive at the point of sale.

As this table implies, the acceptance of the marketing concept is an acceptance of a focus on profit and growth opportunities. These growth opportunities do not have to necessarily be at the expense of traditional competitors. They can be in new markets, as noted in this quote:

> When a company sets out to increase its sales, . . . by the application of research and insight to the task of creating new markets — indeed, new businesses — then we know that we are dealing with a management that has fully embraced the marketing concept.[10]

One cannot say without contradiction that all U.S. companies do not face production problems today. There exist a number of industries that have had such problems. For instance, the color television field had perhaps 10 years of production problems before finally perfecting a color set that would remain relatively repair free. Although the demand for color television would be enormous in view of the sale of black and white television sets, it took years for the industry to overcome production and technical problems that would deliver such a product.

---

[10]J. B. McKitterick, "What Is the Marketing Management Concept?" in F. M. Bass, *The Frontiers of Marketing Thought* (Chicago: American Marketing Association, 1957), pp. 77–78.

TABLE 1-3 Some of the Essential Differences between Production- and Marketing-Oriented Organizations

Business Element or Function	Characteristics		Organizational Effect or Viewpoint
	Marketing-Oriented	Production-Oriented	
Top authority	Consumer considerations dominate	Company considerations dominate	*Marketing:* Marketing personnel in highest-level executive positions *Production:* Production and engineering personnel in highest-level executive positions
Product line	Broad	Narrow	*Marketing:* Making and selling what will sell *Production:* Selling what we make
Organizational arrangement	Decentralized	Centralized	*Marketing:* Organization chart tends to have fewer levels with more product rather than function heads. Staff functions more proliferated. More horizontal jurisdiction *Production:* Organization chart emphasizes levels of authority which flows vertically. Strong centralized staff activities with emphasis on control
Objectives	External influences dominate	Internal influences dominate	*Marketing:* Goals more long-range. More emphasis on strategy and planning *Production:* Goals more short range. More emphasis on efficiency and method
Research	Market research	Technical research	*Marketing:* Heavy in analytical research *Production:* Heavy in scientific research
Financial	Emphasis on market price rather than cost	Emphasis on cost rather than selling price	*Marketing:* Thinks in terms of what customer will pay, how competition will react *Production:* Thinks in terms of how to do things well and cheaply

Business Element or Function	Characteristics		Organizational Effect or Viewpoint
	Marketing-Oriented	Production-Oriented	
Product development	Suggestions stem from customer needs and whims	Suggestions stem from functional performance and cost improvements	*Marketing:* Sales and market testing *Production:* Laboratory testing
Product design	Style and appearance prime considerations	Performance and applications prime considerations	*Marketing:* The stylist dominates *Production:* The engineer dominates
Packaging	Viewed as sales tool	Viewed as shipping and protection device	*Marketing:* Chief concern is advertising and sales-promotion effectiveness *Production:* Chief concern is engineering materials-handling and packaging machinery
Manufacturing	Flexibility in production	Production less flexible	*Marketing:* Everything starts with determination of market opportunity *Production:* Everything starts with what production is able to produce

Source: Ferdinand F. Mauser, *Modern Marketing Management* (New York: McGraw-Hill Book Co., 1961), pp. 10 and 11.

The U.S. space program also represents an industry that has encountered numerous technical and production problems. Although much of the theory and mechanics of building space apparatus is presently known, the delays in developing such equipment are caused by production problems.

In the future many production problems have to be overcome in order to meet the needs of our society. For instance, the increased public interest in producing a pollution-free automobile has spurred industry research to develop such an engine. At this stage, one can see that many years of solving production and engineering problems lie ahead, for in the view of many scientists the gasoline engine is still the most efficient way we have today of propelling automobiles.

On the other hand, most industries have the capacity to produce all kinds of products if they can find a market for them. Hence the interest in the marketing concept as a way of conducting the firm's business.

To better understand the importance of the marketing concept to the firm, one should consider the sequence of marketing activities. Figure 1-4 illustrates the sequence of events that most firms engage in when marketing a product. The six-stage cycle involves a complete circle of events that starts and ends with the consumer.

The Marketing Sequence

The Marketing Sequence   **FIGURE 1-4**

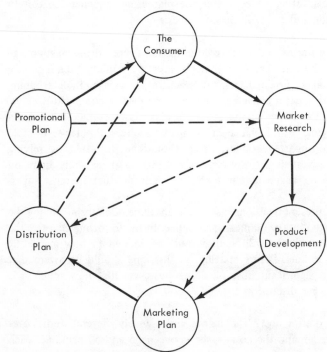

Source: Adapted from Gordon Medcalf, *Marketing and the Brand Manager* (Elmsford, N.Y.: Pergamon Press, Inc., 1967), p. 3.

The initial stage requires that management develop information that relates the needs of the consumer to a product that can be produced. Thus H. J. Heinz Company determined that their well-established name could be used on all kinds of food products. As a result, they decided to enter the soup market with the Great American Soups – a premium product priced substantially above the dominant soup producer, the Campbell Soup Company. The information concerning the possibility of a premium-priced soup was obtained through marketing research. This development triggered the marketing sequence to the stage of product development, which resulted in the planned production of the Great American line of soups.

Simultaneously, as Figure 1-4 indicates, other plans in the sequence are underway. The information derived from performance of the research function is being used to (1) develop a marketing plan, (2) develop a distribution plan, and (3) develop a promotional plan. All these activities are conducted under the marketing manager and represent a coordinated effort to produce and launch a salable product. The last step in the marketing sequence involves total coordination to market the product to the consumer, thus closing the sequence.

Of course, marketing does not stop here. The firm, through research, is constantly monitoring these products to determine whether or not changes must be made. Thus the addition of other kinds of products to the present line would call for a further recycling of the marketing sequence, and the same procedure would be followed.

In summary, the marketing concept and the marketing sequence are closely related in that they begin and end with the consumer.

The Marketing Sequence and Decision Making

Although the marketing sequence represents the steps most firms must engage in, it does not explain the role that management plays in completing the sequence and forging its continuance. For management is constantly engaged in determining the steps to be taken to meet a consumer's needs or to meet a competitive move. The role that each of the stages in the sequence plays is in essence based on a decision by management. For instance, a company such as Procter & Gamble determines that its toothpaste product, Crest, should be marketed by relying heavily on television advertising. Conversely, Campbell Soup may rely more on their ability to command a substantial space for their product in most supermarkets.

These differences represent decisions made by management, choosing among the many alternatives dictated by the marketing sequence. In the following chapters the steps in the marketing sequence will be discussed and related to how marketing management makes decisions. Before starting on this, one should be aware that marketing represents a significant cost of doing business. Just how much is a question that requires some discussion.

The Cost of Marketing

How much does marketing cost? The answer varies widely. Several studies over the years have been made, and the costs range between 35 and 59 cents per each dollar spent.[11] Fifty cents of every dollar spent goes for marketing is an often-quoted amount.

---

[11] Stanley Hollander, "Measuring the Cost and Value of Marketing," *Business Topics*, Summer 1961, pp. 12–22.

Table 1-4 gives an indication of the cost of marketing in the food field, where the average family spends approximately 25 percent of their total dollar.

Here one sees two food products, meat and cereal, contrasted. In the case of meat, an analysis of a breakdown of the costs involved in bringing the product from the farmer to the consumer seems to indicate that of each dollar spent by the

Distribution of the Consumer Food Dollar (Retail Store Purchases, 1963)   TABLE 1-4

	Meat ($)	Cereals ($)
Farm value	0.59	0.22
Food manufacturing	0.11	0.48
Purchased transportation	0.03	0.05
Wholesale costs	0.06	0.07
Retail costs	0.21	0.18
Total	1.00	1.00

Source: Adapted from G. A. Marple and H. B. Wissmann, eds., *Grocery Manufacturing in the United States* (New York: Praeger Publishers, Inc., 1965), p. 274.

consumer 41 cents is charged to either the cost of distribution or manufacturing. Careful examination of the data shows that 30 cents is directly chargeable to marketing costs (retail, wholesale, and transportation). In addition, one can conclude that part of the 11 cents of the cost attributed to food manufacturing also is part of the cost of distribution, and the balance is perhaps directly chargeable to manufacturing processes involved in readying the meat for the wholesaler. The farmer in this case receives 59 cents for the meat he brings to the marketplace.

Cereal, a widely advertised product, shows a similar pattern. From a payment of only 22 cents to the farmer, the wholesaler, retailer, and transporter account for over 35 cents (or 35 percent) of the total product. Manufacturing costs in this case, however, are 48 percent of the total selling price.

The high manufacturing costs in the case of cereal would seem to indicate that the food manufacturer engages in performing many more functions than the meat processor. In particular, the food manufacturer will no doubt spend substantial money in advertising and packaging the cereal product.

One must conclude that marketing costs represent a considerable proportion of the total selling price of a product. The next logical questions are: Is it worth it and are these costs necessary?

The answer to the first question is obvious, in that it is undisputed that the American consumer has the highest standard of living in the world. In essence, what this means is that the U.S. economy delivers more goods per dollar of worker income than any competing economy. This would seem to indicate that the U.S. technology delivering these goods to the mass markets is efficient. Thus the costs represent productive inputs into the economy.

However, one should be aware that the competitive nature of the U.S. economy tends to force less efficient firms to change or perhaps become insolvent. That is, firms operating inefficiently or incurring unnecessary costs tend to decline over the long run if they do not make an adjustment, since they are performing functions at an unnecessarily high cost.

An excellent example of this happening can be found in the history of the variety store since World War II. Well into the 1950s the variety store was primarily situated in the downtown area of practically every major U.S. city. Most numerous were the national chains, such as F. W. Woolworth, Kresge, W. T. Grant, J. J. Newberry, and a host of others. It was widely recognized that the variety chain was one of the most *inefficient* distributors of manufactured goods, since as late as 1957 these stores required a higher markup than full-service department stores. About that time the apparel discount house came into being and attracted many of the variety-store customers. In addition, the location of the variety store became less profitable since the downtown stores began expanding to the suburban areas of most major cities. It became apparent that the variety-store customers had shifted elsewhere and perhaps were doing a great deal of their shopping in the new suburban department stores. At this point, the variety store was either headed for bankruptcy or was forced to yield to its more efficient competitor, the discounter — a group that was operating at almost half the cost of the variety store. The variety store did react — by establishing its own discount stores and closing the downtown stores wherever possible. During this period and up to the present, stores such as Woolco (Woolworth) and K mart (Kresge) were started and represented a dramatic contrast to the earlier high-cost, less-efficient downtown variety store, which had been forced to become more efficient and thus deliver goods to the consumer more efficiently and at a lower cost.

Criticism of Marketing

In spite of the high standard of living in the United States and its accompanying material benefits, marketing during the past decade has undergone severe criticism. It is a growing view among certain segments of our society that simply delivering a high standard of material goods is not all good.

Several of these criticisms are dealt with in our discussions of consumerism and advertising. However, it is worthwhile at this point to recognize some of these arguments. They usually fall into the following categories:[12]

1. Marketing is unproductive. This concept has developed from making a comparison with the production division of manufacturing. Production by definition changes the form of goods, from perhaps a raw material to a finished product. This of course strikes one as productive work in the sense that it changes the character of the goods.

The answer to this argument lies in the fact that marketing creates intangibles; that is, it offers goods place, time, and ownership utility.

Place utility is created by the transportation function. Thus a dress hanging in a manufacturer's showroom in New York has much less value than the same dress hanging in a department store in Salt Lake City, ready for sale. This difference is created place utility.

---

[12]For an excellent detailed summary of these criticisms, see R. R. Gist, *Marketing and Society* (New York: Holt, Rinehart and Winston, Inc., 1971), pp. 26–41.

Time utility is created in that a product that is not needed at this particular time has less value than a product that is available at a needed time. Thus toys sitting in a warehouse in April are more valuable in terms of timing in December for the Christmas buying season. Time utility is created by the storage function and is particularly valuable when there exists an imbalance between production and consumption.

Ownership utility is created through the advertising and other promotional activities of the firm that attempt to get the goods into the hands of consumers that need them.

Ordinarily, the creation of form utility is considered the major contribution of production. However, with the growth of product development in many firms, this activity is shared with marketing in that they may engage in making changes in the product attributes, such as the recent move by the makers of Brillo to add more soap to their product.

2. Marketing costs are excessive.   As noted previously, marketing costs can be a considerable fraction of the total cost of a product. This criticism is difficult to answer in the sense that if one accepts the premise that marketing does provide needed services and performs needed economic functions, as noted previously, then the issue becomes one of determining whether or not these functions are performed efficiently or not.

The answer lies somewhere between two extreme views.

3. Marketing creates products that people do not need.   When one examines the myriad of products that the consumer is presented with, one can easily arrive at this view. One could well wonder why the public needs to be presented with perhaps 10 different brands of products, when one meeting government standards could easily do.

The fact that the public is questioning many of these new products and, for instance, the packages that they are wrapped in is evidence enough that marketing must undergo a serious reconsideration of many of its previous practices. It is noteworthy, however, that the development of consciousness on the part of marketing firms has come about through a desire to satisfy the consumer.

In addition, one could easily argue that with the tens of thousands of products on the market, and the freedom of choice on the part of the consumer, only a foolish manufacturer would make a product that the consumer neither needs nor wants.

Of course, one could argue that through advertising and promotional manipulation one could persuade the consumer to buy something he doesn't want or need. Although this may be true in many instances, it is also equally true that many products are not advertised. For example, most apparel firms spend very little on advertising, and one would be hard pressed to name more than a handful. One could also argue that in many cases (particularly food products) the ability of advertising to persuade one to buy what is not needed is rather limited.

It is assumed that our present economic system awards those that reach a certain level of efficiency and penalizes those that do not. The variety store experience (see p. 20) would seem to support this view. Overall, however, one would assume that the costs of these functions are needed and wanted by consumers.

SUMMARY

Marketing is concerned with the flow of goods from the producer to the ultimate consumer. The functions performed can be viewed as following a sequence, starting with the consumer and ending with the consumer. Steps in the sequential flow include marketing research, product development, the marketing plan, the distribution plan, and the promotional plan. The concentration on the consumer indicates that the marketing department subscribes to the marketing concept; that is, they produce products that are consumer oriented, in contrast to an earlier period when products were produced and then the firm's effort went into selling. This is of particular significance when we consider that marketing accounts for 35 to 59 percent of the price that the consumer pays.

QUESTIONS

1. Why is it important to study marketing?
2. How does the consumer-oriented firm differ from firms in previous years?
3. What functions does the marketing department perform?
4. How does the organization function differ in Figure 1-2 from that outlined in Figure 1-1?
5. What is meant by the marketing sequence?
6. What is the importance of the marketing sequence?
*7. Table 1-4 indicates that the retailing costs of meat are 21 cents, whereas the retailing costs of cereal are 3 cents less. Why?
8. Why has marketing become so interested in the "marketing concept"?
9. It is estimated that marketing cost ranges from 35 to 59 cents of the total dollar spent by the consumer. Is this cost too high?
10. Shouldn't the production department determine the products a firm will make?
11. In Figure 1-1, under the old concept Finance and Accounting were responsible for forecasts and budget controls. How and why is this changed in Figure 1-2?
12. In producing a new product, a firm proceeds through the steps identified as the "marketing sequence." Does this procedure occur once or twice? Why?
13. Must all steps be followed in the marketing sequence?

*In-depth question.

Management
Decision Making

2

SUMMARY KEY

Firms selling similar products may approach the marketing of such products differently. This indicates that companies put stress on different marketing tools. The decision to use different marketing tools in essence represents marketing management.

Management refers to the performance of various functions – determining the objectives of the firm; planning, which includes developing strategies and tactics; organizing and coordinating activities; staffing and assembling resources; operating and directing the firm; and analyzing and evaluating performances based on measurements.

Objectives of the firm include the grand design and the more specific objectives. The specific objectives are of major concern to the operating objectives and are usually presented in the form of sales volume, market share, and profit targets.

Sales include setting sales goals and meeting these goals and engaging in sales analysis, which may include making growth comparisons with either the industry or other firms in the same industry.

Market share of an industry is watched, as any slippage may indicate a failure on the part of management. In some industries market-share data are not available.

Profits are measured as a ratio of sales from year to year. The most closely watched ratio, however, is return on investment, which indicates how efficiently management is spending its money.

Once a firm has established its objectives, it then makes plans as to how these objectives will be achieved. By choosing among the many alternatives, management engages in decision making.

What do managers make decisions about? They make decisions about the goods and services to be offered, the communication with the potential customer, and the physical distribution of the product. These three major areas are called the *marketing mix* or the *marketing effort*. These three areas are also important in that they are controllable by management.

The determination of the mix that is best suited to the firm is governed by the environment. This environment includes the consumer, competition, legal forces, and social pressures. These are uncontrollable. Marketing information is a force that

23

feeds back information to management concerning many aspects of its environment.

Most decisions that are made in a firm are routine and made in the natural course of the business. However, major decisions require a great deal of study and the consideration of endless alternatives. By attaching probabilities to many of the most promising alternatives, one can actually quantify some decisions.

In performing the last function of management, that is, establishing controls, the firm can use the specific objectives as a means of measuring the firm's performance. These would include share of the market, sales, and profits. Just as important would be the firm's interest in making expense comparisons with other industry firms.

The contrast between Magnavox and RCA illustrated in the first chapter tells us several things about marketing departments of firms. The first is that firms selling similar products may approach the marketing of the product in a different manner. In the case of Magnavox, the product is sold directly to the retailer, whereas in the case of RCA the product is sold through wholesalers or distributors. Similarly, Revlon sells cosmetics through retail outlets, while Avon, the largest cosmetics firm in the country, sells directly to the home.

In addition, firms put a greater stress on different steps in the marketing sequence. Thus Wrigley's supports its chewing gum products with a strong advertising campaign. In contrast, the Hershey bar is sold by putting strong emphasis on price, distribution, and packaging with little national advertising.

All this indicates that companies put stress on different marketing tools. In a sense the procedures a manufacturer follows represent a very deliberate and carefully thought out way of reaching a market. In essence, this is marketing management. In the following sections we shall discuss this important aspect of marketing; what is marketing management, what does it do, and what does it decide?

Management

Managing any type of business enterprise involves performing several important functions. Although the listing and depth of the functions referred to may differ, the basics remain the same. Management performs the following functions:

1. Determines the objectives of the firm.
2. Plans including strategies and tactics (decision making).
3. Organizes and coordinates the firm's activities.
4. Staffs and assembles other resources.
5. Operates and directs the firm.
6. Analyzes and evaluates performances based on measurements (control).

These functions are performed by managers whether they are running a $100 million corporation or a charitable organization such as the Red Cross.

In the pages that follow, all these functions will be discussed. However, the second function, *planning,* will be elaborated on in Chapter 3, due to its importance as the center point for all corporate strategy and budgeting operations.

Determining the firm's objectives represents the first major function of management. It also happens to be the most important. For once management clearly spells out the firm's objectives, they, in effect, offer the lower echelons of the organization the necessary guidelines to function day to day. For example, if management is concerned with gaining a substantial share of a high-quality sportswear market, the advertising director will have a clear picture of the types of magazines that he can run his advertising in. Additionally, he also has guidelines as to the type of advertising copy he will write. Without these guidelines, he would find it difficult to make these decisions.

Firm objectives usually take two forms: they are (1) the broad basic objectives of the firm and (2) the more specific objectives of the firm. Most operating people in the firm are interested in the specific objectives, since they are usually set in quantitative form. Thus a firm may have as a goal a profit margin of 10 percent of sales, or a return on investment of 20 percent.

Nevertheless, the specific objectives of the firm must be within the broad context of the firm's basic objectives.

Although marketing represents an important part of the business enterprise, it is concerned mainly with activities that deal with the customer. Finance, personnel, and manufacturing are concerned with other operating aspects of the firm. As noted in the previous chapter, it is the goal of top management to coordinate all these activities in such a way that the firm meets the needs of the customer and thereby earns an adequate profit.

To better coordinate these activities, the firm must establish broad objectives that offer the various departments guidance in making many other decisions. These objectives, referred to by one author as the *grand design* of the firm, precede all marketing, financial, personnel, or manufacturing plans or goals.[1] They are a necessary prelude to any specific merchandising or financial plans a firm may make.

The importance of clearly stating the firm's grand design or objectives can be seen in the following hypothetical situation. Suppose that you were asked by a magazine publisher to write an article on traveling for a forthcoming issue. What would you write? Could you accomplish this (assuming you have traveled a great deal) within a short period of time?

The answer to these questions is clearly based on the type of magazine that asks you. For example, if a photography magazine asked you to write such an article, the article would include mostly pictures of your travels, and a limited amount of actual writing. On the other hand, if a magazine that caters to children asked you to do the same thing, the article would be quite different. If the article was commissioned by a consumer-oriented magazine, it would require still another slant.

The point of this is to indicate that each business enterprise should have a clear statement of objectives, so that the various management groups within the firm can guide their responsibilities in the proper direction.

The grand design need not involve a complicated and long statement of all the thoughts that occur to top management. It may for example be a fairly simple

---

[1]C. H. Granger, "The Hierarchy of Objectives," *Harvard Business Review,* May–June 1964, p. 64.

Determining the Objectives of the Firm

Broad Objectives

statement of fact. For instance, a firm engaged in marketing mechanical sealing devices described its objectives or grand design as "stopping the leaks around the world."[2] As strange as this statement may seem, it clearly spelled out the firm's intent and indicated the world scope of this intention.

Conversely, the Mark Cross Company, a Fifth Avenue leather-goods store catering to high-income groups, stated its broad objectives in this manner.[3]

I. Objectives of the Mark Cross Company Unpublished Paper, by Phyllis G. Winkler, former treasurer of the firm, 1964.

A. *Market Which We Will Serve*

1. To conduct a leather-goods specialty store.

2. To concentrate our efforts towards the customer in the upper-middle or higher income group.

3. To serve the customer who recognizes and is willing to pay for superior quality.

4. To operate a main store at 55th Street and 5th Avenue, a mail order business and such additional branches as deemed advisable by the Board of Directors (outlined in F objective).

B. *Merchandise*

1. To concentrate and emphasize and guard zealously the leather-goods classifications which, throughout the competition of more than a hundred years, have earned for Mark Cross a distinguished and unique place in the retail world.

2. To provide the highest standards of quality, both in merchandise and service.

3. To be active in the creation or selection of new distinctive styles, functional designs and new items. This will be in line with our history and background as the store which discovered the "wrist watch" and the "thermos bottle" in America.

4. To provide the best in design, material and workmanship and function at the best possible price (this price will be relatively high).

C. *Service*

1. To provide our clientele with the finest service available in any retail establishment. These facilities will also include the maintenance of the merchandise we sell, for as long as it is in existence.

D. *Personnel*

1. To employ in our organization, from "maintenance" to our "Board of Directors," those people who are qualified to carry on the traditions of our company.

E. *Management*

1. To provide management whose main goal is perpetuation of our company and its tradition in a competitive society.

2. To provide management whose goal is an adequate return on the capital invested by our shareholders.

F. *Growth*

1. To constantly seek, investigate and develop additional outlets or branches for the distribution of our merchandise. Growth objectives can

---

[2]*Ibid.*, p. 68.

[3]D. J. Rachman, *Retail Strategy and Structure* (Englewood Cliffs, N.J.: Prentice-Hall, Inc., 1969), p. 20.

be developed only if they are consistent with the quality standard objectives of our business.

G. *Sales Promotion and Advertising*

    1. To demonstrate to the public that not only is Mark Cross the finest leather-goods store in the world, but that Mark Cross has interesting and exciting items which are not necessarily expensive.

    2. To develop Fifth Avenue traffic who may become acquainted with the store.

    3. To generate an attitude among our salespeople and staff of excitement, interest, and enthusiasm.

    4. To re-emphasize the role of Mark Cross as an innovator.

    5. To make it clear that in our promotion of novelty items we are not in conflict with our basic philosophy of quality.

The objectives as stated by the Mark Cross Company make it clear to those entrusted with selecting the firm's merchandise the type and quality of goods that can be inventoried in this firm. One would surely not consider purchasing dollar plastic wallets; nor would one consider buying low-priced leather goods for sale. If one would agree that the firm would spend most of its monies on high-quality, unusual leather products, the statement of the objectives of the firm have accomplished their purpose, that is, to serve as a guideline to the executives in the business.

Whether the firm spells out its objectives in either of these two ways, certainly they must meet two major criteria: they should be realistic in terms of (1) the internal resources of the firm, and (2) the external environment of the firm.[4] For example, if the firm sets a goal of a certain percentage of earnings, it must consider the present business cycle (which may be in a recession) in making this an operating objective. The internal resources of the firm are always a major consideration in setting any objectives or goals.

In essence, the firm that establishes a clear set of corporate objectives will more than likely avoid misdirected effort among the firm's various departments. Once the objectives have been established, the various departments can then set their budgets and plans for the coming year or years.

Since the marketing department is the major business-getting division of the firm, a substantial part of the burden of reaching these objectives falls upon them.

The flow of management procedure from that of establishing the grand-design objectives of the firm into developing a strategy based on their expectations, resources, and needs is depicted in Figure 2-1. Here one sees the development of strategies based on many factors. When the firm creates a strategy that does not meet one of the criteria, it may arrive at a "no go" decision. This results in management reconsidering its strategies and eventually in the development of a well-planned strategy that meets the internal restraints or controls management has set for the firm. Eventually, management will develop a strategic plan that they believe will help them achieve the goals. From this strategy management is then in a position to develop lower-level operational goals. Meeting the operational goals of the firm is the basis for most of the activity among the lower management levels during the planning period.

---

[4]Granger, *op. cit.,* p. 68.

FIGURE 2-1 Strategy Cycle

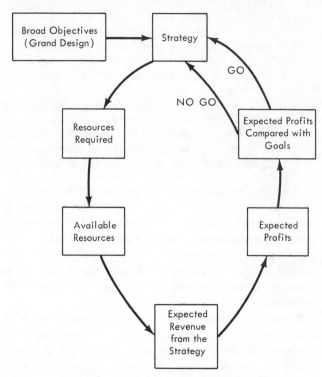

Source: Adapted from D. J. Luck and A. E. Prell, *Market Strategy*
(New York: Appleton-Century-Crofts, 1968), p. 8.

Perhaps an example would clarify these differences. Should a firm desire
to increase its sales volume in the coming year by 10 percent, management may
decide that the only way this can be accomplished is by increasing the number of
stores carrying the firm's product lines. Thus the strategy becomes one of trying to
accomplish this during the forthcoming planning period.

To carry this out, the firm establishes an operational goal of getting each
salesman to open up one new account a month until 500 new stores are now
carrying the firm's product. This now clearly shows the salespeople what they must
accomplish in the coming year.

Of course, if the strategy of opening up new accounts is not feasible (for
instance, there may not be many new stores that are not carrying the product),
then the firm must rethink its strategy and set different operational goals.

Operating
Targets
Although the policy of the firm may be spelled out in general terms, eventually
the executives in the firm must specify the objectives of the firm in rather specific
ways. Thus, although the company may pursue a quality market, it may determine
to obtain 50 percent of that market. That would represent a rather specific target
or goal for the marketing department. In other words, the objectives of the firm
become a goal for those charged with meeting the objectives of the company. How

they will meet these objectives becomes the task of those charged with planning. This aspect will be considered later. What specific targets do companies set for the marketing staff? The major goals include

1. Sales volume.
2. Market share.
3. Profits.

Sales Volume

Since sales represent one of the key goals of the marketing firm, a measurement of sales growth is usually considered to be a specific objective for many firms. For instance, a firm may have as a target for the coming year a 10 percent annual increase in its sales volume. As will be noted later in a section on forecasting, this 10 percent increase may be based on a carefully considered examination of both the industry and economic conditions for the coming year.

At some point the firm makes a forecast of sales and then, at some later point, examines the results to determine what happened. Prediciton of sales-volume increases are filled with problems, as one can see from the lists of results presented in Table 2-1. In this group, one finds a listing of some of the firms in the top 500 in the United States. The sales-volume changes range from a massive 22.8 percent decline for General Motors, a modest decline of 0.1 percent by E. I. du Pont, to a substantial gain by Westinghouse of 22.9 percent.

Several comments can be made about these changes. First, of course, is that the increases ranged widely and no pattern seems to have developed. As a matter of fact, most of the sales increases are illusory in that they are a result of inflationary price increases. Thus only a few of the firms were able to increase the physical volume of the firm.

Second, upon close examination there are explanations for some of the decreases and increases that occurred. For example, the sharp decline by General Motors was due to a strike. The increase by Westinghouse was due to acquisitions rather than an actual increase in sales volume from its present operations. During this same period, Westinghouse's number one competitor, General Electric, showed a sales revenue rise of only 3.3 percent.

Sales Analysis

Aside from viewing a year-to-year sales comparison in determining whether or not a firm has reached its stated goals, many firms engage in sales analysis in great depth. Sales analysis is a term that usually describes the attempt of the marketing department to analyze sales changes in greater depth than simply a year-to-year comparison.

Figure 2-2 compares the growth rate over a 7-year period of the Heublein Company, a liquor producer and distributor. Note that the firm has increased its sales at a rate twice that of the liquor industry and more than twice the increase in the gross national product. This indicates to management that the firm is beating its competition.

TABLE 2-1   Sales Volume of the Top 33 U.S. Firms

Rank 1970	1969	Company	Revenues ($000,000)	Change Over 1969 (%)
1	1	General Motors	18,752	−22.8
2	2	American Telephone and Telegraph	16,955	8.1
3	3	Standard Oil (N.J.)	16,554	10.9
4	4	Ford Motor	14,980	1.5
5	5	Sears, Roebuck	9,262	4.5
6	6	General Electric	8,727	3.3
7	11	International Telephone and Telegraph	7,611	13.1
8	7	International Business Machines	7,504	4.3
9	9	Mobil Oil	7,261	9.7
10	8	Chrysler	7,000	−0.8
11	10	Texaco	6,350	8.2
12	12	Great Atlantic & Pacific Tea	5,754	5.8
13	13	Gulf Oil	5,396	8.9
14	15	Safeway Stores	4,860	18.6
15	14	United States Steel	4,814	1.3
16	21	Westinghouse Electric	4,313	22.9
17	16	Standard Oil (Calif.)	4,188	9.5
18	17	J. C. Penney	4,151	10.5
19	22	Kroger	3,736	7.4
20	23	Standard Oil (Ind.)	3,733	7.6
21	18	Ling-Temco-Vought	3,710	−1.1
22	24	Aetna Life and Casualty	3,697	11.9
23	33	Boeing	3,695	30.6
24	19	E. I. du Pont	3,653	−0.1
25	20	Shell Oil	3,590	1.5
26	25	General Telephone and Electronics	3,439	5.4
27	27	RCA Corp.	3,292	3.3
28	26	Goodyear Tire and Rubber	3,195	−0.7
29	32	Travelers	3,130	10.5
30	28	Swift	3,076	−1.0
31	30	Union Carbide	3,026	3.2
32	36	Procter & Gamble	2,979	10.0
33	31	Bethlehem Steel	2,935	0.3

Source: *Forbes,* May 15, 1971, p. 79.

Aside from making an industry comparison, sales analysis attempts to make comparable comparisons. For instance, a firm experiencing a sales decline of 10 percent during the summer months may find that this is a relatively good record when a comparison is made with the firm's previous summer's experience. One of the principles usually followed in sales analysis is to compare like periods of time. This usually means comparing comparable months, seasons, and even comparing

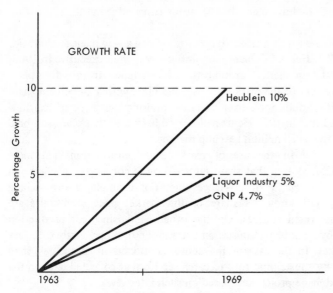

GROWTH RATE

Percentage Growth

10

Heublein 10%

5

Liquor Industry 5%

GNP 4.7%

1963   1969

Source: S. D. Watson, *Marketing in a Changing Society*, presentation to the New York Society of Security Analysts on March 21, 1969 (Hartford, Conn.: Heublein, Inc.).

comparable years, especially when a recession may have had a strong influence on a previous period.

Sales analysis can go much deeper into a problem than just making overall comparisons. Good sales analysis may very well break down sales increases or decreases by customers or by the type of products being sold. Thus one may find that 80 percent of the firm's sales come from 5 percent of the firm's customers. One may find that the same ratio applies to the product line, that is, 80 percent of the sales come from a small percentage of the product line. Accurate sales analysis can show the company where it is going and particularly where it is not meeting the needs of the market.

Market Share

Related to sales analysis is the concept of market share. This concept, if stated in its simplest form, is that it is the objective of many companies to maintain their share of their market at all times. Thus General Motors may have as its goal the maintaining of a 50 percent share of the total automobile business. Any slippage in this share would seem to indicate a failure on the part of the management of the firms.

The top level of many companies watch only changes in the firm's market share, as it indicates to these firms that marketing is or is not doing a proper job. One major oil company subscribes to a research service that publishes quarterly the changing shares of the market for each oil company throughout the year. The oil executives are particularly careful to watch changing shares among companies that have made changes in their marketing programs. One change that was watched carefully was the advent of games at filling stations during the late 1960s. When shares started to change rapidly, many of the major firms joined in the promotion at the station level.

Market share is often used as a major target for judging a new management. For example, when the H. J. Heinz Company appointed a new chief executive in 1965, their share of the ketchup market at that time had slipped from a first-place position holding 30 percent of the market to a second place with a 24 percent share of the market. (Hunt's Foods took over first). In praising the work of the new executive, it was noted that in 1970 Heinz had moved back into first place and held a 34 percent share of the $170 million ketchup market.[5]

A few problems arise in the use of market-share information that most companies are aware of. One is that share information is not always available, in that it is not easy to calculate or not accessible. For example, a firm selling children's shoes may not know its share of the market since retail sales are unavailable from most retail sources. On the other hand, since car production figures are collected by an industry source, an automobile firm may easily calculate its share of the market. In the case of the above-mentioned oil companies, they solved their problem by subscribing to a research service that collected data on the basis of interviews and made projections based on such interviews.

The major issue, however, concerning market shares is that although a company may be able to increase its share of the market it is not always profitable to do so. For instance, it is quite possible that if a manufacturer of a product wishes to increase the product's sales and thereby his share of the market, he can do so in several ways. One way may be to reduce the price of his product and thereby sell more. Another may be to send a salesman into lightly populated areas of the country and reach people who are not in the prime marketing areas. In both cases the company could very well increase its share of the market. However, in both cases the cost of increasing the share of the market may be at the expense of profits, since the lower prices and increased cost of reaching a rural customer simply may not result in a sufficient increase in revenue to overcome the additional costs of doing business. In effect, many companies have found that increasing their share of the market can result in decreasing the profitability of the firm.

Profits

Most managements would agree that profits are the ultimate criterion of any organization's efficiency and ability to manage its business properly. Thus many set achieving a certain level of profits as a target.

On this type of firm one usually finds that all new product ventures are measured on the basis of the firm's ability to generate sufficient profits. Thus one finds many of these firms have specific profit goals. Should one bring a new product idea to such a firm, one might be asked a specific question relating to profits, such as will this new product idea generate a certain percentage of return on our invested money over the next 5 years?

---

[5]"The Good Steward," *Forbes*, March 1, 1971, pp. 24, 28.

The most common measurement of profits is to relate them to sales. Thus a firm earning $1 million in profits in a given year would have a profits-to-sales ratio of 10 percent if the company's sales were $10 million.

Manufacturing Corporations' Relation   TABLE 2-2
of Profits After Taxes to Stockholders' Equity and to Sales: 1970

Industry Group	Ratios of Profits to Stockholders' Equity (%)	Profits per Dollar of Sales (cents)
Total	**9.3**	**4.0**
Durable goods	**8.3**	**3.6**
Motor vehicles and equipment	6.1	2.4
Aircraft and parts	6.8	2.0
Electrical machinery, equipment, and supplies	9.1	3.3
Machinery, except electrical	9.9	4.6
Fabricated metal products	8.6	3.1
Primary iron and steel industries	4.3	2.5
Primary nonferrous metal industries	10.7	6.1
Stone, clay, and glass products	6.9	3.4
Furniture and fixtures	7.9	2.5
Lumber and wood products, except furniture	5.9	2.5
Instruments and related products	14.2	7.3
Miscellaneous manufacturing, including ordnance	10.0	3.4
Nondurable goods	**10.3**	**4.5**
Food and kindred products	10.8	2.5
Tobacco manufactures	15.7	5.8
Textile mill products	5.1	1.9
Apparel and related products	9.3	1.9
Paper and allied products	7.0	3.4
Printing and publishing	11.2	4.2
Chemicals and allied products	11.5	5.9
Petroleum refining	11.0	9.3
Rubber and miscellaneous plastic products	7.1	2.7
Leather and leather products	9.4	2.5

Source: *Statistical Abstract of the United States* (Washington, D.C.: Government Printing Office, 1971), p. 473.

Firms today, however, are also becoming interested in another ratio, return on investment, that is, profits measured as a percentage of the firm's investment in the business to stockholder's equity. Table 2-2 lists a comparison of major industry net profits after taxes as a *ratio of sales* and *stockholders' equity*. The variance between industries is obvious. The range of return on investment extends from a low of 4.3

percent (primary iron and steel industries) to a high of 15.7 percent (tobacco manufacturers). This variance indicates why firms in different industries must make their comparisons within the same industry. In addition, the table reveals another important concept. It shows that the two firms reporting the highest and lowest *return on investment* did not have the highest or lowest ratio of sales to profits.

FIGURE 2-3   Return on Investment: Heinz and Four Competitors

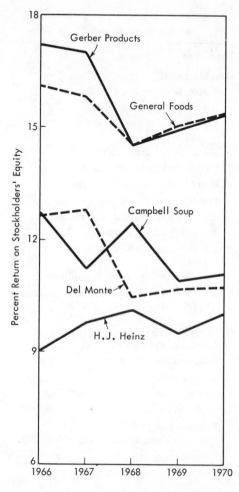

Source: *Forbes,* March 1, 1971, p. 28.

Return on investment can be used to make comparisons among competitors. In Figure 2-3 one can see a recent comparison of H. J. Heinz and four major competitors. Note the variance, the high of over 15 percent for General Foods, and the Heinz return of about 10 percent.

Return on investment, as compared to profits to sales, is considered by management to be a better indicator of the efficiency of the firm and, in effect, an evaluation of the firm's decision-making ability for several reasons. The first is that return on investment in a sense is easy to understand and is commonly used by the individual in evaluating various investment opportunities for his funds, such as the opportunity to place his savings in a bank versus the other opportunities for profits he can obtain by putting his money into a business, buying stocks or bonds, or perhaps lending monies to others.

Thus a firm in a sense is investing its money in all aspects of its business and should expect a return that is superior to other available opportunities. It may be expected, therefore, that when a firm makes a decision to increase its investment in inventory the resultant return on the inventory investment must be superior to other opportunities.

Another important reason for using return on investment as a criterion of evaluation is that this concept can be easily communicated to the lower management levels. Thus a manager of a warehouse can be expected to produce a certain return on the inventory investment in his warehouse as measured against the sales that can be directly related to the same distribution point. A manager of a firm's product can be held responsible for the profits of that product, and it can be related to his investment in all aspects of promoting the product and producing it.

Once the objectives of the firm have been established, the firm then develops a plan that includes a determination as to how objectives can be reached.

The carrying out of this function will be discussed in greater detail in Chapter 3. Nevertheless, it is important at this point to understand how planning fits into the role of marketing management.

Planning implies making decisions concerning how the firm will reach the previously stated objectives. To do this, management has to choose among alternatives. This is important to remember, because if there were no alternatives, there would be no decisions to be made. For instance, a child of 13 must attend school in his state because of the law. He, therefore, has no choice, no alternatives (unless his parents want to end up in jail), and thus he cannot make a decision. A student considering going to college has other alternatives (he can go to work instead, do both, or just stay home), and thus he can engage in decision making.

Planning and Strategy Decision Making

What do marketing managers make decisions about? The answer simply lies in our understanding of what they control. They control the elements that are incorporated in the marketing plan. Thus the manager can control the *goods and services* to be offered, the *communication* with the potential customer, and the *physical distribution* of the product. These three major areas make up what has been described as the *marketing mix* or the marketing effort. The mix is important in several ways:

1. It is the part of the firm's business that is controllable; hence the firm can feel free to choose among the many alternatives the mix offers.

2. Since it is controllable, the choices among the vast alternatives become spelled out in the marketing plan in the form of a strategy.

In Figure 2-4 are depicted these several relationships. Note that each part of the marketing mix is made up of several components. The choice of using one of these components in reference to another represents the area of decision making.

Controllable Forces—The Marketing Effort

FIGURE 2-4 Marketing Strategy

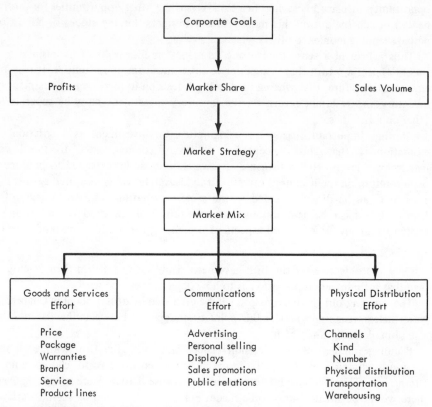

Source: Adapted from E. J. Kelley and W. Lazer, *Managerial Marketing, Perspectives and Viewpoints,* 3rd ed. (Homewood, Ill.: Richard D. Irwin, Inc., 1967), p. 528.

Uncontrollable Forces—The Marketing Effort

What determines what decisions the executive will make? Or, why does a company decide to use a strong advertising campaign to reach potential customers while another firm may not?

To make such decisions, the marketing manager must consider several factors. The first is the firm's view of the motivation of the consumer. All decision making in marketing is predicated on some interpretation of how the consumer will buy the product. The consumer, therefore, represents an unknown, and is thus depicted as the uncontrollable part of the firm environment. In a sense, therefore, the firm is constantly adjusting the mix to the whims of the consumer. Interpretation of what the consumer wants or his reaction to a product represents a *restraint* on management. Thus the unfortunate experience of the Rheingold Brewery in attempting to market a low-calorie beer (Gablinger's) was predicated on the false assumption that the beer consumer was interested in reducing calorie intake. Hence the whole marketing effort went for nothing.

The firm is faced with other restraints on their ability to market a product profitably; these are *competition* and *legal and social pressures* (consumerism). In a sense the difficulty of getting useful information as a feedback in order to make a proper decision also represents a restraint. The latter, of course, can be improved by developing a systematic means of obtaining useful feedback information. However, most decisions are made without formalizing the collection of data. Nevertheless, the information feedback acts as a positive force in helping manufacturers make the right decision.

Marketing Management **FIGURE 2-5**

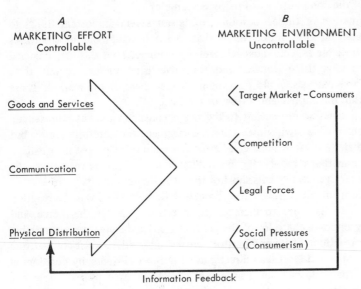

Figure 2-5 indicates this pattern of controllable *versus* uncontrollable systems that management faces. Under A is the total effort of management as depicted by the goods and services, communication, and physical distribution mix. The restraints (B) are represented by the consumer, competition, legal forces, and social pressures. Marketing information is depicted as a positive force helping management by feeding back information concerning the consumer and the environmental forces.

The problem of dealing with the environmental and uncontrollable factors in devising a marketing strategy can be seen in the battle Procter & Gamble is staging for a share of the all-purpose cleaner market.

Procter & Gamble's major entry in this household cleaning market is Mr. Clean, a product that was introduced in 1958. After being on the market for 1 year, this product held the number one position until 1970, when it was forced to yield to Colgate-Palmolive's Ajax liquid cleaner. The stakes in this market are high in that the estimated volume is approximately $115,000,000. To improve its position, the marketing team at Procter & Gamble decided to take two steps to improve the product. First, they added a "lemon-refreshed" formula that improved the odor.

Restraints
on Strategy

Second, they increased their advertising budget slightly to $3 million, and changed the theme to emphasize the floor-cleaning capabilities of the product. At the start of this campaign, Mr. Clean was slightly behind Ajax. However, it is reported that it is now in a virtual tie for first place. Estimated shares of the market are 13 percent for Ajax and 12 percent for Mr. Clean.

Will the strategy of Procter & Gamble be successful? The answer lies in several areas. First, one must consider the quality of the advertising by asking was it better directed and did it make the points that management believes are necessary? Second, will these changes be of interest to the target customers? Third, what will be the reaction of the competitors of Procter & Gamble?

Careful examination of these questions points out several important things to remember. Perhaps the most important is that in the development of the firm's strategy the controllable aspects must be carefully planned. Thus this firm changed the product, the advertising dollars, and the advertising theme. It was their judgment that these changes would gain them a larger share of the market. These changes were within the controllable effort of the firm.

Whether the changes were relevant to the target consumer market represents a part of the uncontrollable environment that management can carefully study; but they are aware that they can make a great error. Through using proper information sources, they can perhaps reduce the possibility of error, but, nevertheless, the information they receive usually falls short of their total requirements.

A further uncontrollable problem that Procter & Gamble faced was the reaction of its competitors to its move to increase its advertising, change the theme, and most importantly improve the odor of the product. This is the great uncontrollable variable, and the reactions of its competitors proved interesting. Most competitors avoided engaging Ajax and Mr. Clean directly as all-purpose cleaners; by positioning their products as spray cleaners, or disinfectant cleaners, they captured a segment of the market that would be difficult for the all-purpose cleaners to penetrate. Some of the more effective specialized cleaners were American Cyanamid's Pine-Sol, 7.5 percent of the market; Morton-Norwich Texize division's Janitor-in-a-Drum, 5 percent; Lehn and Fink's Lysol, 5 percent; and Noxell's Lestoil, 4 percent.[6]

One can see that the strategy designed by Procter & Gamble must take into consideration not only the firm's controllable mix, but an estimation of the environmental factors, particularly competition and its planned strategy in reaction to Procter & Gamble.

Quantifying Decision Making

The ability to select the proper strategy for a firm is of course the major task of management. However, although in most of this book we shall be discussing various strategies, one is impressed with the many combinations that management must deal with. In effect, management is constantly considering the alternatives among its three major controllable variables, that is, goods and services, promotion, and physical distribution.

For instance, a company selling cosmetics can consider at least five different media for advertising a product. These include television, radio, newspapers, magazines, and billboards. In addition, the firm can consider *not* to advertise as an

---

[6]*Advertising Age,* June 7, 1971, p. 3.

alternative. One can also deal with several other alternatives in the promotional mix. For example, they could consider using couponing or point-of-sale promotional literature.

As one delves into these many alternatives, one soon realizes that the combinations available could easily exceed 1,000.

How then does management eventually make a decision? One answer lies in the view that many decisions are routine and thus can be made easily. However, in this book we are concerned with crucial marketing decisions, that is, those which can have an important effect on the success or failure of the firm.

In dealing with these decisions, management must concern itself with eliminating most of the alternatives and concentrating on those which seem to be the most fruitful. Thus, because of the many possible alternatives, management must dismiss most alternatives in its decision-making process.

At some point management considers perhaps a handful of alternatives, and, drawing upon its experience and perhaps research information, makes a decision. One might expect that its decision will be based on the probability of success of that alternative that offers the highest profitability. On the other hand, there are many instances when the decision to choose an alternative may be based on things other than maximizing the profits. A firm, for instance, may select the easiest alternative, or the alternative that has the highest probability of success with the least risk to the company. Perhaps an example can better illustrate the relationship of these concepts, and indicate how they can be quantified.

Consider for instance the apparel manufacturer that is contemplating spending a considerable amount of money on advertising during the coming fall season. The problem being faced is whether to spend most of the monies on advertising the firm's heavy winter coats or perhaps spend most of its money on advertising the firm's lighter-weight women's coats.

To make this decision, the firm must first consider the most important variable, the weather. To accomplish this they would probably check the past weather in the particular area where they plan to market their products. Perhaps they may examine the records for the past 10 years and determine that the probabilities are as follows for the fall season:

Unseasonably warm fall weather	30%
Unseasonably cold fall weather	20%
Average fall weather	50%

These figures could be determined from checking the temperature reports for the past 10 years and determining what temperatures constitute being unseasonably cold, warm, or average.

The next problem that management can deal with is to determine the profits that would accrue to each alternative if the weather conditions were as follows:

Probability of Occurrence of Fall Forecast

	Unseasonably Warm 30%	*Average* 50%	*Unseasonably Cold* 20%
Profit from selling heavy coats ($)	5,000	10,000	20,000
Profit from selling light-weight coats ($)	8,000	9,000	3,000

Expected profit:

> Heavy coats: $5,000 × 0.30 + $10,000 × 0.50 + $20,000 × 0.20 = $10,500
> Light-weight coats: $8,000 × 0.30 + $9,000 × 0.50 + $3,000 × 0.20 = $7,500

Here we see that the expected profit, that is, applying the probability of occurrence to the estimated profits seems to indicate that advertising heavy coats offers a profit projected at $10,500 versus $7,500 for light-weight coats. More will be said on this subject in Chapter 3.

Other Management Functions

Although a great deal of management's time is taken up with the first two functions, establishing objectives and planning and choosing among various strategies, several other functions are of importance. Although most of the following chapters will concentrate on the performance and decision-making aspects of the latter function, it should be recognized that the proper performance of all marketing management functions requires several other steps. Included in this group are organizing and coordinating the firm's activities, staffing and assembling its resources, operating and directing the firm, and analyzing and evaluating the firm's performance.

Organizing and Coordinating the Firm's Activities

One of the major changes noted in Chapter 1 is the change in the organizational approach of the marketing department. However, in all firms and institutions it is the task of management to organize and coordinate the firm's activities.

In marketing it is of particular interest, since the implementation of the basic philosophy of the marketing concept relies on a particular method of organizing that stresses coordination. It is a basic philosophy of the marketing concept that the marketing department coordinate all marketing activities with the activities performed in the nonmarketing departments of the firm. In effect, the task of the marketing department is to coordinate its activities, particularly with the production and financial departments of management. All planning and forecasts must be coordinated with these areas. Within the marketing department coordination is particularly important, since the marketing sequence relies on a constant cycle of activities, which begins with the consumer and ends with the communication of the product to the consumer. The coordination must be carefully organized, since constant adjustments must be made in the procedure due to field or research experience.

Staffing and Assembling Resources

Although this book will devote little time to personnel selection and its impact on the marketing department, it is nevertheless an important management function.

In coordinating the firm's activities the marketing department must take into consideration the personnel needs of its department. Although, from an activitiy point of view, the marketing department may devote most of its coordination efforts to the production and finance departments, the personnel department should be a vital link in their efforts.

Although management has the authority to carry out its work, the use of this power is rather limited in the marketing department. There are several reasons for this. The first is that many marketing activities are conducted outside of the firm. That is, a salesman may be given a large territory to cover and may spend most of his time traveling without the direct supervision of top management. Second, many of the promotional activities of a firm are not easily measurable so that management can judge whether or not a marketing employee is performing efficiently. Third, many marketing jobs are staff positions in which only advice is offered and creativity is the full measure of a man's ability, another factor that is difficult to measure.

It can be seen, therefore, that the ability to operate and direct marketing activities must rely less on using authority and more on management's determination to get employees to strive for self-motivation. This represents the major challenge to a management that hopes to accomplish the firm's objectives.

Analyzing and Evaluating Performance Based on Measurements

Once the firm has established its objectives and carried out the many functions, it is necessary at some point to evaluate the performance and particularly to establish adequate controls.

In previous sections, most of these controls have been discussed. In particular, market share, sales measurement techniques, and profits and return on investment seem to offer management an excellent means of evaluting, and thereby controlling, the organization.

Aside from these controls, the firm controls its operations through expense control.

Expense Control

A cost or expense ratio is one of the most common measurements of performance by a firm. In fact, most budgets and systems of large organizations are based on previously computed cost and expense ratios.

An *expense ratio* is simply an expense expressed usually in relationship to the firm's net sales. Thus a firm with a sales volume of $10 million annually and sales expense of $1 million has incurred a sales expense ratio of 10 percent.

Expense ratios are only valuable when a firm has some criteria or standard to judge the firm's performance against. Thus many firms collect data from various sources and make comparisons against their own company's performance. For instance, in Table 2-3 one sees the typical operating statistics of several manufacturers. Management, at some period of time during the year, will make comparisons with their firm's operating ratios and perhaps make changes or examine areas where they are out of line.

In some cases the firm may find that one of its expenses is higher than the industry average. This knowledge keys management in to a particular problem within the firm.

TABLE 2-3 Expense Ratios of Manufacturers, 1970

	Paint, Varnish, and Lacquers	Industrial Chemicals	Perfumes, Cosmetics, and Other Toilet Preparations	Wines Distilled Liquor, and Liqueurs	Women's Dresses
Net sales	100%	100%	100%	100%	100%
Cost of sales	68.9	80.5	60.4	76.4	76.7
Gross profit	31.1	19.5	39.6	23.6	23.3
Selling and delivery expenses	15.0	6.9	16.0	11.8	9.9
Officers' salaries	2.9	1.9	2.0	1.5	2.7
Other general administrative expenses	8.0	6.5	15.7	3.8	8.5
All other expenses	1.1	1.0	2.0	1.4	1.2
Profit before taxes	4.1	3.2	3.8	5.1	1.1

Source: *Annual Statement Studies* (Philadelphia, Pa.: Robert Morris Associates, 1971).

Problems develop, however, when one uses industry average figures. For instance, suppose a firm discovered that its expenditures for advertising were considerably above the industry average. The question then arises as to why the advertising expenditure is above the national average, and, second, should it be above average? A firm may have above-average advertising expenses, and yet have a profitable operation, since the firm may choose to emphasize its advertising skills and choose to cut back in some other area, such as personal selling. Thus, on balance, the firm may still find that its total average operating statistics are below average. The point is that management recognizes that many comparative statistics do not take into consideration the fact that companies differ in their emphasis on the marketing mix, and hence cannot be expected to always match the operating reports of other firms in the same industry.

Yet, in spite of its weaknesses, many firms use operating statistic reports as a basis for comparing their firm with other similar organizations. Even though a particular firm may put a stronger emphasis on some part of the marketing mix, management can at least compare other firms in the same industry with their organization.

SUMMARY

In this chapter the major functions of management have been outlined and discussed. Their functions include the determining of the firm's objectives, both general and specific, the planning and development of strategy (this is an important procedure in decision making), organizing, coordinating, staffing, and assembling the firm's resources, and, finally, the evaluating process, better known as the control of marketing activities.

The functions performed by the marketing department were introduced as the "marketing sequence," and, in effect, represent the total effort of the firm. Essentially, management is pursuing its plan, making decisions concerning the emphasis on each of the marketing mixes — the *goods and services, communication,* and the *physical distribution.* Choosing among the alternatives represents management's major role and the challenge of decision making.

The restraints on decision making are many. They are represented by the uncontrollable factors — the consumer, competition, and legal and social pressures (consumerism). Feedback information, particularly concerning the consumer, helps management make the right decision.

QUESTIONS

1. How does the management of a small store differ from that of General Motors?
2. Which functions performed by management are the most important in marketing? Why?
3. How would the objectives of the Rolls-Royce Company differ from that of Volkswagen? How are they similar?

4. Why is it necessary to set objectives for a firm?

5. How are the firm's objectives translated into specific goals for the marketing departments?

6. Distinguish between return on investment and profit to sales as a measure of firm efficiency.

7. What is meant by the marketing mix? Is it controllable or uncontrollable?

8. Are the consumers uncontrollable? Why or why not?

9. Under what condition could one conclude that Heublein's 10 percent sales increase (see Figure 2-2) was not adequate?

10. It is the task of top management to set the company objectives and the marketing department's job to operate within the confines of these objectives. True or false? Explain.

***11.** Examine Table 2-3 and explain the difference in operation between perfume and industrial chemical manufacturers.

12. Discuss the role of market share as a specific target for a firm. What are the negative aspects?

13. Write out the objectives, as you see them, of any major store in your city.

*In-depth question.

Marketing Planning

3

SUMMARY KEY

Marketing planning is about the most important procedure management engages in. Without change there would be little need for planning. Planning is nothing more than a formalized or systematic approach for management to consider the many alternatives and choices it faces.

Planning has become a more formalized and well-established procedure in recent years for many reasons. The most prominent are changes in technology, which cause the development of new competitive products.

The marketing plan, although the most important plan business must make, is just one of several plans made in a firm. The marketing plan in all cases must be consistent with the total plan of the corporation and must tie in carefully with the stated objectives of the firm. For instance, if it is the stated objective of the firm to earn a certain percentage on net worth, all new products planned for the year must take that fact into consideration. Steps in marketing planning include

1. *Reviewing the past performance.* At this point executives sit down and review the past and, particularly, try to explain what happened.

2. *Forecasting the future.* Accurate forecasts are the key to good planning. Firms engage in two types of planning procedures, informal and formal. Informal procedures are usually made up of meetings of top executives where some estimate of future sales is arrived at based on their past experience. Although these procedures are subjective, they are widely used because of their simplicity. Formal procedures include forecasts of the general economy, the industry, and then the firm. In developing forecasts correlation analysis is sometimes used to show relationships between economic factors and the company products.

3. *Selecting alternatives.* Once forecasts have been made, the firm may select several different alternative marketing programs. In selecting alternatives they may simply consider the sales and profit possibilities of each alternative or may engage in formally attaching probabilities to each of these alternatives and making a calculation of expected profit.

4. *Monitoring and directing the plan.* Here the firm relies on accounting data to determine how well the plan is proceeding. Marketing research may also determine the status of the plan at any given point in time.

In planning, the firm should have developed various theories that will help them anticipate the reaction of consumers. For instance, in developing a forecast of dresses several theories may be considered: trickle down, trickle up, designer, and media theories.

In a firm no one department is completely responsible for the total marketing plan. Ordinarily, the marketing manager or vice president is responsible for setting the planning objectives; however, the research, sales, and other administrative departments are also involved.

Marketing planning is about the most important procedure management engages in. Although the firm's total planning program starts with the chief executive, the marketing plan is the core of the organization's direction for the coming year.

After the firm has established the objectives as noted in Chapter 2, it then becomes incumbent upon marketing to establish the necessary planning information to develop the proper strategies and choices among alternatives to accomplish the plans.

In addition to the overall plans, the firm, through its organizational procedures, will ask all the people in the line of authority to establish additional plans to achieve individual goals. Thus the sales manager will establish selling norms for each of his salesmen for the forthcoming period, in line with the overall plan. The individual salesman will establish a sales goal procedure for himself in order to accomplish this norm.

Planning and Change

Without change, there would probably be little need for a manufacturer to engage in planning new strategy during the coming period. However, as most of us are aware, a firm's environment is constantly changing, and management, as a result, is under pressure to rethink last year's strategy and alternatives.

To develop a useful strategy, a manufacturer must choose among perhaps hundreds of alternatives. Although several alternatives may result directly in his achieving his company's objective, there is little doubt that the selection of most of these alternatives may cause the company to fall short of its objectives.

Planning, in essence, is nothing more than a formalized or systematic approach for management to consider the many alternatives and choices they face. In most cases, management prefers to act on the basis of facts that are available. But in most cases management must rely on the experience and intuition of its executive staff.

In recent years, more and more firms are taking formal planning seriously. Many firms have established planning procedures and planning boards at the top executive level. The reasons for this tendency toward more formalized planning are many. The most important would seem to be the following factors:

1. Changes in technology.
2. Changes in government policy.
3. Changes in aggregate economic activity.

Changes in technology have been particularly important in marketing. Through the vast government expenditure program since World War II on defense-related research projects, many firms have developed technical abilities that have resulted in the development of new products. Although more will be said about this in our chapter on products, it is important to recognize that this new technology has resulted in offering even medium-sized firms an opportunity to produce products in competition with some of the giants of industry.

In addition to its impact on new products, many firms have found that technological growth has influenced their internal operations. For instance, the growth of computers and the accompanying programming techniques have made it possible for manufacturers to set the size of their inventories and maintain control over their warehouse stocks with much greater precision than has ever before been possible. All these developments, of course, require careful and systematic studies and fall into the decision-making powers of those engaged in planning.

Changes in government policy in recent years have placed more pressure on the firm to plan strategy carefully. When one speaks of government, one may be referring to not only the federal but also the state and local government. For instance, distillers of liquor selling in New York State found themselves faced with a state law that directed their firms to sell to New York wholesalers at the lowest price available in any of the other 49 states. One need not be experienced in business to realize the havoc this caused to the dozens of large distillers who sell perhaps 10 or 15 percent of their output in New York State. Decisions of that type require careful consideration for all aspects of business and again fall into the jurisdiction of the planning group within the firm.

Constant shifts in economic activity, a natural occurrence in our society, also require that a firm carefully plan its future strategy. Should, for example, a recession occur or an economic forecast fall considerably below the previous year, the burden falls upon management, and particularly the planners, to adjust this environmental fact to the firm's plans for the forthcoming year.

Changes in the degree and character of competition seem to be always occurring in the environment. This competition need not come only from present firms, but may occur as a result of imported goods from foreign markets. For instance, in recent years the major shoe manufacturers have been pressuring the United States Congress to increase tariffs on shoes as a result of the huge quantity of imported shoes entering the United States. For those firms faced with meeting this competition, the alternatives would seem to be many, and planning to meet this competition has to be at the highest level of the firm.

Changes in social norms and attitudes are particularly relevant in today's world. For instance, the changing values of young people toward the clothes they wear and the movies they wish to see are just two indicators of these changing norms in our society. The changing attitudes toward movies, that is, the demand for more

[1]W. W. Haynes and J. L. Massie, *Management: Analysis, Concepts and Cases,* 2nd ed. (Englewood Cliffs, N.J.: Prentice-Hall Inc., 1969), p. 250.

relevant and realistic plots, has had a particularly important effect on the large movie producers. The ultimate effect has been a growth of large numbers of small independent movie-making concerns and the decline of the major studios. Its impact on the industry in terms of both profit and the importance of major stars is obvious.

The last factor that has affected the tendency and need for planning is the constant change in the markets that firms serve. Although more will be said about these changes in our chapters on the consumer, it is important to note that even population shifts from year to year cause firms to reconsider their past marketing strategies.

Planning

After setting the firm's objective, the next step in any management procedure is planning. At the planning stage, management must determine what problems it faces, examine the strategies to overcome these problems, and then make a choice among these alternatives. Once the plan is developed, the organization is then ready to move ahead developing specific budgets and formulating policies that will help make the plan a reality.

By proper planning, a firm can get a much firmer grip on its future. By carefully examining the alternatives and making a choice, the manufacturer can use careful planning to control his progress. Once the company has planned where it wants to go and be by a certain period of time, it has developed guidelines for the total organization. Thus, should the company consider developing a new product, it becomes important that short-run management decisions be coordinated with the long-run strategy of the firm. Only if management has set up a specific plan can coordination result at all levels and can the members of the organization commit themselves fully to the necessary tasks.

By planning, the firm's management is in effect attempting to control its own destiny.

Marketing Plan

Establishing a plan for the firm's total marketing program is perhaps the major project management must engage in before a business period gets underway. Yet the marketing plan is just one of the many plans management must develop. It, of course, must be consistent with the total plan for the corporation and must tie in carefully with the stated objectives of the firm. For instance, if it is the stated objective of a firm to increase its return on net worth during the year, then all new products must be planned to achieve this goal.

The other major sections of the business organization — manufacturing, personnel, and finance — must also develop plans with these goals in mind.

Steps in Marketing Planning

Although an exact sequence of marketing planning may vary from firm to firm, it has been recognized that most planning does involve the consideration of several steps. The most notable are

1. Reviewing the past performance.

2. Forecasting the future.
3. Selecting alternatives.
4. Monitoring and directing the plan.

These will be discussed next.

Reviewing the Past Performance

In making a marketing plan, the firm at some point in time must review the past. Thus the executives in the firm must examine what has happened, and at this point develop theories as to why things happened and what things are happening that can affect their future opportunities.

In reviewing the past, the firm may simply compare the previous period's *objectives* with the *accomplishments*. Thus a firm with a planned objective of a 20 percent return on investment may carefully examine the reasons why this objective may not have been reached.

To evaluate the past, the firm must rely on people who are familiar with not only the company operation, but can interpret outside economic changes and consumer behavior. As a result, many firms are sure to bring the marketing research department into this evaluation, as well as top executives and advisors.

Forecasting the Future

All planning involves a careful forecast of the future. In a sense it is this forecast that becomes a goal of the firm's management. Thus a firm may forecast the total sales potential for the industry in the period ahead. This forecast then becomes a target market for those engaged in planning. Although forecasts can eventually be developed in the form of dollars, many forecasts involve the listing of happenings that can take place that can affect the forecast. For instance, inflation or a business recession usually affects all firms and their future. Perhaps a shifting in government policy, such as a reduction of expenditures for housing, would affect firms in the construction industry.

It is important to remember that accurate forecasts are the key to good planning. Should the forecasts be wrong, all the subplans within the firm will be inaccurate. For example, should the company sales plan fall below estimates, the manufacturing division may overproduce, the personnel department may hire too many people, and the finance division will be spending too much money.

An example of how forecasts can cause havoc in an industry is seen in the sales of snowmobiles in the 1970 winter season. Since 1964, sales of snowmobiles have increased by 50 to 100 percent each year. During the 1970–1971 season, sales increased by only 10 to 12 percent, and estimates from one source (Anderson and Company, an accounting firm) indicated that somewhere between 100,000 and 150,000 snowmobiles remained unsold. The reason for this slide in sales was attributed to economic considerations, or more specifically the recession of 1970–1971.[2]

---

[2]"Snowmobile Sales Hit the Skids," *Business Week,* March 13, 1971, p. 134.

In spite of these problems, all planning starts with a forecast of the firm's sales for the coming year. Once the forecast is made, the firm can set its specific planned expenditures into action; that is, it can then set its advertising budget so that it can achieve these specific goals.

Types of forecasts. Forecasts are developed on the basis of two procedures, informal and formal. Informal (or judgment) procedures are perhaps the most common means of developing a sales forecast. To accomplish this, a firm usually relies on the judgment of executives or perhaps technicians in the firm to estimate the firm's sales potential for the coming period.

The information procedure may be as simple as executives sitting around a table discussing the sales potential for each major product in the company's line. This group may include sales, marketing, financial, and production executives. Their estimates in this case are based primarily on their vast years of experience and their evaluation of any new developments in the foreseeable future.

This procedure suffers from some serious defects. First, it is much too subjective and depends on the particular feelings of the group at this period of time. It fails to come to grips with the realistic measurable happenings taking place. It also may result in making the same forecast as the year before, since it is perhaps safer to do so. Thus, when a company may be forecasting a sales increase of 5 percent a year, one usually finds that a similar forecast is made year after year. Also, one might raise the issue that once this sort of forecasting makes a prediction it is self-fulfilled, because the team then has its goal for the year, and will not expend the effort to exceed the set goal.

Perhaps the most useful means of forecasting involves the use of formal techniques. Formal techniques involve several steps, but eventually result in some kind of mathematical computation.

The formal method is illustrated in Figure 3-1. Note should be made that the forecasts are eventually integrated with the firm's plans during the forthcoming period.

Advantages of formal forecasts. Although formal forecasts do not ignore the information flow from informal forecasts, they do differ in several ways. The ways can be considered to represent clear advantages that accrue to this method. Some of these advantages are as follows:

1. Formal forecasting represents a more orderly and systematic method of collecting pertinent data. By following a set procedure, the company is assured that consideration will be given to all variables that are pertinent to a company forecast. For example, it is possible that a firm using an informal approach could conceivably forget to examine past data. Or they could fail to perceive a correlation with economic statistics, such as the relationship between the sale of paint and new housing starts in an area of the country.

2. Formal forecasting, if done properly, results in a detailed, logical plan that eventually results in a complete integration of production schedules, inventories, and distribution to meet the forecasting goals.[3] Thus a formal forecast produces such detailed forecasts that the end result is a whole series of meaningful figures that all levels of the firm can use to plan their next period's activities.

---

[3] N. L. Enrick, *Market and Sales Forecasting* (San Francisco: Chandler Publishing Company, 1969), p. 6.

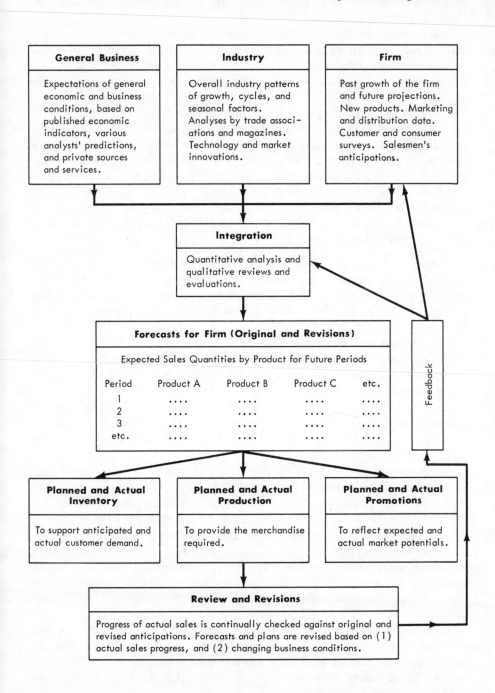

General Business	Industry	Firm
Expectations of general economic and business conditions, based on published economic indicators, various analysts' predictions, and private sources and services.	Overall industry patterns of growth, cycles, and seasonal factors. Analyses by trade associations and magazines. Technology and market innovations.	Past growth of the firm and future projections. New products. Marketing and distribution data. Customer and consumer surveys. Salesmen's anticipations.

Integration

Quantitative analysis and qualitative reviews and evaluations.

Forecasts for Firm (Original and Revisions)

Expected Sales Quantities by Product for Future Periods

Period	Product A	Product B	Product C	etc.
1	....	....	....	....
2	....	....	....	....
3	....	....	....	....
etc.	....	....	....	....

Feedback

Planned and Actual Inventory	Planned and Actual Production	Planned and Actual Promotions
To support anticipated and actual customer demand.	To provide the merchandise required.	To reflect expected and actual market potentials.

Review and Revisions

Progress of actual sales is continually checked against original and revised anticipations. Forecasts and plans are revised based on (1) actual sales progress, and (2) changing business conditions.

Source: N. L. Enrick, *Market and Sales Forecasting*, (San Francisco: Chandler Publishing Company, 1969), p. 5.

Formal forecasting procedures. All formal forecasts start with a consideration of general economic trends for the economy, the industry, and the firm (see Figure 3-1).

The first step involves an evaluation as to the general economic trends in the nation's economy. An evaluation of this sort relies on the professional and expert estimates of both government and private economic advisors. Many firms hire outside economic consultants to make these predictions for the coming forecasting period.

An economic forecast may be in the form of an estimate of growth in several economic indicators in the economy. Predictions may be made as to the overall rise in the gross national product, or a change in the amount of unemployment. Generally, however, a forecast indicates to a firm the general trend in the period ahead in terms of consumer spending. Thus a firm may find that in the coming year they can expect a 6 percent rise in total output in the economy. This forecast becomes a base for any predictions the firm will make. It must be remembered that a forecast of a recession ordinarily affects all industries. It is rare indeed that an individual firm will not be affected by a negative forecast for the general economy.

Industry and company forecast. Once the firm has determined a forecast for the economy, the next step is to examine the industry forecast and relate it to the company sales. The industry forecast is made up of a collection of historical data and consists of an attempt to relate the industry sales to the general economic forecast.

Once this relationship is established, the firm then faces the challenge of relating the industry sales forecast with the firm's forecast. Here again, a formal approach can be used. The firm, for instance, can use share-of-the-market data and apply it to the industry forecast. Thus, in 1972, the Ford Motor Company reportedly had 30 percent of the U.S. automobile market. Any industry forecast by Ford would be made on the basis of Ford's maintaining this ratio. If the industry forecast in a particular year is for the sale of 9 million autos, then Ford will perhaps forecast total sales of at least 2.7 million cars.

The fact that Ford has maintained this share of the market for a number of years would seem to indicate that they will continue to do so. However, a change in their marketing plans would, of course, cause them to readjust their estimates. For instance, with the development and marketing of the Pinto, Ford may feel that through this new product they will increase their share of the total market.

In any case, at this point a firm now has an estimate of the industry market and the firm's share of that market. The firm can further refine its forecast by estimating the sales of each of its major products for the forthcoming period. In the case of Ford, the company may make estimates of the sales of the Lincoln Continental, Mercury, and Ford divisions.

Once this is completed, the company is then in a position to let its various divisions go to work and make their own forecast and determinations. Thus the factory can now plan its production scheduling and the inventory required, and, finally, the marketing department can now make plans based on achieving the expected sales forecasts (see Figure 3-1).

The marketing department would perhaps now take the estimated sales figure and relate it in some meaningful way to sales by area. Here again, past experience and records would indicate rather clearly the expected sales for each of the area divisions of the firm.

Correlation analysis. To relate industry sales to the sales of the individual company, correlation analysis may be used.

Correlation analysis is a statistical method whereby it is possible to estimate the value of one factor by reference to the value of an associated factor. Thus a manufacturer may note a relationship between his sales and an economic statistic. More specifically, a manufacturer of automobiles may note a strong relationship between the sales of his cars and disposable income.

Economic and Demographic Indicators Related to Selected Product Lines   **TABLE 3-1**

Product Lines (Dependent Variables)	*As Related To*	*Economic and Demographic Indicators (Independent Variables)*
Consumer expenditures for:		
Baked goods		Retail grocery store sales
Crackers, cookies, and other tidbits		Disposable income per capita
Frozen foods		Consumer expenditures for non-durables
Frozen prepared foods		Consumer expenditures for non-durables
Frozen vegetables, fruits, and juices		Consumer expenditures for food
Candy and chewing gum		Number of households
Canned foods		Consumer expenditures for non-durables
Canned baby foods		Number of households
Canned juices		Consumer expenditures for food
Canned milk		Total U.S. population
Canned soups		Consumer expenditures for food
Canned vegetables		Number of households
Condiments, dressings, spreads, and relishes		Number of households
Cereals		Retail grocery store sales

Source: Lionel O. Edie & Company, Inc., New York.

The first step in using this technique in making a forecast is to look about for relationships that will aid in making these forecasts. Table 3-1 shows a whole series of these relationships. For instance, to make a projection for baked goods, one should relate projected grocery store sales. Grocery stores sales also seem to be a good indicator of consumer expenditures for cereals. On the other hand, consumer expenditures for canned vegetables seem to be more closely related to the number of U.S. households.

Once one suspects a relationship exists, its existence can be determined by establishing a scatter diagram. Figure 3-2 shows the relationship between a primary metal production index and the sales of a sulphur company. By plotting the sales of the firm on the vertical axis (Y) and the production index on the horizontal axis (X) and drawing a straight line through the dots, one can determine whether a relationship exists or not. It is obvious that some relationship does exist between the production index and the sale of sulphur of this firm.

FIGURE 3-2 **Scatter Diagram and Freehand Trend Line for Sulphur Company Sales Related to Primary Metal Production**

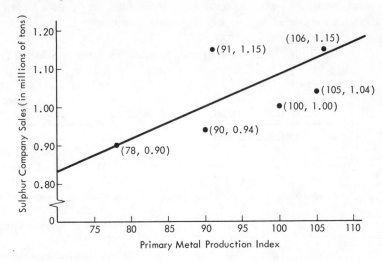

Source: Adapted from F. J. Charvat and W. T. Whitman, *Marketing Management* (New York: Simmons-Boardman Publishing Corporation, 1964), p. 138.

One can see that it is possible to draw several different straight lines through the data freehand, since the line depends on the slope one draws. To determine the line of best fit, a mathematical technique called least squares has been devised to aid us in drawing such a line. This line is calculated to be:

$$Yx = a + bx$$
$$= 0.4405 + 0.00625X$$

The line is called a regression line, and it is used to measure the relationship between the data. In effect, if the line were to cut through all the dots (or actual data), it would mean that there is a perfect relationship between the production metal index and the actual sulphur sales. Thus, given the production index, one could forecast sales exactly. In reality, there is rarely a perfect correlation.

In the case of the sulphur sales, by simple calculation one could determine that when the index registers 100 (1967) the sales will be 1.06 million tons.[4] In

4 Year	Y Alpha Sulphur Co. Sales (millions of tons)	Y²	X Production Index	XY	X²
1965	1.151	1.3248	106	122.006	11,236
1966	1.052	1.1067	104	109.408	10,816
1967	1.000	1.0000	100	100.000	10,000

actuality the sales were 1.00. This, of course, indicates that the estimate is rather good, and forecasting based on the production index should yield accurate results.

Much of the forecasting that is done today in this manner involves more complex sets of variables and complicated mathematical formulation. Nevertheless, the principles of relating sales to a variable or a set of variables is the basis for most formal forecasting methods.

To understand the forecasting procedure, one should consider the following illustration, prepared by Lionel D. Edie & Company, for determining the future potential for eight companies in a variety of industries. The approach was twofold in that it depended on statistical analysis and on interviewers to obtain qualitative information.

Forecasting Illustration

Statistical Analysis

The first step is to examine the major product lines of these eight companies and thereby determine growth rates for their industries. Table 3-2 presents the results. Here one can see that they range from an annual growth rate of 4.1 percent for food to a high of 11.0 percent for ethical drugs.

As a second step the forecast then applies their growth figures to that portion of the company's present sales that can be identified from Table 3-1. In the case of the

Year	Y Alpha Sulphur Co. Sales (millions of tons)	Y^2	X Production Index	XY	X^2
1968	0.904	0.8172	78	70.512	6,084
1969	0.941	0.8855	90	84.690	8,100
1970	1.152	1.3271	91	104.832	8,281
	6.200	6.4613	569	591.448	54,517

With these data it is now possible to calculate the normal equations in order to find the Y intercept (a) and the slope of the line (b).

$$
\begin{aligned}
Y &= Na + bX \\
XY &= aX + bX^2 \\
6.2 &= 6a + 569b \\
591.448 &= 569a + 54{,}517b \\
a &= 0.4405 \\
b &= 0.00625
\end{aligned}
$$

Estimating equation:

$$
\begin{aligned}
Y_x &= a + bX \\
&= 0.4405 + 0.00625X \\
&= 0.4405 + 0.00625(100) \\
&= 1.06 \text{ estimated sales (1967)}
\end{aligned}
$$

Source: F. J. Charvat and W. T. Whitman, *Marketing Management* (New York: Simmons-Boardman Publishing Corporation, 1964), p. 139.

Green Giant Company, the food category would be applied to most of the firm's sales. In the case of the Gillette Company, cosmetics and toiletries are the applicable category. The results are shown in Table 3-3.

TABLE 3-2   Growth of Major Product Lines of Companies

Product	*Billions of Dollars* *1966*	*1977E*	*Expected Annual Growth Rate (%)*
Food	99.4	155.0	4.1
Textiles	19.5	36.0	5.7
Cosmetics and toiletries	2.50	5.23	6.9
Proprietary drugs	1.39	2.20	4.3
Ethical drugs	3.07	9.65	11.0
Medical and health	1.70	3.77	7.5
Household supplies	4.63	7.50	4.5
Other[a]	4.17	11.22	9.4

E = estimated.
[a]Photographic equipment, pens and mechanical pencils, and rigid and semirigid plastic containers.
Source: Lionel O. Edie & Company, Inc., New York.

TABLE 3-3   Growth Prospects of Major Market Product Lines in the Next 10 Years for Each Company[a]

	Millions of Dollars			*Average Annual Rate of Increase*	
	1962	*1966*	*1977E*	*1962– 1966*	*1966– 1977*
Abbott Laboratories, Inc.	5,940	7,797	16,827	7.1	7.2
Chesebrough Pond's, Inc.	4,295	5,983	12,010	8.6	6.8
Gerber Products Company	5,748	6,699	10,282	3.9	4.0
The Gillette Company	3,534	6,069	14,675	14.5	8.4
Green Giant Company	5,242	5,849	8,065	2.8	3.0
Kendall Company	2,421	3,217	7,659	7.3	8.2
Miles Laboratories	3,605	5,150	13,139	9.3	8.9
Richardson-Merrell, Inc.	8,093	10,895	22,064	7.7	6.6

E = estimated.
[a]The series shown for each company represents the additive total of all the market products that can be classified and identified with each company.
Source: Lionel O. Edie & Company, Inc., New York.

One may question this statistical analysis at this stage in that it assumes that the projected growth ratio will stand up in the future. To avoid this problem, the firm developed three models of forecasts as follows:

Model 1 assumes the company's share of the market will be the same in 1966 as 1977.

Model 2 assumes that the trends of market penetration by product lines will change in the future as they did in the past 5 years.

Model 3 assumes that the percentage of distribution of a company's sales by product line will change in the future as they did in the past 5 years.

The point of Model 1 seems obvious. However, models 2 and 3 require some explanation. Model 2 assumes that the firm's penetration of the market will continue into the forecasted period at the same rate as the previous 5 years. Thus Gillette's dollar sales of razors and blades went from $92.5 million in 1961 to $111.0 million in 1967; the forecast would assume this growth to be maintained up to 1977.

In model 3, the assumption is that razors and blades would maintain their share of the Gillette Company's product line in the future. Thus from 1961 to 1967 the share of the companies' total output for razors and blades declined from 36.5 to 25.9 percent. This decline would continue to 1977 for this product line.

The results of analyzing these models are seen in Table 3-4. In the case of the Gillette Company, the forecasts for each model are 8.4, 8.1, and 7.9 percent.

Interviews

Since the forecasts made in Table 3-4 are statistical in nature, it occurs to firms engaging in this activity that the caliber of management could affect the accuracy of these estimates. For example, if the Green Giant Company changed management recently, this could result in a substantial improvement in sales at a range far above the forecasted amount.

To make this determination, Lionel D. Edie & Company interviews knowledgeable industry people to determine the quality of management of these firms.

A summary of the interviews concerning the Green Giant Company is as follows:

Management: Generally, Green Giant is regarded as having a very strong marketing and management team. They are considered to be very aggressive, good innovators, and shrewd advertisers. Part of Green Giant's growth was achieved by its marketing efforts, which have allowed the company to sell higher quality foods.

Problems: So far the company has not suffered from lack of diversification. However, it cannot continue to make the same strides as in the past due to the fact that competition is increasing. Much of its success has been because the company has created a strong brand image. Up to now buyers do not seem to resist Green Giant's price structure because it is riding on a good product quality image. How long this will last is difficult to ascertain. History certainly indicates that competition chips away at the quality advantage over time. The price umbrella invites new entry into the industry.

Growth prospects: New growth areas for Green Giant include institutional feeding, further upgrading of food products and the addition of new vegetable and specialized items. As long as the company can continue this trend, it will be less vulnerable to private label food products.

TABLE 3-4 **Three Growth Models for Selected Companies**

Company	Model 1[a] $ Million 1966	$ Million 1977E	Growth[d] 1966-1977	Model 2[b] $ Million 1977E	Growth[d] 1966-1977	Model 3[c] $ Million 1977E	Growth[d] 1966-1977
Abbott Laboratories, Inc.	266	574	7.2	807	10.6	622	8.0
Chesebrough Pond's, Inc.	157	248	4.2	283	5.5	356	7.7
Gerber Products Company	195	299	4.0	370	6.0	300	4.0
The Gillette Company	396	958	8.4	933	8.1	915	7.9
Green Giant Company	140	193	3.0	468	11.6	193	3.0
Kendall Company	181	430	8.2	403	7.5	492	9.5
Miles Laboratories	166	423	8.9	574	11.9	400	8.3
Richardson-Merrell, Inc.	248	501	6.6	553	7.6	583	8.1

E = estimated.
[a]Model 1 – Assumes total company's share of market in 1977 will be the same as in 1966. Share of market is total company's sales as a percentage of combined sales of industries in which it participates.
[b]Model 2 – Assumes the trends of market penetration by product line will change in the future as they did in the past 5 years.
[c]Model 3 – Assumes the percentage distribution of a company's sales by product line will change in the future as it has in the past 5 years.
[d]Compound annual growth rates (%).
Source: Lionel O. Edie & Company, Inc., New York.

In establishing a plan, management must choose among many alternatives, particularly in making a marketing plan. Rarely is management faced with one choice. The alternatives involve the development of a strategy for a firm that will help management achieve its objectives. The strategy includes the proper selection of the marketing mix that will apply to achieving such a goal and objectives. As noted in Chapter 1, the Magnavox Company has attempted to sell television sets by choosing a strategy that involves selling through franchise dealers. In contrast, the major seller of television sets, RCA, has chosen another plan, selling to practically all dealers.

The very nature of marketing makes it necessary for all marketing executives to consider a wide variety of choices in establishing a choice, alternative, or strategy for accomplishing the firm's objectives.

Although much of what will be discussed in the remaining chapters is concerned with how management views the many alternatives it is faced with, and how it ultimately makes a decision, it must be remembered that management can make decisions in many ways. Thus a major decision can come out of a meeting of top executives, where the discussion is the major input of information. In some cases the firm may have a special research study that will indicate to management that the decision should go in a certain direction. In all cases, management usually attempts to estimate all the possibilities and examine carefully the alternatives.

In some cases management can formalize its decision making by resorting to mathematical caculations. Some of the more recent developments in this area involve the use of subjective probabilities to give us an expected value of a proposed strategy.

To more clearly understand the use of probability and expected values, consider the case of the business executive who is faced with the problem of calling on a customer who lives 800 miles away. He knows that it will cost him $200 to call on this executive. He also knows that the most profit he could make would be to sell him a $2,000 piece of equipment on which he earns $700. He also knows from previous experience that the probability of selling a customer is one for each five sales calls made. The question, obviously, is should he make the sales call?

The executive then proceeds to make the following calculations:

Expected profit on this sale:

$$\$700 \times 0.2 = \$140$$

Expected value of the trip:

$$\text{Expected profit} - \text{cost of trip} = \text{expected value}$$
$$\$140 - \$200 = -\$60$$

In this case the executive should not make the trip. This does not necessarily mean that he will not make a profit, but it does mean that in the long run these probabilities will hold up and in only one in five cases will he make a sale. Thus, he should either look for customers that will spend more money on purchases or those who are closer to home so his trips will cost less and his opportunities to make a profit will increase.

Figure 3-3 indicates this same concept in more detail. Here one sees a firm considering the possibility of setting its market strategy at one of three levels, 10, 20, or 30 percent. As noted in the first box, if the kind of season (state of business) is good, the firm will generate sales per week at three different volumes using each of the markups. If it is a fair season, the sales will decrease to a lower level for each markup choice. If perhaps the firm runs into a poor season, the resultant sales figures will be the lowest.

FIGURE 3-3 Expected Value of Three Markup Strategies

	(1)	(2)	(3)	(4)	(5)
	Strategies	**States of Nature**			
		Good Season	Fair Season	Poor Season	
	Markup, %	Anticipated Sales ($1000 per week)			
a	10	100	50	20	
b	20	35	25	15	
c	30	30	20	10	
		Anticipated Profit, $1000 per week = Markup % x Anticipated Sales			
d	10	0.10 x 100 = 10	0.10 x 50 = 5	0.10 x 20 = 2	
e	20	0.20 x 35 = 7	0.20 x 25 = 5	0.20 x 15 = 3	
f	30	0.30 x 30 = 9	0.30 x 20 = 6	0.30 x 10 = 3	
		Probability, %, of Good, Fair, or Poor Season			Expected Value of Strategy ($1000 per week) = (2) + (3) + (4)
		20%	60%	20%	
		Expected Profit, $1000 per week = Probability % x Anticipated Profit			
g	10	0.2 x 10 = 2.0	0.6 x 5 = 3.0	0.2 x 2 = 0.4	2 + 3 + 0.4 = 5.4
h	20	0.2 x 7 = 1.4	0.6 x 5 = 3.0	0.2 x 3 = 0.6	1.4 + 3 + 0.6 = 5.0
i	30	0.2 x 9 = 1.8	0.6 x 6 = 3.6	0.2 x 3 = 0.6	1.8 + 3.6 + 0.6 = 6.0

Source: N. L. Enrick, *Management Planning* (New York: McGraw-Hill, Inc., 1967), p. 94.

In the next box the firm has calculated its anticipated profit for each of these markup levels. Thus, if business is good and the firm maintains a 10 percent markup, the *anticipated* gross profit would be $10 ($100 × 0.10 = $10).

The next problem for management in making a determination of this strategy is to make a subjective estimate as to the probability that business will be good, fair, or poor.

Their forecasts seem to indicate that the greatest probability of occurrence seems to be that business in the coming period will be fair, and they have thus assigned a probability value (p) of 0.6 to this outcome. The remaining possibilities of good and poor are assigned values of 0.2. These values all add up to 1.0 or 100 percent. By simply multiplying each of the *anticipated* profits by the probability of occurrence, one can conclude that the 30 percent markup would have the greatest expectation of profit per week, that is, $6,000.

This calculation does not mean that this event will take place if the firm chooses the strategy of establishing a 30 percent markup. It does mean, however, that if these probabilities are applied over a period of time they will average out to the calculations as indicated in this table.

The key question in these calculations is how does management arrive at these probabilities and estimates of the sales that will occur? The answer lies in two major areas, their own *subjective experience* and perhaps *research studies,* or *past calculations* that could prove helpful.

Monitoring and Directing the Plan

The balance of the marketing plan involves most of the activities of the marketing department throughout the year. In this aspect of its function, the marketing department actually organizes the firm and directs its resources toward accomplishing its stated objective. In addition, the marketing group is faced with the task of monitoring the results, that is, determining how well the firm is accomplishing its stated objectives.

In directing the organization, the marketing people are roughly organized in the manner spelled out in Figure 1-2. Here one sees the various departments in the marketing department, which include advertising and sales promotion, product planning, sales, product service, and marketing research. Although each firm has its own organizational arrangement to suit its own needs, most marketing departments of major firms include most of these parts within the setup. When a firm, for example, has several major products, they may have this organization reporting to a brand manager. For instance, General Foods Corporation has a complete organization reporting to the brand manager of Yuban coffee and Maxwell House coffee, two of the firm's major products.

To monitor a marketing plan, management relies mainly on quantitative data available to the firm from the accounting department or the marketing department research unit. Accounting department data may be in the form of sales comparisons or profits. The latter are usually presented in the form of profits as a percentage of sales or return on investment.

The marketing research department may develop the share-of-the-market reports for the firm, as noted earlier. This same department may indicate to management the changing attitudes of the consumer toward the firm's products.

Monitoring is a continuous process and is charged with keeping management fully informed of the firm's status in regard to the plan at all times.

Theory and Planning

The planning process includes, as noted earlier, choosing among the many alternatives that management has available. Underlying their choices is a theoretical view of how the consumer will react to the many different alternatives. For example, if the firm is marketing clocks, they must determine the possible reactions of the consumer to any activities the firm may engage in. Should the firm decide that massive advertising will help them achieve their particular objective, it may be weighed against the use of price cuts, which may accomplish the same thing.

When choosing among the many alternatives, management has to theorize about the reactions of the consumers to each or any combination of actions one may take. In the example, management may determine that price cuts are the best means to the end, rather than engaging in a strong advertising campaign, simply because they will get a more meaningful response from the consumer.

All these tentative views concerning the consumer's reaction to either advertising or price cut are theoretical. That is, they represent a preconceived notion of what might happen under certain existing conditions.

Should management theory be borne out by the marketplace, then one may conclude that the theory is a valuable one. Under these conditions, management may store that theory and use it again when similar conditions arise. On the other hand, should management find that the consumer reacts negatively to a price decrease or the additional revenue derived from such a price decrease falls far short of the firm's expectations, management will probably choose to reevaluate its theory concerning consumer behavior.

Essentially, management is constantly developing theories about the consumer and using them in establishing its basic market plan. In some industries, it is a matter of survival to establish useful theories that can be applied to the marketing of the product. An important example can be found in the apparel industry, which accounts for a substantial proportion of consumer expenditures and is related to several other important industries.

Theory becomes particularly important in this industry when dress manufacturers are trying to establish what fashions or styles will be important in the forthcoming season. In recent years, the controversy over the midi, maxi, and mini has tended to emphasize the importance of understanding not only consumer behavior, but the influence on this same consumer. In determining the influence on styles and fashions, the firm must develop a theory that leads to an understanding that can be used to develop a forecast of the fashion market. In this case management must choose among several prevalent theories:

Trickle-down theory.　The fashion theory that subscribes to the view that what the rich wear ultimately becomes the standard style for the masses within a given period of time. Thus, if the socially prominent and wealthy women are wearing, let us say, maxi-coats during this season, the theorists suggest that during the next season or the season afterward the masses will be wearing the same coat.

Trickle-up theory.   This theory has developed in recent years and emphasizes the importance of the youth cult. It is, in a sense, the opposite of the "trickle-down theory" in that it supports the view that many styles are starting with the young, a relatively low-income consumer. The advocates of this theory point to the many bizarre styles of today as emanating from this source, and in particular they lay claim to the mini style as having its origins in the "streets of London" during the 1960s.

Designer theories.   The advocates of this theory support the view that Paris showings by major couture houses strongly influence the fashion trend throughout the world. These showings held once a year in Paris display the designs of some of the major fashion designers. Since many major department and specialty stores go to great lengths to copy these fashions, the theory suggests that eventually the mass manufacturers of apparel gain much of their design patterns from these showings.

Media theories.   This theory suggests that the major fashion media tend to communicate and thus influence the selection of fashions among the masses. The influence of the major fashion magazines, trade publications, such as *Women's Wear Daily,* and other such media are said to have a strong bearing on what is produced and eventually sold.

One may ask at this point, which theory is correct? The answer is that perhaps each theory has some bearing on what is eventually bought. In addition, the point has been made that each theory may be paramount during different periods of time. As noted above, the "trickle-up theory" has more than its share of influence during the present era. In combination with this, the media have maintained a prominent role in influencing fashions. In any case, the apparel manufacturer planning his next season's fashions must carefully consider the role of each of these theories and select the one that applies to his market.

Responsibility for Market Planning

The responsibility for all phases of marketing planning falls on many departments within the marketing division. In some divisions most plans are made and developed by the marketing vice president. In many firms he makes practically all the planning decisions. In other firms the financial and control administrators are deeply involved in establishing all expenditure plans. In other firms much of the sales forecasts are developed by the marketing research departments.

In Table 3-5 one can see the responsibilities for marketing planning for Eastern Airlines within the firm's marketing division. Here one notes that the marketing vice president has primary responsibility for setting the objectives and strategies for the firm. This responsibility in this firm is not shared by any of the other major departments of the marketing department. In engaging in other planning activities, the vice president shares the planning with other divisions in the firm. For instance, in establishing department plans, the responsibility is shared with eight different departments.

It is obvious that the marketing research department plays perhaps the most important role in developing a marketing plan. They are particularly important in determining the economic conditions and the competitive moves that can be expected in the future.

The field sales force for Eastern mainly engages in sharing responsibility with other divisions. For instance, in examining travel trends primary responsibility lies with the marketing research division; however, the sales force contributes to the

TABLE 3-5   **Eastern Airlines: Responsibilities for Marketing Planning**

Within Marketing Division

	Administration	Advertising	City Ticket Offices	Market Research	Reservations	Sales – Field	Sales – Cargo	Sales – Passenger	V.P. – Marketing
1. Introduction	X								
2. a. Economic conditions and trends				X					
b. Attitudes and travel trends			O	X		O	O	O	
c. Competition				X		O	O	O	
3. a. Equipment availability and schedules				X					
b. Routes				X					
c. Competitive moves				X					
d. Fares				X					
4. a. Current position versus industry				X					
b. Current position versus last year's plans				X					
5. Objectives and strategies									X
6. a. Sales forecast – total				X		O	O		
b. Sales forecast – detailed						X	O	O	
c. Sales forecast – industry and EAL percentage				X					
d. Expense forecast	X	O	O	O	O	O	O	O	
7. a. City pair – potentials				X					
b. City pair – sales and schedule plan				X					
c. City pair – action programs		O	O	O	O	O	O	O	X
8. a. Departmental plans	X	X	X	X	X	X	X	X	X
b. Plans summary	X	O	O	O	O	O	O	O	O
c. Performance standards	X	X	X	X	X	X	X	X	X
9. Timetable	X								
10. Responsibilities	X								O

X = Primary responsibility
O = Contribution responsibility
Source: E. C. Miller, American Management Research Study 81, *Marketing Planning, Approaches of Selected Companies* (New York: American Management Association, 1967), p. 40.

development of these evaluations since they are actively engaging the customer and are in a position to understand competitive changes.

One can see, however, that the various departments within Eastern Airlines contribute in several ways to the development of a marketing plan.

SUMMARY

Change at all levels causes firms to engage in marketing planning. In establishing a plan, the firm must review the past, present, and future, select alternatives, and monitor the plan. In forecasting the firm may use informal or formal procedures. The latter require the use of statistical methods and the identification of important consumer indicators to make a forecast of sales. Accurate forecasts are the key to good planning.

In choosing alternative plans, management must rely on its understanding of consumer behavior. An example of three theories available to the management of apparel firms was offered.

QUESTIONS

1. What is marketing planning?
2. Relate marketing planning to change.
3. Relate marketing planning to the firm's objectives.
4. Discuss the four major steps in marketing planning.
5. Discuss the two types of forecasts a firm may make. Which is the most accurate?
6. What are economic indicators? How are they related to a company forecast?
*7. What economic indicators would you select (from the monthly publication, *The Survey of Current Business*) for a firm in the following industries:
   a. baby foods
   b. appliances
   c. automobiles
   d. trucks
Why would you choose each?
8. How are economic indicators related to an industry forecast?
9. How is the industry forecast related to the firm forecast?
10. In Table 3-2, why do the annual growth rates for the product lines vary? Why are ethical drugs the highest and food the lowest?
11. In Table 3-3, why does Gillette have a higher growth rate than the Green Giant Company?
12. What are forecasting models? What role do assumptions make in developing models?
13. What is the relationship between theory and planning?

*In-depth question.

14. What theory underlines the view of the marketing department that
    a. Customers will purchase just as many shirts if the price is $5.00 instead of $4.50.
    b. It is more profitable to sell a line of television sets to as many dealers as possible, in each area of the country.

Restraints on
Decision Making

4

SUMMARY KEY

Restraints exist outside management's control. They include consumerism, competition, and the legal framework of society. Consumerism is a paralegal force that has developed in the past 5 years as an important consideration in making decisions. By definition, consumerism is the term that describes the efforts by organized groups to call attention to business activities that are seen to be detrimental to the best interests of the consumer groups they represent.

Consumerism has had an evolutionary growth. The history includes the beginnings of the civil-rights marches in the South tied in with a general defiance of authority through boycotts and other nonviolent techniques. The challenges to major American business interests by Ralph Nader are a part of this movement.

Consumerism takes hold on many levels. In the form of laws, one finds state and local laws that benefit the consumer. Many of these laws are aimed at pricing policies of retailers, credit policies, and rate structures of utilities. At the national level the President has established a consumer advisor and the Congress has tended to hold public hearings that call attention to areas where the consumer is not getting his money's worth.

There exist at this time three views toward consumerism: the extreme ones hold that consumers are surrounded by sharks (businessmen), or that the marketplace will eventually supply the consumer with a product that meets his needs and thus laws are not necessary. The most widely held view at this point is the more moderate view, which recognizes that the marketplace in some cases will produce the product the consumer needs. However, it also recognizes that there exist many areas where the consumer can be protected through legislation and/or information.

The impact of consumerism has been tremendous. It has caused the formation of study groups and a more general harder look by those in power at many of the products and services sold in our society.

Consumerism has a cost, and it is noted that in some supermarkets the cost of installing and maintaining unit pricing can go as high as 4 percent of sales. However, this cost is always balanced against the consumers' getting better and more accurate information.

Businessmen spend a great deal of their time in trying to differentiate themselves from their competitors. In industries where concentration is heavy, they are not as concerned about differentiation. Yet even in industries where concentration is high, the consumer can shift to other products. If, for instance, cotton commands a monopolistic price, the consumer can buy nylon products.

In some cases concentration is brought about through marketing practices, whereas in other industries concentration may be brought about because of a monopoly of the sources of supply.

Imported merchandise has caused an increase in competition and has made it difficult for a firm to maintain a monopolistic position.

Legal restraints upon the manufacturer can be found at many levels. The major laws at the federal level are the antitrust laws, which include the Sherman, Clayton, Celler-Kefauver, Wheeler-Lea, and Robinson-Patman Acts.

In most cases the Federal Trade Commission and the Justice Department enforce these acts.

A growing group of laws that affect manufacturers are the environmental laws that have been passed at all levels of government, for instance, laws that restrict the amount of lead content in gasolines, laws banning the use of phosphates in detergents, and in the state of California laws that set pollution standards for automobiles.

In choosing among the many alternatives that are available to management and developing a meaningful strategy to reach the target market, management is well aware of the restraints that are outside their control. These restraints include consumerism, competition, and the legal framework of our society.

The fact that these restraints exist makes management's job difficult. The fact that they are outside the control of management makes them even more challenging. Management, for example, can do little about the fact that a certain law exists. True, they can lobby in the congress, state legislature, or perhaps city government to have it repealed or changed. However, as a firm, they can do little to reverse the course of legislation. In the same sense, they can do little about competition except to put forth a stronger effort in some direction to attempt to eventually neutralize its effect. However, here again they may find that the competition will react even stronger against this additional pressure.

Since management cannot control these elements in their environment, what they must do is to develop a greater understanding of each element and attempt to market their products within the confines of these uncontrollables.

Consumerism

The legal restraints on the manufacturer will be outlined later in this chapter. A nonlegal, but yet a somewhat paralegal, force that has developed in the past 5 years is referred to as *consumerism*. Although consumerism is still in an evolutionary stage, its force has become so powerful that it is affecting all levels of business. Although no definition can adequately describe consumerism at this point in time, it nevertheless has certain characteristics. First and foremost, as a social force, it represents consumer groups. Second, it is usually viewed by businessmen as being somewhat antibusiness. Third, its means of operation are to call public attention to its activities.

If one were to define consumerism, one might suggest the following: *Consumerism is the term that describes the efforts by organized groups to call attention to business activities that are seen to be detrimental to the best interests of the consumer groups they represent.*

Effect of Consumerism

Within a few short years, this force has had a strong effect on legislation and the actions of many firms. Laws establishing unit pricing[1] (presently in effect in New York City and the State of Massachusetts), setting safety standards for automobiles, or those establishing pollution controls in industrial areas are all a direct or indirect result of the growing tide of consumerism.

History of Consumerism

The history of consumerism has yet to be written. However, it is clear to many observers that several happenings have had a direct effect on the growth of this movement.

Perhaps the basis for the growth of consumerism is the early civil-rights marches and campaigns launched in the South and in many northern cities. Although consumerism was not directly related, several phenomena developed from these movements that gave impetus to the movement.

The first aspect was the *activism* seen in the marches through the streets of Montgomery, Alabama, and many other cities. Although this phenomenon was not particularly new in the rest of the world, it was a rather recent addition to the American scene.

The second aspect was the *challenging of authority* through many useful devices, such as boycotts, again a phenomenon of the civil-rights movement. The challenge of authority took place through the ignoring of local laws against demonstrations, and the willingness to go to jail in defiance of such laws that were considered to be unjust. The boycotting occurred wherever the movement found it useful to boycott merchants and thus cause a local economic crisis to occur.

The civil-rights tactics were used by other activists in the consumerism phenomenon. For example, in the early 1960s a large group of Denver housewives successfully used the economic boycott and marches to challenge high prices and the use of trading stamps by Denver supermarkets.

Naderism

The challenge to authority was probably best demonstrated by the growth in stature of Ralph Nader. Nader came into national prominence upon the publication of his book *Unsafe at Any Speed,*[2] a book that pointed out that many American cars were unsafe and that most car manufacturers had little interest in car safety. As a result of Nader's challenge to the authority of some of America's

---

[1]This law requires that the food store operator show clearly the price by weight, volume, or other unit of measure on each item of merchandise sold.

[2]Ralph Nader, *Unsafe at Any Speed* (New York: Grossman Publishers, 1965).

largest business interests, the Congress and many states passed and established auto safety standards, the end of which is still not in sight.

Although Naderism started in the area of car safety, it is branching out into all areas where the feeling is that the consumer or public interest is at issue. Thus the work of the Federal Trade Commission and all other federal agencies is being carefully scrutinized by people closely associated with this movement.

Other Developments

Consumerism is developing and growing in many ways. On the local level one finds groups challenging the credit policies of stores and banks. Many of these groups have banded together to challenge the rate structure of the telephone and electric power companies.

The cities and states have taken more interest in the growth of this movement and have started to enforce and plan legal techniques to protect the consumer. For instance, in New York State an installment contract with a seller of merchandise does not take effect until 3 days after it is signed. Thus, when a door-to-door salesman sells a consumer a product on an installment basis, the consumer need not carry out the terms of the contract if he notifies the firm of his intent not to honor the terms of the agreement. This law was passed in order to avoid the problems that ensued when people unknowingly signed a contract, only to find out at a later date that they did not know what they had signed.

On a national level one finds several changes. First is the fact that the President has been forced to recognize the growth and challenges of consumerism by appointing a consumer advisor. Under the Nixon administration, presently Mrs. Virginia Knauer holds that post.

Second, Congress has recognized consumerism as a political challenge and many have taken up the cry. For instance, hearings have been held in Washington by various Congressmen investigating the pricing policies of food chains in ghetto areas of the major cities. Congress recently enacted a credit bill that makes it mandatory for firms charging interest to indicate the annual rate on each bill to the recipient.

The aggressiveness of many of the participants in these hearings can be seen in the testimony of Robert B. Choate, who testified before the Subcommittee of the Consumer Committee on Commerce of the U.S. Senate.[3] His testimony was based on a chart and study that he prepared, which is shown in Figure 4-1. Here he indicates the nutrient content of the 60 major cereals marketed in the United States. He also noted the cost per ounce to the consumer. One can see that the cost per ounce is not necessarily related to the nutritional value of the product. For instance, his study indicated that the cost per ounce for the top 20 brands with the highest nutritional value was 3.8 cents, 4.5 cents for the middle 20, and 4.4 cents for the bottom 20. Aside from the cost relationship to nutrition, Mr. Choate presented several other important observations. First was the fact that over 50 of the 60 cereals are sugar frosted, sugar coated, or sweetened at the factory. This he believes has serious implications for children's teeth.

Most importantly, he points out that the cereals being touted by many of the companies on television rank low nutritionally. Of the nine Kellogg "television"

---

[3]"The Seduction of the Innocent," July 23, 1970.

FIGURE 4-1 Rating Chart: Cumulative Nutrient Content of Dry Breakfast Cereals[a]

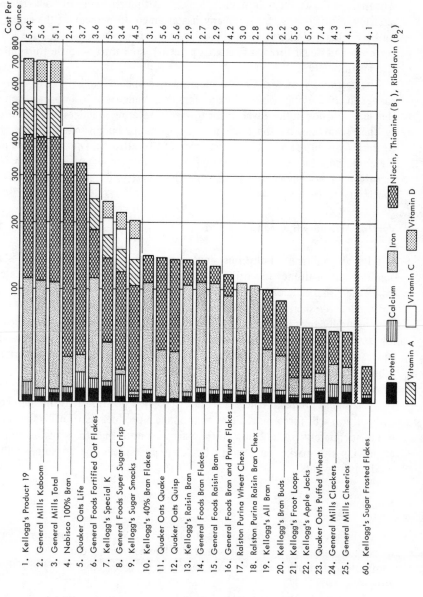

1. Kellogg's Product 19
2. General Mills Kaboom
3. General Mills Total
4. Nabisco 100% Bran
5. Quaker Oats Life
6. General Foods Fortified Oat Flakes
7. Kellogg's Special K
8. General Foods Super Sugar Crisp
9. Kellogg's Sugar Smacks
10. Kellogg's 40% Bran Flakes
11. Quaker Oats Quake
12. Quaker Oats Quisp
13. Kellogg's Raisin Bran
14. General Foods Bran Flakes
15. General Foods Raisin Bran
16. General Foods Bran and Prune Flakes
17. Ralston Purina Wheat Chex
18. Ralston Purina Raisin Bran Chex
19. Kellogg's All Bran
20. Kellogg's Bran Buds
21. Kellogg's Froot Loops
22. Kellogg's Apple Jacks
23. Quaker Oats Puffed Wheat
24. General Mills Clackers
25. General Mills Cheerios
60. Kellogg's Sugar Frosted Flakes

Cost Per Ounce

5.4¢
5.6
5.1
2.4
3.7
3.6
5.6
3.4
4.5
3.1
5.6
5.6
2.9
2.7
2.9
4.2
3.0
2.8
2.5
2.2
5.6
5.9
7.4
4.3
4.1

4.1

Legend:
- Protein
- Vitamin A
- Calcium
- Vitamin C
- Iron
- Vitamin D
- Niacin, Thiamine (B₁), Riboflavin (B₂)

[a]The sum of percentages of minimum daily requirements in nine nutrient categories.
Source: Robert B. Choate and Associates, Washington, D.C., June 1970.

71

cereals, he observed that only two are in the top 20 nutritionally. Of the cereals promoted by other major cereal manufacturers on Saturday morning shows (each with a budget exceeding $500,000), none are in the top nine nutritionally, and, he adds, all contain sugar. One of the major advertisers (but not a Saturday advertiser), Wheaties, ranks twenty-ninth nutritionally. Although many of Kellogg's products rank low nutritionally, the company has attained 43 percent of the cereal market. Its best sellers, Kellogg's Corn Flakes (9 percent of the market), Rice Krispies (5 percent), and Sugar Frosted Flakes (5 percent), rank thirty-eighth, thirty-ninth, and last nutritionally.

The testimony of Mr. Choate received widespread publicity and caused some change in the buying habits of many families. Aside from its impact, it represents a changing attitude in the government toward marketing practices of some firms.

The recent ban by the Federal Trade Commission on television advertising of cigarettes would seem to be an extension of this attitude. One might also note that the continuing interest in environment and pollutants, whether it be waste from a factory or a no-deposit bottle scarring the countryside, are prime targets for this continuing force.

Varying Attitudes toward Consumerism

Like all political discussions and controversies, there exist many shades of opinions and attitudes toward consumerism. Among the extreme advocates, there exists the "shark theory." This is that the consumer is all alone in the water and surrounded by sharks (businessmen) who are out to devour him. Holders of this view naturally take an extreme position regarding most products and usually press for strong government intervention on behalf of the consumer. Few of these advocates believe that the consumer has sufficient knowledge or information to protect himself from the "sharks."

At the other extreme, one finds the "marketplace" theory, usually subscribed to by business interests. These advocates take the position that the marketplace or competition will force most firms to produce a product that fulfills the consumers' needs adequately. In addition, these partisans note that the growing emphasis on employing the marketing concept by firms guarantees the consumer will get the products he wants.

Moderate

At the present time groups on both sides tend to accept a more moderate view of consumerism. This view holds that the two extreme groups hold positions that contain much truth, but, by overstating their case, tend to ignore the middle ground.

Subscribers to the moderate view hold that product problems arise mostly in products when the consumer lacks knowledge. The variance in product knowledge can be substantial. Thus the purchaser of chewing gum has a great deal of knowledge based on previous purchases at a relatively low cost. Since most gum is made in a similar fashion, his choice usually satisfies his needs. One might add that the cost of chewing gum makes the choice even less critical.

At the other extreme, one might find a product for which the consumer has practically no knowledge. Diamonds may represent this extreme. Here the consumer has little knowledge and relies on experts to support his purchase. Even experts disagree, as anyone can attest to who has had a diamond appraiser determine the value of a stone. Drugs, car maintenance, and furniture perhaps represent other products and services of this type.

The holders of the moderate view recognize that competition and the marketplace play a role in controlling the quality of many products. Thus, should a product not measure up to standards, the consumer has the choice of not repurchasing that product on his next trip to the store. Or one may find that a competitor may be quick to point out its failings – even including differences in ingredients. Thus, in the New York area, the Dannon Yogurt Company, faced with a challenge by the Sealtest Company, a much larger competitor, was quick to note in its advertisements that the Sealtest Yogurt contained artificial ingredients not found in Dannon Yogurt. Volvo, a Swedish-made car, has placed great emphasis on its durability, a factor the firm believes the consumer does not obtain in American-made cars.

Nevertheless, the consumerists holding the moderate view believe there are many areas where government or organized consumer interests should play a role. Thus they advocate more government controls of new drug products. They suggest that the U.S. government set standards of quality for such products as tires and foods and vegetables. They recognize that there are many areas where competition may force a manufacturer to produce a product that is actually detrimental to the lives of consumers, in order to meet competition. They point to competition in the tire industry, where manufacturer's classifications, such as premium, may be meaningless, in that such a tire may not meet minimum safety standards for turnpike driving.

Attempts to deceive may include reducing the contents of a cereal package, yet maintaining the same size box. Failure to carry or spell out warranties is also an area that has attracted even moderate consumer advocates.

Impact of Consumerism

The growth of consumerism has had a direct impact on government on all levels. Much of this action has affected both legal and quasi-legal actions of each of these bodies.

On a national level the impact on the federal government has grown substantially. The government's reaction has been both direct and indirect.

Directly, the consumer movement has resulted in the federal government passing laws establishing important guidelines for business that will hopefully aid the consumer. The laws have ranged from federal government control over consumer information on credit to forcing automobile dealers to post manufacturer's suggested list prices on all new automobiles. As noted previously, the government establishment of a presidential advisor on consumer affairs represents direct action by this same body.

Indirectly, government action has been just as persuasive. This action has taken the form of Congressional hearings that attempt to expose the failings of many companies to deal with serious consumer problems. For example, in May of 1971 the Senate held hearings concerning the maintenance costs involved in caring for automobiles. Much of the testimony revolved around the fact that American consumers spend millions of dollars on parts and maintenance. One witness was Ralph Nader.

The federal government also uses many of its directive and publicity devices to act on the consumer's behalf. For example, recently the Federal Drug Administration issued a release that noted that swordfish has such a high mercury content that it was judged to be dangerous. The FDA has taken the position that mercury in food can cause tumors, mouth ulcers, produce birth defects, cause kidney disease, and affect the central nervous system.

In recent months the FDA has started a program of reexamining drugs now on the market to determine whether they are as effective as the manufacturers supplying and the physicians using the drugs believe. This power derives from a law passed in 1962, which gave the FDA the power to determine both the effectiveness and safety of drugs on the market.

The government has also engaged special study groups to examine problems related to the consumer. For example, recently the government established a National Commission on Product Safety. After many months of study, this commission reported that there are many products that are unacceptable risks for the consumer. Some of these are listed in Table 4-1. They range all the way from

TABLE 4-1   Products Posing Unacceptable Risks to Consumers

Product	*Hazard*
Architectural glass	Insufficient use of safety glazing
Color television sets	Fires resulting from high voltages
Fireworks	Explosion, fire
Floor furnaces	Floor grate temperatures of $300-400°F$
Glass bottles	Weak or thin glass that explodes or shatters
High-rise bicycles	Poor stability, unsafe design features
Hot-water vaporizers	Easily upset, spilling scalding water
Household chemicals	Petroleum distillates, caustics, and corrosives found in dishwasher detergents, furniture polishes, drain and toilet bowl cleaners
Infant furniture	Bars on cribs, easily-toppled highchairs
Ladders	Lack of nonslip feet, treads, end tips; sharp corners
Power tools	Lack of hoods, guards; shock hazards
Protective headgear	Lack of standards for sport and motorcycle helmets
Rotary lawn mowers	Lack of guards, hoods; failure to meet industry's own safety standards
Toys	Electrical, mechanical, and thermal hazards; deafening noise
Unvented gas heater	Carbon monoxide
Wringer washing machines	Lack of safety release mechanism long available for use

Source: *Business Week,* July 4, 1970, p. 37.

architectural glass to the wringer washing machine. Some, of course, represent small product markets, but in the case of television sets, they can be damaging to markets that represent a major industry.

In most cases, when the commission reports point an accusing finger at an industry, the firms in the industry may take action to avoid government restrictions. Many times the industry responds by setting up minimum industry standards to overcome publicized product failings. Although this may *not* have been the industry practice in previous years, with the growth of the consumer movement, many industries are reluctant to ignore such reports.

This is not difficult to understand, since many of these reports uncover damaging information. For example, the *National Commission on Product Safety* had this to say about glass bottles:

> . . . we find that glass bottles used for carbonated beverages present an unreasonable risk to consumers. When one of these bottles fails, the glass under internal pressure bursts into splinters. Because of this pressure, bottles of carbonated drinks are more hazardous than those containing inert beverages.
> Although explosions are the most dramatic cause of injury from glass bottles, they are not the most common. Insurance companies reported more claims related to glass bottles than to any other consumer product.
> . . . Responses to our inquiries from the six largest bottlers indicate that 5,000 to 7,000 injuries are reported annually. Hospital records confirm that glass bottles consistently rank high among products connected with injuries treated in emergency clinics.

State and Local Levels

On the state and local levels similar approaches are used. Many states have attempted to aid the consumer by concentrating on the powers of the state's law official (usually the attorney general). This official has the power to conduct investigations of consumer complaints and advise the legislature on possible legislation that is needed. The law office has the power to institute legal proceedings against corrupt firms and stop firms, which in his opinion are defrauding the consumer, from conducting business in his state.

At the local or citywide level, many consumer affairs departments have been instituted to help alert the consumer to business practices that are considered to be detrimental. New York City, in recent years, has established just such a department that presently is actively engaged in many programs on behalf of the consumer. Many of these practices are publicized by this department, which calls attention to short weighing, misleading packaging, and high fat content in hamburgers.

Not all campaigns for consumerism are waged by governmental bodies. For example, the Allstate Insurance Company (owned by Sears, Roebuck) has waged a strong and well-publicized campaign to get American car manufacturers to produce cars with bumpers that will absorb punishment. In these ads Allstate has noted that a collision at 5 miles per hour can cause extensive car damage. The firm goes on to state that they will automatically reduce insurance premiums to anybody buying a car that will absorb the impact of a collision at speeds of 10 miles per hour.

Cost of Consumerism

From the firm's point of view, consumerism can be costly. In some cases, many of the steps that are necessary to meet the demands of consumer groups can increase costs substantially. Many of these changes can result in higher prices and thus, in effect, the consumer may end up paying for consumerism.

In Table 4-2 one sees the results of a recent study of the cost of establishing a unit pricing system in food chains. In this table one can see that stores with sales volume of up to $100,000 in chains with 20 or less stores incur costs that exceed 4 percent of sales. In chain stores having 90 or more firms, one sees that the costs drop dramatically. In the very large sales volume stores, that is, those with sales exceeding $2 million, the cost for the largest chain drops to less than 1 percent. One should also note that regardless of the sales volume those chains with 20 or less stores incur the highest cost of unit pricing in all volume groups. In essence, therefore, this study seems to indicate clearly that the smaller grocery chains incur the highest cost in order to carry out unit pricing.

TABLE 4-2   Direct Cost of Unit Pricing as a Percentage of Sales

Sales Volume of Stores ($)	*Number of Stores in Chain*			
	20	*40*	*60*	*90*
Up to 100,000	4.15	3.61	3.43	3.31
100,000 to 150,000	2.49	2.16	2.06	1.98
150,000 to 300,000	1.38	1.20	1.14	1.10
300,000 to 500,000	0.78	0.68	0.64	0.62
500,000 to 1,000,000	0.42	0.36	0.34	0.33
1 to 2 million	0.21[a]	0.18	0.17	0.17
More than 2 million	0.12	0.10	0.099	0.095

Source: T. David McCullough and Daniel I. Padberg, "Unit Pricing in Supermarkets: Alternatives, Costs, and Consumer Reaction," *Search Agriculture,* Vol. 1, No. 6, January 1971 (Cornell University Agricultural Experiment Station, Ithaca, N.Y.), p. 9.

Other important points are also raised in this study. It was noted that only about half the consumers perceived and understood unit pricing, and, most importantly, those least likely to understand are the disadvantaged groups, that is, those who are held to be needing help the most.

Those opposed to consumerism also point out that if many of the consumer pressures are acted upon by business the consumer may end up paying a high price for these efforts. In addition, many feel that the steps taken may not help those most in need of such protection.

To balance this cost, one must consider that consumerism has forced business to become more aware of its relationship with the consumer. This pressure has forced marketing people to study the past buying experiences of consumers and in many cases assume responsibility for many of the failures of their products. The recall of thousands of American cars (one might add even the Rolls-Royce) to make changes because of safety problems is a good example of this changing attitude.

All decisions made by marketing management are made with competitors in mind. Although throughout this text the role of competition will be recognized, the structure of competition and its impact on marketing will be discussed here.

Most businessmen are aware of competition. In a sense many of their efforts are directed at differentiating themselves from competition. How well they accomplish this depends on many factors, one of which is certainly the structure of the industry. By structure one refers to the number and size of competitors. Thus, should a manufacturer operate in an industry where there are tens of thousands of small firms, he will most likely find it extremely difficult to distinguish his product line. Conversely, in industries where the numbers are much smaller a firm may find it easier.

Aside from competitors, manufacturers are also careful to watch new products that are being made available and particularly those that may be classified as substitutable. Thus United States Steel is very conscious of the price of aluminum when they establish prices for their products. Similarly, General Motors is not only aware of the pricing plans of its arch competitors, Ford and Chrysler, but must also consider the prices of many of the foreign small car imports.

Concentration

The ability of the firm to control its activities and environment may be attributed to the concentration within the industry to a great extent. The concentration ratio simply indicates the share of the market held by a small number of the firms in the industry. Table 4-3 indicates the share of market held by the 4,

Concentration Ratios in Selected American Industries, 1967   TABLE 4-3

Industry	Total Number of Companies	Percentage of Value of Shipments Accounted for by		
		4 Largest	8 Largest	20 Largest
Chewing gum	19	86	96	100
Soap and detergents	599	70	78	86
Envelopes	172	32	44	63
House slippers	125	22	37	63
Distilled liquor	70	54	71	88
Women's hosiery	302	32	44	64
Luggage	325	34	45	59
Flour	438	30	46	76
Radios and TV sets	303	49	69	85
Cotton weaving mills	218	30	48	68
Commercial printing	11,955	14	21	29
Fur goods	1,304	5	8	15

Source: *Census of Manufacturers, 1967*, Vol. 1 (Washington, D.C.: U.S. Department of Commerce, Bureau of the Census, 1967).

8, and 20 largest firms in several industries. Note for instance that in the soap industry the top four firms control over 70 percent of the total shipments. In direct contrast, the top four fur-goods manufacturers account for no more than 5 percent of the total shipments in their industry. In further analyzing the soap industry, one might note that the four companies that control most of the industry represent less than 1 percent of the total number of soap firms.

One should be careful, however, in jumping to conclusions concerning monopoly and its impact on the marketing of products. First, one should be aware of the fact that consumers can shift to different industry products when they encounter a monopolistic price. For instance, when a consumer finds the price of a cotton product to be unrealistically high, he can shift into buying products made from synthetics. This has always been true in the raw materials suppliers areas, where producers find they can easily shift from steel-made products to aluminum or plastic products if the price becomes unrealistic.

One should also be aware of the fact that much of the concentration ratios may be due to good marketing practices on the part of companies that enable them to deliver goods to the public at a price that is extremely low and looked upon favorably. For instance, the largest soap companies have engaged in furious price competition over the years, although as noted the concentration ratios are considered to be high.

One factor to be considered in evaluating the impact of a highly concentrated industry on market control is the reason the firm has managed to maintain such control. Thus, in the case of a basic raw materials industry, such as aluminum, the concentration may occur simply because a few companies can control the basic raw material supplies. On the other hand, the control of soap products in this country is primarily due to the ability of the firms to identify markets and develop brands that people prefer. Thus, in the case of the soap company, the barrier to entry is the *product preference* by consumers, whereas in the case of the aluminum industry the barrier to entry may be the *control of the sources of supply.* In the former case, one can safely say that marketing has made the company a factor in the industry. Marketing could also be a contributing factor in the case of aluminum; however, it is likely that control of the sources of supply would be the major governing force.

The impact of concentration ratios in the marketing of consumer products can be seen in Figure 4-2. Here one sees that the top 200 companies in the United States, representing 135 industries, account for a substantial proportion of the business in several industries. For instance, in industries where the four leading companies made over 75 percent of the shipments, companies among these 200 accounted for 87 percent of the business. In direct contrast, the largest corporations made only 14 percent of the shipments in industries where four-firm concentration was under 25 percent.

When consumer products industries are divided by the degree of product differentiation, the 200 manufacturing firms account for almost three quarters of all shipments. These industries would include heavily advertised products, such as cereals or household soap products. Here again is indicated the importance of marketing in causing this concentration of business among these firms.

One should also remember that although a company in the United States has control over a market on a domestic level it does not necessarily mean that they do not face competition. For instance, it is true that the big three automobile companies control perhaps more than 85 percent of the total automobiles sold in this country. It is also true, however, that foreign competition has started to become a major consideration in the marketing policies of the major manufacturers. In recent years one has seen this in the sales growth of the Volkswagen and the Japanese cars. As a direct result, the U.S. car makers have been forced to produce a whole series of minicars to meet this competition, in spite of their strong hold on domestic sales.

What causes the variance in concentration ratios among manufacturing firms? Why do the four largest soap companies control upward of 70 percent of the market, whereas the top four manufacturers of fur goods perhaps account for 5 percent of industry sales? The answer seems to lie in two related and yet different factors: *product differentiation* and *barriers to entry.*[4]

Share of Value Added Held by Top 200 in 135 Manufacturing Industries, 1963   FIGURE 4-2

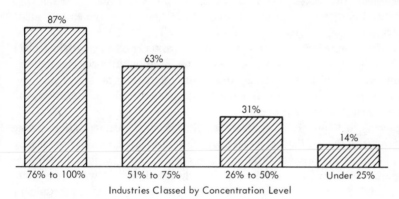

Industries Classed by Concentration Level

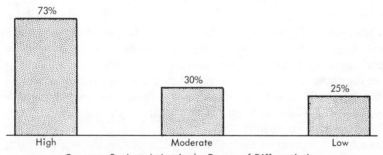

Consumer Products Industries by Degree of Differentiation

Source: *Economic Concentration,* Hearings, Subcommittee on Antitrust and Monopoly of the Committee on the Judiciary, U.S. Senate, Ninety-first Congress, First Session, 1969, p. 215.

[4]Richard Caves, *American Industry: Structure, Conduct and Performance,* 2nd ed. (Englewood Cliffs, N.J.: Prentice-Hall, Inc., 1967), p. 16.

Product differentiation refers to the ability of a manufacturer to make his product distinctive from others on the market. One could define marketing as all the effort exerted by the manufacturer to differentiate his product from his competitors. This differentiation must be relevant to the consumer. It may be real or imagined, but nevertheless is meaningful.

This is not to say that all products are differentiated from each other. In the *industrial* field, where manufacturers sell to other manufacturers, many of the products are graded and may be treated alike. Thus the miller may order No. 2 wheat from a farm cooperative at a given market price. He may have little interest in where the wheat is grown or which of the thousands of grain elevators expedites the delivery.

Similarly, General Motors, needing a certain strength steel for its automobiles, may search for a supplier that can deliver the steel at a competitive price.

Although many of these industrial products seem to be undifferentiated, it does not necessarily follow that all products from given firms are treated exactly alike. For instance, although United States Steel may sell a similar steel product as Bethlehem Steel, United States Steel, in a given market, may have a larger plant capacity than Bethlehem and thus be in a better position to meet the delivery requirements of General Motors. Thus product differentiation takes into consideration not only the product itself, but the many times the services, location, and perhaps the availability of the product.

As a general rule, one is most likely to find product differentiation among *consumer goods* products, that is, goods that are sold to the consumer for use by his family. Much of the product differentiation occurs simply because the firm has done a superior job in marketing. Hence, a well-advertised product with a particular theme may catch the interest of the consumer and become a part of the consumer's preference schedule. A consumer, through advertising and promotion, may come to prefer a *particular brand* – a term that is almost synonymous with product differentiation.

The manufacturer selling his product through a retailer may find that through careful selection of outlets he may be able to differentiate his product and therefore gain consumer acceptance. For instance, the American Tack Company produces and distributes tacks, usually on a small cardboard square, throughout the United States. By careful and unusual distribution policies, they have managed to maintain a substantial fraction of the market in an industry where the product itself can be easily copied by other manufacturers.

Even products that seem quite similar can be differentiated through marketing. For instance, although certain grades of oranges look alike, the Sunkist marketing cooperative has managed to develop an identification that has some effect on consumer buying habits.

Why are manufacturers interested in increasing the differentiation of their products? The answer lies in the *impact* on the demand for his product. The wheat farmer or granary in the preceding example will be unable to raise his asking price above the market, because the buyer (in this case the miller) does not distinguish between wheat. By the same token, he would be foolish to ask for less, because he can obtain the going market price. In addition, by asking for less, he may trigger a price war, because the product is undifferentiated.

On the other hand, the producer of a differentiated product may be in a position to hold his price above other producers simply because a large segment of the market prefers his product because of whatever characteristics it may have. Thus the makers of Schweppes Quinine Water may maintain a market price above other competing products simply because the consumer does not feel they are similar.

Barriers to Entry

If competitors find it difficult to enter an industry because of substantial barriers, then a manufacturer can increase his share of the market and thereby maintain greater control over an industry. The barriers may be in many forms.

From a marketing point of view, the above-mentioned product differentiation may loom as the largest and most effective barrier to the entry of new firms. Nothing is more imposing to a potential entrant than one firm holding a substantial share of the market. Thus a potential new entrant into the electric typewriter market may be discouraged by the fact that IBM commands over 60 percent of the office typewriter market.

There exist other formidable barriers to entry. A firm holding a long-term patent may defy competition during this period of time. Other barriers relate to the potential cost of entering a market. Thus it surely would cost a firm hundreds of millions of dollars to enter the steel industry, with little guarantee of being profitable. Many firms have established a distribution system that bars only the most hardy from entering their industry. For instance, suppose that a cosmetic manufacturer was planning to compete with Avon products by also selling directly to the housewife. Entering the market would include at least the following steps:

1. Recruiting and training a national sales force to sell door-to-door.
2. Hiring regional managers to supervise the sales force.
3. Establishing warehouses to maintain a stock of products to deliver to salesmen.
4. Either contracting for production or developing your own factories to produce the products.
5. Hiring a total marketing team to design and promote a new line of cosmetic products.

No doubt, these are only some of the parts that would have to be coordinated to be a major threat to Avon. All this, of course, would involve a substantial investment, and here again there is little guarantee of success, since Avon is one of the most profitable and efficiently run cosmetic companies in the world.

It is interesting to note that should this same company decide to compete with Revlon, a firm that sells only through retail outlets, the investment and risk would probably be less, simply because it would not be necessary to maintain huge stocks of merchandise through all areas of the country. In addition, in competing with Revlon, the firm would not find it necessary to recruit such a large sales force, since they are selling through stores that reach thousands of women shoppers. This would, no doubt, reduce the investment requirement and thus a substantial barrier to entry.

Small Firm Competition

Barriers to entry are particularly imposing to a small firm. However, small firms are not always at a total disadvantage in competing against large firms. They do have some advantages. Most of their advantages revolve around their ability to remain flexible. For example, the small grocery store can manage to compete against the large chain supermarket by being flexible. The small store may choose to open earlier and close later than its larger competitor. This same store may change its window prices at any time and may, if it so chooses, offer the consumer free delivery. For the chain to follow any of these competitive moves would require a major change in firm policy, which in turn would affect hundreds of stores.

By stressing flexibility, the smaller marketing firm can often neutralize the power of the large firm in a similar manner. Many times this ability takes a strange turn. For instance, when Procter & Gamble was testing Head and Shoulders, a dandruff shampoo in the early 1960s, they tested the product's saleability in four different markets. Alberto Culver, a much smaller firm, observed this testing and actually produced and marketed a similar product called Subdue. By accomplishing this quickly, they actually beat Procter & Gamble to the market. As a result, the powerful Procter & Gamble was put in the position of forcing itself into a market where Subdue was first.[5]

Foreign Competition

Although one usually thinks of competition in terms of other manufacturers in this country, the realities of marketing today are such that foreign competition is an important consideration. For instance, by 1970 the Japanese had captured approximately 30 percent of the United States market for television sets. They did this in several ways. The first was by selling their regular production run television product at prices reported to be 15 to 20 percent below the retail prices in Japan.[6] Second, in some cases they marketed a superior or at least a high-quality product aimed at a substantial segment of the U.S. market. Falling into this category are the Sony and Panasonic products.

Foreign competition in recent years has hit several industries hard. Notable are the shoe and apparel industries. In recent years the men's wear industry has fallen victim to products brought in from Asia.

To combat this problem, industries have put pressure on Congress to raise tariffs. Others have turned to either manufacturing in many of these countries for the U.S. market or purchasing through foreign firms. Recently, Chrysler Corporation purchased a Japanese manufacturer of automobiles.

Legal
Restraints

Perhaps no stronger force exists to restrain the decisions that marketing managers may make than that of the legal environment he must contend with. The legal environment consists of all the laws and interpretations of the laws that are

---

[5]*Dun's Review and Modern Industry,* Jan. 1964, p. 96.

[6]*Forbes,* May 1, 1971, p. 16.

aimed at the many facets of the firm's activities. These laws include not only those at the federal level, but the state and local level as well.

The role of the government in restraining the activities of the marketing department of the firm has expanded greatly in the past 10 years. It is probably true to say that almost any decision made by the marketing department must consider the legal implications. This can include advertising programs, pricing, functional discounts offered channel members, promotional allowances of all kinds, and even planned company acquisitions. Government involvement many times is not subtle. Many advertising agencies now seek Federal Trade Commission approval before launching an advertising campaign.

A summary of some of the major laws is shown in Table 4-4.

Antitrust Laws

Most of the powers of federal government over marketing are derived from the antitrust laws and their amendments that have developed throughout the better part of this century. Court cases that have been decided have made clear to most firms the factors they must weigh in making a business decision.

Sherman Antitrust Act. The Sherman Act passed in 1890 was the first major piece of legislation enacted by Congress that attempted to restrict what was considered to be conspiracies in restraint of trade.

Both Sections 1 and 2 of this act were aimed at controlling either persons or companies that attempt to monopolize or "conspire" to monopolize trade. The effectiveness of the Sherman Act can be seen by examining the many court cases that have evolved over the years. The Act as it has been interpreted bans all collusive actions on the part of firms to establish prices or restrict competition. In addition, the Act has been used to force companies to either split up or avoid establishing a monopolistic share of a product's market. In a number of cases the Act has been interpreted to exclude many territorial agreements. In the famous Sealy Mattress case the courts ruled that the Sealy agreement to give exclusive territories to each dealer was in effect a horizontal price-fixing arrangement, and thus represented a collusive means of control.

Clayton Act and Federal Trade Commission Act. It was the view of many observers that the Sherman Act was weak simply because it did not spell out many of the things that could be considered illegal. The Act, for example, failed to indicate what types of price discrimination could be a violation of the Act.

As a means of becoming more descriptive of such violations, Congress passed the Clayton Act in 1914. This Act spelled out more explicitly the actions that sellers in particular could not engage in. For instance, Section 2 of the Act forbids price discrimination between like purchasers; in addition, price discrimination is permitted only where cost savings can be justified.

In conjunction with the passing of the Clayton Act, Congress also passed the Federal Trade Commission Act, which empowered this new body to enforce many of the provisions of the antitrust acts. The main difference between antitrust enforcement previous to the new acts was the fact that the government could take actions before a violation occurred, whereas previously they had had to wait until

TABLE 4-4   History of Major Federal Laws Affecting Marketing

Year	Act	Main Impact	Amended (by)
1890	Sherman	Monopoly or restraint of trade. Sections affecting price, product, place, and size.	By Clayton Act: Product and Place.
1914	Clayton	Lessen competition or create monopoly. Section 3: Product, Place, and Price. Specific practices spelled out.	By Miller-Tydings Act: permitted vertical price-fixing in Section 2. By Celler-Kefauver Act: Antimerger. By Robinson-Patman Act: Section 2 on price discrimination
1914	FTC	Misleading practices: regulatory agency; unfair competition; basing points.	By McGuire Act: nonsigner's clause approved. By Wheeler-Lea Act: specified practices and strengthened in three ways
1936	Robinson-Patman	Price discrimination: quantity discounts, brokerage and promotional allowances.	Basic legislation and judicial interpretation.
1937	Miller-Tydings	Permits vertical price-fixing.	Amended Section 2. Sherman Act.
1938	Wheeler-Lea	Unfair competition: Outlines specific practices.	Amended FTC Act: strengthened three ways.
1950	Celler-Kefauver	Antimerger.	Amended Clayton Act: more control over mergers.
1952	McGuire	Collusion permitted for nonsigner's clause.	Amended Section 5 of FTC Act.

Source: William T. Ryan and Roger H. Hermanson, *Programmed Learning Aid for Principles of Marketing* (Homewood, Ill.: Richard D. Irwin, Inc, 1971), p. 123.

there was a breach of the law. As a result, the FTC was given the power of deciding what constitutes an act that tended to lessen competition. In addition, the FTC was given the power to control false advertising, since its use tended to lessen competition.

The aggressiveness of the FTC has become quite noticeable in the past few years in case after case. For example, recently the Commission attempted to force the Coca-Cola Company to pay $100 each to thousands of unsuccessful contestants in a promotional game called "Big Name Bingo." An undisclosed rule of the contest, according to the government, was that certain questions required more than one correct answer. Only 800 prizes were awarded. However, 1.5 million persons participated. If the FTC pursued this tactic, Coca-Cola could be obligated to pay out $150 million in prize money.[7]

It was the government's view when the FTC was formed to establish guidelines for business through prosecuting cases. In this way the government establishes ground rules, which in effect act as guidelines for businessmen.

However, as time went by it became clear that this approach was becoming less and less effective. The reasons became clear. First, establishing precedents takes time. In contrast, one finds that new marketing practices are proliferating, and by the time cases are established and decisions reached, marketing may be moving down another road. While cases are being argued, the business's legal advisors are probably not able to offer any meaningful advice that will hold up over a long period of time.[8]

The tendency in recent years has been for the FTC to offer businessmen advice on what practices constitute a violation of our antitrust laws. To accomplish this they have established industry guidelines, advisory opinions, trade regulation rules, and policy statements.[9]

The Celler-Kefauver Act. The Celler-Kefauver Antimerger Act of 1950 was aimed at firms that attempted to avoid prosecution under Section 7 of the Clayton Act, which prohibits firms from buying stock of competing firms and thus lessening competition. This act was an amendment to Section 7 and plugged a loophole in the original section by also including not only stock purchases, but buying of assets also. By doing this the government hoped to limit the mergers of firms in competing businesses.

The Wheeler-Lea Act. The Wheeler-Lea Act passed in 1938 broadened Section 5 of the Federal Trade Commission Act. As a result of an adverse court decision, the government found that the court interpreted Section 5 to include only violations when an act tended to lessen competition. In a fraudulent advertising case the court ruled that since the advertising did not tend to lessen competition it was not a violation, even though the consumer was obviously hurt. The Wheeler-Lea Act broadened the FTC Act to include cases when the continuance of such a practice would tend to be detrimental to the consumer's interests.

---

[7] *The New York Times,* July 9, 1970, pp. 1, 61.

[8] W. F. Mueller, "The FTC and Current Marketing Interfaces," from Reed Moyer, ed., *Changing Marketing Systems* (Chicago: American Marketing Association, 1967), p. 34.

[9] *Ibid.,* p. 34.

Robinson–Patman Act. Probably the most controversial law that is presently a restraining force in the marketing field is the Robinson–Patman Act of 1936. This act amended Section 2 of the Clayton Act.

It was aimed at controlling large buyers, and in reality was a direct result of the activities of the Great Atlantic & Pacific Tea Company during the depression. A&P was considered to be pressuring suppliers of food and gaining discounts by doing so. Many of these discounts were not available to others.

As a direct result, the Act was aimed at preventing price discrimination favoring large buyers. Under the Act the seller cannot discriminate in price between buyers of like grade and quality – and he cannot discriminate if it tends "to lessen competition." Its intention originally was to prevent buyers from gaining discriminating discounts. The interesting aspect of the act is that when it was finally drawn up it strengthened the FTC's enforcement against the seller. An indication of this was noted in 1966 in that of the 1,100 cease-and-desist orders only 30 or 3 percent were issued against buyers.[10]

The Robinson–Patman Act also contains provisions against offering price discounts in other forms, such as cooperative or merchandising allowances, unless they are offered proportionately to all buyers.

The problem for both the FTC and the defendent is that it may be cheaper for a manufacturer to sell to one firm than to another. Thus a manufacturer of basketballs will certainly find it cheaper to sell 10,000 basketballs directly to Sears, rather than a dozen each to 800 small stores. Still and all, this has to be proved, and if forced to, a firm may feel it too costly to fight a cease-and-desist order. For example, General Electric spent $100,000 for a study justifying its quantity discount for radio and television tubes.[11]

If justified, the seller can offer quantity discounts. This, of course, does not stop him from offering trade discounts to buyers on different levels. For instance, a manufacturer of radios can offer a large retailer a different price than a wholesaler, since they are not in the same channel level.

Effects of Robinson–Patman Act. Most observers admit that the Robinson–Patman Act has not succeeded in its intention of reducing discrimination. However, it has had the effect of making sellers and buyers more cautious in their dealings. The problem arises in that it has never been too clear as to how it can be enforced. For example, consider the case of the buyer representing a department store. Suppose that a manufacturer offers him a product at a given price. The buyer at this point has no information as to the price the manufacturer has been selling to other retailers. The price offered could be higher or lower than others are paying. He has no way of knowing and in effect could find himself in violation of the Robinson–Patman Act. For that matter, the FTC does not know the manufacturer's costs either. The enforcement of the act, of course, has not stopped price discrimination. For instance, one soap manufacturer indicates he gets around the proportional provisions by offering smaller buyers discounts he knows they will not participate in.[12]

---

[10]*Business Week,* Nov. 12, 1966, p. 66.

[11]*Ibid.,* p. 68.

[12]*Ibid.,* p. 3.

Other firms simply buy the total output of a small firm and avoid the problem. In any case, this act has caused the buyer and seller to think carefully before making a pricing decision.

Enforcement of the Acts

The enforcement of these acts falls under the jurisdiction of both the FTC and the Justice Department. The FTC is solely responsible for enforcement of the FTC Act; both are entrusted with enforcing the provisions of the Clayton Act and its many amendments. As a general rule, the Justice Department enforces the Sherman Act.

Within recent years a whole new series of laws has been developing that attempts to curb what is considered to be the pollution of the air, water, and land. These laws, numbering in the hundreds, are being legislated on all levels of government, that is, federal as well as state and local.

Environmental Laws

Some of the more prominent environmental laws presently cover the following products:

1. The use of lead in gasoline is presently being scrutinized by many states. Some states have already placed an additional tax burden on leaded gasoline. Federal legislation is expected momentarily.

2. The labeling of the phosphate content of detergents is now common. Some states, cities, and counties have banned the sale of phosphate detergents completely.

3. Some cities are presently considering the banning of nonreturnable bottles; others are considering placing restrictive taxes on their use.

4. The uses of insecticides are being regulated and their production is being made more difficult.[13]

The development of and intensive interest in these laws are a direct outgrowth of the consumerism trends described earlier in this chapter. Their impact on the marketing of products even at this early stage has been considerable.

Perhaps one of the most important effects has been the setting of standards for firms in the same line or business. This has meant that many firms that may have chosen polluting as a means of saving money have now been forced to operate under the same conditions. For example, although the use of phosphates, at least at this stage of development, will most likely make clothes cleaner, the restrictions placed on phosphate detergents will force most companies to either come up with a substitute or eventually reduce the phosphate content of their detergents. In addition, firms have been faced with the problem of phasing out an old successful product and replacing it with a more pollution-free product.

The challenges to the firm due to the development of environmental laws reach into the cost aspects of their operation. For instance, the firm usually finds that most of the changes require additional expenditures that must be passed on to the consumer. However, in some industries these additional costs, because of

---

[13]R. H. Aldrich, "Environmental Controls: The Growing Impact on Industrial Marketing," *Marketing Review,* May, 1971, p. 9.

competition, must be absorbed. This fact of course raises new problems and social issues, particularly in industries that are relatively high on pollution but low on their ability to absorb the additional costs of reducing pollution.

Agencies
of the
Federal
Government

Several government agencies also act at times to curb the activities of firms. One of the most active agencies within the federal government is the Food and Drug Administration. This agency is entrusted with carefully evaluating all food and drugs sold in the United States. Enforcement by the FDA includes seizure of lots of foods that are produced and injunctions to stop such production. However, the most potent weapon available to the FDA today has been recognized as its ability to generate unfavorable publicity for an unsafe product. The agency does this by publicizing products that they feel are a definite hazard to health.

State and Local

The manufacturer in some cases must concern himself with laws on the local and state level. On the local level one finds restrictions such as when a county forbids the sale of detergents containing phosphates. In addition, a city may restrict the products certain retailers may sell and the location of retail outlets.

On the state level several types of laws can restrict the manufacturer. For example, the state of California has several laws that will force automobile manufacturers to adjust their product to adhere to pollution standards in the near future. New York State requires that distillers sell their product at the lowest prices to liquor wholesalers. Some states restrict the use of credit and trading stamps. Others have a minimum markup law that sets minimum price standards for products such as milk and cigarettes.

SUMMARY

In this chapter the restraints that represent the uncontrollable environment of the manufacturer have been discussed in detail. These restraints include the consumerism movement, competition, and the legal system. The newest and yet perhaps the most potent force faced by the manufacturer is consumerism. This force takes the form of organized groups and, more recently, governmental bodies, whether they be commissions or official government posts. In developing a marketing strategy management must take into consideration the growth and importance of this movement.

The remaining restraints in this chapter are competition and the legal framework within which the firm must operate. In making all decisions the firm must consider the reactions and opportunities to competition. This consideration varies with the amount of monopoly a firm has. In industries with high concentration ratios, considerations of this sort vary. However, even where the ratio is high, management must be aware of foreign competition. In addition, management must consider its source of monopoly. For instance, its position if derived from a control of a basic material supply is no doubt safer than if its position is derived from the ability to differentiate its product from the competitors through advertising or other marketing activities. Its position would seem also to be safer when the barriers to entry of other firms are formidable in terms of the capital investment required or when a pecular system of distribution is unavailable to competitors.

Legal restraints are found in the form of several major laws, especially the Robinson–Patman Act and many of the antimerger acts and antitrust laws. Local and state laws are also becoming particularly sticky for the firm, and again consumerism is represented in the development of environmental laws.

QUESTIONS

1. What restraints does management encounter in its attempt to market its products?

2. Consumerism is another word for consumer legislation. Comment.

3. Consumerism is antibusiness. Comment.

4. Develop some arguments against consumerism.

5. One of the ways of monopolizing an industry is to engage in effective marketing and promotional programs. Comment.

6. From Table 4-3, explain why in one industry the four largest firms control 86 percent of the business, while in another listed on this table only 5 percent is controlled by the top four companies.

7. What role does product differentiation play in the marketing of products? How is it accomplished?

8. What is meant by "barriers to entry" in an industry? What role does marketing play in "barriers to entry"?

9. Under the Robinson–Patman Act, quantity discounts are not allowed. Comment.

*10. List several recent laws in your state or city that can be considered environmental laws or a direct result of the consumerism movement.

11. Why does the FTC consider advertising to be an important area of concern?

12. Can a manufacturer offer a quantity discount to a customer who buys a large amount of merchandise from his firm? Discuss.

13. How important is foreign competition in restricting the monopolistic powers of American manufacturers? Name some major industries where foreign competition is an important factor.

*In-depth question.

THE MARKET

II

That the consumer is the target of all marketing activities goes without saying. It is the ultimate purpose of the business to sell its product to the consumer at a profit. To accomplish this the firm must have as clear an understanding as possible as to the makeup of the consumer. Thus the firm spends much of its time on studying and analyzing the consumer

The study of the consumer divides itself into two major areas. In Chapter 5 these areas are introduced along with the concept of segmenting a consumer market. In Chapter 6 the first of these areas is introduced, the quantitative or demographic characteristics of the consumer. Here one speaks of population, age, and income of the population, as well as other measurable aspects.

In Chapter 7 the reader is introduced to the study of consumer behavior, which is less measurable through the use of quantitative data, but none the less important to the manufacturer who is striving to understand his markets.

Chapter 8 is concerned with collecting information from the market. Here we discuss market research and other forms of gathering information.

The Consumer Target

5

SUMMARY KEY

The target of all the activities and forces that make up the total marketing mix is the consumer.

Marketing in this textbook is mainly concerned with consumer goods, that is, goods and services intended for the consuming public. There exists, however, another important area that uses marketing of products and services, the industrial markets. These goods are ordinarily used in the production of other goods. Although there exist similarities in the way these products are marketed there are many differences. Most firms selling industrial products do not place much of an emphasis on advertising; buyers are less emotional and more interested in technical data; more servicing and post selling consultation are necessary; sales are for larger quantities; bids are an acceptable way of doing business; and fashion and style play a minor role.

To understand the consumer, management may rely on several types of information. The most usable seem to be demographic in the form of statistical information, and behavioral, which includes psychological or sociological data, such as interpretations of the status of the consumer.

The consumer we study is usually the ultimate consumer or the person who ultimately uses the product. However, one must recognize that the buyer may be only representing the user of the product. One should also recognize that buying behavior is only one aspect of human behavior. Since it is virtually impossible for a manufacturer to sell his product to everybody, he must direct his marketing activities to segments of a market. A market segment must contain enough people to make a profitable market. In addition, this segment must be identifiable so that the firm can implement a marketing strategy.

To begin the study of how the consumer functions, one should consider the purchasing process depicted as a model, which includes such major elements as

1. The consumer has only a general noncommital view of the industry's products.

2. At this point he allocates his income to various expenditure areas.

3. He engages in general shopping.

4. He makes a product decision.

5. He selects a brand and store, and ultimately makes a specific purchase.

His reactions to the purchase govern the manufacturer's opportunity to serve him again.

The purchasing process makes it clear that consumers go through stages and develop varying attitudes and changing patterns. Here again one can see that demographic and behavioral information are important to the manufacturer.

The most widely used and easiest source of data for the manufacturer is demographic information. In most cases where behavioral information is used it is in conjunction with demographic data. As an example of this, consider the data showing that 70 percent of the users of toothpaste were concerned with tooth decay. The balance of this demographically identified market were concerned with "whiteness," an emotional or psychological factor, since it is difficult to precisely determine which toothpaste gets your teeth whiter.

The target of all the activities and forces that make up the total marketing mix is the consumer. It is the consumer who ultimately decides which firms are going to survive and which firms will falter.

Although this textbook concentrates on marketing and its role in producing consumer goods, it is worthwhile at this point to digress for a brief time to discuss industrial marketing.

Marketing, as noted earlier in the text, is concerned with the flow of merchandise and services from the producer to the consumer, who purchases goods for his or her family's use. Hence merchandise and services that are produced with the intent in mind of meeting the needs of the consuming public are referred to as *consumer goods.*

Aside from these goods, there exists a whole vast area of marketing referred to as the *industrial markets,* where goods and services are produced to be used in the production of other goods. Thus a company may market a line of tools and dyes to be used in the production of other goods. A firm may produce a cleaning agent to be used in factories to clean equipment. These represent industrial goods.

The industrial market also includes products that can be classified as raw materials and semifinished products. Among raw materials one might find such basic products as coal, oil, iron ore, copper, zinc, and bauxite. Semifinished products may include watch movements, motors, textiles, and some fresh foods.

It is also true that many products are produced and sold in both markets. General Electric, for example, produces and sells a large line of light bulbs. Many of these light bulbs are sold in supermarkets to the housewife for use in her home. This product when sold in this manner represents a *consumer product.* On the other hand, General Electric sells many of its bulbs to owners of office buildings and factories. This market represents an *industrial market.*

Although many of the concepts that have been developed in consumer marketing can be applied to industrial marketing, it is true that there are important differences in each market. Although more will be said about this market, it should be noted that the industrial market is much more compact and the lines of distribution are much shorter and more direct.

Perhaps more striking is the fact that there are many similarities in these markets, the most obvious being that companies selling in each of these markets have the same goals. That is, they intend to operate as efficiently as possible, and to increase their share of the market and the profits they will earn. They must also study their market carefully, determine the buyer's motivations, and most of all use the same basic techniques. For instance, their decision making involves the same three controllable aspects in each market — decisions concerning products, promotion, and physical distribution.

Differences

The differences arise in the emphasis on each of these major controllable variables. Most firms in the industrial field do not place as strong an emphasis on the use of advertising as one may find among many consumer-oriented firms. Many industrial firms never advertise their products in magazines and newspapers. In addition, even when they advertise, they rarely spend substantial amounts of money.

There is, of course, good reason for this. First and most importantly, the industrial market is usually more concentrated than the consumer market. A firm, for instance, selling a product that can be used in the airplane industry need only concentrate its efforts among less than a dozen firms, most of which are located on the West Coast. A firm selling a product to the automobile industry would need only to reach four major firms in the United States. A rather recent example of the concentration of industrial markets can be seen in Mobile, Alabama, where the interest of Japanese steel companies in low-sulfur coal (to reduce air pollution) has caused a revival in this dormant coal market. Many Japanese firms have placed orders from this area of the country to be shipped at prices well above the current U.S. rates.[1] It is interesting to note that most of this type of coal is concentrated in this area and the bordering areas of Kentucky and Tennessee.

Other major differences also exist. The motivation of the buyer would seem to differ among consumer and industrial buyers. The latter is usually considered to be much more rational in making all decisions. Thus the purchasing agent for a manufacturing firm is said to look at the more technical aspects of the product being sold, checking delivery dates, the credit of the seller, and perhaps the firm's previous experience with this same seller.

In contrast, the consumer buyer is more likely to make judgments on the basis of emotional values such as the color or fashion appeal of an item rather than its more technical attributes.

One should not be lulled into the view that all industrial buying and marketing are involved in examining products from the point of view of rational buying motives. For instance, there is a growing view that when products are basically the same, and this involves a great many industrial products, the decision to favor one company over another may be made on the basis of such non-rational and non-product-related criteria as the personality of the salesman, friendship, or the possibility that the company selling the product could become a potential buyer of the buyer's product. There is also a growing view in the industrial design field that

---

[1]*Business Week,* May 15, 1971, p. 45.

products designed with a modernistic look may sell better. For instance, one expert claims that the IBM electric typewriter has managed to gain almost three quarters of the office market by designing its typewriter in a modernistic and impressive manner. Many computers are also designed in the same way.

There are, however, some clear differences between industrial and consumer marketing. For example, the industrial product usually requires much more servicing and consultation before a sale is made. Since much of the consultation and time spent on selling is with technicians such as engineers, their interest would naturally be in terms of what the product can do under varying factory conditions. Thus the user of aluminum, which ultimately is used in the production of airplanes, is interested in the type of aluminum that can withstand temperature extremes and air pressure changes.

Most transactions in the industrial field involve large-volume transactions. It is not unusual for a major automobile manufacturer to purchase 1 million tires at one time or a coal user to buy 10 trainloads of coal. In contrast, the ultimate consumer buys in much smaller units.

The tendency to buy in large quantities in the industrial field has several effects on the way marketing is conducted. The worth of the large order makes it profitable for the manufacturer to deal directly with the buyer rather than through intermediaries. Thus it is quite understandable that manufacturers of expensive machine equipment deal directly with large firms. In contrast, it is also understandable that chewing gum is sold through wholesalers.

This tendency toward large orders also means that the seller can spend more time on the sale of his product than a consumer marketing firm. In reality, much of the time spent on selling in the industrial field is spent on preparation, whether it be in the form of specification letters, formal contracts, or bids.

The use of bids to obtain orders is particularly common among companies selling to governmental bodies. Many cities and state governments have laws governing the acceptance of bids. Some state that the order must go to the lowest bidder. As a result, many of the firms actually plan their bidding strategy based on their previous experience and the expected behavior of their competitors. The tendency of the federal government to give contracts to the lowest bidder is voiced in the comment of the astronaut who when asked what he thought of flying in space capsules for thousands of miles replied, "How would you like to travel at such speeds through the empty space in a vehicle that was built by the lowest bidders?"

Perhaps the major difference firms find in dealing in the industrial field as compared to the consumer markets is that fashion and style play a rather minor role. The emphasis on industrial products is their utility, and thus such things as design changes take place only after it can be demonstrated that they will improve the use of the products.

The influence of women is perhaps at its lowest point in the industrial marketing field. The influence of women, however, in consumer marketing is well recognized and considered by many companies to be the only influence. This is certainly true in the selling and marketing of family apparel and food products, perhaps the two major categories of consumer consumption.

Finally, the salesmen in the industrial marketing field are required to go through a much longer sales training period than salesmen of consumer goods. This is due to the technical nature of the products. One of the major problems of the industrial firm is to find salesmen who are trained technically, but still are capable of perceiving the motivation of the purchasing agent. As noted previously, the view that the salesman's personality and social abilities play a role has gained support. There is thus a tendency to look for salesmen who possess both abilities.

In 1970 it was estimated that manufacturers of women's dresses accounted for over 2 percent of the total output of our economy. Yet this industry was in what can only be called a turmoil during 1970 because of the inability to determine fashion trends, that is, the midi versus the mini skirt. Combined with a recession during this period and the consumer indecision, the industry experienced one of its poorest profit years perhaps since World War II.

Segmenting the Consumer Market

Businessmen are always in the process of examining and reexamining the consumer, for it is the consumer that makes the ultimate judgment as to the worthiness of the firm's efforts. Yet it is also quite true that the consumer is perhaps the missing link in the marketing executive's knowledge. Many marketing executives have full knowledge concerning their internal operations. That is, they may know the exact internal costs involved in making many of their decisions. Thus General Motors is well aware of the fact that if one of its divisions is able to produce and sell 350,000 cars in any given year they will make a profit; this knowledge is backed up by virtually an army of cost accountants who in turn have dozens of previous years of experience to rely on. The one unknown in the equation necessary to make a General Motors marketing executive completely at peace with the world is the reaction of the consumer to their latest cars. This always remains the unknown.

It doesn't necessarily mean that General Motors is completely ignorant of what will happen during any given model year; they do have history on their side, and they can usually expect history to repeat itself to a great extent. Therefore, the Cadillac division can expect to sell a substantial fraction of the same number of cars they sold the previous year. During relatively stable years they can usually expect to sell more. Their basis for this determination lies in the conditions of the luxury car market and the firm's interpretation of how the consumer reacts to the product. The conditions of the automobile market are such that no major firm has entered the luxury car field in many years. There are many reasons for this, the most important being that a competitor would have to invest millions of dollars to enter the luxury car field. Even more important, a competitor would have to establish dealerships, an almost impossible task in today's competitive market. If any competition did develop, it would most likely come from the two major competitors of General Motors, Ford, or Chrysler. However, General Motors would ordinarily not be worried about its large domestic competitors surprising it with a new car this year, since these corporations are always aware of changes in their competitors' product line. Recently, when Ford introduced the new mini car the Pinto, General Motors came out with a similar type car, the Vega.

General Motors may have several other good reasons for believing that Cadillac will have a profitable year. First, they have an established dealership system for Cadillac, which they know from study is all-important in selling and servicing new cars. Second, they may have several consumer studies showing that "Cadillac owner loyalty is the highest in the land."[2] Other studies may show that Cadillac owners on the average trade their old cars in every 4 years. Tying this in with the owners' loyalty, it would seem that General Motors can make fairly reasonable estimates of the Cadillac's sales in the coming year.

Third, and most important, it may be the conclusion of the management that status is the most significant reason for purchasing a Cadillac. This information may be derived from research studies or simply management's evaluation based on their past experience. It may also be management's opinion that status will maintain itself in the present market, and management will be sure to stress this fact in the coming promotion of the automobile.

Finally, as an adjunct to status, management may have studies showing that family income will continue to increase substantially during the coming year with a large percentage of the population moving into the over $18,000 a year bracket, an income dividing line that distinguishes the luxury car owner.

It is interesting to observe from the preceeding that the marketing team at General Motors relied on several sources of consumer behavior. The latter was what is known as *demographic* information, that is, statistical information that can be put in quantifiable form and analyzed. The family income information would fall into this category, which includes mainly vital statisitics, such as ages, births, and incomes, of large groups of population.

The second source of information is what is loosely called behavioral information, that is, information that attempts to interpret from a sociological or psychological basis the motivation of the consumer. The interest in status, a value not indentifiable from vital statistics, would be an example of behavioral information. *Status* represents an attitude and has deep psychological meaning; nevertheless, the ability of General Motors to understand this state of mind would seem to be extremely important to all decision makers in the firm.

The *loyalty* of the consumer is the type of information that can be derived from research analysis of either internal records or can be developed directly from consumer interviews. Since loyalty also has deep psychological underpinnings, many analysts would classify this fact in with the consumer behavior information.

Based on all the information presented above and the executive's experience, management will develop a *consumer theory* of how the Cadillac purchaser views their car and their company.

All firms must engage in this process, that is, develop accurate theories of how the consumer views their product. Like all business theory, it must be based on reality. And like all theory the answers must act as a guideline to management's decision-making areas. Thus, once the theory of *why* and *how* the Cadillac buyer prefers the Cadillac has been established, the advertising department has a clear guideline as to what to say in their advertising. All they have to do is follow management's view that the Cadillac buyer is (1) extremely loyal, (2) possesses a well-above-average income, and (3) is likely to respond to status appeals.

The reader should note that management could possess other theories. They could believe that the Cadillac buyer is more concerned with the mechanical features of the car. They could also believe that price is a factor or perhaps dealer

---

[2]Quoted from the "Cadillac 1971" sales brochure.

servicing. Although management is aware that these factors do play a role, the pervading values would probably be the three given.

In a sense, therefore, it is up to management to gain as much information as possible concerning their consumer so that they may be able to develop workable theories and guidelines for the firm. Many firms have been developed simply on the basis of possessing superior knowledge of the consumer.

The Consumer

Before discussing the various approaches to gaining an understanding of the consumer, one must first be aware of certain characteristics and generalizations about consumers.

The first factor is that *everyone is a consumer.* That is, we all make purchases or influence purchases at some time during a given week. Although babies do not make purchases, by their very existence they do influence the types of purchases that are made. As they grow, a very strong case can be made as to their influence as children on all purchasing.[3]

Thus, when one considers the market for a particular product, one considers all people as possible users of the product. However, as we shall see, firms do discriminate.

When we discuss the consumer, we refer to the *ultimate consumer,* meaning purchases for the family that are used ultimately by the family. Here one must distinguish between *the buyer* and *user of a product.* One must recognize that the *buyer* may *represent* the *user* in the marketplace. Thus a husband may purchase perfume for his wife. However, in most cases he purchases only that perfume that she uses regularly or prefers. In contrast, a wife may purchase beer for her husband at the local supermarket. Naturally, her husband's preferences determine the brand of beer she buys.

In the case of children this division is even more pronounced. In most cases it is the mother who purchases a breakfast cereal for her children. However, she is aware that many children have strong preferences for certain cereals, and will most likely yield to their tastes rather than take the chance that they will not eat the cereal.

The second factor that must be realized concerning consumers is that *consumer behavior is only one aspect of human behavior.* In studying the consumer one is only interested in that aspect of his total behavior that bears on his buying behavior and its relationship to marketing. Although a person may be brought up in a household where strict standards of behavior were maintained, one would have little interest in this background information. On the other hand, should one establish that a goodly fraction of female buyers are influenced in their purchasing habits of a single commodity by the environment they were raised in, this could be of interest to us in analyzing their present consumer behavior. The supermarkets are well aware of the fact that many female food shoppers follow in the footsteps of their mothers and purchase meat from independent butchers, whereas in buying other food commodities they prefer supermarkets. This behavior pattern would of course be of great interest to us in marketing.

---

[3]For example, see J. U. McNeal, *Children as Consumers* (Austin, Tex.: The University of Texas Bureau of Business Research, 1964).

Finally, one must bear in mind that consumers see the same things differently. In studying consumer behavior we accept this fact, although in some cases one might be interested in why consumers view similar things differently. However, since this is a peculiarity of consumer behavior, one must be well aware that it therefore follows that a firm selling a product will find itself unable in most instances to get the same reaction from all consumers. More will be said about this fact next.

Market Segments

One important concept in marketing is that it is virtually impossible for a manufacturer or for that matter any institution to meet the needs of all buyers of its product. There are several logical reasons for coming to this conclusion.

First and foremost, as noted previously, even if the products were the same, consumers may very well view the products offered quite differently. Several examples of this type of behavior can be offered. For example, many people are aware that aspirin must meet the standards set by the federal government. All producers of this product adhere to these minimum standards. It has often been pointed out to readers of the consumer press that all aspirin products that meet these standards will relieve a person's headache. Thus it would seem logical that most purchasers of aspirin, especially if they are aware of this fact, would purchase the most inexpensive aspirin. Yet it has also been shown by company studies that, in spite of this fact, many aspirin products that sell for three and four times the least expensive aspirin have maintained substantial shares of this market. One fact seems certain; people view the aspirin products of companies very differently.

Consider another medical fact. There is no cure for the common cold. There are no drugs, nor medicines, nor anything that one can take to hasten the exit of cold viruses. Yet should one decide to pass on this information to friends, one would find that in spite of the information most people would still retain their belief in how best to treat a cold symptom, ranging from staying indoors, to drinking hot tea with perhaps a dash of lemon or something stronger.

Admittedly, these examples are extreme; however, they make the point that people with their complex backgrounds and perceptions view similar products in different ways.

Manufacturers have other reasons for realizing that it is practically impossible to meet the needs of all consumers. One of the most important is that to reach all people would require a fantastic effort in terms of money, and a tremendous waste would incur. Thus, although all people who earn over $8,000 per year may represent a potential market for a small foreign-made automobile, it would be more efficient for the manufacturer to try to reach suburbanites meeting the income standards, since they are more likely to need a second rather inexpensive automobile. To reach this market, the manufacturer may choose to advertise in newspapers directed to the suburban market. Additionally, one must remember that since most major manufacturers are engaged in selling to mass markets the manufacturer can do little to tailor his product to the special needs of each individual buyer.

Another reason for manufacturers concentrating on a market segment is that it is not necessary to design a product that has only one appeal to one group. Most products are designed in such a way that the consumer may find just enough attributes in that product to cause him to buy the product, although he may reject most of the product's other appeals. Thus a person stopping at a franchised hamburger outlet may not care too much for hamburgers; however, he may be attracted by the convenient location on this occasion, plus the rather reasonable price to satisfy his appetite. Other customers of the same restaurant may find that the hamburger does not satisfy their hunger. In essence, one is saying that both customers and sellers in our mass production society are constantly compromising their choices. The buyer cannot always satisfy all his needs by using product A. Conversely, as much as he may try, the manufacturer can rarely produce a product that will appeal to everybody. He must also compromise. What results is a product that appeals to a large enough number of potential customers to satisfy the needs of the manufacturer who must maintain a profitable firm.

Usefulness of Market Segments

Once a manufacturer has established and identified a useful market segment, he is in a position to throw all his energies into the task of developing and marketing a product(s) to fulfill the needs of this market. In specific terms, the manufacturer will attempt to

1. Design a line of products that meets the needs of this market. Once knowledge of this market is collected and digested, the next most obvious step is to produce a product or line of products that meets the needs of the bulk of the consumers in this market. Implied in the designing, of course, is the proper pricing and packaging of the product.

2. Design a promotional campaign that reaches and communicates effectively with this market. In this endeavor the firm will select media and outlets that will reach this market most efficiently, establish the advertising and sales appeals, and establish the timing of all this promotional effort.

3. Establish a constant monitoring system that will alert management to any changes that are taking place within this profitable segment.

Segments of the market *must* be large enough to make it profitable for a manufacturer to concentrate his resources on such a market. For example, one may be able to identify people who are neurotically concerned about price. These people may spend most of their waking hours shopping and thinking about ways they can save money. Although one might agree that there exists in our society a number of such people (perhaps we may even know a few) it would be doubtful that they exist in such numbers that it would be worthwhile trying to reach such a market.

The neurotically price-conscious potential consumers offer still another problem, even if they do exist in adequate numbers. This involves the problem of identification. It would be most difficult to attempt to identify this segment of the market; for they cannot be identified by many of the characteristics we discuss later. This type of person would not belong to groups with similar characteristics, nor would they live in an area that could be identified. It is doubtful that income or education or any of the other variables used in segmenting markets would easily identify such a market. In effect, therefore, *a market segment must contain enough people* to make a profitable market and *must be identifiable* in order to implement such strategy.

Consumer Purchasing Model

To understand the ways manufacturers can segment markets, one should first examine the purchasing process of the consumer.

FIGURE 5-1   Model of the Purchasing Process

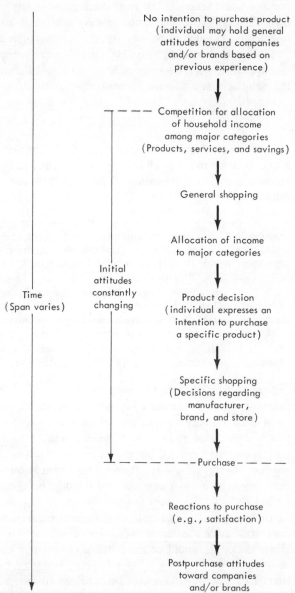

Source: Adapted from R. W. Pratt, Jr., "Consumer Behavior: Some Psychological Aspects," in *Science in Marketing,* George Schwartz, ed. (New York: John Wiley & Sons, Inc., 1965), p. 131.

In Figure 5-1 a model of the purchasing process is depicted. Although simplified, it indicates the steps or growth of the consumer from a noncommitted state, to making a product decision, and then to making an actual purchase.

The model starts with the assumption that the consumer has only a general attitude toward company products. At this point the consumer has no intention to purchase a product.

The second step depicts the consumer deciding the allocation he will make of his income after taxes. In general, he can buy products, services, or elect to *save* his income.

Although much will be said about this in Chapter 6, the general trend in our society at this stage will be to spend more proportionally on services and less on goods. Savings remain relatively the same.

This general trend toward services is not due to any wish or special effort on the part of manufacturers, but simply represents a consumer preference at this stage in our development. Perhaps a decade from now this trend will again reverse itself. However, there is little a manufacturer can do to stem this tendency.

At this step the next procedure in the purchasing process is for the consumer to allocate his income to various categories, such as food, rent, household goods, education, insurance, and so on. This allocation could follow along the general lines noted previously. Education and insurance could represent a substantial proportion of the expenditure for services. Food could constitute a sizable part of the expenditure for goods.

If one continues following the purchasing process, the consumer will eventually make a decision concerning a specific product. For instance, the consumer may determine that he wants to purchase a television set.

At this point the consumer engages in a *search activity* that will result in making a decision regarding the brand to purchase and the store to make the purchase in. This search activity will conclude when the consumer has purchased a specific item. In this case it could be an RCA television set.

Of course, the total purchasing process does not end here. The consumer does not simply buy and forget the experience. There is always a postpurchase reaction. This postpurchase reaction is composed of the immediate satisfaction one gets from buying a product and the later postpurchase attitude toward the company, store, and perhaps the brand.

Quantitative and Behavioral Information

As one can see from the purchasing-process model described, the consumer undergoes a constant change in attitudes toward purchasing products. The decision-making efforts are subject to reversal or patterns that most marketing departments must be familiar with. It is also fair to state that, although an individual has made a choice at a certain period of time, whether she will continue making a similar choice in the next time period will depend on what she has learned through the act of purchasing.

One can see that the purchasing model as depicted in Figure 5-1 represents several potential areas of study. The first is the quantitive area, where one can study and determine the economic characteristics of the consumer. This is discussed in

Chapter 6 in greater detail. Here one recognizes the expenditure patterns and population movements that influence this part of the purchasing process.

One should remember, however, that, given the spending characteristics of consumers, all consumers do not spend their monies alike. They make different selections and purchase at different outlets.

One can easily conclude from studying quantitative data that the consumer process cannot be explained in terms of spending and demographic information. Ultimately, one must conclude that other factors also play a role in determining and understanding the consumer purchasing process. These other factors are identified as behavioral in nature and include three major categories:

1. *Individual factors:* cognition, perception, learning, personality, motivation, and attitudes.
2. *Social factors:* group membership and social influence.
3. *Sociocultural factors:* social class, subcultures, and cultures.[4]

In essence, what is being said is that the choice of many products is not only a function of spending ability, but of factors that may be more important, such as group acceptance or the individual personality. These factors will be discussed at some length in Chapter 7.

Demographic Illustrations

Demographic characteristics are the most widely used in marketing for determining consumer characteristics that can be used to identify markets. The reason is apparent; demographic characteristics are easily obtainable and in most cases relatively easy to understand. For example, take the case of Ivory soap. One of the most obvious characteristics in selling this product is the factor of age, since it is associated closely with babies. Identification of the size of this market is available through data from the Census Bureau. Similarly, a firm may plan to market a soap that appeals to older women who have complexion problems, again a characteristic that can best be identified in terms of age.

Behavioral Characteristics

The easiest means of identification is using demographic characteristics. Most behavioral identification techniques are used in conjunction with demographic information. For instance, in recent years it has become apparent that most users of toothpaste are concerned with tooth decay in their choice of a dentifrice. Demographically, one can identify the size of the toothpaste market and the number of users of toothpaste in the typical family. Research at one point indicated that 70 percent of these families were concerned with tooth decay.

After examining the statistics, Macleans toothpaste discovered that the remaining 30 percent of the market were emotionally concerned with the concept of "whiteness," the cosmetic effect of brushing their teeth.[5] "Whiteness" is an

---

[4]T. S. Robertson, *Consumer Behavior* (Glenview, Ill.: Scott, Foresman and Company, 1970), p. 9.

[5]*Grey Matter,* Nov. 1965, Grey Advertising, Inc., New York.

emotional and thus psychological factor, since it would be difficult to determine by any means which toothpaste gets teeth whiter. The impact of the Macleans advertising program aimed at just this market has been impressive.

Perhaps a more dramatic example can be offered by the marketing of malt beverages as an example of using both demographic and behavioral characteristics in order to delineate a market. For many years the industry has been aiming its marketing programs at the youth market, a market that can be easily identified in terms of age. It was suggested by one author that instead of concentrating on just *this one segment* the industry could consider several other segments, many of which could be only identified using a behavioral approach.[6] These segments are outlined in Table 5-1.

Possible Malt Beverage Market Segments for Additional Cultivation   TABLE 5-1

Upper social class, "snob" appeal	via	Ale, imported beers
"With-meals" market	via	Advertising and store promotions depicting with-meals use
With snack foods	via	Promotion such as Coca-Cola's "Nothing beatsa Coke n' Pizza," or "Coke n' Burger" promotions
Women	via	Feminine appeal brand name, small package sizes, recipes using beer, as the wine industry does[a]
Those who prefer strong beers	via	Malt liquor, some imports
Draught beer lovers	via	Bottled draught beer (for example, Michelob)

[a]These measures would be introduced to foster greater consumption of beer by women, in addition to the fact that they buy most of the beer sold in grocery stores (now over 40 percent of total beer volume – and growing steadily) as their families' purchasing agents.
Source: L. Adler, "A New Orientation for Plotting Marketing Strategy," *Business Horizons,* Winter 1964, p. 44.

One obvious application of the behavioral approach to cultivating the malt beverage market is the identification of an "upper social class, 'snob' appeal" market. This market has been cultivated in recent years, particularly by those companies that import beer into the United States. Although many of these products sell for two or three times as much as the domestically brewed product, they still find a rather hefty "snob" market in the United States. Careful study of this

[6]L. Adler, "A New Orientation for Plotting Marketing Strategy," *Business Horizons,* Winter 1964, p. 44.

market and determination of the necessary appeals would seem to rely mainly on information available from sociology.

The balance of the table contains purchasing behavior types for the same product. Again this information cannot be determined in terms of straight demographics; it must be obtained as a direct product of further understanding of the consumer decision-making apparatus. Much of this information may be determined from marketing research studies. In any case, all the proposed segments would seem to indicate that management needs more information than is usually found in demographic data.

This analysis also points out several other facts concerning behavioral information. The first is that behavioral information need not be psychological or related to sociology exclusively. It can, for instance, be only a description of how people purchase merchandise based on some study that is available. Thus it may simply be a statement based on research that heavy users of a product prefer to purchase brands, or that the product is purchased on impulse.

Second, behavior information can be combined with demographic information in many instances. For instance, demographically one may determine that the major markets contain several occupational groups, such as blue-collar, professional, and white-collar workers. From a behavioral point of view one may determine that the major purchasers of our product are the blue-collar workers. Assuming that this group can be identified as a major user of our product, it falls upon sociology to explain the behavior of this group, so that our firm's effort can be more carefully aimed at this market. This is not an unusual situation.

It is becoming recognized that demographic information, although easy to obtain, is limited and needs an additional dimension, since

1. People identified from similar demographic groups based on age, income, and educational background may have very different purchasing behavior.

2. People who can be identified as buyers of a product through some demographic characteristic may still not be a narrow enough group to be of any value. Suppose it was determined that only high-income people purchase expensive pipe tobacco; however, since only a small proportion of these high-income people purchase this expensive pipe tobacco, it becomes particularly relevant that we learn more about this relatively small number of purchasers. It would seem in this case that we can only add to our knowledge of this small segment by delving further into the behavior of this market.

Use of Market Segments

Once a firm has carefully identified a market, they are then in a position to apply their accumulated knowledge to the total effort of the firm. The effort includes producing a product for this market, communicating its availability, and distributing the product so that it reaches this market in such a way as to maximize its sales.

Consider, for example, cosmetics as a product for which firms have segmented their markets into much different categories. For instance, Charles Revson, one of the founders of the Revlon Company, indicated that his firm does not sell cosmetics, "they sell hope."[7] The success of Revlon is well known, and the amount of money the firm puts into packaging and store displays is also obvious to even the untrained professional eye. In contrast, there exist many cosmetic firms that concentrate on selling cosmetics with an eye on the price-conscious market. Their cosmetics may be found in variety stores and many discount houses.

These two markets require much different approaches and affect all aspects of the firm's efforts. Revlon would certainly be obliged to spend more of its money on packaging, advertising, and in-store displays than a price competitor. The firm would also be obliged to see that its product is sold in stores that fit in closely with the image it is trying to present to the public. Thus the channels of distribution would be carefully monitored, and its pricing policy would try to meet the needs of these channels. One would also suspect that taking this route would oblige the Revlon firm to carry a wider variety of products than if it were selling to the price market.

Since the snob market would seem to be more willing to consider products that create "hope" more readily than the price shopper, it would affect the type of product being offered. For example, one could visualize the price operator selling cold cream, while Revlon-type companies now have moved from this one product by introducing cleansing, vanishing, nourishing, hormone, astringent, and wrinkle creams. These products are the result of further segmenting the market in terms of age, motivation, and changing attitudes.

SUMMARY

The consumer market differs from the industrial market in many ways. In particular, in the industrial market the individual sales transactions are large, sales are preceded by longer periods of consultations, advertising is less of a factor, customers are usually more concentrated in different areas of the country, and the motivation of the industrial buyer is considered to be more rational than the consumer buyer.

Manufacturers are interested in developing several types of information concerning the consumer, demographics being the most useful in that it is quantifiable. Behavioral information is particularly relevant, but is not quantifiable and requires a much deeper understanding of norm behavior.

Firms strive to study market segments through the gathering of demographic and behavioral information. In Chapters 6 and 7 some of this information is presented.

QUESTIONS

1. How are industrial marketing and consumer marketing related?
2. How do industrial marketing and consumer marketing differ?
3. In the marketing of an industrial product, such as steel beams, how does the approach differ from a product sold in a consumer market?

---

[7]*Ibid.*, p. 42.

4. What is meant by demographic information?

5. Why do manufacturers concern themselves with only segments of a market?

6. In what ways can a manufacturer segment a market?

7. Is "snob appeal" a demographic or behavioral characteristic?

8. The industrial product requires more consultation than sales in the consumer market. True or false? Explain.

9. The buyer of the product is always the key person to observe. True or false? Explain.

10. How important are theories of consumer behavior in marketing a product? What theories could be applied to an airline that could affect their (1) advertising and promotion, and (2) pricing?

11. Is education a demographic or behavioral characteristic? Explain.

12. Delivery is of great interest to both the ultimate consumer and industrial buyer. Which buyer finds it the most important?

*13. How can consumer behavior differ from human behavior? Give an example.

*In-depth question.

The Consumer:
A Quantitative View

6

SUMMARY KEY

Manufacturers are always monitoring demographic data that concern the consumer market. These data include population, occupation, education, marital status, race, and income. Some of these statistics are summarized as follows:

Population. U.S. population is increasing at a rate of a little under 2 percent annually. States in the South and West are increasing more rapidly than in other areas. Population within cities has moved to the suburban areas. For example, two thirds of the population growth in the 1960s took place in the suburbs.

Age of Population. Forty-five percent of the population is under 25 years of age. Almost 10 percent of the population is over the age of 65. Projections seem to indicate a decline in the growth of the former and a continued rise in the latter. Age of the head of household shows clearly that those families headed by persons in the 35 to 44 age groups have the highest potential income of all groups.

Education. This group may represent a sophisticated market for goods. Also, it contains the highest income families.

Employment. The trend has been a decrease in farm workers and an increase in professional and white-collar occupations. Although unskilled work has declined, skilled labor has increased in total. This trend indicates a movement to higher paying occupations. Two thirds of all female workers are married.

Income. Of major interest to marketing people are disposable income, which is income after taxes, and discretionary income, which is income that can be spent or saved without consideration of current need or prior commitment. Personal income refers to all income from any source. Discretionary income is watched closely, since it is the amount available for spending on luxuries. The rise of income and its distribution can be seen in the fact that over one fifth of American families have an income of over $15,000 annually; in 1950 almost 80 percent of the families had incomes under $5,000.

Expenditures. Most income goes for food and housing. The discretionary portions seem to be moving in the direction of foreign travel and education. The proportion of the income spent on food is declining, an important consideration by supermarkets contemplating selling nonfood products. Within income groups the patterns differ. Families earning over $15,000 a year spend a little more than twice the money on food as the national average; for clothing, however, their expenditures are roughly three times the national average.

Before the manufacturer can delve into the behavior and nuances of the consumer, the firm must first establish how large the market is, where it is located, and its many characteristics.

Much of the data available to the marketing manager in establishing this information are derived from published statistical sources, mainly supplied by the federal government. Most statistical information is derived from various censuses taken on a regular basis by departments within the government. In addition, the marketing manager has available to him many of the private studies that supply such information.

Quantitative or demographic information consists of population characteristics such as size, location, and age of the population, occupation, education, marital status, and income. Firms engaged in marketing products are constantly monitoring these variables in order to detect change, which then must be related to their marketing problems. As will be shown later in this chapter, a firm noting the rapid population growth of the State of California may be forced to reconsider its present warehouse system, since many of its potential customers may now reside in that state. Or, noting the decline in population in another state, this same firm may decide to retrench and reduce its sales staff and shift the emphasis to growing states. Regardless of their decision, most major companies maintain a constant vigilance over statistical changes that are vital to their existence.

Population

It is axiomatic in consumer marketing that people make markets. Thus a firm is interested in where people are located, where they are moving, and in what numbers.

In collecting population statistics the firm relies on the *Census of Population* in order to discover the whereabouts of these markets. The census is taken every 10 years by the government and serves to spot many of these changes. However, since one out of five American families moves every year, it is necessary for the firm to collect information on population movement in between the 10-year census. Here again the government makes estimates of the population between each major census. In some cases the firm may rely on local, state, and private sources in order to maintain its population monitoring system.

Table 6-1 indicates that the population of the United States between 1960 and 1970 increased by 13.3 percent. The total increase in U.S. population during that period averaged a little under 2 percent per year. This total population represents the total market in the United States for consumer goods and services.

Closer examination of this table shows, however, that the overall average of 13.3 percent was not experienced by all regions in the country. Specifically, it shows that states in the South and West exceeded the average, while the balance of the country did not. Most startling is the finding that the Pacific area increased its population over this period by a little over 25 percent. This gain is almost double

Population Rank — Percentage of Change — States and Puerto Rico, 1960-1970   TABLE 6-1

State or Other Area	Population (1,000)		Percent Change 1960-1970
	1960	*1970*	
United States	**179,323**	**203,212**	**13.3**
Regions:			
Northeast	44,678	49,041	9.8
North Central	51,619	56,572	9.6
South	54,973	62,795	14.2
West	28,053	34,804	24.1
New England	**10,509**	**11,842**	**12.7**
Maine	969	992	2.4
New Hampshire	607	738	21.5
Vermont	390	444	14.0
Massachusetts	5,149	5,689	10.5
Rhode Island	859	947	10.1
Connecticut	2,535	3,032	19.6
Middle Atlantic	**34,168**	**37,199**	**8.9**
New York	16,782	18,237	8.7
New Jersey	6,067	7,168	18.2
Pennsylvania	11,319	11,794	4.2
East North Central	**36,225**	**40,252**	**11.1**
Ohio	9,706	10,652	9.7
Indiana	4,662	5,194	11.4
Illinois	10,081	11,114	10.2
Michigan	7,823	8,875	13.4
Wisconsin	3,952	4,418	11.8
West North Central	**15,394**	**16,319**	**6.0**
Minnesota	3,414	3,805	11.5
Iowa	2,758	2,824	2.4
Missouri	4,320	4,677	8.3
North Dakota	632	618	-2.3
South Dakota	681	666	-2.2
Nebraska	1,411	1,483	5.1
Kansas	2,179	2,247	3.1
South Atlantic	**25,972**	**30,671**	**18.1**
Delaware	446	548	22.8
Maryland	3,101	3,922	26.5
District of Columbia	764	757	-1.0
Virginia	3,967	4,648	17.2
West Virginia	1,860	1,744	-6.2
North Carolina	4,556	5,082	11.5
South Carolina	2,383	2,591	8.7
Georgia	3,943	4,590	16.4
Florida	4,952	6,789	37.1
East South Central	**12,050**	**12,803**	**6.3**
Kentucky	3,038	3,219	5.9
Tennessee	3,567	3,924	10.0
Alabama	3,267	3,444	5.4
Mississippi	2,178	2,217	1.8

TABLE 6-1   (cont.)

State or Other Area	Population (1,000)		Percent Change 1960– 1970
	1960	1970	
West South Central	**16,951**	**19,321**	**14.0**
Arkansas	1,786	1,923	7.7
Louisiana	3,257	3,641	11.8
Oklahoma	2,328	2,559	9.9
Texas	9,580	11,197	16.9
Mountain	**6,855**	**8,282**	**20.8**
Montana	675	694	2.9
Idaho	667	713	6.8
Wyoming	330	332	0.7
Colorado	1,754	2,207	25.8
New Mexico	951	1,016	6.8
Arizona	1,302	1,771	36.0
Utah	891	1,059	18.9
Nevada	285	489	71.3
Pacific	**21,198**	**26,523**	**25.1**
Washington	2,853	3,409	19.5
Oregon	1,769	2,091	18.2
California	15,717	19,953	27.0
Alaska	226	300	32.8
Hawaii	633	769	21.5
Puerto Rico	**2,350**	**2,712**	**15.4**

Source: U.S. Department of Commerce, Bureau of the Census, *Census of Population.*

the national average and almost three times the increase shown by the Northeastern part of the United States, the section with the highest income per capita.

Table 6-1 illustrates the changes in the states located in these various regions. Although one of the most impressive increases can be seen in the state of California (now the largest state), both Arizona and Nevada in the Western region showed that, although they rank low in total population, their growth has been well above the national average. Much of Arizona's growth has been due to the interest in a climate that is particularly appealing to those with certain illnesses, or at a retirement age. California, on the other hand, although blessed with a favorable climate, has developed mainly on the basis of a growing commerce and a favorable location. Although its climate does appeal to older people, its growth in commerce has made it an important factor in many industries. California's population is growing at the rate of about 2.5 percent per year, whereas its commercial rival, New York, is growing at the rate of 0.7 percent per year, a figure that is substantially below the national average.

The most rapidly developing Southern state in terms of population growth is Florida, where the growth rate is three times the national average. Here again climate plays an important part in a rapidly developing area. In addition, as we shall observe later in this chapter, growing discretionary income will help this state develop even more rapidly in the future.

The growth of the population by states has not been the only population factor that has interested the marketing firm. Perhaps even more important in their analysis is the fact that over two thirds of the population increase in the United States has taken place in the suburban areas. For example, although between 1960 and 1970 the population of New York City has decreased slightly, the surrounding region has grown at a rate that is well above the national average. This same change has taken place from coast to coast. Figure 6-1 indicates that more people now live

Suburban-Central City Population, 1920-1970   **FIGURE 6-1**

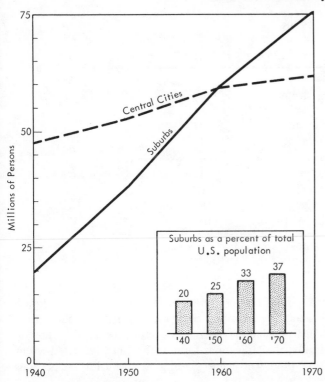

Source: "Number of Inhabitants, United States Summary," *1970 Census of the Population,* PC (1)-A1; *Statistical Abstract of the United States,* various years; *The Statistical History of the United States from Colonial Times to the Present,* Farrfield Publishing, Inc., 1965.

in the suburban areas than in the central cities. Almost 40 percent of the total population lives in the suburbs.[1] The impact of this development on firms selling to consumers is immense. For instance, one can safely say that a distribution system developed 20 years ago is not relevant to today's market. Although more will be said about the changing character of the suburban consumer, it should be noted here that this consumer does differ in her purchasing power, habits, and outlook from the typical city resident. A manufacturer must be assured that he has outlets in the suburban areas as well as the older downtown areas. Specifically, a

---

[1] The balance, about 31 percent, live in nonmetropolitan areas, which equals the number now living in the central cities.

manufacturer must maintain sufficient outlets in the shopping centers in the suburbs, and also be adequately represented in the towns comprising these same areas.

Population Projections

The census deals with the past. As a matter of record, much of the detailed data from the census do not make an appearance until at least 2 years after the data are collected. Although the past may indicate a trend that allows us to examine the present, most firms at some point rely on population projections into the future.

TABLE 6-2   **Population Growth in the 1970s**

Change from 1968 to	1975 (%)	1980 (%)
National	+ 7	+13
New England	+ 5	+10
New York	+ 5	+ 8
Middle Atlantic	+ 9	+15
East Central	+ 3	+ 7
Chicago	+ 6	+12
West Central	+ 4	+ 7
Southeast	+ 9	+15
Los Angeles	+18	+32
Remaining Pacific	+14	+25

Source: *Frozen Foods and the Expanding 70's,* General Foods Corporation, June 1, 1970.

Table 6-2 represents a population projection made by the General Foods Corporation, a company which produces and sells products that are sold in food stores. It shows that national population increases will perhaps be equal to those in the past 10 years. Specifically, the projections for growth from 1968 is 7 percent by 1975, and 13 percent by 1980. This increase seems to be equal to the previous census increase.

When the population projections are examined by regions, one quickly notices that the East and New England areas will continue to lag as they did in the most recent census. Additionally, the projections suggest strongly that the country's population will continue to move in the direction of the West, with particularly heavy population increases experienced by California; the Pacific states will continue to grow at twice the rate for the rest of the United States.

Though since World War II the U.S. population has been constantly growing, preliminary evidence from the 1970 census and the most recent samplings seems to indicate that the growth rate will not continue. For instance, during the first nine months of 1972 it was reported that the fertility rate dropped below the replacement level for the first time.[2] Such a rate, if it persists, would bring the U.S.

[2] *The New York Times,* Dec. 18, 1972, pp. 1 and 56.

growth level down to that of most European countries. This change could have a significant impact on the marketing of products in the years ahead.

Although the number of people and their location is an important indicator of the potential market for consumer goods, the age of the population adds an important dimension to the population information.

Age of the Population

In Table 6-3 one sees the age distribution of the population of the United States. It shows, for example, that over 45 percent of this population is under the age of 25. This figure is not surprising, in that it has been long forecasted that our population was getting younger due to the vast increase in births following World War II. On the opposite end of the age scale, one finds that those over the age of 65 comprise 9.9 percent of the population.

Age and Projections of the Population (percentages)   TABLE 6-3

	Under 25	25 to 44	45 to 64	Over 65
1960	44.4	26.1	20.1	9.2
1970	45.8	23.7	20.5	9.9
1980[a]	43.2	27.8	18.9	10.4

[a]D projections, Bureau of the Census.
Source: U.S. Department of Commerce, Bureau of the Census, *Current Population Reports.*

When making comparisons with the previous 10 years, one notes that both these groups have increased in their growth rates. Table 6-3 indicates that these groups will perhaps vary in their growth in the years ahead. For instance, the over 65 group will increase from 9.9 percent to 10.4 percent between 1970 and 1980. However, the projections for the under 25 group would seem to indicate that gains will cease by 1980.

What is particularly important in these findings is their potential effect on the marketing of products. For example, should the over 65 market maintain itself in the years ahead, the cosmetic companies may become even more interested than they are now in producing products that appeal to these groups, such as creams that hide the various skin problems, or products that hide wrinkles. The same firms would also be interested in the growth of the youth market and may promote cosmetics to meet the special needs of this market. Perhaps they may put some emphasis on tan lotions, and medicated creams that help to reduce the skin eruptions that younger people encounter.

Age of the Household Head

In addition to the individual age of the population, the marketing man may examine the age of the head of household as an indication of the economic status of the family unit. Table 6-4 represents an example of the type of information that can be useful in analyzing this factor.

Although we have pointed out the growth of the under 25 market, one sees that the head of the household under 25 represents about 6 percent of the total U.S.

115

TABLE 6-4   Household Characteristics by Age, 1966 (percentages)

	All Households	Under 25	25 to 34	35 to 44	45 to 54	55 to 64	65 and Over
Households (millions)	58.1	3.6	10.0	11.9	11.7	9.7	11.2
Percent distribution	100.0	6.1	17.2	20.5	20.0	16.7	19.3
Average size	3.3	2.9	4.0	4.4	3.6	2.5	1.9
Distribution all persons. . . .	100.0	5.3	21.1	27.6	22.1	12.8	11.1
Household income ($)	100.0	100.0	100.0	100.0	100.0	100.0	100.0
Under 3,000.	22.5	20.3	8.9	9.6	13.4	23.8	59.4
3,000 to 5,000	17.5	26.3	17.8	14.3	14.4	18.0	20.9
5,000 to 7,500	24.3	35.1	33.5	26.6	22.5	23.3	11.6
7,500 to 10,000	15.6	11.8	21.2	20.5	19.2	13.2	4.3
10,000 to 15,000	14.8	5.9	15.6	22.1	19.8	14.3	3.8
15,000 and more	5.3	0.6	3.0	6.9	10.7	7.4	—
Distribution all income ($) .	100.0	4.7	18.2	24.8	25.4	17.3	9.6
Under 5,000.	100.0	6.7	11.0	12.2	14.0	17.4	38.7
5,000 to 10,000	100.0	6.8	23.3	24.7	21.6	15.6	7.9
10,000 and over	100.0	1.8	15.5	29.9	30.9	18.2	3.7
Households owning homes . . .	57.0	10.0	39.0	62.0	66.0	66.0	65.0
Households owning automobiles.	78.6	79.6	86.6	87.5	84.7	77.4	56.4
Two or more	25.1	16.0	23.3	34.0	36.5	24.8	9.1

Source: Adapted from *The Conference Board Record*, Aug. 1968, p. 25.

households but accounts for less than 2 percent of the families earning over $10,000 per year.

Households in this group have a lower income, less education, and are less likely to own their own homes or automobiles. A firm looking for a market for certain types of products may be totally uninterested in this segment of the market, particularly one interested in selling products used by home owners.

The over 65 group involves an interesting contrast with the younger family households. In the former group one finds many retired workers. In addition, the educational level of this group is the lowest among all the various age groups in the table. The most dramatic aspect of the over 65 group statistics is the household income breakdown, which shows almost six out of ten households earning less than $3,000 per year. This is an indication of the fact that many of these households are living off pensions and social security.

The segment in these age groups that seems to indicate the widest market for most of the goods and services being sold in our economy is the 35 to 44 age group. Within this group one would find what one might call the typical family in terms of income distribution and number of children. Here one finds the highest ratio of children and the highest percentage of suburban dwellers.

Education

The relationship of education and income can be seen in Table 6-5. When the family head is a college graduate, over 40 percent of such families have incomes that exceed $15,000 per year. In contrast, when the family head is a high-school graduate, this income level is achieved by only 14.5 percent of the families in this grouping. Closer examination indicates that families headed by college graduates account for over half of all families earning over $25,000 per year.

Several other observations about education should also be made. The first is that today about two out of five young people go to college. Second, the educational gap between the young members of the family and the head of the household has been widening over the past 10 years. For instance, when the family head is over 65, only 8.0 percent have graduated from college, whereas in the 25 to 34 age group 27.3 percent have completed college.[3] A third observation is that families in which the level of education is higher can be expected to be more sophisticated in their choice of goods and services. Many firms have found this group to be an excellent target market for encyclopedias, travel, and specialized magazines, in addition to the many other goods and services a person would ordinarily buy at this high income level.

The level of education has other profound effects on the future of marketing. For instance, the better educated groups are by definition more interested in new ideas. They are more likely to accept something new and act upon it. As any travel agent can attest to, many of these higher educated people are quite willing to take trips to exotic places where even friends and neighbors have never been.

The better educated groups in addition develop specialized tastes and needs that ultimately result in the segmentation of very narrow and specialized marketing opportunities for manufacturers. This ability to discriminate results from a long educational process, and can change the product offerings of many firms. Many people claim that the type of movie fare today is a direct result of the growing

[3]F. Linden, "The Education of the Family," *The Conference Board Record,* Oct. 1970, p. 42.

TABLE 6-5   Family Characteristics by Educational Attainment, 1969

	Total Families	Elementary School	Some High School	High-School Graduate	Some College	College Graduate
Age of family head						
Under 25	100.0%	100.0%	100.0%	100.0%	100.0%	100.0%
	6.6	2.1	7.7	9.1	10.8	4.5
25 to 34	20.3	8.1	19.8	26.3	26.1	27.3
35 to 44	21.7	15.5	22.3	23.6	22.8	28.3
45 to 54	21.1	19.5	22.9	22.3	20.8	19.3
55 to 64	16.3	24.6	16.6	12.0	12.0	12.7
65 and over	14.0	30.2	10.7	6.7	7.5	8.0
Family income ($)	100.0%	100.0%	100.0%	100.0%	100.0%	100.0%
Under 3,000	10.0	21.1	9.4	5.3	4.0	2.6
3,000 to 5,000	11.5	20.3	12.6	8.0	6.5	3.3
5,000 to 7,000	13.8	17.4	16.9	13.7	9.6	5.9
7,000 to 10,000	23.2	20.6	25.8	27.4	23.3	15.1
10,000 to 15,000	25.8	15.0	24.6	31.1	32.6	32.5
15,000 to 25,000	12.9	5.1	9.7	12.5	20.2	29.2
25,000 and over	2.8	.5	1.0	2.0	3.8	11.4
Families $25,000 and over	100.0%	5.0%	6.1%	22.1%	14.0%	52.8%

Source: Adapted from *The Conference Board Record*, Oct. 1970.

sophistication of the population, caused by a rising educational level. One need only look back at many of the old movies from the 1940s, particularly those aimed at the mass movie goer, to understand the many changes that have occurred.

Another example of this growth in sophistication may be in the use of wines and the interest in gourmet cooking among the better educated. The proper use of fine wines from different areas of the world requires an appreciation of subtle differences in quality and taste.

In the area of employment several factors have taken effect that will have a direct impact on marketing in the years ahead. One involves the general tendency toward more professional and managerial occupations. Second, and also important, is the tendency for more women to enter the work force.

Employment

Occupational Trends

The relative change in the types of occupations has become quite pronounced in recent years.

Employed Persons by Major Occupational Groups as a Percentage of the Work Force   TABLE 6-6

	1950	*1960*	*1970*
White collar	37.5	43.1	48.3
Professional	7.5	11.2	14.0
Clericals	12.7	14.6	17.3
Blue collar	38.8	36.1	35.2
Service workers	10.8	12.3	12.3
Farm workers	12.3	8.0	3.9

Source: U.S. Department of Commerce, Bureau of the Census; and U.S. Department of Labor, Bureau of Labor Statistics.

Table 6-6 shows some of these trends. One important development has been the decline of farm workers from a total of approximately 12 percent of the workers in the United States in 1950 to 3.9 percent in 1970. This is in keeping with our earlier noted tendencies of population growth in the large metropolitan areas of the United States.

The decline in this group has been offset by an increase in higher-level professional and white-collar clerical occupations. Over this same period of time the professional work force has about doubled, and clerical workers have increased by about 40 percent. These groups are usually considered to be middle- and higher-class occupations.

Among laborers there has been a slight decline over this period. However, within this group certain tendencies have occurred that warrant our consideration. Unskilled laborers (and the above-mentioned farm laborers) have declined in their share of the total number of occupations. However, this slack has been partially taken up by the increases in skilled labor.

The decline of some occupational groups and increases in others has been a favorable happening in the view of those engaged in marketing. The increases in effect have been among those occupations that have traditionally been higher paying occupations. The declines have been among those occupations that have been among the lowest paying jobs. Additionally, confirming the previous discussion, the growing occupations have been those that usually require a higher educational level.

Female Work Force

One of the most impressive changes in the work force in the past 20 years has been the increase in the ratio of married females in the work force.

In terms of just females, the female work force has increased by 13 million since 1950, and this trend is expected to continue. The most startling change has been the fact that about 63 percent of these workers are married. This is in direct contrast to the year 1940 when two thirds of the female work force consisted of single females. In addition, one might also note that a larger proportion of the working women have had some exposure to college and hold white-collar occupations.

This development has had a tremendously complex effect on all phases of marketing. With the female in the household working, it has, for example, limited the time she has available for cooking foods and shopping. This explains the trend toward instant and frozen food products. Lack of shopping time has forced retailers to extend the shopping days by opening longer hours and keeping their stores open on Sunday. This trend has created markets for wash-and-wear clothing. The added income in the family created a situation where families could purchase homes in suburban areas, and buy more home furnishings possessions than ever before in our history. It has also created a market for fashion merchandise simply because the working wife must dress differently when employed.

Consumers' Income and Expenditures

Growing family income and how people tend to spend this income represent one of the most important considerations in developing a marketing plan. Changing family income in the past 20 years created many new industries and opportunities for many firms.

The income of the consumer makes up the basic demand factors for a company's product. However, it is obvious that the consumer does not get to spend all his money. Hence, in discussing family income one must take into consideration the various types of income that are available for spending. The most important may be defined as follows:

1. Personal income: The income to individuals in the form of wages and salaries, proprietors' and rental income, interest, social security, and related benefits.

2. Disposable income: Personal income less taxes – federal, state, and local.

3. Discretionary income: Income that may be spent or saved without consideration of current need or prior commitment.

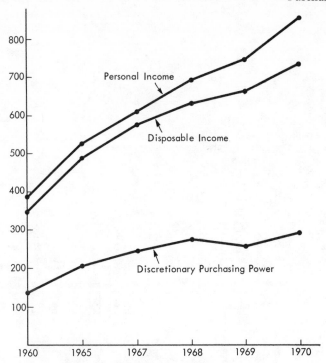

Growth of Disposable Personal Income and Discretionary FIGURE 6-2
Purchasing Power, 1960-1970

Source: *Survey of Current Business,* April 1971, p. 19.

Personal Income and Disposable Income

Both personal income and disposable income have been on the rise during the past 20 years. Figure 6-2 shows the close relationship between these two statistics. Thus any upward movement in personal income results in an almost automatic increase in disposable income.

Although there has been a rapid increase in income over this period, the increase has not been evenly divided among all states. Figure 6-3 shows the wide discrepancy in income among the states. Per capita income, for example, ranges from a low of $2,561 in the state of Mississippi to a high of $5,519 in the District of Columbia. Connecticut is the state with the highest per capita income.

The manufacturer watches per capita income data by state carefully since it affects his estimate of the potential of a market area and is a major factor in determining his sales forecast.

Discretionary Income

Discretionary income represents, in effect, the amount of money available for spending on luxuries. In actuality, the consumer with discretionary income can either save his money or choose to spend it on goods and services. Consumers with large amounts of discretionary income make excellent markets for luxurious cars,

121

FIGURE 6-3   Per Capita Personal Income, 1970

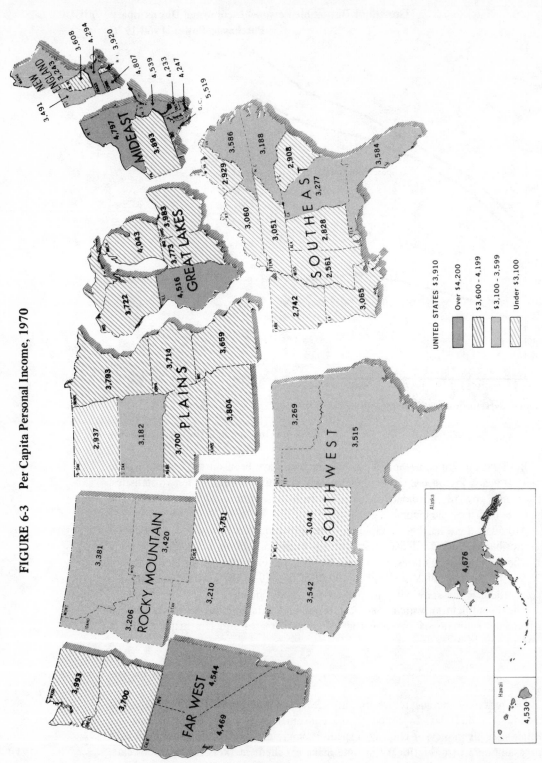

UNITED STATES $3,910

Over $4,200 $3,600 – 4,199 $3,100 – 3,599   Under $3,100

Source: *Survey of Current Business*, April 1971, p. 19.

jewelry, furs, boats, and better homes. In Figure 6-2 one can see that discretionary income has been increasing at a rapid rate. In 1970 it reached a peak of $300 billion.

As will be seen later in the chapter, the availability of discretionary income has caused many new patterns of consumer spending in the past 10 years. Some of this money has gone into travel, personal services, and education.

Family Income

In Table 6-7 one sees the distribution of family incomes for over 60 million American families. Note should be made of the fact that over one fifth of the American families has an income over $15,000 annually.

On the other end of the scale, one out of three families has income of under $7,000 annually. As noted earlier, the higher income groups are characterized by over-representation of those who are college graduates or have had some college. Over 40 percent of those families headed by a college graduate earn $15,000 or more. In the lowest income groups one finds an overrepresentation of untrained workers and blacks.

The dramatic shift upward in incomes in our society can be seen in Table 6-7 where one sees that in 1950 76.8 percent of the total families had incomes of under $5,000. In 1969 only 20 percent had incomes that fell below $5,000.

One other noteworthy fact about incomes is that there seems to be a direct correlation between high incomes and residence. That is, the higher the income the more likely the family will be living in the suburban areas. Thus of those families living outside the central cities, fully 51 percent earn over $10,000 annually, whereas only 40 percent residing in the central city earn that much.

Products and Income

The usefulness of family income data in analyzing markets can be seen in the relationship between income and purchases of automobiles.

For instance, in households with earnings of under $5,000 a year 57 percent own cars. In contrast, for those families with incomes between $5,000 and $10,000, the ratio is 92 percent. It is even greater for families with even higher incomes.[4]

The relationship of automobile ownership to income is interesting, in that if one takes an overall look at the market it seems saturated, in that today four out of five families own automobiles. Yet when one examines the market by income there appears to be important differences.

Should one choose to examine car ownership by another factor such as age, one would develop different answers. Is car ownership related to the age of the head of the household? The answer is *no* with one exception. When income is kept constant, the ownership of automobiles is remarkably similar for all age groups with the exception of the over 65 category.[5] Since the over 65 group has a decided

---

[4]Fabian Linden, "Automobile Ownership in 1975," *The Conference Board Record,* March 1968, p. 62.

[5]*Ibid.*

TABLE 6-7 Money Income – Percentage Distribution of Families, by Income Level

Income Level in Dollars (percent distribution)

Race of Head and Year	Total	Under 1,000	1,000 to 1,999	2,000 to 2,999	3,000 to 3,999	4,000 to 4,999	5,000 to 5,999	6,000 to 6,999	7,000 to 9,999	10,000 to 14,999	15,000 and Over
All Families											
1947	100.0	10.8	16.6	22.0	19.7	11.6	7.7		8.9		2.7
1950	100.0	11.5	13.2	17.8	20.7	13.6	9.0	5.2	5.8		3.3
1955	100.0	7.7	9.9	11.0	14.6	15.4	12.7	9.5	12.9	4.8	1.4
1960	100.0	5.0	8.0	8.7	9.8	10.5	12.9	10.8	20.0	10.6	3.7
1965	100.0	2.9	6.0	7.2	7.7	7.9	9.3	9.5	24.2	17.7	7.6
1968	100.0	1.8	3.4	5.1	6.1	6.0	6.9	7.6	23.4	25.0	14.7
1969	100.0	1.6	3.1	4.6	5.3	5.4	5.9	6.4	21.7	26.7	19.2

Source: U.S. Department of Commerce, Bureau of the Census.

problem in meeting physical requirements for driving and contains a large number of retired people, it would not seem startling to conclude that ownership in this group is somewhat below the levels for the other age groups. However, in the age groups up to the age of 65 no meaningful distinction can be made between these groups by age.

Table 6-8 lists the expenditure patterns of consumers between 1955 and 1969. The top part of the table, which is concerned with aggregate dollars, indicates clearly that all expenditures for all merchandise in our economy have increased substantially over that period of time. For example, expenditures for food have increased from approximately 72 billion dollars in 1955 to over 131 billion dollars in 1969. Clothing expenditures have increased similarly, as well as housing, personal care, and housing operations. One should also note that expenditures for medical care have increased. However, the increase has been much sharper than that for the above-mentioned groups.

One can learn a great deal by studying these statistics. For example, the statistics show, as indicated by the change between 1955 and 1969, that consumers are increasing their expenditures more rapidly in some areas and less rapidly in others. As mentioned, medical care expenses have increased dramatically. It should also be noted that expenditures for recreation, private education, and foreign travel have more than doubled over this period of 15 years.

These data would seem to indicate that the consumer is becoming more interested in several new areas of purchasing. For instance, the consumer is spending much of his discretionary income on foreign travel and, of course, on education. Although he is not spending less money on food and beverages, the growth as indicated by this table would not seem to be as rapid as some of these latter mentioned areas.

The ratios tabulated and presented in the bottom of the table would seem to indicate this change. For example, in 1955 the consumer spent roughly $28.40 out of every $100 on food, beverages, and tobacco. By 1969, however, the same consumer spends less than $23.00 for these items for every $100 of total expenditure. Looking at the same part of the table, one sees that the consumer's expenditures for clothing have remained relatively stable when shown as a percentage of total expenditures. The question may then be asked, what is the consumer spending his money on proportionately? The answer can be seen in this same table where expenditures for foreign travel have increased by one third, and education has increased by four times. In 1955, $5.00 went for medical care expenses. By 1969, over $7.00 went for the same medical care.

The question is often asked, why should a firm be concerned if its ratio of consumer expenditures is declining, but the total expenditures are still increasing? For instance, referring back, you will note that in 1955 only 72 billion dollars was spent for food, beverages, and tobacco, whereas by 1969 approximately 130 billion dollars was expended in this area. Yet although food expenditures increased in total dollars, the share of the consumers' dollars going into food has declined rather drastically. The reason for the concern among food firms lies in several directions.

First, a decline in ratio indicates that the consumer is becoming less concerned with expenditures for food. For example, supermarkets find that out of the total

TABLE 6-8 Personal Consumption Expenditures by Product[a]

Type of Product	1955	1960	1965	1969
Total consumption	254.4	325.2	432.8	577.5
Food, beverages,[b] and tobacco	72.2	87.5	107.2	131.9
Purchased meals and beverages[b]	13.8	16.2	20.1	26.1
Food (excl. alcoholic beverages)	58.1	70.1	85.8	105.3
Alcoholic beverages	9.1	10.4	13.0	16.4
Tobacco	5.0	7.0	8.4	10.2
Clothing, accessories, and jewelry[c]	28.0	33.0	43.3	59.4
Women's and children's, except footwear	12.4	14.8	19.7	27.2
Men's and boys', except footwear	7.0	8.0	10.7	14.8
Jewelry and watches	1.7	2.1	2.9	3.9
Shoes, and shoe cleaning and repair	3.8	4.7	5.7	8.0
Personal care	3.5	5.3	7.6	9.7
Housing	33.7	46.3	63.5	84.0
Household operations[c]	37.3	46.9	61.8	81.5
Furniture, equipment, and supplies	19.5	22.8	30.8	41.6
Electricity	3.5	5.1	6.6	8.9
Gas	2.0	3.2	4.1	4.9
Water, other fuels, and ice	4.7	5.5	7.2	8.3
Telephone and telegraph	3.1	4.5	6.4	9.0
Domestic service	3.1	3.8	4.0	4.9
Medical care expenses	12.8	19.1	28.1	42.6
Personal business	10.0	15.0	21.9	31.9
Transportation	35.6	43.1	58.2	78.0
User-operated transportation	32.6	39.8	54.4	73.0
Purchased transportation	3.0	3.3	3.8	5.0
Recreation	14.1	18.3	26.3	36.3
Private education and research	2.3	3.7	5.9	9.7
Religious and welfare activities	3.3	4.7	6.0	8.2
Foreign travel and other, net	1.6	2.2	3.2	4.3
Percent	100.0	100.0	100.0	100.0
Food, beverages,[b] and tobacco	28.4	26.9	24.8	22.8
Clothing, accessories, and jewelry	11.0	10.2	10.0	10.3
Personal care	1.4	1.6	1.8	1.7
Housing	13.3	14.2	14.7	14.5
Household operations	14.7	14.4	14.3	14.1
Medical care expenses	5.0	5.9	6.5	7.4
Personal business	3.9	4.6	5.1	5.5
Transportation	14.0	13.3	13.4	13.5
Recreation	5.5	5.6	6.1	6.3
Other	2.8	3.3	3.5	3.8

[a]In billions of dollars, except percent. Prior to 1960, excludes Alaska and Hawaii. Represents market value of goods and services purchased by individuals and nonprofit institutions, and value of food, clothing, housing and financial services received by them as income in kind. Includes rental value of owner-occupied houses, but not purchases of dwellings.
[b]Includes alcoholic beverages.
[c]Includes items not shown separately.
Source: *Statistical Abstract of the United States* (Washington, D.C.: Government Printing Office, 1971), p. 308.

dollars the consumer has to spend only 23 percent is being spent on products that they sell, whereas 15 years ago a little over 28 percent was being spent. This could mean that the consumer has less of a concern for food expenditures and hence tends to pay less attention to promotional activities of the food firm. Perhaps the food chain may also experience less reaction to price reductions than in previous years.

Second, from the point of view again of the supermarket, it also means that the consumer has more money to spend, but in effect is spending less of it in the supermarket. This can represent a challenge to a supermarket operator, and thus we have seen many supermarkets develop what we call nonfood areas; that is, they are selling apparel, housewares, and even phonograph records. This represents their attempt to get a larger share of the consumer's dollars.

Of course, in the sale of some products perhaps an industry can successfully increase their sales through "trading up," that is, trying to get the consumer to spend more money for the product. Although a manufacturer might find that people are spending less of their income on his product, he may make a strong attempt to interest the public in buying accessories or perhaps buying a much more luxurious model. Through this device he may be able to gain a larger share of the total expenditures. An industry such as the toy industry may try to get consumers to buy their products throughout the year, rather than just during the Christmas season.

From another practical point of view, this shift in consumption expenditures can hurt an industry and, more particularly, a firm. For example, most industries experience rising expenses and wages over a long period of time. It is more difficult for a firm to pay these increases and still maintain a profitable firm if its share is declining.

Family Income and Expenditures

One problem associated with income analysis relates to the tendency for family income to increase. A question often asked among marketing analysts is what happens to a family expenditure pattern as income increases? This is a particularly pertinent question since, as we observed in previous sections, rising incomes appear to be a permanent characteristic of our economy.

Table 6-9 indicates that in all major spending categories absolute expenditures do increase with an increase in income. For example, families earning pretax income below $3,000 annually spend $600 for food. This amount is roughly one half of the national average for all groups. At the extreme end of the scale, families earning over $15,000 a year spend more than twice as much for food as the national average and four times as much as the low-income family.

In other expenditure groups the evidence is similar. Expenditures for clothing and accessories are roughly three times the national average for those families earning over $15,000 annually. Reading and education expenditures in the higher-income families are more than 15 times higher than in the lowest income groups. Expenditures for alcoholic beverages, for example, are more than 10 times as high in the higher-income groups than in the lowest. Even the middle-income groups spend half as much as higher-income families for alcoholic beverages. As one

TABLE 6-9   **Consumption Expenditures by Family Income**

Expenditures for Current Consumption[a]	Total	Under $3,000	$3,000 to 5,000	$5,000 to 7,500	$7,500 to 10,000	$10,000 to 15,000	$15,000 and over
	100.0%	100.0%	100.0%	100.0%	100.0%	100.0%	100.0%
Food, total	24.4%	29.4%	26.3%	24.8%	23.9%	22.7%	20.0%
Alcoholic beverages	1.6	1.0	1.4	1.5	1.7	1.6	1.9
Tobacco	1.8	2.1	2.2	2.0	1.8	1.5	1.1
Housing and household operations	24.0	30.3	25.1	23.8	22.9	21.8	23.7
House furnishings and equipment	5.2	4.1	4.8	5.3	5.5	5.5	5.4
Clothing and accessories	10.2	7.1	9.0	9.9	10.6	11.5	12.2
Transportation	15.2	8.6	14.5	16.0	16.1	16.7	14.9
Medical care	6.6	8.5	7.0	6.6	6.3	6.2	6.1
Personal care	2.9	3.0	3.1	2.9	2.9	2.8	2.5
Recreation and equipment	4.0	2.3	3.4	3.8	4.3	4.8	4.7
Reading and education	1.9	1.3	1.4	1.7	1.9	2.5	3.5
Other expenditures	2.2	2.3	1.8	1.7	2.2	2.3	4.0
Food, total	$1,259	$600	$1,015	$1,318	$1,624	$1,970	$2,550
Alcoholic beverages	81	21	55	81	117	152	242
Tobacco	93	42	84	105	123	126	134
Housing and household operations	1,236	620	968	1,263	1,552	1,889	3,002
House furnishings and equipment	269	83	185	284	376	476	690
Clothing and accessories	525	145	348	528	720	1,001	1,550
Transportation	781	176	560	848	1,093	1,450	1,891

TABLE 6-9 **Consumption Expenditures by Family Income (cont.)**

Expenditures for Current Consumption[a]	Total	Under $3,000	$3,000 to 5,000	$5,000 to 7,500	$7,500 to 10,000	$10,000 to 15,000	$15,000 and over
Medical care	342	174	269	350	425	539	771
Personal care	148	61	118	156	194	241	312
Recreation and equipment	205	48	133	201	291	419	597
Reading and education	100	26	55	88	126	215	440
Other expenditures	113	47	69	93	147	201	508
Total	$5,152	$2,043	$3,859	$5,315	$6,788	$8,679	$12,687

[a]Totals vary slightly due to rounding.
Source: National Industrial Conference Board, *Expenditure Patterns of the American Family* (New York, N.Y.: NICB, 1965).

firm in this industry noted, the high-income person is more likely to live in the suburbs, entertain many more people, and maintain a home bar that requires an initial investment in liquor stock exceeding $100.

In the upper half of Table 6-9 one can see that the percentages spent on each of these major expenditure categories are sometimes dramatically different as income increases. For example, the highest income family in this table spends 20 percent of his income and expenditures on food, whereas the poorest income group spends almost 30 percent on food. In direct contrast, one finds that expenditures for clothing and accessories increase rapidly as family income increases. And here one finds that the lowest income groupings spend approximately 7 percent of their expenditures on clothing, whereas the highest income group spends over 12 percent.

The differences in the expenditure patterns for both food and clothing can be explained by the nature of food and clothing expenditures. As family income increases, a family can only consume so much food. Naturally, food expenditures can increase if a family perhaps buys prime cuts of meat and gourmet food items. And there is no question that higher-income families eat better quality food than lower-income groups whose diets are more restricted and emphasize starchy meals. However, the amount that any family can consume is still limited, and hence as the income level keeps rising, the ratio of food expenditures to total expenditures will decline.

On the other hand, families can buy almost unlimited amounts of clothing. In the purchase of clothing there is no limit on either the price one wishes to pay for a given item or the number of items one may purchase. Therefore, as family income increases, it is usual for not only the total dollars spent on clothing to increase, but the ratio of clothing expenditures to total family expenditures to increase as well.

SUMMARY

This chapter is concerned with quantitative measurements of the market. Several important characteristics are studied:

1. Population – its growth and movement between sections of the United States and within the metropolitan area.

2. Age of the Population – its growth in terms of two contrasting segments, the under 25 and the over 65.

3. Education – preponderance of college graduates in the over $15,000 family income group.

4. Employment – an increase in white-collar workers and the decline of blue-collar and farm workers. Growth of the married female in the work force.

5. Consumer income – growth of personal, disposable, and discretionary income. Increase in family income, which now includes one out of five families in the over $15,000 income group.

6. Consumer expenditures – growth in dollar expenditures in all groups. Decline in proportionate food expenditures and rapid growth for medical, travel, and education.

1. Table 6-1 indicates the population growth by regions and states between 1960 and 1970. What areas are growing the most rapidly and why?

*2. What effect has suburban population growth had on the manufacturer of: (a) automobiles; (b) chewing gum; (c) men's suits?

3. What kinds of firms will be affected by the data in Table 6-3? In what way will they be affected?

4. How important is the under 25 group to the manufacturer of expensive furniture?

5. Are income and education related? Be specific.

6. What trends in employment are presently under way? How can this affect marketing?

7. Distinguish between personal income, disposable income, and discretionary income. How important is the latter to the manufacturer of food?

8. What important changes in family income have taken place in the past 20 years? How has this affected marketing?

9. What has been the trend in recent years for food expenditures?

10. How has the trend in food expenditures affected the supermarket?

11. As family income rises, more dollars are spent on food. True or false? Explain.

12. Travel is an increasing expenditure group since 1955. Why?

13. As family income increases, more money is spent proportionately on clothing. True or false? Why?

*In-depth question.

Behavioral Characteristics
of Consumers

7

SUMMARY KEY

Aside from collecting statistical data concerning the consumer, management has a need for understanding the behavior of the consumer in terms of his being an individual, as a member of society, and as a purchaser of products.

In accomplishing this the firm can draw on principles derived from several behavioral sciences, such as psychology, sociology, social psychology; and cultural anthropology.

The question behavioral information addresses itself to is why people of similar economic characteristics act in different ways in response to a similar stimulus.

The consumer as an individual has certain basic needs, which are further classified into physiological and psychological, the former referring to the need for water, food, air, temperature regulation, and sex. The latter refers to safety, social, and egotistical needs. All these needs are met to some extent by an individual relating to a product or service he may have purchased.

Several psychological concepts are particularly relevant. The need for *self-esteem* on the part of the individual is certainly satisfied by many products; the consumer's *perception* of these goods and services determines how much a product will go to satisfying the consumer's need. Consumers obviously perceive products in different ways. Since all consumer behavior is *learned*, its relationship to *reinforcement* and habit is also pertinent to understanding the consumer. The role of *frustration*, which affects *habits* and learning, is also of interest.

Attitudes are predispositions to act in a certain way. Marketing people are interested in how they are formed, simply because the more favorable a consumer attitude the more likely the consumer will use the product.

Aside from the consumer as an individual, one should consider the consumer as a member of groups, social classes, and a certain culture. In terms of groups the marketing interest revolves around the reference groups of the individual. The social class is also an important determinant of his interest in goods and shopping behavior. Warner's six social classes are still relevant to today's identification needs.

Here one can identify a relationship between store selection and class.

Culture is of particular importance today since the United States is made up of many ethnic groups and those with different cultural outlooks, particularly in regard to goods. The American Black is representative of this group.

Aside from psychological factors, the behavior of the consumer in making a purchasing decision indicates a valuable source of information. Of particular interest are:

1. Sources of product information, which are identified as those that are controllable by the manufacturer (i.e., advertising) and those that are not, such as past experience or information from friends.

2. Studies of brand loyalty, which indicate the level of loyalty a consumer has toward a brand or a store. This could include loyalty ranging from undivided loyalty to divided or no loyalty. Changes over a period of time and the amount of impulse buying seem also relevant to the study of loyalty.

3. Planned purchasing and the variance of time spent on preplanning a purchase, which give us insight into consumer behavior.

4. Heavy users of a product, who are particularly important in that they help the manufacturer to identify his major buyers. Thus in one study it was indicated that although 89 percent of consumers use margarine, 45 percent of these total customers account for 83 percent of the total margarine sales.

In the previous chapters we discussed the means of identifying consumers on the basis of statistics that are available to the firm. In this manner it was shown that the firm can locate potential markets measured in terms of income, expenditure patterns, and other characteristics such as education and age. The need to segment these markets was also discussed in some length.

The reader should recognize, however, that at no point did this information reveal to any useful extent the purchasing behavior of the consumer toward either products or stores. To accomplish this, one must look at human behavior or, more accurately, consumer behavior.

The difference between these two observations is becoming increasingly more important to firms because marketing and, for that matter, our society are becoming more complex. The barrenness of just knowing the statistical size of the market can be seen in the problem of the boating firm that tries to identify and sell to a market of high-income people. The firm would have little difficulty in locating high-income groups throughout the country. They could if necessary locate the areas within each state where many of these people are located. If they cared to, they could perhaps secure lists of people who owned boats previously and are perhaps in the market for a new boat or one that is more expensive. If this is the totality of the firm's information about boats, they would be unable to answer several important questions. For instance, where do people purchase boats? Who do they consult before making a purchase? What motivates them to purchase a boat? If a firm had this knowledge, it would find itself in a better position to write ads, establish channels for distribution, and above all design a product that would appeal to the motivation of this group.

Management would of course like to have the answers to the questions raised by the boating firm for most any product. Again, they do not get these answers from quantitative data.

In studying consumer behavior management is concerned with only certain aspects of it. Some of the areas they study are more in the form of background; others are directly attributable to the company's product.

Those interested in the behavioral aspects of the consumer are concerned with the following:

1. The consumer as an individual.
2. The consumer as a member of society.
3. The consumer as purchaser of products.

To achieve a greater understanding of the consumer and how he acts, the tendency in marketing in recent years has been to apply many of the principles and studies that are available to use from the behavioral sciences. The behavioral sciences that apply to marketing include the following:

1. *Psychology,* which is a study of the individual and how he thinks and the motivation behind his everyday activities.

2. *Sociology,* which is a study of groups, and how they are formed and function.

3. *Social psychology,* the science that combines psychology and sociology by studying the individual and his relationship to the many groups in our society.

4. *Cultural anthropology,* the study of man and his words, which includes his customs, taboos, and activities such as gift giving, and many of his primitive styles.

Each of these behavioral sciences can throw light on consumer behavior. For example, psychology can offer us much information on the consumer as an individual, particularly in determining his needs and motivation.

The consumer as a member of society can best be served by information from sociology and social psychology. Here one can gain a great deal of information as to how consumers relate to groups and, particularly, the group's importance in selecting merchandise.

Direct information concerning the consumer and how he actually makes a buying decision can be obtained from research studies, which are intertwined with information from the behavioral sciences. Thus a statistical study that obtains data based on a previous definition of social classes and relates the answer to this definition can prove to be valuable.

One major problem, however, in trying to arrange and collect such information is that the federal government's statistics do not make such breakdowns in the data. For instance, although the government recognizes occupation, education, or age as an important population characteristic, it has not delved into many of the social classifications, such as social classes, as necessary adjuncts of population studies. On the other hand, one can perhaps make assumptions about social classes based on the occupation of the head of the household.

The importance and crucial nature of behavioral factors can be best understood in terms of a stimulus–response analysis of consumer behavior. For example, one would agree that two individuals viewing a similar commercial on television would not respond in the same way. One might go right out and buy the advertised item, whereas another may decide at that point to never purchase the same item. The question marketing men have been asking is why people with similar economic characteristics act in different ways in response to a similar stimulus.

Behavior and Behavioral Variables   **FIGURE 7-1**

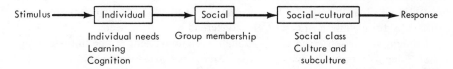

The answer lies in the intervening variables that can be seen in Figure 7-1. Here one sees that these intervening variables include individual, social, and sociocultural factors that affect the response one gets from an individual. Thus a person of a certain social class may respond more favorably to an advertisement for foreign travel than someone from a lower social class. As many airlines have noted, the response to the stimulus (advertisement) may be more closely related to class than to income.

One should also note that the stimulus response of the individual usually changes over time. Thus one may respond to a certain stimulus in one way at one stage in the life cycle and in another at a later point in life.

In the following pages consumer behavior is studied from the point of view of the individual, social, and sociocultural factors.

The field of psychology contains information concerning the individual that can be related to marketing. The most important aspect of the individual that is of obvious importance to marketing is an understanding of his needs. Individual needs are of major interest to marketing analysis since buying products is a way people have of fulfilling these needs. In effect, this fulfillment represents the motivation of the individual and is an important part of human behavior.

Fulfilling human needs is not the only aspect of human behavior. Perception and learning make up the total behavior pattern of the individual. Perception is the process by which one turns sensory stimulation into a meaningful picture of the world. Learning as a process is a more active part of consumer behavior and is based on actual experiences of the individual. Naturally, it is strongly affected by the striving to fulfill needs, and particularly the way the cognitive processes work in the individual. These three major aspects of human behavior will be discussed next.

The Consumer
as an
Individual

Basic Needs

Human behavior is initiated through the needs of an individual. Psychology has recognized that man has two levels of needs, those that are physiological in nature, and those that are psychological.

Basic physiological needs refer to the human beings' need for food, water, air, temperature regulation, and sex. In our society, it is felt that most of the basic human needs are met to a greater extent than in any other present or previous society. Thus it has been noted by one observer that the United States is perhaps the only country in the world that has an overeating problem.

On the other hand, it is also true that not *all* Americans have satisfied their basic needs. It is also not particularly true that one needs to completely fulfill all basic needs to turn to fulfilling his *psychological* needs. Most people in our society do not fulfill all of their basic needs. However, one can conclude that they have been sufficiently fulfilled in most cases to be concerned with other needs.

It should also be observed that although basic food needs can be fulfilled in our society there is growing evidence that even basic needs are subject to either expansion or at least change. For example, it was shown in the section on expenditures that the typical family with rising income was spending less of its total budget (proportionately) on food. Yet it is also true that the budget of the typical American family is turning more and more to better quality food and more exotic items from all over the world. Thus one finds an increasing consumer interest in gourmet foods, wines, and organic and health foods in our society. Even thirst seemingly cannot be satisfied by drinking water; in recent years the sale of bottled pure spring water has increased tremendously.

In essence, therefore, man can probably never fulfill all his basic needs, since they are constantly expanding. However, most people in our society have fulfilled these needs at least to a point where they can consider a higher level of needs — psychological needs.

Higher Needs

Higher needs are those that are beneficial to the complete development of the individual, but not necessary to continue life. These needs only come into focus when the lower physiological needs are satisfied. These needs are defined as[1]

1. *Safety needs:* Man's need for protection against danger, threat, and deprivation.
2. *Social needs:* Man's need for belonging, for association, for acceptance by one's fellows, for giving and receiving friendship and love.
3. *Egotistic needs:* Man's need for self-esteem and needs that relate to his reputation, that is, the need for status, recognition, appreciation, and for the deserved respect of one's fellows.

According to psychologists, these categories not only delineate a higher level of man's needs, but also indicate the order in which man seeks to satisfy them. Thus,

---

[1]Douglas McGregor, *The Human Side of Enterprise* (New York: McGraw-Hill Book Company, 1960), pp. 36–40.

when physiological needs are reasonably well satisfied, needs at the next highest level (safety) dominate a person's behavior. When the person has fulfilled this need sufficiently, he then assumes more interest in the next level — social needs. The last level — egotistic — is, as has been pointed out by a number of authors, one that is rarely fulfilled.

What do the three higher-level needs mean to marketing management? As demonstrated earlier, the basic needs of human beings offer rational themes for advertising and for all communication with consumers. The higher levels would seem to offer fewer possibilities; yet possibilities do exist. Safety needs would seem to be fulfilled by individual products rather than by the image projected by a retail store. For example, intangible products such as life insurance or medical insurance would seem to offer opportunities for a marketing man to develop a meaningful strategy aimed at the demands of people concerned with this need. On the other hand, both the social and egotistical needs of people offer more promise in developing a retail strategy. Social needs refer to the consumer as he functions in a group.

It is interesting to note that the last set of needs — the egotistical — is of great interest to the retailer as well as the manufacturer. This is because status is a prime factor here; and status can be symbolized by the store one shops in and in another sense can afford. Status naturally varies according to one's life goals or levels of aspiration. If the consumer feels that his aspirations (or goals) are met by shopping in a particular store, then his association with this store will continue for a long time to come.

In choosing these life goals, individuals differ considerably. Most either lower or raise their goals, depending on their success or failure. In psychological experiments it has been shown that even those with minimum qualifications will raise their goals to higher levels as they achieve success. Many individuals set their goals in terms of income and status. And a sure indicator of status is to have the means to shop at stores that cater to higher income levels. In one sense the retailer stamps certain individuals as having attained status and therewith a certain level in their aspirations or goals. Consumers understand this and are no more perplexed by it than by the motivation of a person buying a Cadillac. Certainly, few buy this product because of its excellent mechanical features.

Need for Self-esteem

One must bear in mind that goods and services are merely symbols to the purchaser of a product. If one accepts the fact that the individual through his interactions with parents, teachers, and groups he associates with forms a personality, which in effect is a self-concept of himself, then one should be curious as to how products and services purchased relate to the self-concept. In effect, goods are a communication device for the individual.[2]

Thus, when the consumer is purchasing goods that are seen or conspicuous, his choice revolves around his self-concept. His choice of stores is also an important symbol in the sense that he must relate his self-concept to the store. Thus one may

---

[2]E. L. Grubb and H. L. Grathwohl, "Consumer Self-Concept, Symbolism and Market Behavior: A Theoretical Approach," *Journal of Marketing*, Vol. 31, Oct. 1967, p. 24.

draw some conclusions concerning the personality and self-concept of the individual who purchases an expensive automobile. However, it does not necessarily follow that a person of high income would purchase the same automobile. Among individuals with even the same high income, one will find a much different view of the automobile as a communications symbol. That is why one finds millionaires driving around in older, inexpensive cars in direct contrast to another individual driving a Rolls-Royce.

Knowing the symbols and their relationship and interaction with the individual's mental processes would seem to constitute valuable information and understanding for the manufacturer of most products. This understanding could help direct his advertising, selling, and pricing policies, which establish the firm's product image.

Perception

How does the consumer satisfy the drives we have outlined above? One way is by going out and searching for satisfying products and services. He becomes aware of these ways through his senses; however, these perceptions are also influenced by his experiences. Perception (or cognition) has been defined as "the process of becoming aware of objects, qualities, or relations by way of the sense organs. . . . What is perceived is influenced by . . . experience. . . ."[3]

A consumer's choice of objects and the like is strongly influenced, therefore, by the mental processes related to his perception of the object he is considering. In evaluating products the consumer in a typical supermarket is faced with many choices. His decisions in this case are based on how he perceives the product and his understanding of the meaning of the product in relationship to his goals and drives. His memory may play a part and his past experiences, if applicable, may also help him to arrive at a decision. The consumer's evaluation of the product he is considering may be made on the basis of its outward appearance, the information contained on the label of the product, its color, its smell, and the appeal of the display that promotes the product.

No two people see the same thing alike. Our perception is always colored by our experiences, physiological characteristics, and psychological makeup.[4] There is much supporting evidence for this view. For example, in a classic study done many years ago it was learned that children tended to overestimate the sizes of coins as compared with discs of the same size. This perhaps is understandable. However, it was noted in analyzing the data that poor children exaggerated the size to a greater extent than wealthy children "presumably because of the greater value the coins have for the former."[5]

Our perceptions of stores are similarly affected by our makeup and experiences. For instance, most supermarket customers have varying views as to which store has the lowest prices or offers the best values. Although it is almost impossible for even

---

³E. R. Hilgard, *Introduction to Psychology,* 2nd ed. (New York: Harcourt Brace Jovanovich, Inc., 1957), p. 587.

⁴Robertson, *op. cit.,* p. 14.

⁵B. Berelson and G. A. Steiner, *Human Behavior* (New York: Harcourt Brace Jovanovich, Inc., 1964), p. 117.

the trained analyst to make an exact compilation of the lowest supermarket prices in town, the fact remains that consumers make these judgments. It is therefore obvious that the consumer makes these judgments on his perception of a selection of food items and their relative value. What the customer observes and makes this judgment on is perhaps only known to him. However, retailers running such stores attempt to make this determination, and thus are prone to instigate price cuts in product categories that seem to rank high in perception.

Price perception offers one a fertile field for study. For instance, in one study it was judged that women who are self-confident are less likely to use price as an indicator of quality.[6] In other tests of the ability of consumers to recall correct prices of products, the researchers discovered that those in the lower classes were more likely to correctly identify the price of a commodity than those in the upper social classes.[7] Both studies seem to indicate that a certain psychological makeup can color the perception of consumers.

Learning

All consumer behavior is learned. Thus one interested in understanding the consumer as an individual must come to grips with the problem of how consumers learn. Perhaps, in a more specific way, the marketing man must concentrate on how people learn about his brand.

Learning comes about through the process of experience. It is not instinctive for consumers to acquire product buying habits; they are learned. Thus, when a consumer prefers a Buick automobile or a Kodak camera, one can say that this behavior is learned.

The benefits from understanding how a consumer learns about your product are immense. For instance, when one introduces a new product, the firm can direct its introduction to those things that encourage learning. In addition, one can design promotional techniques that can more effectively encourage learning behavior.

Although learning theory as applied to marketing of products is at a rather crude stage at this point in time, one can still identify two important occurrences in the learning process – *reinforcement* and *habit* formation.

Reinforcement occurs when the consumer purchases something and has a rather happy experience with the item. If at some later date he has occasion to buy the same item again and it brings a similar gratification, it is extremely likely that this procedure will continue. What actually takes place is a process of learning, and one may expect that this transaction will be repeated again and again. In a sense, this reinforcement enhances the chance that he will purchase a product again.

On the other hand, frustration plays the converse by a similar role. For example, in Table 7-1 one sees that as incomes rise consumer frustration toward shopping increases. Thus it can be assumed that people with higher incomes are more likely to become more frustrated and thus will switch to a different store in this case.

---

[6] B. P. Shapiro, "The Psychology of Pricing," *Harvard Business Review,* July–August 1968, p. 24.

[7] *Ibid.,* p. 15.

From the marketing man's point of view, consumers will look for a different product when the occasion arises.

TABLE 7-1   Index Ratings of Frustration by Income Group (100 = extreme frustration)

	Income $0 to $5,999	*Income $6,000 to $11,999*
Must return several times to shopping center to get what you want.	71.0	80.9
Advertised goods out of stock before you get to store.	64.3	75.8
Store out of weight or texture of clothes you desire.	67.0	71.9
Store out of color you desire.	56.3	90.6
Clerks slow to serve you.	68.7	75.0
Clerks pounce on you as soon as you enter.	71.3	78.5
Clerks sell aggressively.	73.0	85.2

Source: C. J. Collazzo, Jr., "Effects of Income upon Shopping Attitudes and Frustrations," *Journal of Retailing*, Spring 1965.

Habit.   Should a favorable reinforcement continue, eventually the consumer will develop what one calls a purchasing habit. As a matter of fact, one could define marketing as that function that attempts to develop habit toward purchasing a

FIGURE 7-2   Learning Response Curve

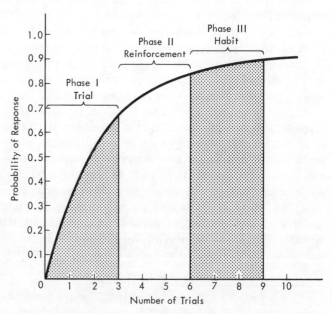

Source: Paul, *op cit.*, p. 324. Adapted from John A. Howard, *Marketing Management: Analysis and Planning*, rev. ed. (Homewood, Ill.: Richard D. Irwin, Inc., 1963), p. 36.

company's products and services. This development of habit, of course, is a major goal of most firms. For if a consumer develops a purchasing habit for your product, his purchasing may become more or less automatic, and in spite of what your competitors may do, the consumer will rarely consider his option.

The relationship of reinforcement and habit to the learning of the consumer is illustrated in Figure 7-2. If a person purchases an item three times, there is about a 70 percent probability that he will purchase the same product on the next trip to the store. This process continues. Once we approach the sixth trial the buying is now practically a habit. The probability of buying the product on any of the succeeding purchases exceeds 90 percent.

At Phase I, the trial phase, the consumer is just learning and is trying to solve the problem of fulfilling a need. At Phase II the consumer is now committed to this product and the decision is now more likely to favor one product. At Phase III learning is now over, and the purchase becomes automatic.[8]

Attitudes

Attitudes are predispositions to act in a certain way.[9] They develop as a result of our total experience, the groups we associate with, our environment, and the culture we are immersed in.

Marketing people are interested in attitudes formation from the point of view of its status among present and potential consumers. Their interest stems from several important realizations. The initial ones are that

1. The more favorable the consumer's attitude toward a firm's product, the higher the usage.

2. The less favorable the consumer's attitude toward a firm's product, the less the usage.

3. The more unfavorable the consumer's attitude toward a product, the more likely he will stop using it.[10]

Marketing people recognize that a favorable consumer attitude toward their product requires less effort on their part to maintain than if they were forced to change an unfavorable attitude.

To maintain a favorable attitude, the firm only finds it necessary to reinforce attitudes already held. Whether they do this effectively or not may not matter, since the consumer will probably retain this attitude unless they are given a good reason for changing.

On the other hand, an unfavorable attitude presents a problem to the firm that must change it. This is understandable, since the development of an attitude may take place over a period of many years. For example, the attitude of the residents of Atlanta, Georgia, toward Rich's, the famous department store, has developed over a period of 75 years. This attitude has a deep origin in that it represents several decades of family shopping habits. Rich's need only reinforce this favorable attitude. They do this by stressing their leading role in the community; participate

---

[8]C. G. Walters and G. W. Paul, *Consumer Behavior* (Homewood, Ill.: Richard D. Irwin, Inc., 1970), pp. 324–325.

[9]*Ibid.,* p. 311.

[10]Robertson, *op. cit.,* pp. 65–66.

in community activities; and maintain stocks of merchandise that are in keeping with their tradition.

One can see that the role of a competitor of Rich's is to change customers' attitudes, and, in essence, this is the task of all marketers producing a product.

Changing attitudes. Do attitudes change? The answer is yes — but the real question is what causes a consumer to change? There are several aspects to consider; the most important would seem to be

1. *Product change.* How the producer changes the product and thereby attempts to change attitude.

2. *Change the strength of the attitude.* Consumers with weak attitudes or almost-neutral positions toward products can be most easily swayed.

3. *Change in communication.*[11] Existing products receive a new look through changing communications. Thus one may give an old product a new label. Or one may develop new information and communicate this new information.

These represent specific areas where management can effect a change in attitude, and they do so in many cases.

The Consumer as a Member of Society

To further understand the consumer and his behavior, one must recognize that although he is an individual he functions in society. As a result, one must consider that he is subject to many pressures both consciously and unconsciously. In this section some of these pressures will be discussed — mainly groups, social classes, and the relevance of culture.

The Influence of Groups

Most individuals in society are in constant contact with groups. One may in a formal way be a member of an organized group of people, such as the Scouts, fraternal organizations, or perhaps the people one works with. These are usually referred to as membership groups and represent most of the people that one comes into regular contact with.

It is probably true that many of these groups which one associates with also act as reference groups. *Reference groups* are those groups which an individual identifies with to the extent that these groups become a standard or norm which influences the behavior of the individual. Thus the views of the members of an organization one belongs to may strongly influence one's attitude toward a store or a product or a purchase. It does not necessarily follow that all membership groups influence the purchasing or shopping behavior of an individual. It is perhaps more truthful to say that some of these groups have greater influence than others.

Research seems to indicate that reference groups do have a strong influence on the development of a person's self-concept and eventually his shopping behavior. It is also true that the importance of reference groups tends to vary with the type of product being purchased. For example, such research has determined that reference groups have little influence on either the product or brand chosen in the sale of products such as laundry soap and peaches. Conversely, reference groups were

---

[11]Walters and Paul, *op. cit.,* p. 310.

particularly important in determining whether one would buy a car and also the actual brand selected. Similar findings were reported in the sale of cigarettes and beer.

In product categories such as air conditioners, instant coffee, and televisions, reference groups influence the actual purchase of the product, but have little influence on the brand chosen. On the other hand, the brand was specifically influenced by reference groups in the purchase of clothing, furniture, and magazines. However, in these same categories of goods, the reference group had little, if any, influence on the decision to purchase these products.

Here again one can see that group influence varies considerably by product. A question, however, may be asked — how can such knowledge be useful to a company marketing a product? The answer can only come about after the firm marketing a product has carefully examined the importance of a group on the sale of their product. In the case of the firm that markets the Water-Pic, their view was that the most important influencer in the sale of their product is a dentist. Thus the firm campaigned to create interest among dentists in their product. Many dentists received free samples of the product and were carefully instructed as to its use. Through such encouragement the firm found that many dentists in turn recommended their product.

Firms producing drug products for instance, have determined that to get other doctors to prescribe their drug they must be able to gain the cooperation of a small group of doctors in most large cities that have a strong influence on the majority of those in the medical profession. Several of these firms have discovered that without the complete approval of these medical people, sometimes referred to as "influencers," the product has little chance of success. The "influencers" may not be large in number; however, the drug firms have discovered that it is important to identify them.

One may ask, who are these "influencers"? The answer perhaps is that they are doctors who are associated with medical colleges in a teaching capacity and also maintain private practices. In addition, they may be people who engage in medical research and perhaps publish articles in some of the prestigious medical journals. In any case, they are looked upon favorably by most doctors in the area.

Social Classes

Are there social classes in America? The answer to that question seems to be yes. Accepting this, one asks the obvious question; if there are social classes in America, can they be identified? and if so, why is this information useful in marketing?

What are social classes?. Social classes are groups in our society who (1) share the same goals, and (2) hold common views toward the environment and other groups. This would seem to indicate that one can distinguish between social classes not by their income, but by their views. For example, the limited outlook and educational level of the working-class group would tend to indicate that this class is relatively conservative in its outlook on life and other people. Terms such as "hard hats" or "blue collar workers" tend to indicate a working-class group that has similar views toward life in general and the particular social problems of the day.

Conversely, many upper-middle-class people who reside mainly in the suburban areas maintain similar views in terms of their children and tend to be characterized as leaning further left in their political views than the above-mentioned working-class groups.

The importance of social classes.   Social classes are groups of people who share to an extent similar goals and consider themselves equal to one another in terms of their status. Thus a skilled carpenter earning $15,000 a year may be of a similar social class as a truck driver perhaps earning $5,000 less per year. Both of these people may be of an entirely different social class than the elementary school teacher who may earn $8,000 per year.

The marketing man is interested in social classes particularly in the way they differ from each other. It has been observed that social classes represent important variations in life style.[12]

In essence, members of different social classes tend to perceive the product differently, and harbor a variety of attitudes that sharply differ toward products and ideas.

Warner's social classes.   In a sense the term social class has a negative connotation in American society. Most people if asked if there are social classes in America would probably deny the fact. Also, if forced to indicate the social class they belong to, most Americans would probably place themselves in a very descriptive and all encompassing class, the "middle class." Nevertheless, although there is some disagreement among sociologists, most would agree that there are social classes in this country. It is also important, and becoming even more important in recent years for marketing people to understand social class as an indication of consumer behavior.

In Table 7-2 we find an outline of Warner's six social classes with an estimation of the percentage of the United States population that falls within each group. As one can see, the overwhelming number of Americans fall into the lower-middle and upper-lower classes.

In the top groups one usually finds the highest incomes, and they include families of substantial wealth, doctors, lawyers, and top corporation executives. Most of these classes are college educated.

The total middle-class group is perhaps the fastest growing segment of U.S. society. In the upper middle, one finds professionals, owners of businesses, and middle-management people. The lower middle and the upper lower are the average American types — the latter considered to be factory and semiskilled workers in the main. The bottom rung of the social class includes the poorly educated, unskilled, and those who work irregularly.

What impact does social class have on marketing? The answer lies in the different behavior patterns of each of the social classes. For example, as will be noted later, lower classes are reluctant to shop in department stores, whereas this type of store has developed a reputation as a solid middle-class enterprise, supported in the main by this class. On the other hand, the working classes are more apt to be concerned

---

[12] J. W. Newman, ed., *On Knowing the Consumer* (New York: John Wiley & Sons, Inc., 1966), p. 13.

Social Class	Membership	Population Percentage
1. Upper upper	Locally prominent families, third- or fourth-generation wealth. Merchants, financiers, or higher professionals. Wealth is inherited. Do a great amount of traveling.	1.5
2. Lower upper	Newly arrived in upper class. "Nouveau riche." Not accepted by upper class. Executive elite, founders of large businesses, doctors and lawyers.	1.5
3. Upper middle	Moderately successful professionals, owners of medium-sized businesses and middle management. Status conscious. Child and home centered.	10.0
4. Lower middle	Top of the average-man world. Nonmanagerial office workers, small business owners, and blue-collar families. Described as "striving and respectable." Conservative.	33.0
5. Upper lower	Ordinary working class. Semiskilled workers. Income often as high as two next classes above. Enjoy life. Live from day to day.	38.0
6. Lower lower	Unskilled, unemployed, and unassimilated ethnic groups. Fatalistic. Apathetic.	16.0
Totals		100.0

Source: C. G. Walters and G. W. Paul, *Consumer Behavior* (Homewood, Ill.: Richard D. Irwin, Inc., 1970), p. 399. Adapted from Charles B. McCann, *Women and Department Store Newspaper Advertising* (Chicago: Social Research Inc.).

with their homes and thus are excellent markets for do-it-yourself products and all labor-saving devices. Most lower-class groups are rather provincial and limited in their choice of stores.

The upper classes and the upper-middle class represent the most ambitious people in our society. It thus follows that they are more likely to be concerned with status and to engage more readily in conspicuous consumption.

Social class and shopping habits.   Aside from their views and attitudes toward life style, social classes may have varying shopping habits. For instance, in Table 7-3 one can see clearly that the lower upper and upper upper and both middle classes have a much stronger preference for the regular department store than the lower classes. Conversely, both lower classes prefer or at least frequent a discount department store much more often. This table also seems to show that the mail-order catalog store is more attractive to the lower classes than the upper classes. These findings are not surprising if one considers that the department store has generally tried to maintain an image that would appeal to the middle class and upper classes in the country. As a matter of fact, most of the effort reflected in the advertising of products sold has always had a particularly strong middle-class appeal. Thus one finds the branch department store carrying garden supplies, home furnishings, and fashion merchandise (particularly sportswear) in their stores

TABLE 7-3   Kind of Favorite Store of Cleveland Women, by Social Class

Kind of Store	Social Class					
	L–L	U–L	L–M	U–M	L–U	U–U
Regular department	51%	60%	77%	83%	88%	91%
Discount department	14	11	6	2	–	9
Variety and junior department	2	6	6	5	–	–
Mail order	9	14	5	2	3	–
Medium to low specialty	2	2	1	–	6	–
Neighborhood	11	2	1	1	3	–
Others	11	5	4	7	–	–
Total	100%	100%	100%	100%	100%	100%
Number of cases	132	346	265	206	36	11

Source: S. V. Rich and S. C. Jain, "Social Class and Life Cycle as Predictors of Shopping Behavior," *Journal of Marketing Research,* Vol. 5, Feb. 1968, p. 231.

located in surburban areas of the city. These stores appeal directly to home owners, most of which make up the broad middle class that has been moving to the suburbs at varying rates since World War II.

Nevertheless, there do exist to some extent three general types of department stores, that is, those which can be considered high fashion, those with broad appeal, and stores emphasizing price appeal. When the data for a study conducted in the early 1960s are broken down by the preferences of Cleveland shoppers for these three types of stores, here again one sees a strong division between the varying social classes. This division is outlined in Table 7-4, indicating that the upper classes have a considerable preference for the high fashion store, lower classes for the price appeal store, and the middle classes for the rather broad appeal department store.

TABLE 7-4   Kind of Department Store Favored by Cleveland Women, Group Influences

Kind of Department Store	Social Class					
	L–L	U–L	L–M	U–M	L–U	U–U
High-fashion store	4%	7%	22%	34%	70%	67%
Price appeal store	74	63	36	24	19	18
Broad appeal store	22	30	42	42	11	15
Total	100%	100%	100%	100%	100%	100%
Number of cases	67	208	204	71	32	10

Source: S. V. Rich and S. C. Jain, "Social Class and Life Cycle as Predictors of Shopping Behavior," *Journal of Marketing Research,* Vol. 5, Feb. 1968, p. 48.

Social classes also differ in their attitude toward products. Pierre Martineau has noted that upper-upper-class women respond well to style and fashion advertising that uses adjectives such as aristocratic, well bred, and distinguished, and in general they tend toward independence from fluctuations in current fashions. In contrast, the middle- and lower-class women react negatively to high style. They prefer descriptions of styles that use the word "smart," and, interestingly, respond to styles favored by movie stars who in Martineau's view have glamour, which this class interpreted as "femininely pretty."[13]

Taste preferences among social class have also been observed. For instance, upper income classes reportedly prefer bitter dry tastes, irregular weaves in fabrics, and less pungent fragrances. In contrast, low-income groups reportedly prefer a sweet chocolate taste, rubbery fabrics, and strong fragrances. In interpreting this finding, sociologists indicated that it seems that high-income people perhaps could discern better the "weak stimuli," or perhaps lower classes reacted only to stronger stimuli. Still other authors have suggested that this preference among higher classes for weaker stimuli may be in actuality a learned ability to distinguish and "appreciate finer differences" due to their higher education.[14]

As a general rule, upper-class women in particular engage in many more activities outside the home. They are more likely to join clubs and organizations, shop alone, and spend less time engaged in household chores.

Lower-class women are much more involved in taking care of their homes and spend relatively little time making friends outside of their immediate environment. Much of their activities revolve around family and typically a Sunday will be spent visiting relatives.

When viewing advertising, upper-class people are more critical and suspicious of its claims and emotional appeal. Although upper-class and middle-class people are critical of advertising, they still respond to it. The approach, however, must be sophisticated and appeal to the objects and symbols that are important to this class.

On the other hand, lower-status people are relatively more receptive to advertising, particularly that which shows practical solutions to everyday requirements and social relationships.[15]

The main differences in social class, however, occur from their different views toward life in general and products in particular.

In Table 7-5 are presented the differences in outlook between middle-class and lower-class groups. One finds, for example, that the whole attitude of the middle class is pointed toward the future, whereas the lower-class is concerned with the present and particularly the past. Lower classes are much concerned with security, whereas the middle classes are perhaps more willing to take risks. This perhaps may explain the success of the union movement among lower classes and its lack of success in organizing white-collar workers.

In view of earlier comments, the reader should note the tenth item which indicates that the lower classes are more concerned with their immediate family problems.

Influence of Culture

If one agrees that a child born and raised in Japan will have a much different outlook on life than another child born and raised in the city of Des Moines, Iowa, then one subscribes to the view that culture can strongly influence one's

---

[13]*Motivation in Advertising* (New York: McGraw-Hill Book Company, 1957), pp. 168–169.

[14]C. R. Wasson and D. H. McConaughy, *Buying Behavior and Marketing Decisions* (New York: Appleton-Century-Crofts, 1968), pp. 122–123.

[15]Newman, *op. cit.,* throughout the book.

self-concept and the related perception of objects. By culture one refers to the pattern of behavior of groups and the strongly underlying beliefs and norms they have established.

TABLE 7-5   Patterns of Social Classes

Middle Class	*Lower Status*
1. Pointed to the future.	1. Pointed to the present and past.
2. His viewpoint embraces a long expanse of time.	2. Lives and thinks in a short expanse of time.
3. More urban identification.	3. More rural identification.
4. Stresses rationality.	4. Nonrational essentially.
5. Has a well-structured sense of the universe.	5. Vague and unclear structuring.
6. Horizons vastly extended or not limited.	6. Horizons sharply defined and limited.
7. Greater sense of choice making.	7. Limited sense of choice making.
8. Self-confident, willing to take risks.	8. Very much concerned with security and insecurity.
9. Immaterial and abstract in his thinking (Idea-minded.)	9. Concrete and perceptive in his thinking. (Thing-minded.)
10. Sees himself tied to national happenings.	10. World revolves around his family.

Source: Pierre Martineau, "The Pattern of Social Classes," in R. L. Clewett, ed., *Marketing's Role in Scientific Management* (Chicago: American Marketing Association, 1957), pp. 246-47.

Although one may make a case for the fact that the United States is a particular culture, from a marketing point of view one is more interested in the extensive subcultures found in our society. Most subcultures are predicated upon the existence of groups who may maintain a common language or religion, or be of similar race. They may, through the influence of these factors, develop their own pattern of behavior, which may in many cases differ markedly from the culture norms established in a country.

One of the most obvious and familiar subculture groups within the United States is that of the American Black. In recent years, with the growing affluence of this group, many firms have successfully determined needs and particularly behavioral patterns relating to the consumption habits of these groups. As a result, these same firms have successfully marketed products by carefully planning appeals that are welcomed by this subculture.

Hundreds and perhaps thousands of similar subcultures have come up in our society. Large groups interested in purchasing kosher products are found in New York City, subcultures related through religion are found in Boston, Milwaukee, and Chicago, and subcultures of blue-collar work forces are found in many of these same cities.

Marketing is interested in subcultures, for they can represent distinct markets. However, since all members of these groups live within our society, they represent a fusion with the totality. No society is homogeneous; it is made up of thousands of groups.

Our overall American society does subscribe to certain cultural patterns, however. Many of these patterns directly affect marketing. Some that seem particularly relevant are[16]

1. The belief that work is good and material comforts, which derive from hard work, are necessary to our society.
2. The emphasis on technological advances and innovations.
3. The emphasis on youthfulness as a prized cultural characteristic.
4. The emphasis on personal achievement.

These four characteristics establish the major reasons for the emphasis in our society on goods and marketing. Knowing these characteristics, one can see the direction that the marketing program can take.

One could, perhaps, note the recent national political campaign as an area where great emphasis is placed on our cultural values. The emphasis on youth is obvious, in terms of the endless visitations by candidates to college campuses. The recent discovery that one of the major presidential aspirants had dyed his gray hair lends support to the importance of youthfulness.

Further evidence can be found from the comments of candidates supporting and sympathizing with the typical American "working man" and the negative attitude toward any of those forced to live on governmental subsidies. The support of increased social security payments, since they represent benefits for those who have worked, is still another indication of the recognition by politicians of our cultural patterns. Although subcultures exist in this society, the members of these groups acquire many of the general cultural attributes. And although they represent markets that appear to be distinct, they may be closer to the majority of the population than one thinks. Many in these groups will invariably purchase similar products as the balance of society.

One should be cautioned also that culture does not only refer to ethnic characteristics, but also to such quantifiable groups as senior citizens or teenagers.

The Consumer as a Purchaser of Products

Although one can learn a great deal from studying the consumer as an individual and in relationship to the society he lives in, all the conclusions from such study are theoretical. Although all decisions must have a good theoretical underpinning, marketing executives are always interested in studies that throw light on their understanding of the consumer. Through careful study of the reports, the executive can gain valuable insights into the results of consumer behavior.

In the following section are presented some of the types of studies that represent practical observations of consumer behavior. They concern such topics as sources of

---

[16]Walters and Paul, *op. cit.,* p. 416.

product information, brand loyalty, planned purchasing, and the heavy users of products.

Sources of Information

In Table 7-6 are summarized the findings of a study of purchasing behavior for small electrical appliances. In this study the author was interested in determining what information sources the purchaser found both helpful and useful. In tabulating these sources of information he distinguished between controllable sources and noncontrollable, controllable being those that the manufacturer or the retailer had some influence over. In examining the data, one finds that newspaper advertising and mail-order catalogs and circulars seem to have the strongest influence on the purchaser. These findings suggest something the retailer has been aware of for years — newspaper advertising is perhaps the most effective way he can reach the consumer.

TABLE 7-6   **Out-of-Store Sources of Information**

Sources of Information	*Percentage Finding Helpful*[a]	*Percentage Finding Most Useful*[b]
Controllable		
Newspaper advertising	25.0	9.6
Mail-order catalogs and circulars	20.7	10.2
Magazine advertising	15.0	2.4
Television advertising	14.2	3.7
Radio advertising	7.0	0.4
Noncontrollable		
Past experience with the product brand	50.2	33.2
Discussions with friends, relatives, neighbors	33.9	18.7
Consumer rating magazines (e.g., *Consumer Reports*)	9.1	3.0
Telephone calls to stores	3.5	1.0

[a]Percentages do not total 100% because many respondents mentioned more than one source of information; in addition, the less frequently mentioned sources are not shown in the table.
[b]There were 10% who could not recall obtaining helpful information from any source of information other than visiting a store.
Source: J. G. Udell, "Prepurchase Behavior of Buyers of Small Electrical Appliances," *Journal of Marketing,* Vol. 30, Oct. 1966, p. 51.

It is interesting to note upon further examination of the table that the noncontrollable sources of information seem to be overwhelmingly in favor of past experience with the product brand. However, discussions with friends, relatives, and neighbors also seem to rank high.

One should not jump to the conclusion here that the findings of this study can apply to other products. One must remember that in the sale of small electrical appliances brand is much more important than almost any other product characteristic.

Loyalty

Since manufacturers spend a great deal of their effort attempting to create continuity in purchasing among consumers, one can legitimately ask, does consumer loyalty toward a product exist? And even more basically, what is meant by consumer loyalty?

One should recognize that several types of consumer loyalty exist. They may be classified as follows:

1. Undivided loyalty. The consumer buys brand A in the following sequence: A A A A A A.

2. Divided loyalty. The consumer buys brands A and B in the following sequence: A B A B A B.

3. Unstable loyalty. The consumer buys brands A and B in the following sequence: A A A B B B.

4. No loyalty. The consumer buys brands, A, B, C, D, E, and F in the following sequence: A D E B C F.[17]

Analysis of Classifiable Families According to Brand Loyalty   **TABLE 7-7**

Item	Undivided Loyalty	Divided Loyalty	Unstable Loyalty	No Loyalty
Margarine	21.1	13.8	27.5	37.5
Toothpaste	61.3	6.5	17.7	14.5
Coffee	47.2	18.1	29.5	5.2
All-purpose flour	73.2	7.1	14.1	5.6
Shampoo	44.0	10.4	12.3	33.3
Ready-to-eat cereal	12.5	22.7	18.2	46.6
Headache remedies	46.1	23.1	5.8	25.0
Soaps and sudsers	16.8	20.0	26.2	37.0
Concentrated orange juice	26.8	7.0	39.4	26.8

Source: G. H. Brown, "Brand Loyalty – Fact or Fiction?" *Advertising Age,* Jan. 26, 1953, p. 76.

In a study of nine products a great deal of variation as to loyalty toward products sold in a food store was found. The data are found in Table 7-7. The interpretation of this table rests on the definition of what is considered to be brand loyalty. If one considers that brand loyalty is met by the criteria of "undivided loyalty," then five of the nine products, with loyalty ratings exceeding 40 percent of the purchases, would seem to command such loyalty. If one includes in your definition the "divided loyalty" tabulation, the 40 percent or higher grouping

[17]G. H. Brown, "Brand Loyalty – Fact or Fiction?" *Advertising Age,* Jan. 26, 1953, p. 76.

would still remain the same. However, should one consider that "unstable loyalty" should also be included, then all products except ready-to-eat cereals would command a sizable proportion of loyal customers.

It is interesting to note that the two products with the highest proportion of loyal customers represent products where a brand has a sizable proportion of the market. In this case, toothpaste with 61.3 percent of loyal buyers represents an industry where two products, Colgate and Crest, have maintained a strong image and share of the market. In the case of flour, the name Pillsbury is synonymous with flour, and here one finds a strong customer preference for a brand and an indicated loyalty.

Conversely, in the case of soap one might note that no one brand has a solid share of the market, and thus consumers have many preferences. In addition, one might conclude that users of soaps probably agree that most soaps are similar and hence a purchase may be made on the basis of price inducements.

TABLE 7-8   Brand Loyalty: Percentages of Agreement between Various Years

	Preferences with Preferences		
Category	Total Sample 1941 to 1953	1941 to 1961	1953 to 1961
	(1)	(2)	(3)
Coffee	35	31	37
Typewriter	36	26	54
Automobile	24	19	47
Gasoline	33	22	45
Razor	38	39	61
Magazine	36	24	41
Watch	35	29	50
Toothpaste	27	18	41
Soap	31	20	41
Cereal	23	26	46
Bread	31	20	30
Tire	34	29	24
Gum	29	24	52
Average	32	26	44

Source: Adapted from Lester Guest, "Brand Loyalty Revisited, A Twenty Year Report," *Journal of Applied Psychology*, Vol. 48, April 1964, p. 95.

Time

Do people change their loyalty to brands over the years? The answer lies in our interpretation of the data as presented in Table 7-8. These data are based on a study of about 175 people. The respondents were questioned during their childhood (preschool through high school) and up to 20 years later concerning brand preferences for products. In reading this table one can see that 35 percent of those indicating a brand preference for coffee in 1941 had the same preference in 1953. By 1961, 31 percent had the same brand loyalty. On the average for all brands, by 1953 32 percent had the same brand preference and 26 percent indicated the same preference by 1961.

This would seem to indicate (1) consumer loyalty to the same brand would seem to be considerable, and (2) as time goes on our childhood preferences tend to change.

Column 3 in the same table seems to indicate, however, that in adulthood we tend to remain brand loyal. One can see, for example, that when a comparison with 1953 for all brands is made with the 1961 survey the brand-loyalty average increased to 44 percent.

All in all, however, one must conclude that a substantial number of buyers remain loyal to a product over the years.

Can a firm identify brand-loyal customers by socioeconomic characteristics? Several attempts have been made to determine the characteristics of loyal buyers of brands through correlation with education, income, occupation, race, and so on. Attempts to identify loyalty would seem to be of no avail.

In summarizing several major studies of brand loyalty toward food products, Ronald Frank observed: (1) brand-loyal customers lack identifiability in terms of either socioeconomic or personality characteristics; (2) loyal customers do not purchase in greater quantities nor are they more sensitive to pricing or retail advertising than nonloyal customers.[18]

In effect, brand manufacturers, although engaged in developing consumer loyalty as a marketing policy, are probably not able to identify the potential market through the usual techniques of market segmentation.

Impulse Buying

Manufacturers are well aware of the importance of impulse buying by the consumer. As will be shown later, manufacturers devote a great deal of their marketing effort in developing point-of-purchase displays and offering consumers attractive price-off deals in order to increase sales within the store. Although it is difficult to develop a definition of impulse buying that will suit everybody, usually we consider that an unplanned purchase is a suitable definition for such purchasing. Typically food items, chewing gum, and cigarettes are often considered to be impulse items. In contrast, purchases of appliances, automobiles, homes, a great deal of clothing, and perhaps a service such as life insurance, are considered by most marketing experts to fall in the category of planned purchases. These purchases are usually well thought out, and most consumers will make several trips to different sources before making a final decision.

Nevertheless, unplanned purchases would seem to be an important part of the marketing pattern. In a study conducted several years ago, one author discovered that a considerable number of purchases made in food stores were unplanned. In making a comparison between actual expenditures and anticipated expenditures of food shoppers, he noted that many consumers purchased much more than they had

[18]R. E. Frank, "Is Brand Loyalty a Useful Basis for Market Segmentation?" *Journal of Advertising Research*, Vol. 7, June 1967, p. 33.

anticipated. In Table 7-9 one can see some of his findings. Here we see, for example, that expenditures for total food were within 10 percent of total anticipated expenditures for only 19 percent of the almost 200 families included in this report. In contrast, 20 percent of the families had actual food bills that differed from the anticipated expenditures by more than 50 percent. When one examines the individual food products, one finds that beverages, sugar, sweets, and nuts are high on the list of unplanned purchases.

TABLE 7-9   **Comparison of Anticipated and Actual Expenditures of Individual Families[a]**

Product Class	Percentage of Families with Actual Expenditures Differing from Anticipated by		Percentage of Families with Actual Expenditures Larger or Smaller Than Anticipated by More Than 10 Percent	
	Less Than 10 Percent	*More Than 50 Percent*	*Larger*	*Smaller*
Total food at home	19	20	39	42
Dairy products[b]	22	32	31	48
Fats and oils[b]	25	47	38	38
Fruits	12	51	46	43
Vegetables	15	43	47	38
Meat, poultry, and seafood[c]	16	34	42	42
Bakery and cereal products	12	35	53	35
Sugar, sweets, and nuts	20	60	48	32
Beverages[d]	31	41	37	32
Cooking aids	52	39	29	19

[a]Based upon two reports from each of 199 families.
[b]Butter is included in fats and oils.
[c]Includes eggs.
[d]Not including fluid milk or fruit juices.
Source: J. D. Shaffer, "The Influence of Impulse Buying, or In-the-Store Decisions on Consumers Food Purchaser," *Journal of Farm Economics,* May 1960, p. 321.

It would seem that in an examination of most studies concerned with food purchasing the one consistent conclusion that most seem to come to is that a large proportion of food purchase decisions are made in the store. It is thus understandable why grocery manufacturers, food distributors, and brokers spend a good part of their money on in-store promotion and missionary salesmen, that is, salesmen whose major role is to maintain stocks in the supermarkets. For example, the Nabisco Company maintains not only a warehouse for their products in each major marketing area, but also a staff of missionary people who receive a salary and a commission on all sales. The major task of these people is to see that the store manager places orders of sufficient quantity for their hundreds of varieties of products. In addition, it is the task of the missionary salesmen to actually set up the displays of all the Nabisco products on a weekly basis.

A planned purchase is one for which the potential purchaser has considered the alternatives before making a decision. One of the important ingredients in making a planned purchase is the time factor. Although time may range from a period of several weeks to a few minutes, it is an important distinguishing factor in differentiating a planned purchase from an unplanned purchase.

In Table 7-10 one sees the estimated length of the purchase-planning period for selected appliances. Here one sees the range of time in planning varies from 16 weeks to 1 week. However, one should be aware that certain products, due to their special nature, will naturally involve less preplanning than others. For instance, the air conditioner, although an expensive product, has a relatively short planning period because it is a seasonal item in most sections of the country. Thus, although the price of an item may be a significant factor, the usage may tend to be almost as relevant.

**Estimated Length of the Purchase-Planning Period   TABLE 7-10
for Selected Appliances (rounded to nearest week)**

Clothes dryer	16
Tape recorder	13
Refrigerator	12
Washing machine	10
Blanket	9
Hair dryer	8
Vacuum cleaner	7
Television	4
Room air conditioner	4
Iron	4
Electric fan	3
Electric skillet	2
Radio	1

Source: R. W. Pratt, Jr., "Consumer Buying Intentions as an Aid in Formulating Marketing Strategy," in R. L. King (ed.), *Marketing and the New Science of Planning* (Chicago: American Marketing Association, 1968), p. 300.

The marketing implications of such planning-period variation are of concern to many manufacturers.[19] Limited preplanning periods for a product would seem to indicate that the manufacturer follow a strategy based on the sale of impulse products, that is, wide distribution, strong local advertising campaigns, and heavy emphasis on displays.

---

[19]R. W. Pratt, Jr., "Consumer Buying Intentions as an Aid in Formulating Marketing Strategy," in R. L. King, ed., *Marketing and the New Science of Planning* (Chicago: American Marketing Association, 1968), pp. 296–302.

Conversely, long planning periods would seem to indicate a strong reliance on national advertising, more limited distribution, and more concentration on developing an important quality image.

FIGURE 7-3 Annual Purchase Concentration in 18 Product Categories

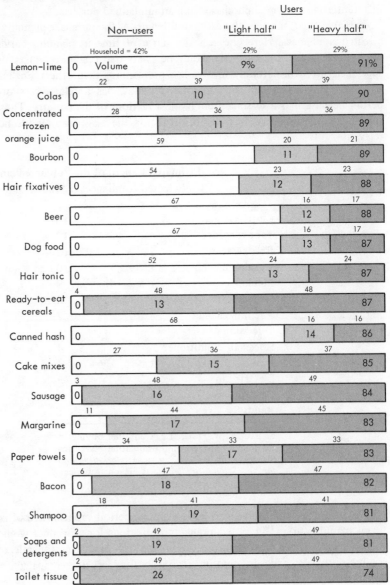

Source: D. W. Twedt, "How Important to Marketing Strategy Is the 'Heavy User'?" *Journal of Marketing,* January 1964, p. 72.

Aside from the various behavioral characteristics of buyers of a product, firms sometimes resort to using raw purchase data to gain insight into the type of buyer they are dealing with. The most useful type of data for certain convenience products is the classification known as "heavy users."

A tabulation of this sort is seen in Figure 7-3 for 18 products, most of which can be found in food supermarkets. The users of each product are divided into three categories, heavy, light, and nonusers. It is the purpose of this table to indicate the share of sales volume accounted for by the first two groups. The figure also indicates the share of the consumers that accounts for each grouping. Thus, in the case of margarine, 11 percent of the consumers do not purchase the item; that is, they are nonusers. Conversely, 89 percent of the consumers use margarine. According to this same table, the heavy users, who represent 45 percent of the total consumers, account for 83 percent of the total margarine sales volume. Conversely, the light users, who represent 44 percent of the consumers, account for only 17 percent of margarine sales volume.

Careful study of these figures shows some interesting and useful contrasts. For example, heavy beer drinkers, who represent only 17 percent of all consumers, account for 88 percent of all beer sales. Another interesting statistic is that 67 percent of the consumers are nonusers of beer.

Having this knowledge, the beer firm can attempt to segment this rather small group (17 percent) and concentrate their selling and promotional efforts in their direction.

SUMMARY

Aside from collecting statistics concerning the consumer, the marketing team must develop a clear understanding of consumer behavior as it is acted out in the marketplace. To understand consumer behavior, one must deal with human behavior, simply because the former is only one aspect of the latter. To aid us in this understanding, one can call on several behavioral sciences — psychology, sociology, social psychology, and cultural anthropology.

One has a greater understanding of consumer behavior by examining the following:

1. Individual needs, which include basic needs and higher needs.

2. Individuals as members of groups, particularly those groups used as a source of reference in making a purchase.

3. The individual as a member of a social class and a certain culture; in the case of the latter, marketing is concerned with subcultures within our society.

4. The individual as a purchaser of products. Here one can study how the consumer gets product information, the importance of loyalty to a product, the planning that goes into purchasing, and the heavy users of a product. All these indicate the manner in which consumer behavior operates in the marketplace.

1. Of what value are the behavioral sciences to the manufacturer?

2. If one clearly understands the needs of a person as an individual, this is the main information that is necessary to know in order to sell products. True or false? Explain.

3. Basic needs take precedence over all other needs of the individual. True or false? Explain.

4. Relate the basic needs of the individual to the operation of a variety store. A travel agency.

5. In what ways does the concept of self-esteem reflect on a consumer's choice of a retail outlet?

6. Would the choice available in question 5 change if one were buying a gift for a friend?

7. Relate learning theory to habits, frustration, and reinforcement.

8. How does a manufacturer aid the consumer in forming habits toward his product?

9. Why are consumer attitudes so important to the seller of a branded product?

10. Are there social classes in America? Explain.

11. Explain why we study social classes in marketing.

*12. Explain the problems one might encounter in selling an industrial product in a different culture, such as Japan.

13. What sources of information are available to the buyer of a television set? How could a manufacturer of such a set take advantage of this knowledge?

14. What are some characteristics of products that command a considerable amount of brand loyalty?

15. Are products that command brand loyalty also products for which a great deal of preplanning is necessary before purchasing?

16. Demonstrate how one may use the information furnished in Figure 7-3.

*In-depth question.

Collecting Information
from the Market

8

SUMMARY KEY

Most marketing decisions are made without the aid of complete information. However, in making most decisions some information is available either in the form of information from previous experiences or in the form of formal data collections available from secondary sources or combined with a formal method of research collection called marketing research. Every decision in the firm is made on the basis of an executive's past experience, whether or not the firm commissions a research study or not. Most decisions are made without the aid of marketing research because costs are many times prohibitive, things move too fast for research in some industries, in testing a new concept or product the competitors may learn of it, and there are numerous recorded cases where research has produced inaccurate information.

High on the list of marketing research studies in firms are forecasting, new product and competitive product studies, and studies to develop market-share information.

The steps in marketing research studies include defining the problem through exploratory research, specifying methods of data gathering, designing question-naires, developing a sampling plan, collecting the data, tabulating and analyzing the data, and presenting the report.

In defining a problem, management's first step is to develop a tentative hypothesis, that is, a tentative solution that might solve the problem. When formal research is used to test a hypothesis and demonstrates that it does solve the problem, it is no longer a hypothesis but a solution.

To determine a proper hypothesis for study, the research manager designs an exploratory study, which involves interviewing, in an informal manner, middlemen, people in the field, and the company's own personnel. It also involves checking secondary information, which consists of internal records of the company and many other library sources. External data would consist of trade association studies and reports, government data, and the many periodicals that study and report on various industries. In collecting data the research department uses survey, observation, and experimental techniques.

159

The most widely used method is survey research, which refers to direct interviewing of a person selected from a sample. Direct interviewing is done through personal interviews, mail, or over the telephone. Personal interviewing is the most expensive method but the most accurate; through motivation research, a form of in-depth personal interviewing, the research department hopes to understand underlying psychological motives of consumers. Telephone is the least costly and gets the quickest response. However, the interview must be short and can only reach those with listed telephone numbers. Mail can cover a large geographic area at little cost, but requires a literate person to answer the questions. In addition, many people do not answer mail questionnaires.

Observation studies can be used to study consumer behavior in a store or to observe activity, such as counting cars for a potential site; experiments are patterned after the scientist's laboratory tests by testing a consumer response. The reaction of consumers to a television commercial would be an example of an experiment.

In writing a questionnaire, care must be taken to avoid bias and to make sure the respondent understands the question.

In selecting a sample properly that is representative of the total population, every member of the population must have an equal chance of being selected.

In collecting data the research firm must use trained interviewers. In the case of motivation research an interviewer must be trained in psychological techniques.

In tabulating and analyzing data the job is made easier if the tabulations are anticipated when writing the questionnaire. By cross tabulation, depth information can be developed.

In writing a report, the results and recommendations must follow from the findings of the study.

Due to the increasing complexity of business firms, they have developed marketing information systems that tend to create information flow from all sectors of the business rather than just the marketing research department. This flow can originate in financial areas or production areas as well as the marketing departments.

Perhaps one of the severest restraints on making the right decision in marketing is the lack of complete information needed to make a decision. Practically all marketing decisions are made with only incomplete information. This is true even of those decisions made with the aid of marketing research. When one looks at the decision process in either a successful or unsuccessful marketing program, one is sure to recognize that many decisions that have to be made are made without the aid of sufficient information.

Thomas Berg describes the problems associated with making marketing decisions in his discussions concerning the attempt of the Dow Chemical Company to market a new antifreeze automobile product under the name of Dowgard.[1] On a technical basis Dowgard was superior to the antifreeze products sold in discount stores and in the service station. It was proved to Dow's satisfaction that their product could remain in the average car for at least two winter seasons and thus avoid the annual ritual of flushing out the car radiator and adding antifreeze. From a technical point of view, Dow, no doubt, had come across a technical change that would seem to warrant a strong effort on their part, particularly since the antifreeze market had been in the doldrums for many years. It was rather easy for the firm to estimate

[1]T. L. Berg, *Mismarketing* (Garden City, N.Y.: Doubleday & Company, Inc., 1970), p. 13.

their share of a sizable market. Nevertheless, the firm still had to make several determinations before entering the market.

Several obvious problems that were identified and had to be solved were: Would the consumer pay a substantially higher price for Dowgard in exchange for a product that would last longer? Was the consumer interested in a product that would last longer? And, finally, are consumers of antifreeze more concerned with price or with the functional aspects of the product?

The answers to these questions were forthcoming in that Dow discovered much too late, according to Berg, that ". . . there was sufficient price resistance and suspicion about the new products to make them cling to older concepts . . . in antifreezes."[2] In addition, the firm soon discovered that service dealers resisted this new product for many reasons, one of which was just general suspicion as to how well the product would work.

To solve this problem Dow would, of course, need a substantial amount of consumer and dealer information. To obtain such information Dow would have to invest in market research projects that would not only cost the firm a great deal of money, but would take valuable time that might allow the firm's competition to beat them into the marketplace. Additionally, even if Dow could anticipate its market, the research could end up being inaccurate. Its inaccuracy perhaps could come about because of some failure in the research technique. The difficulty of utilizing market research techniques was further thwarted by the fact that the product was new and thus it would be difficult for consumers or dealers to imagine the problems associated with a new product.

Obtaining Information

In reviewing the experience of Dow Chemical, one should be aware of the fact that executives practically never have enough information to make a decision. The next obvious question is, where do they obtain information to make their decisions?

The answers lie in two areas: information sources based on their *past experience,* and *formal data collection* available from *secondary sources* combined with a *formal method of research,* usually referred to as marketing research.

Past Experience

Practically all major marketing decisions are made on the basis of an executive's past experience. Even when the firm has commissioned a marketing research study, it is the executive's decision-making ability that makes the final judgment.

There are several reasons for this. First and foremost is the fact that a firm makes so many decisions in a given week that the cost would be prohibitive to design a formal research project for all decisions. Thus, by its very nature, marketing research is limited to collecting information that will help the firm make only major decisions.

Perhaps a second reason is the belief in many industries that things move too fast to research all problems. For instance, many firms must make a decision to produce

---

[2]*Ibid.,* p. 40.

a product and market it simply because their competitors may have been first with a similar product.

Another important consideration is that in testing and researching a new product idea the firm may find that it may have unwittingly let its competitors know what it is planning. There are several recorded cases of this happening.

Finally, as Alfred Oxenfeldt has noted, there are many widely known case histories where the research produced wrong answers. One outstanding failure he noted was in the television industry when General Electric rejected the findings of marketing research that there was no great market for the 14-inch portable television set. In spite of these findings, they went ahead and produced this set, finding that a substantial market did exist. Similarly, RCA has had numerous experiences where consumers expressed preferences for particular designs and features of television sets, but yet they did not buy them when they appeared on the market.[3]

It is important to remember that even if the company goes about developing further information on decisions to be made by formal techniques the final decision is still made by an executive when he combines his past experience, skills, and evaluation of research to arrive at a decision.

Role of Marketing Research

Management's role and growing interest in marketing research can be seen in Table 8-1. Here one can see the great variety of activities that manufacturers, retailers, and wholesalers engage in. High on the list of activities are forecasting, new and competitive product studies, and studies to develop market-share information.

Advertising research activities are carried out mainly by large firms that spend substantial sums in advertising. Consumer goods manufacturers are more prone to carry out a wider assortment of research activities. Both retailers and wholesalers are less likely to engage in the listed activities. This is as expected, since the middlemen are not concerned with selling individual products nor do they manufacture products. They simply add value by distributing the manufacturer's output through the various channels and finally into the hands of the ultimate consumer.

Formal
Methods
of Data
Collection

The formal collection of data involves several important steps. Although the actual steps differ from project to project, it has been recognized that in most completed market research projects the following steps are followed:

1. Define the problem through exploratory research.
2. Specify methods of gathering needed data.
3. Design questionnaires.
4. Develop a sampling plan.
5. Collect the data.
6. Tabulate and analyze the data.
7. Present the report.

---

[3]*Marketing Practices in the Television Set Industry* (New York: Columbia University Press, 1964), pp. 78–79.

The first step in conducting any research study is to carefully define the problem that will be subjected to formal study. In accomplishing this one must use a combination of exploratory research and logical reasoning. Exploratory research includes in-depth discussions with knowledgeable people and examination of secondary sources of data from libraries and company files.

The most crucial aspect of marketing research is the careful definition of the problem and the application of logical reasoning.

Once the problem has been defined, it is then studied carefully through the process of exploratory research before any attempt is made to actually conduct a field study.

Carefully defining a problem is filled with pitfalls and in a sense represents the most important step in research. An excellent example of these pitfalls is given by James H. Myers and Richard R. Mead; they present a problem faced by an insurance company concerning a study of why people let their insurance policies lapse.[4]

In defining such a problem, management may develop what is called a *tentative hypothesis,* that is, a tentative solution that might solve the problem. When formal research tests a hypothesis and demonstrates that it does solve the problem, it is no longer a hypothesis but a solution. In the case of the lapsed insurance policies, one hypothesis was that people who let their policies lapse early were simply ignorant of the many benefits attached to the policy. To test this hypothesis, the company interviewed 200 policy lapsers and found that 66 percent were unaware of more than three out of ten benefit provisions found in their policies. Could we then conclude that a large percentage of lapsers are ignorant of the many benefits found in the policy and thus tend to let the policies lapse? The answer is no, if one carefully examines the logic of our conclusions. The question can only be settled if one knows the percentage of nonlapsers who are unacquainted with the policy benefits. When this was done, the firm found that among nonlapsers 67 percent were ignorant of the benefits. Thus the hypothesis as suggested was stated incompletely and should have read: *Lapsers are ignorant of the major provisions of their policies and thus a test of lapsers versus nonlapsers would show that the lapsers know less about these benefits.* Under these conditions, the hypothesis was not supported by the research. One should note the role that logic plays in clearly defining the problem and the suggested tentative solution.

To understand the challenge of defining a problem and developing a logical solution, consider the predicament of the soda pop manufacturer who was faced with declining sales in his market. His market consisted of most of the states in the New England area. He assigned the research department the task of determining why the sales of his company had declined.

To accomplish this, the research manager spent some time thinking in a logical fashion about the decline. First, he considered that the decline could perhaps be due to a trend in that area of the country that was affecting all firms selling soda. If this were true, then it might explain the firm's decline. On the other hand, if it were

---

[4]*The Management of Marketing Research* (Scranton, Pa.: International Textbook Company – College Division, 1969), pp. 64–65.

TABLE 8-1 Marketing Research Activities, by Type of Company

Activity	All Companies[a]	Percentage of Companies Doing the Activity		
		Consumer Goods Manufacturers	Industrial Goods Manufacturers	Retailers and Wholesalers
Advertising research				
Motivation research	32	60	22	23
Copy research	38	71	38	22
Media research	47	70	51	35
Studies of ad effectiveness	49	81	58	34
Other	13	17	14	7
Business economics and corporate research				
Short-range forecasting (up to 1 year)	61	95	95	51
Long-range forecasting (over 1 year)	59	90	94	49
Studies of business trends	60	87	93	46
Profit and/or value analysis	53	90	87	43
Plant and warehouse location studies	46	83	81	49
Diversification studies	49	85	86	38
Purchase of companies, sales of divisions	45	79	86	37
Export and international studies	41	75	78	23
Linear programming	33	68	51	23
Operations research	36	62	55	28
PERT studies	29	55	52	18
Employee morale studies	36	64	62	32
Other	7	8	9	5

Percentage of Companies Doing the Activity

Activity	All Companies[a]	Consumer Goods Manufacturers	Industrial Goods Manufacturers	Retailers and Wholesalers
Product research				
New-product acceptance and potential	63	98	95	34
Competitive product studies	64	95	95	35
Product testing	53	95	81	27
Packaging research design or physical characteristics	45	86	62	28
Other	6	9	8	3
Sales and market research				
Development of market potentials	67	98	97	51
Market-share analysis	66	98	97	51
Determination of market characteristics	69	98	97	49
Sales analyses	65	99	96	53
Establishment of sales quotas, territories	56	95	94	38
Distribution channels and cost studies	50	91	83	37
Test markets, store audits	37	87	35	30
Consumer panel operations	41	80	20	22
Sales compensation studies	43	85	78	34
Studies of premiums, coupons, sampling, deals	32	77	11	19
Other	5	7	6	1

[a]1,701 companies responded; besides manufacturers and middlemen, the survey covered other types of businesses such as broadcasters, publishers, advertising agencies, banks, and public utilities.

Source: D. W. Twedt, ed., *1968 Survey of Marketing Research* (Chicago: American Marketing Association, 1969), pp. 41–44.

not true, then he must consider that the firm is doing something wrong, and thus he must examine the many varieties of possibilities in this area.

His first step thus consisted of checking studies and sources of information that would indicate the trend in the sales of soda in the New England area. Perhaps he obtained a company study that was available from an industry source. To his consternation he found that sales of soda in New England had been increasing over the past 5 years at an extraordinary rate. He also found that his firm had experienced a similar growth during the first year of this 5-year period, but after that sales started to decline. This decline continued through this period. He was thus left with the view that the company must be doing something wrong in its marketing of the firm's product. Thus his thinking about the problem zeroed in on the major aspects of the marketing mix and he proposed these considerations:

1. *Product.* Perhaps the product did not taste right, was not priced right, was poorly designed, or had a bad image.

2. *Promotion.* Perhaps the product was not advertised to the right markets, the firm was not correct in its choice of media or advertising themes, or its sales effort was faulty.

3. *Physical distribution.* Perhaps the product had not been distributed through the proper channels, or its distribution may not be efficient.

It takes little imagination to recognize that the research director has a monumental task on his hands trying to identify the major possibility that may be responsible for a decline in sales. It should also be recognized that although the research manager has identified the major areas of possibilities it does him little good to conduct a research study at this point; it would be too costly and wasteful to cover all areas since many of them do not apply. For instance, if the firm develops a survey to discover whether or not the product is priced properly, a simple examination of salesmen's reports may indicate that it is priced competitively.

Exploratory Research

To narrow down the list, the research manager would then proceed to conduct an exploratory survey to reduce the possibilities in order to develop a proper hypothesis for study. Thus, if the director can determine that price is a problem, his study could be designed in that direction.

The reasons for conducting exploratory research are many. Some of the more important ones would seem to be

1. They enable a researcher to more accurately define the objectives and scope of the proposed study.

2. They enable him to become more familiar with the industry and industry terms.

3. They enable him to become acquainted with other studies that have been performed previously, thus avoiding duplication of effort.

4. They point to certain problems that may arise from collecting the data.

5. They give the researcher a clearer idea as to the costs that will be encountered and the anticipated results that can be expected from such an expenditure.[5]

---

[5]*Ibid.*, p. 66.

At this point the researcher is looking for information that will give him the answers to all these points. But first on his list is the opportunity to "more accurately define his objectives."

Conducting an Exploratory Study

As noted earlier, the conduct of an exploratory study involves in-depth interviewing of knowledgeable persons and examination of secondary materials.

The in-depth study should always start with the person who assigned the task to the research manager. In the case of the soda company, it might include at least some, and perhaps all, of the following persons:

1. *Customers.* A discussion with some users and perhaps nonusers of the company's brand may give the research manager some idea as to how customers view his product. This type of interviewing is not aimed at being conclusive, but has as its goal the development of usable ideas. Thus it makes no pretense of representing a cross section of the population.

2. *Middlemen.* This group would include a selection of those involved in the distribution of the firm's product. This group may represent the franchised bottlers for the firm's products, some retailers who sell the product, such as supermarkets, and perhaps owners of soda fountains.

3. *Other sources.* These sources would include people associated with the industry's trade association; one might also include interviews with competitors and, of course, the firm's own staff.

Secondary Data

Along with the in-depth interviewing, or perhaps even before this is completed, the research manager should make a thorough search of secondary sources of information. Secondary sources usually refer to material that covers the period prior to the conduct of the study. It includes information that may be available from libraries, government sources, or even within the firm's own files. One usually identifies two types of secondary sources, (1) internal records and (2) external data.

Internal records may include one or more of the following:

1. Salesmen's reports.
2. Files of the firm's sales and dealings with customers.
3. Company financial journals and records.
4. Firm's published financial statements and public relations releases.

A careful examination of one or more of these records may uncover important information. For instance, by reading the reports of salesmen, the researcher may find out that certain complaints from customers continually crop up in these reports. Perhaps the firm's customers are complaining about the quality of the product or some other defect. In any case, once the researcher has completely examined this vast source of information, he may have identified several interesting possibilities for study.

External Data

To support the exploratory interviews, the researcher usually spends a similar amount of time examining published sources of information. In the sections that follow much of this information will be discussed.

However, management has several problems relating to the importance of secondary information. First, one is aware that much secondary information is not completely relevant to the firm's product. For example in the case of the soda company the firm may find many other studies that have been conducted by firms in areas of the country where the product is not marketed. Thus management may have to determine whether the findings of these studies are relevant to the firm's own soda product. In some instances the researcher may find studies that do not apply exactly to the problem but cover one aspect of it. Again, in the case of the soda firm they may find a study showing that consumers in purchasing soda are keenly interested in price. Since we may conclude from our preliminary interviews that our product is priced right the worthwhile information derived from this study may be minimal.

The user of secondary data must also determine whether the information derived has been properly tabulated and collected. Thus a study that is relied on should contain technical surveying information so that the firm may be able to determine the sample size and the care used in collecting the data. For example, a survey that purports to give the views of people who reside in Atlanta, Georgia, should have surveyed all income groups, especially if they are studying a product that appeals to all these groups. Thus it becomes important that the research study contain all the technical information for management to make such a judgment.

Finally, the user of secondary studies should be aware of the bias of certain groups and should take that into consideration. For example, a study by a local newspaper showing the effectiveness of its soda advertising would seem to be suspect. Similarly, a study by a packaging firm or a packaging institute showing the effectiveness of proper packaging of soda pop would also fall into the same category.

Basically, however, the research manager is looking for information that will give him a lead so that he will be able to solve his problem. The problem in this case is the reason for falling sales of his company's product.

His major sources of information include mainly trade associations and government and industry periodicals.

Trade associations. Trade associations are excellent sources of all types of information concerning an industry or a product. Since associations usually derive their income and reason for being from an industry, they tend to collect all information that relates to their industry. In many instances the trade association may sponsor research studies of the products their industry represents.

Typical of a trade association is the Chicago based National Association of Store Fixtures Manufacturers. Members of this organization represent most of the major manufacturers of store fixtures in the country. In New York one can find the Point of Purchase Advertising Institute, an organization that represents many manufacturers that produce and sell point-of-purchase promotional displays for brand manufacturers. As an organization the Institute promotes meetings among its members, and on many occasions has sponsored studies of the impact of displays on the sales of brand merchandise.

The files of most trade associations are filled with source materials, and the researcher would usually start his study of secondary information from this source.

Although the industry associations are excellent sources of information, one should be aware of the fact that these organizations are in most cases biased. By biased, we mean that they represent an industry, and although they may not actively suppress unfavorable information, they are not prone to publicize it. Thus one would hardly expect a trade association representing wool importers to publicize the fact that the use of synthetics in apparel is growing at a much faster rate. This does not necessarily mean that studies sponsored by a trade association are inaccurate; it does mean, however, that the researcher should treat industry-sponsored studies with caution.

Government sources. Government sources of information can be a useful source of secondary information. Many of the government sources and collected data are listed in the annual *Statistical Abstract of the United States.* This publication lists many of the tables found in the numerous government reports published during the year. In addition, a section of the abstract is devoted to sources of information within these studies.

The government also publishes a monthly catalog that lists the sources of all government data published during the previous month. This is summarized by an annual catalog that lists the departments within the government that publish needed information.

Within the departments of the government, perhaps the Department of Commerce issues most of the major studies that would interest a businessman conducting a study. Within this department are published many of the censuses taken by the federal government. As an example, the Census of Business, which includes studies of wholesaling, retailing, and manufacturing, is published through this department.

Other government bureaus and departments are also an excellent source of information. Thus one may find studies by the Federal Trade Commission of some value, or perhaps a report by the Bureau of Labor Statistics would contain information of interest to a manufacturer.

The drawback to using most governmental information is that the information is usually not too relevant to solving the firm's problem. In the case of the soda manufacturer, the firm may find the government of particular value where the number of soda manufacturers can be identified through analysis of the government's Census of Manufacturers. However, in terms of particular consumer shopping information the data will probably be of only limited value.

Periodicals. Industry periodicals represent a major source of information concerning secondary data. Many of these periodicals concern themselves with one industry and therefore collect every possible bit of information concerning happenings in that industry. Thus manufacturers of boats are serviced by *Boating Industry,* a publication that collects total information on all happenings, whether they be marketing or legislation in the boating industry. Thus a party conducting a secondary search of the boating industry would do well to examine this publication and its research files. The same holds true for most other major industries.

In addition, one can find information concerning an industry in many business magazines that are not wholly dedicated to an industry. For example, one may find an in-depth analysis of a particular industry in a regular monthly magazine, such as *Fortune.*

It is important to remember, however, that upon completion of the internal and external collection of data the firm may decide that they have enough information to make a decision. In the case of the soda manufacturer, perhaps the company may have seen a report that indicated the marketing weakness in their product. If the firm is so inclined and believes that the report is valid, they may accept the conclusions and take the necessary steps to remedy the situation.

On the other hand, the firm may at this point clearly see that further research is needed to determine the reason for the failing of the product. For example, the firm may learn from its studying that there are good indications that there is something wrong with the taste of the soda pop. This hypothesis may have come to their attention through examination of other studies or perhaps from discussions that were held with people in the industry. In any case, it is now the job of the research department to plan a formal research project that will have as its goal the determination of whether the taste of the soda is inferior to its competitors.

Methods of Gathering Data

To collect the data the research department has several methods available: survey, observation, and experiments.

Survey Research

The most widely used and useful type of research is survey research. By survey research we refer to a direct interviewing of the person selected from a sample of the population being studied. The data may be collected through direct personal interviewing, or through the use of mail or telephones.

Personal Interviewing

Personal interviewing is perhaps the most expensive way of collecting survey information. Since an interviewer has to collect information directly from a person, the cost and time involved are high.

This is perhaps the major drawback of direct personal interviews. On the other hand, the direct personal interview is perhaps the most accurate way of collecting information in that the interviewers can ask any clarifying questions that they may wish to.

In addition, the personal interviewer can observe sociological or economic information concerning the status of the person being interviewed. Finally, the personal interviewer can usually obtain more information through this technique than any other available.

Usually, personal interviewing is done on a wide scale and those interviewed represent a sample of the population that is to be studied. However, one type of personal interviewing that has gained some stature is what is loosely called motivation research. The development of motivation research came about through the beliefs of many researchers that although the consumer may offer you rational reasons for purchasing a product in reality it is his or her subconscious that dictates this purchase. It is the role of motivation research to gain entrance into the subconscious and thus to better the quality of information available to the manufacturer.

Thus, if one should ask a purchaser why she enjoys baking cakes, one may get answers such as my children or husband love home-baked goods; or I enjoy working around the kitchen; or I find it saves us money. A motivation research expert might reject these answers as being superficial and may claim that the major motivation for a woman baking a cake is that unconsciously it represents the symbolic acting out of the birth of a child. It is the opinion of those engaged in motivation research that this type of understanding of the unconscious cannot be made available through the usual techniques.

How does motivation research differ from investigative research? The answer lies in the techniques used. Motivation research uses psychological techniques in developing information from consumers. Basically, the techniques used are derived from the field of psychology, with many of the applications used being similar to those used by the psychiatrist or psychologist on a patient. Thus a motivation research analyst may use word association and sentence completion tests.

Word association tests can be used in many ways. For instance, in one test an advertising agency asked consumers to name a business that came to mind when they heard the following words; bank, hotel, airline, soda, and so on. After giving these tests to hundreds of people, the advertising agency then compared the results with their present clients in many of these industries to see how well they fared. Perhaps after running special campaigns they could conduct the same type of test again.

In sentence completion studies a similar relationship can be found. A sentence that is to be completed, such as "When I have indigestion, I _____," can give a firm information on product association with this common malady.

Usually, the motivation research expert interviews in depth small groups of people concerning their view of a product or service. Although he may carefully select the individual, he makes no attempt to obtain a valid sample of the population. In effect, what he is looking for by using these tests and interviewing procedures is to be able to attain a keener understanding of the consumer's view of a company's product and thereby offer a firm a sound program based on this understanding.

An excellent example of how motivation research can be applied to solving a marketing problem can be seen in the problem faced by Nescafé in trying to determine why people were not purchasing this instant coffee. In direct interviewing they could only find that the coffee drinkers did not like the taste of instant coffee. However, in taste tests it was determined that instant coffee ranked well with freshly brewed.

By using an indirect device the firm found that the taste was not necessarily the major factor. To accomplish this, they showed women shoppers two shopping lists. The only difference between the two lists was that on one the research firm inserted Nescafé instant coffee, while on the other Maxwell House drip ground coffee was used. The interviewee was asked to characterize the personality and character of the woman shopper.

It is interesting to note that 48 percent of the shoppers identified the housewife with Nescafé on her shopping list as lazy. Only 4 percent identified the other shopper as such. The Nescafé housewife was also described negatively as not being thrifty, failing to plan household schedules and purchases well, and one out of six described her as not a good wife.

The implications of this research are obvious. Instant coffee at that time had a social stigma attached to it, and it would be the job of the firm to overcome this problem.[6]

Motivation research is not without its critics, however. Many critics tend to emphasize the fact that motivation research procedures are not conducted on large groups and hence are not representative of the total population. Critics have also observed that many of the answers put forth by motivation research experts can be obtained through regular research procedures that are more statistically valid. Finally, many critics point out that it is not possible to take the same techniques used by the psychiatrist and apply them to the public at random. In addition, they note that many of the findings uncover mental illnesses or various degrees of neuroses, which only affect a small part of a manufacturer's market. Thus one critic observed that although it is true that some very heavy users of aspirins are underneath it all hypochondriacs this information is of rather limited value to the manufacturer who is attempting to sell to perhaps 60 or 70 million users of the item in the United States.

In any case, one thing does seem clear, and that is that in some applications in motivation research useful information has been uncovered and used by manufacturers.

Mail and telephone. Using the mail or telephone are also ways of gathering data for survey research studies. Mail is less costly than personal interviewing. It is particularly inexpensive when the interviewer is trying to cover a large geographic area. It does have several limitations, however. Perhaps the most serious is that one must compile an accurate and meaningful mailing list in order to use this technique profitably. Since approximately 20 percent of American families move each year, to simply have an updated address list presents a problem. In addition, one must find sources for certain lists. For instance, should the soda pop company want to interview teenagers that drink soda, they could have great difficulty in putting together such a list.

Equally as important is that mail questionnaires tend to be answered by the better educated. This is logical, since a person who has difficulty with the language may find answering a questionnaire to be a terrific chore. Additionally, there is usually a problem of communicating in designing questionnaires for mail survey, and the receiver has little chance to receive any additional information should a question seem to be nebulous.

Since the mail questionnaire does not involve a direct confrontation, the response rate tends to be less than either the personal or telephone interview.

The telephone is perhaps the most inexpensive of the three techniques. It is particularly useful when one wants to get an immediate response. Thus, should the soda company care to get a consumer response to a particular commercial run on a certain day, the telephone interview could gather this information. The other methods require a great deal of lead time, since preparations have to be made.

***

[6]Mason Haire, "Projective Techniques in Marketing Research," *Journal of Marketing,* April 1950, pp. 649–56.

The phone can also reach a larger audience quicker than most other forms of surveying. Several problems arise, however. The first is that telephone interviewing must be shorter than personal interviewing. In addition, since phone coverage requires that the firm rely on the telephone directory, the large number of either unlisted phones or those not owning phones will not be covered in any survey. There is some indication that these groups are overrepresented in either the higher or lower income groups.

It has also been reported that many people dislike telephone interviews since it is difficult to identify who is on the other end of the phone.

Observation. Through observation one can obtain a great deal of information. A typical observation study would be when the potential owners of a site for a gasoline station simply stand near the proposed site and count the number of cars going by. Armed with company statistics that out of every 500 cars passing by 20 will stop into a gasoline station, they can make a decision.

Observation studies are also useful in stores to note travel patterns and to watch consumer behavior. In fact, one major bakery supposedly learned the buying habits of consumers (and capitalized on it) through simple observation. They noted that most people buy white bread in a supermarket by simply squeezing the bread.

Experiments. In more recent years the experimental tests have become of greater interest to those engaged in marketing research. In a sense experiments are patterned after laboratory experiments conducted by scientists. They set up an experimental situation and attempt to measure change.

Testing is a common technique in the advertising field. Through testing the firm can at least attempt to measure the impact of advertising by establishing experimental situations. For instance, a firm can run a television commercial in one city with one approach and at the same time run another commercial in another city with a much different approach. By simply interviewing (by telephone), the firm can measure the effect of one commercial over another.

In the case of the soda pop firm, they can also conduct an experiment, particularly if they believe that there is something wrong with the taste of their product. They can, for example, set up vending machines in various areas with their product and several competing products. At the end of a certain period of time, they can measure the sales and make a judgment as to the selections by consumers. In making these judgments concerning this experiment one must be aware of the shortcomings of the experimental approach. One is that the firm must establish tests that are typical situations that the consumer usually runs into. They must be conducted in areas that are representative. For example, it may be that one of the test areas contains substantially higher proportions of Southerners who may have preference for Coca-Cola. Or it may be that the area has a proportionately higher group of young people, who again have a certain preference. The problem therefore in conducting experiments is that the researcher must attempt to control the experimental area. This is not always possible or feasible. In many cases one finds that no two areas are alike, or one of the areas changes during the study period. In addition, when one is conducting a study in an area, many times those involved in the study are more careful in the attention paid to details than they would ordinarily be. Thus the results are sometimes higher than one would normally expect.

The advantage of this means of collecting useful information is mainly that it represents a close to real-life test of an actual marketing situation. Thus, when a company tests a new product package in a market and measures the results against an area where they did not introduce the new package, the results are based on what is really taking place at the point of sale. This is considered to be an important advantage for experimental research techniques.

Questionnaire Designing

In concluding most surveys the research group must design a data collection form for all those participating in the survey. The reasons are obvious in that all interviewers should ask the same questions.

Most people unfamiliar with research are tempted to believe that most anyone can write questions for a questionnaire. Those who are engaged in marketing research have learned that writing a questionnaire requires a real talent and can only be done properly by engaging in a seemingly endless task of writing, testing, and rewriting.

Mistakes in writing questionnaires fall into many categories, but most can be charged to errors of bias, communication, and errors based on misinformation. In the latter case, one can cite the college alumni survey that asked the graduate his name. This may seem to be the simplest of all questions; however, when the returns came in the researcher soon found that many of the female graduates had changed their names through marriage. Since he needed to know who had replied to his survey, he was faced with the desperate task of trying to match up maiden names with married names!

Errors of bias are of course less obvious. However, we do know that when a person is given a choice of selections, he will often choose the first one he sees in some cases, but particularly when he does not know the answer. Thus the seemingly innocent question

What soap do you prefer?
    Ivory
    Camay
    Dove
    Dial

will collect some votes for Ivory that would not ordinarily accrue to it if it were not always listed first. To overcome this bias, the questionnaire should either rotate the order or leave the question open ended, so that the interviewee can supply his own answers.

Those perhaps not agreeing that the above represents a bias should bear in mind the annual battle that goes on in many states to secure the first line on the state ballot in the voting booth. The politicians recognize the benefits of being first on the ballot.

Perhaps the greatest source of errors is in the area of communication. Here one is usually faced with a misunderstanding as to what the question really means. Take the seemingly innocent question "How many people work in your place?"

Although many answered this question in terms of numbers, most replied about *half* or *three fourths!*

Most market research people are quick to point out that the questionnaire is one of the key ingredients in carrying out an accurate survey.

Sampling

Once we have established the goals of the study and designed the questionnaire, we are faced with the task of selecting a sampling of the population in order to collect our information. The process by which we select a part of the total population, which we expect to be representative of the total, is called sampling.

One could take a complete census of a population; however, in most cases this is too costly. Thus, if we were to take a census of all females over the age of 30 in a city, it could require tens of thousands of interviews. Our option is then to take a sampling of this group. It would have to include rich and poor, old and young, white and black, and any other major characteristics that could affect the validity of our sampling.

To select a sample properly that is representative of the total population, every member of the population *must have an equal chance of being selected*. If this is done properly, the sample should give us the answers we are looking for.

The ability of the research team to select a representative sample determines the validity of the answers. How sophisticated these methods are can be seen in the political polling for the presidential races that are published during an election year. In the most recent presidential campaigns the national research firms were within one percentage point of correctly estimating the percentage of votes the winning candidate would get. In essence, the sampling techniques of these firms represented the voting habits of almost 80 million Americans who went to the polls. Such accuracy indicates that the ability to select samples from large populations has reached a high level of sophistication.

Perhaps even more startling than the accuracy of the presidential polling estimates is the size of the sample that is drawn on nationally. Since, as noted, the polling must represent the voting habits of 80 million voters with many different characteristics, that is, it must be representative of all geographical areas, must include rich and poor, urban and rural dwellers, and so on, the question arises as to the size of the sample that must be drawn on in order to select a representative population. Although most people would perhaps estimate sample sizes of over 10,000, the fact is that most of the national surveys require a sample size of approximately 1,500. One of the most difficult things for the uninitiated to understand is that sample size is not related to the size of the population. It is also true that if the same research company wanted to determine the voting habits of people in East Lansing, Michigan, they would still have to sample 1,500 people. It is not the purpose of this chapter to delve into the subtleties of sampling; however, there is an argument that is used to silence doubters.[7] What would one expect to be the chance of selecting a black ball from a bowl that contained 50 black balls and

---

[7]F. T. Schreir, *Modern Marketing Research* (Belmont, Calif.: Wadsworth Publishing Company, Inc., 1963), p. 137.

50 white balls? The answer is obviously 50 percent. Now what would be the chance of selecting a black ball from a bowl that contained 500 black balls and 500 white balls. The answer is still 50 percent. Thus the size of the bowl has little to do with the chance of selecting a certain unit from the population.

Selection of a Sample

To properly select a sample one should have access to a list of the total population. Thus, if one were to sample those who own automobiles in Arizona, one might obtain a list of registrants from the department of motor vehicles. Once this list is obtained, the firm could then take a random sampling of the list and proceed to conduct the interviews.

The problem arises, however, when a list is not available. For instance, if one were to sample only people who watched a television program last night, there would obviously be no list available. Or if one were to sample people who had traveled to Europe within the past 5 years, a list would also be unavailable. In some cases, even when lists are available one may question the accuracy of such lists.

As a result much sampling is done without the use of a list. Area sampling represents a technique that overcomes the unavailability of a list. In using area sampling one simply divides an area into sampling units. In the case of the research firm wanting to interview those who have registered cars in a city in Arizona, they would simply divide up the city into blocks, select a sampling of blocks, and interview all the residents on those chosen blocks. Thus the principles of random sampling would be upheld; that is, all residents of the city would have an equal chance of being selected and thus the sample should be representative of the city.

Although there exist other forms of sampling that are forms of area sampling, they all must adhere to the principle of random selection.

Collecting the Data

Collecting the data involves the training or use of trained people to conduct interviews. Here bias can creep into the survey particularly when little attention is paid to the quality of the interviewers.

Many firms use the services of outside interviewing firms that maintain contact with interviewers in their area. Most of these interviewers are professionals in the sense that they have handled many different types of surveys.

It has been recognized, however, that survey requirements make different demands on the interviewer. For instance, interviewing housewives in a shopping center parking lot by using a structured questionnaire is much less demanding on the talents of the interviewer than conducting the previously mentioned motivation research study, which requires in-depth interviewing with a relatively unstructured questionnaire. In the latter case, perhaps an interviewer trained in the use of psychological techniques may be required.

Tabulating and Analyzing the Data

The tabulation and analysis of the collected information are related. In a survey the data are tabulated according to the needs of those entrusted with making the analysis.

The mechanics of the tabulation are made simpler by anticipating the tabulation problems and thereby setting up the questionnaire in such a manner that it can be easily handled. With the development of computer tabulation, the physical layout of the questionnaire is in many cases adjusted to ease the transition of the data from the questionnaire to the punch card.

Analysis of questionnaire data requires not only the simple counting of data but also the creative manipulation of the data. This sometimes involves the use of cross tabulations, where the answer to one question is compared with another. In some cases the tabulation may show a relationship that was not previously observed when the data were being added.

A good example of the importance of cross tabulations and their ability to develop depth information can be seen in a survey that attempted to determine who were safer drivers, males or females.

The following tables were constructed:

Accident Rate of Automobile Drivers

	Percentage
Never had an accident while driving	62
Had at least one accident while driving	38
	100

Accident Rate of Male and Female Drivers

	Male	Female
Never had an accident	56%	68%
Had at least one accident	44%	32%

By tabulating the rate of accidents by sex, the second table seems to indicate that females are less prone to have accidents than males. Although some people may think that this indicates that females are less accident prone than males, the author of this study was aware that males drive more than females and thus may be more likely to have at least one accident, since they are exposed to traffic more often. To test this hypothesis, he cross tabulated the sex of the person with the mileage driven and related it to whether they had reported an accident or not. His cross tabulation is seen in the table below.

Mileage Driven, Accident Rates of Both Male and Female Drivers

	Males		Females	
	Drove More Than 10,000 Miles	Drove Less Than 10,000 Miles	Drove More Than 10,000 Miles	Drove Less Than 10,000 Miles
Never had an accident	52%	25%	53%	24%
Had at least one accident	48%	75%	47%	76%

In this tabulation one can now see that when a comparison is made between males and females who drive over 10,000 miles annually, both groups seem to have about equal accident records.

The last step in the research study is to write a report that attempts to answer the questions raised earlier in the chapter. If the project has been conducted properly, the answers will be forthcoming.

Naturally, the results and recommendations must follow strictly from the published findings of the report.

Marketing Information Systems

In recent years firms have been moving in the direction of broadening the role of marketing research. Although the terminology may vary, the organizational arrangement that accomplishes the change is referred to as *management* or *marketing information systems* (MIS). A marketing information system is described as "the interacting structure of people, equipment, methods and controls, which is designed to create an information flow. . . ."[8]

Marketing information systems in a sense represent a broader outlook toward information than the marketing research system. The incorporation of MIS signifies a recognition on the part of management that (1) there exists a need for a constant flow of vital analytical information to management at all times, and (2) there are sources of such information in divisions throughout the firm, the implication being that all useful marketing information is not just found in the marketing division.

Figure 8-1 indicates the types of reports and the sources of information that can create these reports. In examining this report one can see that the marketing research department can create some of this information. In particular, the customer profile would seem to be an obvious area of information that the marketing research department can develop through the use of the marketing studies discussed earlier in this chapter.

FIGURE 8-1   Reports and Information Generated by a Marketing Information System

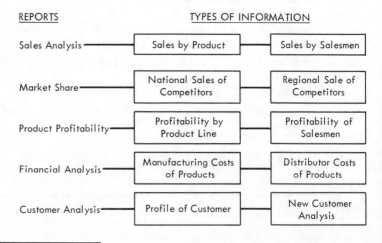

---

[8]Conrad Berenson, "Marketing Information Systems," *Journal of Marketing,* Oct. 1969, p. 16.

On the other hand, other types of reports can be generated from other divisions of the firm. For instance, the financial division can develop information concerning costs and profitability analysis by product lines or customers. A sales administrator on the marketing staff can also develop information concerning sales and profits by product line and by salesman. With little imagination one can see that MIS can generate an information flow that can help management monitor its total operations in a useful way.

The growth and use of the broader concepts of MIS is due to several developments. First and foremost would seem to be the increasing complexity of the business firm. With the growth of the business firm in terms of both the number of products carried and the markets covered, the information demands of management are greater. Companies, on the average, handle many more product lines than ever before and their operations cover a much greater market area.

Aside from the growth of the corporation, one must consider that the introduction of the computer into the corporation has enabled management to collect this information and increase its demands on the quality of such reports. Thus, within a split second the computer in some of the largest corporations can retrieve sales data in several different forms. Most firms, even before the advent of the computer, were collecting similar information. However, the information required long horus of computation. Today, however, this information may be available within seconds.

SUMMARY

To make decisions, businessmen need information. Much of their information comes from their experiences and perhaps most decisions are made on this basis. Firms do have the option of collecting information on a more formal basis by using market research techniques. Market research is used particularly when a business problem arises. The steps are as follows:

1. Define the problem through exploratory research. Once the exploratory research has concluded, the firm may decide that they have the answer and further study is not necessary.

2. Determine the data-collecting procedures. Once it is established that a study should be initiated, the firm may choose any survey (personal interviewing, mail or telephone), observation, or experimental techniques.

3. Design the questionnaire. The data-collection firm should guard against bias and should clearly stay within the goals of the survey.

4. Develop a sampling plan, by which every member of the population has an equal chance of being selected.

5. Collect data through the use of well-trained and professional interviewers.

6. Tabulate and analyze the data. The data must be carefully analyzed, cross tabulated, and interpreted on the basis of the needs of management.

7. Present the final report in a manner that answers the questions management has asked. The results and recommendations must follow the tabulated data.

1. Discuss the role of formal data collection and decision making in the firm.

2. Describe several sources of secondary information.

3. What types of research studies do firms engage in?

*4. Describe four typical studies that a car manufacturer might consider conducting.

5. Why is a proper identification of a tentative hypothesis necessary in conducting a market research study?

6. Why is personal interviewing so costly?

*7. Contrast a motivation research study of aspirin users with a similar study using survey methods.

8. Contrast the use of mail surveys with telephone surveys.

*9. What problems could you envision in asking a consumer the following question in a personal interview: What was your income in the past year?

10. Marketing information systems broaden the role of marketing information. True or false? Explain.

11. Under what conditions would a firm commission a market research study to solve a problem?

12. Why is the response rate to mail questionnaires substantially below other techniques of data collection?

13. If a firm were interested in collecting data from 25 cities in the United States within 24 hours, what collection method would they use? If the same data were collected in one city, would this change the data-collection method?

*In-depth questions.

THE MARKETING EFFORT

III

At this point in our study of marketing one begins the process of examining the marketing mix of the firm. In the following 10 chapters one is introduced to the total effort of the firm, that is, the things that the firm can do to develop and sell products to the target consumer.

In a sense, the following chapters represent the decision variables that a firm has control over. For instance, Magnavox can decide to develop a new product line, perhaps air conditioners. This choice is theirs to make, and whether it suceeds or not will be up to the management of the firm. They can also decide to market these air conditioners through the use of television advertising backed up by a newspaper campaign. Here again the choice is all theirs. Finally, they can sell the product through any channels they choose. For example, they can sell through wholesalers or directly through retailers, as they do now. They can, if they wish, maintain warehouses throughout the country for these air conditioners or they can choose to ship them directly from the factory. Again all these decisions can be made by the company and reflect their view of the opportunities and the chance of success.

The ways and means of accomplishing this are spelled out in the marketing plan, but one must remember that the choices are made with complete freedom.

The total effort and marketing mix of the firm includes the product and pricing described in Chapters 9 to 11, the means of communicating with the consumer described in Chapters 12 to 14, and the selection of channels and the problems of physical distribution covered in Chapters 15 to 18.

Products

9

SUMMARY KEY

Marketing is mainly concerned with products. A product, however, is not only made up of some tangible material but also has psychological attributes. Obsolescence is a major characteristic of products. To understand obsolescence, one must understand that there are two types to consider, fashion obsolescence, which requires a definition of *style* and *fashion,* and technological obsolescence. The former is clearly a result of consumer preferences; the latter is perhaps due to consumer choice and the different quality standards of manufacturers. A major decision area for a manufacturer concerns identifying his product with or without a brand. A brand is a name, symbol, or design used to identify a product. A trademark is a legal term which means that the brand has been awarded to one seller.

Brands are used by manufacturers to differentiate their products and in an attempt to establish customer loyalty. On the other hand, a family brand can cause problems to a manufacturer when one product is rejected by the consumers; this could result in a total rejection of the family of products. Brands can be extremely important. In food stores several major categories are controlled by branded products. Private brands are brands controlled by middlemen, usually retailers. They are in direct conflict with national brands controlled by manufacturers. The major reason for their development is to create store loyalty.

Product classification systems are important in that they influence the direction of the marketing effort. The major classification systems are by shopping behavior (convenience, shopping, and specialty goods) and psychological factors (groupings such as anxiety products and by total personality, such as aggressive).

Although most of the discussion in these chapters is concerned with adding new products, the firm also has difficult decisions to make in eliminating present products. Elimination of a product can have an adverse effect on the sale of other company products in terms of both sales and profits.

Packaging of products can be costly in that some product groups are packaged in containers that exceed one third of the selling price. The overall purpose of a package is to increase sales. However, in most cases this is not the only use. Generally, packages are used to protect, promote, develop a reuse value, increase the use, and meet ecological requirements for the product.

Marketing is mainly concerned with products and their acceptance by the consumer. Most of the discussions and evaluations by management are concerned with making decisions about products. What product shall we make next year? What improvements can be made in our present line of products? What product changes will the consumer be looking for? are all typical but yet important questions that are expected to be answered by the marketing department. In this and the following chapters will be discussed many of these problems and the approaches that companies use to solve them.

Before discussing these problems, let us consider an example of the risks and problems associated with products.

In 1964 the E. I. du Pont Company introduced a new product, Corfam. Corfam was considered to be a substitute for leather, with particular application to shoes. It was du Pont's view that this leather substitute would do for shoes what nylon has accomplished for women's stockings.

The product had many important attributes. It was water repellent, durable, resisted cracking and creasing, and, importantly, it remained uniform. Its drawback was considered to be its price, which seems to be perhaps 20 percent higher than comparable leather shoes. However, it was the view of the company that the price differential would disappear after the product became commonly accepted.

As late as 1966 du Pont reported that demand for Corfam exceeded capacity. From an earnings point of view, Corfam never did well. Perhaps this was attributable to competitive cheaper products that began to appear produced by B. F. Goodrich, Interchemical, and Wolverine.[1] At that point du Pont predicted a price decline, which eventually took place but was more precipitous than they imagined.

No doubt the major causal factor was that the shoe industry was entering a new era in which rapidly changing fashions and styles made the Corfam virtue of durability of limited value.[2] By March 1971, the firm announced it would no longer produce Corfam. The demise of Corfam was costly. Estimates are of a total loss of $100 million and an addition $8 million to phase out the production.[3] Thus after 7 years a major firm had to pay a high price for an error in marketing.

Losses such as experienced by du Pont are not unknown, and at this stage in our marketing knowledge it is doubtful that they can be avoided. The causal factors are ordinarily related to a change that has taken place in the environment. In the case of Corfam, the product ran into serious competitive problems and a changing attitude on the part of the consumer.

In any case, the myriad decisions that firms make concerning products are important decisions in that mistakes can be costly. To avoid these mistakes, the marketing manager must rely on his understanding of the role of his product in the consumer demand schedule. In addition, he must have a clear understanding of what his product represents to his consumers so that every decision he makes builds on this knowledge.

---

[1] "Exit Corfam," *Barron's*, March 22, 1971, p. 1.

[2] *Ibid.*

[3] *Ibid.*

In studying products one soon learns that they are made up of more than tangible or physical attributes. Although many of us would conclude that beer tastes the same, it is true that many beers have a different image in the minds of consumers in many areas of the country. Perhaps the most obvious example is that of aspirin. In the production of this product all manufacturers must adhere to certain minimum standards that regulate the ingredients in the product. In a sense therefore, and for all practical purposes, the ingredients found in all aspirin tablets are basically the same. This applies to Bayer as well as other private-brand products produced under the name of the store selling it. Yet it is also clear that consumers evaluate each brand of aspirin differently. The question is then if aspirin has basically the same material content why do consumers view these various brands so differently?

The answer lies in two explanations. The first is that consumers judge products, in addition to their material qualities, by the firm that produces the product. Thus a product produced by a well-known firm such as Squibb would have an edge on an unknown firm in the selling of many products. In some cases one finds that although adults may prefer to buy a private brand of aspirin for general household use they are more likely to buy a well-known branded aspirin for their children.

In addition to the reputation of the firm, one might choose a product based on the firm's warranty or guarantee that accompanies the sale of the product. For instance, a car manufacturer may be preferred by a customer simply because his warranty may be for 24 months as against 12 months for other firms.

The other means of choosing a product may be simply a psychological feeling toward the firm and its products. It may be tied in with conscious or unconscious attributes of the product that appeal to the buyer. For instance, the package may create some sort of an aura surrounding the product; or it may simply reflect the observation of the buyer as to who is using the product. In any case, the user's choice of product may literally defy explanation.

In summary, what we are expressing here is that a product is more than just material put together in a certain manner. A product is made up of many attributes, some of which we are consciously aware of; others we may not be. These attributes are developed through positive actions on the part of the firm. They include packaging, designing, warranties, channels of distribution, and all those things that tend to satisfy a person's needs.

Obsolescence

One of the major characteristics of the American market is the fact that products tend to become outdated and are replaced more often than in any other country's economy. This has happened so regularly that American producers have been accused of making products that are planned to end up in the scrap pile within a relatively short period of time. In fact, the term "planned obsolescence" has become part of our vocabulary and refers to the actual planning by manufacturers to make a product obsolete so that the consumer will be forced to purchase a new one within a few years.

Before discussing this part of the product planning process, one should distinguish between obsolescence and fashion and style changes, which are a form of obsolescence.

A *style* is a distinctive mode of expression, construction, or design of a product. A *fashion,* on the other hand, is any style that has been accepted for a long period of time. Thus high-heeled shoes may be an important style this summer; however, they only become a fashion after they have been accepted for a longer period of time. In other words, a style does not become a fashion until it has passed the test of time.

One can see, therefore, that in the marketing of certain products where fashion and style play a major part they are automatically going to become obsolete, if fashions change. This is particularly true in the apparel industry, where fashion changes occur regularly. When an important style change takes effect, one can be assured that the present stock of apparel may become obsolete.

The causes of this change and the effective obsolescence are a result of several factors, one being the desire of the manufacturer to encourage this change, and another the desire of the consumer to make these changes. The history of fashion is strewn with manufacturers who tried to push certain changes upon the unwilling consumer.

The second type of obsolescence is the *technological* type that includes also design changes. Here one refers to industries where large manufacturers are in a position to perhaps exert more pressure on the consumer to change. In the apparel industry most firms are relatively small, particularly when they are contrasted with

FIGURE 9-1 Percent of Cars on the Road That Are Eight Years Old around January 1 and Die during the Year

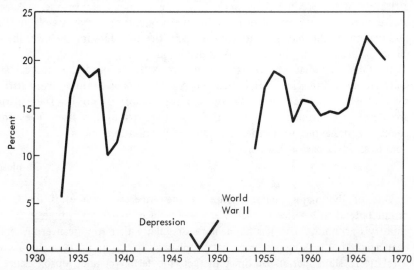

Note: Scattered data indicates the death rate was 15-18% in the 1920s. Other age cars show the same general pattern, i.e., 1934-37 and 1940-41 were equal to 1955-64, but during the 1965-68 period the rate was greater. Particularly note that the 1967 death rate was greater than the 1963-64, i.e., higher mortality in the moderate recession than in extremely good economic times.
Source: "The Automobile Industry – The Road Ahead," industry report, Oppenheimer & Company, p. 4.

the automobile industry in which three large companies control the sale of perhaps 90 percent of the total market. Technological change is an important consideration in the *automobile* industry.

One might ask himself, how long do American cars last? Part of the answer can be found in Figure 9-1. In this chart car life is expressed as a percentage of the number of cars remaining of the original model year sales. It shows that cars purchased during the most recent years have a high ratio of scrapping. Much lower ratios were experienced during the mid 1950s and early 1960s.

The study of automobile statistics seems to indicate that the relative life of the American automobile has seriously declined in recent years. For example, the pre-1960 experience of car life was thought to be 10 years. More recent data seem to indicate that the average is about 9 years.

Why the higher rate of scrappage in more recent years? Are American cars being made more poorly by design than in previous years? Does this represent a deliberate policy on the part of the American companies?

The answers to these questions are difficult to come by, but careful examination of automobile marketing trends can at least give us some insight.

Figure 9-2 seems to dispel the view that all automobile firms maintain the same quality. One can see in this chart that Chrysler's quality has been declining steadily since its peak year of 1966. Conversely, Ford, which reached its lowest level in 1966, has improved its quality quite dramatically since then.

Car Quality Index   **FIGURE 9-2**

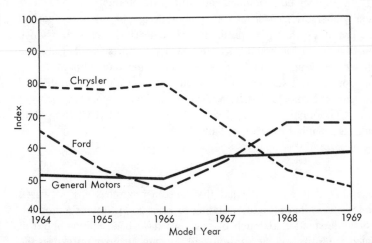

Source: "The Automobile Industry – The Road Ahead," industry report, Oppenheimer & Company, p. 14.

One of the most important developments that has tended to encourage people to scrap automobiles perhaps before necessary has been the growth of optional equipment purchases in recent years. Optional equipment tends to increase the amount of repairs, and has similarly put a greater strain on the car's power. Additionally, the replacement cost of automatic transmissions has caused many car buyers to reach a point, at perhaps the eighth year, where the cost of replacing the transmission exceeds the value of the car. When the car does not have an automatic transmission, the cost of overhauling a transmission does not exceed the value of the car.

Planning Obsolescence

As can be seen, the manufacturer alone does not plan obsolescence. In the case of the automobile it is the consumer who helps establish the type of automobile that will be offered to the public. There is little doubt that a consumer who wants to keep his car for a long period of time would be well advised to buy a stripped down automobile practically devoid of accessories, and surely without an automatic transmission.

On the other hand, the companies by introducing new models cause dissatisfaction on the part of the consumer with their present product. New models are particularly important in the automobile, appliance, and television industries. Most consumer criticism of planned obsolescence occurs in this area of design and new model introductions. Style changes in apparel are treated similarly.

Many firms would reply to this criticism by pointing out that the only reason they introduce style changes and new models is that the American consumers want it that way. Additionally, they point out that there is a psychological need for new products and this need wears thin long before the product itself wears out.

Brands

One major area of decision making for a manufacturer is his determination as to whether he shall produce a product with a recognizable brand name or sell one without such identification. As a matter of fact, the manufacturer has a third alternative, that is, to produce both branded and unbranded products.

A brand is usually characterized as a name, symbol, design, or any other method used to identify a product or family of products. A trademark is a legal term which simply means that the use of the brand has been awarded to one seller. Legally, the trademark may cover the design, symbol, or the words that make up a brand.

Brands are all around us. Examples are Plymouth, Coca-Cola, Del Monte, and Heinz — all brand names. Symbols that have meaning to the customer are the wool mark, the "Flying A Gasoline" Pegasus, Texaco Red Star, and the young child under the umbrella, as a symbol for Morton Salt.

Brand Image

One must remember that much of what the consumer purchases is not based solely on economic values, that is, values relating to price and utility of a product. One would surely understand that much of what we have been talking about in these chapters, such as motivation, perception, and learning, strongly influences the actual selection of products, and, when applicable, brands. A great deal of the purchasing decisions made by consumers are strongly influenced by noneconomic factors.

It has been proven in many cases, as noted earlier, that the label has a strong influence on the purchase of a product. In more specific terms, the brand image of a product, which a marketing firm is constantly attempting to sharpen, usually represents the most important variable in a consumer's choice. Its importance was demonstrated in a study conducted a number of years ago. In this study a group of subjects was asked to distinguish between Coca-Cola, Pepsi-Cola, and Royal Crown Cola. Although the reader may feel certain that in a blindfold test he could easily distinguish between these three brands, the conducters of this experiment found that the subjects could not distinguish through taste. In further experiments in a series of tests, experimenters discovered that even three lesser-known brands could not be accurately identified, and in most cases they were identified as being the three better-known cola brands.[4]

Similar experiments with cigarettes tend to indicate the same results as the cola study. In effect, therefore, these studies tend to support the view that brand image, a psychological factor, can offset even the economic values one may build into a product.

To support a brand name is a crucial decision for a manufacturer to make. For it implies a great deal of effort and commitment on his part. To make this decision, the manufacturer must consider many factors.

Reasons for Branding

The major reason for any manufacturer establishing a brand-name product is to differentiate his product from others, and thus maintain customer loyalty.

To accomplish this, the manufacturer must spend considerable sums of money to gain the support of the consumer. However, if the manufacturer attracts a substantial amount of consumer loyalty, his opportunity to earn profits is raised considerably since he has developed an audience that prefers his product and is not dissuaded by the efforts of his competitors.

Another important reason for using brand names is the value it creates and lends to the other products in the line. Thus, the Campbell Soup Company, which controls perhaps 90 percent of the canned soup business, has developed a name that allows them to offer new products with an advantage. For example, should Campbell decide to introduce a new soup product such as turkey rice, the name Campbell is bound to favorably impress the potential customer. Some marketing people refer to this happening as the "halo effect." One would certainly agree that the Westinghouse name casts a "halo" as to quality over each new addition to the firm's line.

Opposing Views of Branding

Many manufacturers cannot engage in developing brands simply because they do not have the financial resources to spend on advertising and promotion. Others that may have the necessary resources feel that brand names are not too important to the consumer in the sale of their products. This is particularly true in the marketing of apparel. In addition, they point out that in many cases it is more important to select a quality outlet for your product, since the retailer can be the most important factor in the sale of a product. In addition, other problems can arise in a firm that establishes a brand. As noted, a great deal of goodwill can accrue to a product that is introduced into a line that already has an established name. This technique is referred to as *family branding*. On the other hand, the reverse is also true: when a company markets a poor product, the rest of the line can suffer. One

---

[4]M. H. Pronko, and J. W. Bowles, Jr., "Identification of Cola Beverages: III. A Final Study," *Journal of Applied Psychology*, Vol. 33, 1949, pp. 605–608.

of the extreme examples of this happening was the case of a manufacturer of soup under the Bon Vivant label. On June 29, 1971, a purchaser of the firm's vichyssoise died from botulism, a rare disease. Eventually the firm was ordered to recall all soup marketed under their label, and shortly after the company entered into bankruptcy. The Bon Vivant family brand name through this unfortunate circumstance destroyed the company.

On the other hand, a company that develops individual brand names and does not tie them together into a family brand would probably not experience this problem. For instance, Procter & Gamble markets its products as individual brands and rarely identifies the company name to any great extent in their advertising. Few purchasers could identify which soap company makes Duz, Ivory, Salvo, and Comet Cleanser. The problem with individual branding is that the goodwill does not carry over to new products, and a strong advertising effort must be used to introduce all new products.

Brand Strategy Variables

Most firms would prefer to establish a brand name and thereby gain a great deal of consumer loyalty. However, several factors must be taken into consideration.

The first consideration is that the consumer must be receptive to brands. As a matter of fact, the consumer should rate the brand name first over most other considerations, such as the store it is purchased in, color, style, or the service offerings. When brand interest is minimal, such as in the sale of lettuce, the distributor may find it unprofitable to attempt to develop a brand.

Consumer loyalty is particularly important in maintaining the firm's resistance to price competition. Hence Coca-Cola commands such strong consumer loyalty that a large proportion of the public prefers their product to the lower-priced store brands sold by the supermarkets.

Finally, the market should be large enough so that the product can be marketed in large quantities and produced at lower costs as the quantity demanded grows. In this way any increasing consumer loyalty to the firm also increases its total profits.

Importance of Brands

The importance of advertised merchandise can be seen in Table 9-1 where private labels are shown as a percentage of retail sales of 113 retail firms. It is noteworthy that most of the important food groupings are dominated by national brands. Only two products, both highly perishable, dairy and bakery products are exceptions. In the food industry most products sold in supermarkets are either private label or advertised products. Thus in an industry where a substantial proportion of the consumer money is spent, over half the products sold can be classified as advertised items.

Private Brands

In contrast with national brands, private brands are products sold under the name of a retailer or wholesaler. They are sometimes referred to as *distributor brands.* These brands are promoted by the distributor and sold usually under the distributor's name or a brand name controlled by him.

Some private brands have managed to develop a nationally known reputation even though they are *not* promoted by a national manufacturer. Perhaps the best-known private brands are Allstate tires, Kenmore washing machines, and vacuum cleaners, all owned and controlled by Sears, Roebuck and Co. Another major private brand is the Ann Page line of jellies sold in the A & P supermarkets.

Private Labels as Percentage of Sales for Retail Stores, 1964-1965   TABLE 9-1

	113 Retail Respondents
Canned vegetables	26.2
Canned fruit	30.1
Frozen vegetables	48.9
Frozen fruit juices	49.7
Bakery products	53.9
Dairy products	50.2
Coffee	35.8
Bacon	44.8
Wieners	33.2

Source: National Commission on Food Marketing, "Private Label Products in Food Retailing. Case Studies of the Dynamics of Brand Competition," in *Special Studies in Food Marketing,* Technical Study 10 (Washington, D.C.: NCFM, June 1966), pp. 20–21.

Private brands are in direct conflict with national brands sold by and promoted by manufacturers. Many large department stores sell upward of 10 percent of their products as private brands. It is reported that as much as one third of A & P's sales are in private brands.

Retailers who handle private brands represent a threat to manufacturers in that they can put the manufacturer's brand in a disadvantageous position in the store, since the store is where the consumer comes in direct contact with a product. For instance, supermarkets selling a private brand of soda under the store's name usually allot a substantial amount of space to their own product and much less to the nationally advertised major soda products such as Pepsi or Coca-Cola.

Retailers' Views on Private Brands

In view of the fact that the nationally distributed sodas are better known to the public, why should a retailer bother to develop his own brand-name product? There are several answers to this question. From a philosophical point of view the retailer prefers to have private brands in many instances because it allows him the option of using his own abilities to merchandise the store. Previous to private brands, the retailer had to sell only those products that were promoted by the manufacturers.

Retailers who promote private brands hold the view that since they are closer to the customers they may be in a better position to judge what is best for the customers.

Just as important is the fact that once the retailer has developed a private brand the consumer who prefers his product must keep coming back to his store. In this manner he has differentiated his offerings from those of his competitors.

Finally, the retailer usually earns a higher markup on private brands, since he can buy them on the open market from firms that do not incur heavy advertising and selling costs. Since he can buy the private brands cheaper by placing large orders with one manufacturer, the retailer tends to sell the private brands at prices below those of the national brands.

Manufacturers' Views on Private Brands

Manufacturers of nationally advertised merchandise are naturally not too keen about retailers selling competing products, for obvious reasons. However, many manufacturers of nationally advertised merchandise also produce private-brand products for retailers. Some of these firms include Kodak, General Electric, Westinghouse, Goodyear Tire and Rubber, Bell and Howell, and Hotpoint. Naturally, these brands are not identified by name and appear under the store's name.

This does not necessarily mean that all manufacturers sell private-brand merchandise to retailers. The Frigidaire Division of General Motors and Maytag have maintained a policy for years of selling only products under the company's name.[5] Nevertheless, there are many manufacturers that sell private-brand products to retailers.

Manufacturers opposed to retailers selling private brands are quick to point out that the quality of private-brand products tends to fluctuate from year to year, since retailers tend to change suppliers frequently. In the case of a manufacturer of nationally branded merchandise, they point out that since he usually produces his own product he finds it easier to maintain a high level of quality.

Manufacturers who tend to feel deeply about this problem go so far as to point out that it is the nationally advertised and promoted products that tend to bring customers into the store, which in turn enables the retailer to sell his private brands. Of course, this is an exaggerated view in that there are many retailers, for example men's wear stores, that do not carry any nationally branded merchandise in stock. In addition large chains such as Sears and J. C. Penney have managed to sell the consumer on their private brands to such an extent as to exclude most other national brands from their outlets.

Manufacturers are also aware of the fact that private brands represent important weapons to smaller retail firms. For instance, in the food field the small grocers form cooperatives and agree to buy from wholesalers, who in turn supply them with many private brands that are sold in all the cooperative stores. These wholesaler private brands act as effective deterrents to the nationally advertised low markup products put out by canners or food manufacturers.

[5] Leon Morse, "The Battle of the Brands," *Dun's Review,* May 1964, p. 98.

All change is preceded by some sort of appraisal of the product as measured against the competition.

Much of the change information comes in the form of "day in" and "day out" activities. Thus complaints from customers or "feedback" information from salesmen may spur management to reconsider its present product. Those firms with an ongoing research program will receive a flow of information that may very well result in change. As a matter of course, management should always reevaluate its products.

The product appraisal sheet typically points out to management the direction that change can take. The sheet shown in Table 9-2 indicates a firm's appraisal of a ball-point pen in relation to competing pens in a British firm. The exhibit makes comparisons on price, materials, ink supply, and performance. Careful examination of the sheet seems to indicate that the product's point mechanism seems to be superior. On the negative side, management may be concerned that both the price seems high and the product's smearing factor is poor. Whether management will change these negative factors depends on the factors discussed later in the chapter.

Although the appraisal sheet is used primarily to aid in making decisions concerning product change, it can be used in other areas within the management sphere. For instance, the appraisal form may indicate to the advertising department some of the strong points of the firm's product that can be emphasized in relation to the competition. The sales force can also be made more aware of the competition and its basic weaknesses from this appraisal form.

The manufacturer has many different approaches to classifying the products that he sells. Each classification is important in the sense that it influences the direction of the marketing effort for the firm's product.

The classification system used by firms may include a characterization of the shopping behavior of the buyer and a system that relates the psychological personality of the buyer to the product. These systems represent generalizations about consumer patterns of behavior and attitudes. However, as we shall see, these classifications are necessary to the operation of the firm.

Classification by Shopping Behavior

The most common and rather unsophisticated way of classifying products by shopping behavior is by the groupings of convenience, shopping, and specialty goods.

Convenience goods. Convenience goods refers to goods that are sold to the consumer who is unwilling to spend more than a minimal time on shopping for these particular goods. The customer is quite willing to accept substitutions for convenience goods. Implied in this classification is that the consumer has all the information he needs to make a decision on these products; hence his decision can be made quickly and with a minimum of effort and consideration. Some convenience goods are candy, drug products, food snacks, cigarettes, and almost any staple household product. Ordinarily such products are low priced and represent only a minor part of the family's total expenditures.

TABLE 9-2   Product Appraisal Sheet

	Own Product	Competitor A	Competitor B	Competitor C	Competitor D
Price					
Pen	2s. 3d.	2s.	1s.	2s. 6d.	1s.
Refill	9d.	1s.	—	1s. 3d.	
Materials					
Body	Polystyrene	Polythene	Polythene	Polystyrene	Polythene
Clip	Steel	—	Polythene	Brass	Polythene
Point	Steel	Steel	Steel	Tungsten carbide	Steel
Reservoir	Brass	Polythene	Polythene	Brass	Polythene
Ink supply (grams)	1.2	1.4	0.9	1.4	1.2
Performance					
Fast starting	Good	Fair	Good	Very good	Poor
Skipping	Good	Fair	Poor	Good	Fair
Smearing	Poor	Good	Fair	Poor	Good
Fading	Fair	Fair	Good	Good	Fair
Ink clogging	Good	Good	Very good	Very good	Good
Point mechanism	Very good	Poor	Good	Good	Fair

Source: Gordon Medcalf, *Marketing and the Brand Manager* (Elmsford, N.Y.: Pergamon Press, Inc., 1967), p. 69.

Since the consumer will accept substitutes for a convenience good, the producer must get the widest distribution for his products as possible. Thus the manufacturer of cigarettes may sell his product through

1. Food stores
2. Candy stores
3. News stands
4. Taverns
5. Gasoline stations
6. Vending machines (in all kinds of outlets)
7. Drugstores
8. Vendors at stadiums
9. Mail-order firms

No doubt this list is incomplete; but it does indicate at least the extent of the effort that must be made to sell convenience goods.

Shopping goods. In purchasing shopping goods the consumer must spend more time making comparisons among products and hence shopping in several stores. Shopping goods are usually higher-priced items, and most of all the consumer is not as knowledgeable as to their features as he is with convenience goods. Clothing, furniture, and appliances are usually considered to be major shopping goods items.

The apparent willingness of the consumer to shop around indicates that the manufacturer need not sell his product to every store in town. In some instances he may offer his product exclusively to retailers. However, since the consumer will shop around, he prefers that the outlet that carries the product be located near outlets carrying similar merchandise. In today's retail market he would prefer that at least one outlet be located in a shopping center.

Specialty goods. Specialty goods refer to products that have special characteristics or a specific brand name that the buyer is willing to make an extra effort to obtain. Specialty-goods buyers differ from shopping-goods buyers in that they are more aware of the type of product they are looking for, and in most cases they have a brand name in mind. A purchaser of cameras may have a Leica camera in mind; a male may prefer a Hickey-Freeman suit; a female may look for a Koret handbag; all represent specialty-goods buyers.

Although one may get the distinct impression that these product categories are mutually exclusive, after careful study one might question this belief. The problem with this three-level classification system is that the groups overlap in many instances and the specialty- and shopping-goods differentiations are in many cases questionable. For example, television sets are to some people shopping goods in that they shop around for sets in order to gain information. However, in making a second purchase it is now a specialty good, if they have a strong preference for the brand they purchased earlier. This lack of a clear distinction can be seen in the sale of television sets, for RCA sells its product to most major outlets, whereas the Magnavox company offers its sets to only a limited number of dealers in most major cities.

Convenience goods are also a questionable grouping. What is a convenience good to a bachelor may be a shopping good to a married man is a statement often made in marketing circles. Thus a bachelor, with less economic pressure on him, may purchase a television set in the first store he shops in; whereas the average customer may spend more of his time searching. On the other hand, the bachelor may spend more time shopping for an exotic pipe tobacco mixture, whereas the male head of a household may consider that item to be a convenience good.

Nevertheless, firms must attempt to understand the shopping behavior of their customers in relationship to the products they sell, and their analysis can greatly affect the firm's effort to market its product.

Psychological Classifications

Products can also be related to the needs of the individual, either some aspect of his personality or his total being. One of the means of classifying products is to determine the amount of ego involvement of the individual.

One must be cautioned, however, that many products do not involve the psyche of the individual. Although generalizations will be made in attempting to classify various product appeals, it is true that there exist many exceptions to this system of classification.

Goods may be classified in the following six product groupings:[6]

1. Functional
2. Hedonic
3. Prestige
4. Status
5. Maturity
6. Anxiety

Some products are bought for their actual performance characteristics. Goods such as tools, foods such as celery, and thread and needles are all examples of products where psychological factors do not play much of a role. These goods are usually referred to as *functional*. In the sale of these products the ego involvement is almost totally missing. This results in the marketing situation where the consumer has little brand consciousness since her ego is not involved. As a result, the consumer is likely to have little preference for any particular brand over another. Thus in the sale of functional products a marketing firm encounters great difficulty in differentiating its products from other firms.

Hedonic goods refer to products that consumers derive aesthetic pleasure from. Goods such as perfumes, art, and decorative materials fall into this category. Visual factors are usually the most important characteristics of these products. Here again the psychological aspects of the product do not enter into consumer choice. In the case of hedonic goods one may safely say that appeal to the senses is the tact taken by manufacturers selling these products.

Although the characterizing of these first two groups seems to be clearly delineated, the reader should be cautioned that many products fall into more than

---

[6]W. B. Wentz and G. I. Eyrich, *Marketing Theory and Application* (New York: Harcourt Brace Jovanovich, Inc., 1970) p. 198.

one category. For example, one may be inclined to treat a product such as spinach as a functional product, since it is purchased as a food and for its nutritional value. However, among older adults, one may find that if they were raised during the "spinach generation," when all kinds of exaggerated nutritional values were attributed to this food product, the choice may be strongly influenced by childhood behavior.

Prestige products are easily identifiable as those which appeal to purchasers of luxury items. In essence, they serve to reinforce the self-image of the possessor. For example, an expensive car such as a Cadillac symbolizes wealth, conspicuous consumption, and basically indicates success. Other products falling into this grouping include expensive homes, clothing, and perhaps magazines. One might include *Fortune* magazine as a product that has prestige appeal to this group.

A similar type of goods are status products. *Status* products appeal to consumers because they impart class membership. Prestige products impart a view that the individual has unique characteristics, such as wealth or success. Status products indicate that this individual is a member of an approved group. Membership in a club would be an obvious example. A type of haircut or mode of dress would indicate a status product or service. Travel to various parts of the world symbolizes this type of expenditure. Basically, however, this expenditure indicates clearly that the recipient belongs to a group or at least aspires to become a member of a certain group in our society.

Maturity products are products that indicate one is reaching adulthood. Products falling into this category are liquor, cigarettes, and perhaps coffee. In some cases the young person is forbidden by law to purchase such products. In others, custom dictates that they not use such products.

Although a firm selling many of these products must avoid allowing young persons to purchase them, some firms by substituting for these products have developed successful marketing programs. Thus manufacturers of chocolate cigarettes have found a substantial market for their products among youngsters, who can identify with the habits of their parents without indulging in a similar product.

The last classification of products is the anxiety products. *Anxiety* products are sold on the basis of protecting the user against a threat to his ego or social standing. Included in this group are dentifrices, deodorants, toupees, and more recently organic foods.

In selling of these products the marketing firm usually indicates the threat to the individual in its commercial advertising. Reminders that bad breath or body odor can make one socially unacceptable are sufficient reasons to motivate potential users of such products.

Total Personality Classification

Aside from the ego involvement of the individual, one could theoretically relate the personality of the individual to the product he purchases. Attempts over the years have been made by automobile companies to relate the conservative personality or the youthful personality to their product.

In one recent study, the research divided people into three groups: (1) those who move toward people (compliant), (2) those who move against people (aggressive), and (3) those who move away from people (detached).[7]

The *compliant* person was described as one who tries to gain his way in the world by being weak and dependent and relying mainly on others to help him achieve his goals. This person was described as disliking aggression, egotism, and power seeking on the part of others. In general, these people tend to avoid conflict with others, and in general wish to be loved.

In direct contrast, the *aggressive-oriented* person has a strong need to achieve success and prestige. Others around him are seen as competitors. People are in a sense used, and are only seen as being useful if they help the aggressive personality achieve his goals.

The third group, the *detached* personality type, avoids sharing his experiences with others. He does not need other people to achieve his goals and generally has been described as being distrustful of others. Self-sufficiency is an important trait.

In applying these three personality types to product and brand usage, the following relationships were determined:

Men's dress shirts.   It was found in this study that high-aggressive men preferred Van Heusen to other shirts to a greater extent than low-aggressive men. The author also found that a slightly greater percentage of high-detached individuals than high-compliant or high-aggressive individuals did not know what brand they used most frequently. It was generally believed that detached individuals are less concerned with brand names as indicators of social status than aggressive or compliant individuals.

Mouthwash.   The study found that high-compliant people would be more likely to use mouthwash than low-compliant people, the feeling being that high-compliant people would want to reduce the risk of offending others. This was confirmed by the study.

Men's deodorant.   In answering questions concerning men's deodorants, it was found that the aggressive people had a strong preference for Old Spice over other brands. Right Guard, on the other hand, was preferred by compliant and detached people. It was the author's view that Old Spice is thought of as a particularly masculine deodorant.

Toilet or bath soap.   Dial soap was preferred by high-compliant people. Here again it was felt that high-compliant people would be the best targets for strong inner-personal-appeal advertising, since they have a greater concern for offending others. Dial, of course, has pursued this strategy for many years.

Razors.   Three quarters of the aggressive people prefer a manual razor rather than an electric razor as compared to 62 percent of the compliant and detached group. It was felt here again that the manual razor is seen as being more masculine by at least the aggressive males.

---

[7]J. B. Cohen, "An Interpersonal Orientation in the Study of Consumer Behavior," *Journal of Marketing Research,* Aug. 1967, pp. 270–78.

Although much of our emphasis in the next chapter will be on the development and promotion of new products, firms are many times faced with the problem of eliminating products from their offerings. Although this is rather a negative aspect of the marketing job, it nevertheless can be a crucial decision. For instance, in 1971 the Singer Sewing Machine Company, in recognition of the fact that the home sewing market has been growing at an astounding rate, eliminated the sale of home entertainment products in most of its Singer Sewing Centers. Home entertainment products were added to the 1,425 Singer stores during the early 1960s in order to capitalize on a trend that was developing in this field. However, in recent years the growth of home sewing has spurred the sales of fabrics and sewing machines to such an extent that the firm believes the potential is much greater.[8]

The elimination of products that have not been profitable poses several dangers, however. The first is that the elimination of a product could have an adverse effect on the other products in the line. This is likely to happen when the eliminated product is part of a total assortment package of the firm. For instance, if the Ford Motor Company decided to drop its most prestigious automobile, the Lincoln Continental, it could seriously affect the sale of the firm's lower-priced cars, since many of these autos gain prestige from the association with the Continental.

In addition, when the firm eliminates a product that is perhaps a low profit maker, the eliminated profit may have to be picked up by the other products in the line. This is not always possible.

The choice of which products should be eliminated is made in several ways. The most obvious is to eliminate products that show a poor sales trend. Thus a product that has consistently shown either a decline or even a stable sales trend would become a likely candidate for elimination. The same may be said for products when the profits or prices are declining. The latter occurrence would eliminate any possibility of recovery.

Finally, products that conflict with new substitutable products put out by the same firm would also seem to be candidates for elimination. That is, when a company introduces a soap product that for all practical purposes serves as a substitute for one of the older products in the line, the older product may be eliminated.[9]

On the other hand, a firm can still *save* a product that faces competition from either its own line of substitutions or a competitor's. A classic example of such a situation is cellophane, a product produced by E. I. du Pont. This product, during a rapid growth period in the 1950s faced severe competition from various types of plastic film that tended not to rupture in cold weather. Faced with this problem du Pont improved its product by adding a special coating that eliminated winter breakage. In addition, the firm developed lighter grades of this same product. The move helped du Pont maintain its share of the market.[10]

---

[8] *The New York Times,* July 19, 1971, pp. 35, 38.

[9] For a more detailed evaluation of the overall firm consideration in eliminating products, see Conrad Berenson, "Pricing the Product Line," *Business Horizon,* Summer 1963.

[10] D. K. Clifford, Jr., "Leverage in the Product Life Cycle," *Dun's Review,* May 1965, p. 64.

Packaging   One major attribute of a product is the package it comes in. This package and the design, color, and printed matter may represent one of the major selling elements of the total product. Firms spend billions of dollars in the production of packages to suit their products and effectively display them in the retail outlet. As a matter of fact, the package costs more than the ingredients in the product in many industries. This is particularly true in the sale of cosmetics and drug products. For products using Aerosol cans, more money is spent on the can than on the product. It is true, however, that many of these products could not be sold without these expensive packages.

The cost of packaging can be seen in Table 9-3. Here is listed the cost of packaging as a percentage of the selling price for several product categories.

It is interesting to note that similar categories may have similar costs. For instance, cosmetics and drugs incur costs approximating 35 percent of the selling price. Waxes and paints range in cost from 12.5 to 15.0 percent. Food and candy according to this same table average around 23 percent.

TABLE 9-3 **Average Percentage of Manufacturer's Selling Price Represented by Packaging in 19 General Product Fields**

Inks and adhesives	40.0
Cosmetics and toiletries	36.3
Drugs	35.2
Motor oil	35.0
Beer	30.0
Foods	24.1
Candy	21.2
Stationery	20.0
Wax polishes	15.0
Paints	12.5
Toys	9.1
Cigars	8.0
Baked goods	7.8
Meats	6.5
Liquor	5.2
Automotive parts	5.0
Cutlery	5.0
Hardware	4.0
Office machines	1.4

Source: V. L. Fladager, *The Selling Power of Packaging* (New York: McGraw-Hill, Inc., 1956), p. 118.

From this one can conclude that the demand and competition for some products are such that firms are forced to package products in a similar manner.

To properly understand the role of packaging, one must consider the functions that packaging performs; these are to:

1. protect the product,
2. promote the product,
3. develop a reuse value for the product,
4. increase the use of the product, and
5. meet ecological requirements for the product.

Protect the Product

The basic function of any package is to protect the product from damage and the consumer from danger when using the product. Thus many shampoo manufacturers package their products in plastic containers to avoid broken bottles in tiled bathrooms.

An example of a package that protects a delicate product is the egg carton, which is usually made of pulp. In recent years a new egg carton has started to appear in supermarkets, a carton that the buyer can see through in order to examine the eggs. This avoids the problem of consumers opening the carton to examine the eggs before buying, thereby avoiding damage to the eggs. One observer noted that in surveys they found that 80 percent of the shoppers open egg cartons before buying.[11]

Promote the Product

Even a faint acquaintance with products on retailer's shelves would seem to indicate that the product itself usually requires an additional cover or package in order to make the product appealing to the consumer. The product itself in many cases cannot be used for artful display material because of the material it is made of or the shape of its container.

A great deal of artwork and design go into making some products more attractive and appealing to the consumer. Aside from this aspect, the package must be designed in such a manner as to allow the retailer to display it properly. Here again the original container may not be properly shaped to allow the retailer to stack the product on his shelves. Thus the product many times needs an additional cover simply to make it easier for the retailer to display his product in large quantities. That is the reason why soda cans are flat on top, cereal boxes are square, and toothpaste tubes are packaged in square-shaped containers.

Develop a Reuse Value for the Product

A number of products have been designed to encourage their reuse on the part of the consumer. Jellies have been traditionally packaged in a jar that can be reused as a drinking glass. Kraft Parkay Margarine is sold in tight fitting plastic containers, and the consumer is encouraged to consider their reuse to pack leftovers or to start seedlings for gardening. Most products packaged in large jars are used over and over again by housewives for storing leftovers or homemade cooking.

---

[11] *Supermarket News*, July 12, 1971, p. 5.

Increase the Use of the Product

Packaging by its very nature can help increase the use of the product. For instance, the use of aerosol cans has increased the use of many products in a more convenient manner. The whole hair spray industry has developed through the introduction of these cans. Through colorful packaging the makers of facial tissues have brought their product from use in the bathroom or bedroom into other sections of the house.

The makers of cleanser have packaged their product in not only the usual-sized containers but in small packs so that the housewife can keep a can in the bathroom medicine cabinets, and other places where it can be close at hand.

Meet Ecological Requirements for the Product

In more recent years, as noted in an earlier section, all products are coming under closer scrutiny by consumers' groups. One major target has been the packaging industry on several counts. The first is that the package can only be destroyed by causing air pollution. The other is that cans that are strewn about do not oxidize, and thus destroy the beauty of the environment.

In recent months the King Cullen food stores in New York announced in an advertising campaign that they were switching from plastic meat trays in their supermarkets to trays made of paper pulp. They were doing this they noted because pulp will eventually disintegrate and become part of the earth. Also, even when burned they add comparatively little pollution to the atmosphere.

Plastic container manufacturers have not taken lightly to such criticism and have pointed out to the public that, although their products may not disintegrate as rapidly as pulp, pulp products tend to pollute the streams and rivers when being manufactured. They also note that polystyrene is actually a catalyst to thorough burning.[12]

Legal Restraints on Products

In the past several years, the government has taken greater interest in creating closer control over the packaging and labeling of products. The Fair Packaging and Labeling Act (1967) states that a manufacturer must be identified on each package and that the contents must be disclosed under certain conditions. In addition, this act helps the enforcement agencies to deal with certain abuses, particularly in the food field, where the term "cents off" on the package does not always reflect a price reduction to the buyer, or where cereal manufacturers may reduce the net weight of a package but, at the same time, increase the package size.

Other acts, such as the Wool Products Labeling Act (1939), the Fur Products Labeling Act (1951), and the Textile Fiber Products Act (1958) require that the manufacturer provide information that the consumer should have — such as, in the case of furs, the country of origin.

---

[12]*Ibid.*, p. 4.

The product that a firm produces is a result of the choices made by management. It reflects their thinking and views of the opportunities of success. A product is more than just made up of materials; it has psychological meaning to many consumers.

Management is faced with many considerations. Obsolescence is certainly one. The importance of brands and the role of private branding is another. The problem of eliminating products is certainly a challenging problem faced by most firms. The package that the product should have offers many challenges, particularly today.

Presented are several ways of classifying products. These include classifying by shopping behavior, psychologically, and by personality characteristics.

QUESTIONS

1. What is the significance of the statement that products are not composed of tangible and physical attributes only?

*__2.__ Discuss the possible psychological attributes of a cigarette.

3. A consumerist made the statement that practically all American manufacturers engage in planned obsolescence in order to assure a continuing demand for their products. Do you agree?

4. Distinguish between a style and a fashion.

*__5.__ In what way would technological obsolescence affect the marketing strategy of an automobile firm?

6. Should a manufacturer of a private-branded product decide to produce a nationally branded product, what major strategic steps would he have to make?

7. How would the strategy of a producer of a convenience good differ from that of a shopping good?

8. In Table 9-3 it is indicated that over one third of the selling price of cosmetics is accounted for by the cost of the package. Is this necessary? Why or why not?

9. Distinguish between status and prestige products. Is a membership in a yachting club a prestigious happening?

10. What would be the major consideration on the part of General Motors if they considered dropping the Buick Skylark from their product line?

11. Why do retailers prefer to sell private brands?

12. What is meant by family brands? Show how family branding can be an asset to a manufacturer.

13. Are General Motors cars an example of family branding?

*In-depth questions.

New Product
Planning and Strategy

10

SUMMARY KEY

The riskiest part of marketing is the development and distribution of new products. It is safe to say that most new products will fail. In defining what is considered to be a new product, one must distinguish between additions to a line of established products, improvements made in a present line of products, and distinctively new products. Each of these classifications may warrant a different marketing approach.

Firms are concerned with the introduction of new products simply because old products can become obsolete, in the sense that they usually pass through a product life cycle. The cycle, although the time varies by product, includes the following stages: introductory, growth, maturity, saturation, and decline. The length of the life cycle for a given product is related to the *permanence of the product.* In a sense the higher the technological level and skills required to produce the product and the patentability of the product, the longer the life cycle. Fads have short life cycles, whereas an outstanding book can have a short or long cycle depending on public acceptance.

Companies have three major sources of new products: inventions, product improvement, and acquisitions of new companies. The most profitable source can be new inventions; the most likely source is product improvements. It is becoming more and more difficult to develop new products through inventions, mainly because firms through their technological abilities can duplicate most new products.

The decision to add new products to the line depends very much on the firm's production and marketing facilities, competition, and consumer demand. Timing of new product introductions is crucial, based on the view that it is important in introducing a new product to be first.

In measuring new product costs one must include product research and development costs, marketing research and product testing costs, and test marketing costs. The workload involved in developing a new product and introducing it may cover a long period of time. In most cases research and development involve the longest period of time.

New product ideas come from marketing research studies, company staff, or channel members. In appraising the potential of a new product a firm engages in both informal discussions and perhaps formal testing procedures. In addition, a manufacturer must take great care that the retailer does not become antagonistic to the introduction of the new product. This will happen if the new product reduces the value of the present inventory held by the retailer or is sold at a lesser markup by the retailer.

As noted in the previous chapter a firm is constantly reviewing the positioning of its products in all markets. Where a product's share of the market may be dropping or a new competitor appears on the market, the firm may have to reevaluate its present strategy. This review is constantly taking place in the firm and is considered to be a vital part of the marketing management function.

The fact that the riskiest part of managing the firm's products is the development and marketing of new products is unquestioned. It is safe to say that most products that are marketed will fail. Although no reliable statistics are available, it is true that many of the most sophisticated companies have failure rates exceeding 80 percent! This ratio will vary by the type of industry and may have some relevance to the monopoly power a firm may hold. Nevertheless, new product decisions are the riskiest part of the marketing manager's job and require careful study and consideration before any move to market a new product is made.

New Products

In any given year thousands of new products appear on the market in the United States. Some, of course, are simply changes made in products that have been on the market. Others, on the other hand, are new products that have never appeared in outlets around the country. It has been estimated that about 80 percent of all products on the shelves of a supermarket were not on these same shelves 10 years before. In any discussion of products we must carefully distinguish, however, between those products that are actually new and those that represent adjustments in products already available. This will be discussed more fully later.

Yet many new products do appear almost every year. For example, *Fortune* magazine recently discussed some of the new products that made their initial appearance in the previous 12 months. Some of the more interesting ones are[1]

1. Sta-Dri Matches marketed by the Diamond International Company. This product was intended to appeal to the outdoorsman who would have a need for dry matches in inclement weather or under conditions where regular matches might be exposed to dampness.

2. Polyvinyl chloride bottles, which represent the first entirely transparent nonglass containers. These bottles have the distinct advantage of being light, chip proof, and shatter proof. Presently, most of their applications are in the food packaging industry.

3. Biz, Tide XK, Gain, Drive, and Axion represent some of the products that have appeared in the detergent field during this period. They are distinctive in that they contain enzymes and are intended to remove stains that could not be removed by previous detergents. This group of products usually requires a presoak wash cycle. The chemical process was known in Europe for many years.

---

[1] May 15, 1969, p.154.

4. Gatorade was marketed during this period by Stokley-Van Camp. This thirst-quenching drink was heralded as a replacement for salt tablets, a locker-room staple. After an initial heavy advertising program, this lemon-lime flavored drink appeared in most supermarkets around the country.

5. The Kesco Lock was marketed as an important development in the door lock business. The Kesco Lock is unlike its conventional counterpart in that it contains milled holes as a replacement for the notches found in the conventional key. As a result, the company pointed out that the lock is much more difficult to pick.

6. The Allis Chalmers' Terra Tiger travels on both land and water. On land it can reach speeds of 25 miles per hour and 4 miles per hour on water. This 6,000-pound vehicle has one major advantage over previous competitors – it sells for around $1,500.

7. Color Copying Machine is a recent development by the Minnesota Mining and Manufacturing Company. Most copying machines up to the present can only make copies in black and white. This recent development allows the user to copy colors.

8. Litton Industries has purchased an airborne telephone. This allows a party to actually telephone a party directly while they are airborne, much as you would dial a neighbor.

These products represent only a small fraction of the new products that appeared during this 12-month period.

New Product Failures

In spite of the appearance of many new products in the past several years, very few of these products will be around a few years after they are introduced. Most businessmen know that few new products are ever successful. One might also add that even those that survive will not attain the profit goals that management has set for them.

On the other hand, few companies can accurately determine how successful a product will be. That is, firms that have developed new products are many times astounded at the success that they may achieve, far in excess of the original plans.

Many of these new products are critical to the development, and in some cases the very existence, of some firms. Some firms can sustain severe financial reversals that can actually threaten the continuation of the firm.

An example in recent years, of the heavy loss that can occur in developing a new product can be seen in General Dynamics, a major U.S. producer of jet crafts, who lost approximately $425 million in attempting to build the Convair 880 and 990 to compete against the Boeing 707 and Douglas DC-8. General Dynamics was never able to obtain appreciable orders for this plane from any of the major airlines.[2]

Ford's attempt to produce and market an automobile to compete in particular against Buick, Pontiac, and Oldsmobile (all General Motors products) ended in the short-lived production of another fiasco – the 1958 Edsel. Losses on this car were reported to have exceeded $250 million. This car went into production in 1958, and in 1960 production ended. The planning and research involved in producing the car took over 4 years. It was a severe blow to the company, which had hoped to catch its number one competitor in the late 1950s or early 1960s.

---

[2]*The New York Times*, Feb. 20, 1970, p. 81.

In a similar vein, the Campbell Soup Company experienced a fiasco in the 1960s with the introduction of its Red Kettle line of dehydrated soups. For many years this company had been the dominant producer of canned (or wet) soups. Industry estimates are that Campbell holds 90 percent of the canned soup market. Previous to introducing the Red Kettle line, Campbell became aware of the fact that dehydrated packaged soups were growing in popularity and that Thomas J. Lipton, Inc., had managed to capture a respectable share of this market. After several years of study, Campbell introduced its Red Kettle line and ended up absorbing an $8 million loss, with the eventual abandonment of the line.

One can see from these examples that losses from new products can be substantial. In addition, several general comments can be drawn from the experience of these companies:

1. The present position and stake of the company may not necessarily influence the success or failure of a new product (Campbell Soup).

2. Unlimited financial resources of the manufacturer do not guarantee the success of the product (Ford).

3. In some industries the market is so technically oriented that your new product is either accepted or your firm completely loses out; that is, there is no middle ground (General Dynamics).

What is a New Product?

What is a new product is a question that requires an answer. If Heinz adds a large-sized bottle to its line of ketchup, is this considered to be a new product? If Heinz adds spices to their ketchup should we consider this to be a new product?

The reason one raises the issue of definition is not simply an academic exercise, for the development of a new product (such as Heinz's cereals) puts a strain on the marketing forces within the company. These forces must develop a marketing plan and accompanying budgets, a distinctive campaign of action, hire the necessary personnel, establish product identification, and project earnings for the immediate and the future for the new product.

On the other hand, simple changes in established company products put much less of a strain on the marketing organization. In some cases the actual addition of a similar product to a family of products may require little more than developing an introductory advertising campaign, since the channels and marketing promotional arrangements have been established through years of work.

Hence one must distinguish between a new product *addition to a line of established products,* improvements made in *present products,* and *distinctively new products.*

Additions to the Present Line

By additions to a present line of products a firm hopes to increase the total sales of this line. In some instances the firm may find that they are forced to add a product to their line in spite of their estimates that the product may prove to be unprofitable. For example, once Ford introduced the Maverick or Pinto automobile, most major auto concerns were forced to consider producing similar cars, in spite of the fact that the new cars may actually reduce sales of the regular line of products. This represents one of the major problems that manufacturers must deal with, for to add a line that simply subtracts sales from your other products ends up in reducing the overall profits of the firm.

One might quarrel with the view that either the Maverick or Pinto automobile produced by Ford was simply an addition to the line of products sold by Ford, since they represent the smallest autos produced by this company since World War II. However, since the car was a smaller version of a product that Ford has been producing for years, it would seem to fall into the category of an *addition to the line.*

At this point one might ask, how does a company determine whether or not an addition to the product line will result in new customers to the company or result in switching of customers from one product to another? In making this decision the company executives will be guided by both the present competitive situation and perhaps research reports or business views of the people who work on the staff.

Competitive conditions may be such that it is their view that this product will reach a segment of the market that has not been reached previously. In the case of Maverick and Pinto, it was the view of Ford that the foreign-car market was expanding because the American consumer did not have an opportunity to buy a small American-made car. Thus many consumers were turning to the Japanese entrants (Datsun and others) and the highly successful Volkswagen from Germany. These cars particularly appealed to the higher-income suburbanite who needed a second car because the suburbs do not have public transportation systems comparable to the metropolitan areas. Thus it may be Ford's judgment that most of the gains in this market will be made at the expense of the foreign-car markets.

This decision can be supplemented and reinforced by information from the market research department supplied perhaps by consumer surveys posing such a question to suburbanites. In addition, the executive charged with making such a decision would consult, in the normal course of making such a decision, with other executives within the firm and others outside of the company at the distributor level. Nevertheless, many of these decisions are risky and have resulted in failure.

Improvements Made in Present Products

The easiest way a firm can choose to produce a new product is to make improvements in the present product line. An example of this may occur when a soap manufacturer adds an ingredient to his present soap product. For instance, in the 1960s many soap companies added whiteners to their products, thus relieving the housewife of the problem of buying a whitener and pouring it into the washing machine separately. Other firms added a presoak enzyme that helped clothes get cleaner.

Automobile manufacturers are well known for their model changes year after year. Some of the changes include dramatic redesigns of their present line of cars. This event usually occurs every 3 or 4 years because the costs incurred in such changes are high. The usual annual changes include superficial additions of chrome, some minor mechanical change, such as putting the radio antenna in the windshield glass, redesigning the front grill work, and so on. All in all, improvements made in the present product are the most widely used device for introducing new products.

Distinctively New Products

Distinctively new products refer to products that are not additions to the line, but products that put the firm into competition with other types of products. However, this aspect of new product development is not as clearly defined as the two previous areas. For example, if Procter & Gamble adds a new soap product to their line or an ingredient to their soap, these changes merely fall into the two occurrences just discussed. However, should Procter & Gamble add a new product, such as Brillo, to their line, the question arises as to whether or not this is a distinctively new product.

Analyzing this happening, one is sure to notice that this product has never been offered before by Procter & Gamble and thus meets our criterion of being distinctively new. In addition, it is produced in a separate manufacturing facility and again it requires special attention, and in this way is distinctively new. Conversely, the product does complement the many household cleaning items sold by Procter & Gamble and additionally is sold through the same outlets and by the same sales force as those who sell the soap and other household cleaners. So, from that point of view, it is not new in terms of the marketing effort.

The point is that many products that seem to be distinctive are sometimes very closely allied with the present line of products and thus are not as distinctive in their relationship to the other products as may seem on the surface.

On the other hand, one can cite many instances where companies do produce products that are distinct additions to the firm's product line. For example, a company such as Outboard Marine has produced a line of outboard motors for boats (Johnson and Evinrude) for many years. In more recent years they have designed and sold successfully a line of snowmobiles. These products posed different marketing problems and in many instances required different distributors and retail outlets. They were also sold mainly in cold-weather areas of the country in direct contrast to sales of outboard motors. Their selling periods also peak at much different months of the year at both the manufacturing and retailing levels. In this case, one would agree that this product is a distinctively new product as far as Outboard Marine is concerned.

Importance of New Products

Why are companies continually interested in new products? One obvious answer can be observed in Figure 10-1, where one can see the contribution new products have come from new products. In all cases one can observe, as indicated by the the sales increases in textiles, electrical machinery, chemicals, and all transportation have come from new products. In all cases one can observe, as indicated by the shaded area, that new products substantially feed the sales progress of many of our major industries.

A second reason that underlines the importance of new products should also be considered. In Figure 10-2 one can see an important concept outlined – the impact

FIGURE 10-1   Contribution of New Products to Expected Sales Growth, 1963–1967

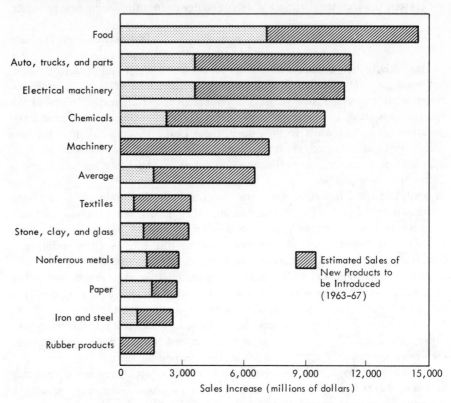

Source: *Management of New Products* (New York: Booz, Allen and Hamilton, Inc.), p. 5.

FIGURE 10-2   Basic Life Cycle of Products

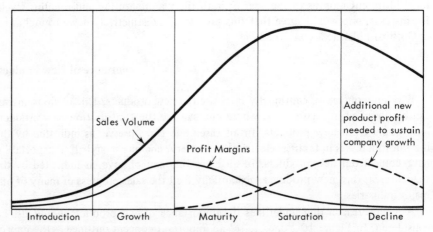

Source: *Management of New Products* (New York: Booz, Allen and Hamilton, Inc.), p. 4

the five stages in the life cycle of a product have on the profits and sales of a firm. Although most products manage to sustain themselves for varying lengths of time, an analysis of each product will probably indicate the following five stages of development:

1. *Introductory stage.* During this stage, because of heavy research and development costs, the profits are usually nonexistent or minimal. Sales volume is usually inadequate to recover such costs.

2. *Growth stage.* Products slowly develop consumer acceptance. As a result, sales start to ascend and profits start to increase at a faster proportional rate than sales.

3. *Maturity stage.* At this stage one usually finds competition enters the market; however, profits of the firm usually peak at the beginning of this stage. One also finds that profits and sales start to stabilize due to competition and the approach of the fourth stage.

4. *Saturation stage.* At this point the company has reached the place where market expansion has stopped due to the concurrent (1) emergence of competition and (2) the fact that all consumers who planned to buy the product have done so. In many cases only a replacement market now exists. During this stage profits decline sharply, although sales may remain fairly stable throughout this period.

5. *Decline stage.* At this point sales start to decline and profits practically disappear due to many factors. One may be the entrance of a new product and a simultaneous change in consumer preference for your product. The second may simply be a technological innovation that undercuts the costs (and eventual prices charged) on the present product. The third may simply be the effect of the saturation stage, which relegates the product to a much smaller replacement market. At this point management may actually decide to discontinue the product.

As one can observe, it is at the fourth and fifth stages that management must be in a position to launch new products to maintain its profits at present levels and thus sustain the growth of the firm.

Length of the Product Cycle

Not all products go through the life cycle over similar time periods. Chemical and drug products usually experience long and gradual changes in their life cycle. Typically, a chemical or drug product could last 10 years. In contrast, a toy manufacturer or apparel firm could experience in 1 year or less a total cycle for a newly introduced product. The reason for the difference in the life cycle is due to many interrelated factors. These factors are sometimes called the *permanence of the product.* This concept refers to the technological work, skills, and patentability of the product. Thus, if a drug product, for instance, required a high level of technological know-how to produce and perhaps was patentable, the life cycle, by definition, would last longer, since competitors would be excluded from introducing the product for a long period of time. Even when the original manufacturer allows competing manufacturers to market the product under a royalty arrangement, the profit flow from these royalties usually guarantees a long life cycle for the original manufacturer. Thus products that require large investments of capital and technology will usually experience a rather long life cycle.

The second concept affecting the length of the life cycle is called the *permanence of the consumer.* Many products, although they do not involve the technological processes just described, still manage to maintain a strong consumer following, which has the same impact. A line of products such as Campbell soups would be an example of a product that is widely accepted by the intended market.

Conversely, many products simply catch the fancy of the consumer for a short period of time and then settle into a rapid decline in favor. Other forms of the same short cycle are *fads*. Fads usually occur among teenagers or children. The hoola hoop craze of several years ago was characterized as a fad. Fads seem to develop mainly in the clothing field and among the young. Several of recent vintage are the shiny, wet vinyl look, hot pants, smile buttons, flower power look, and the rich hippy look, the latter so characterized by *Women's Wear Daily*. As seen in Figure 10-3, the fad is characterized by a rapid growth and an abrupt decline over a short period of time.

FIGURE 10-3   Usual Trajectory of a Fad

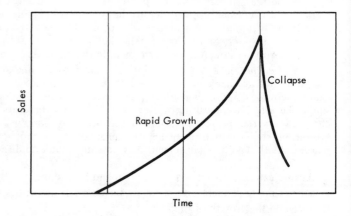

Source: C. R. Wasson, "How Predictable Are Fashion and Other Product Life Cycles?" *Journal of Marketing,* July 1968, p. 38.

Records and books also fall into the same grouping. On the other hand, some books and records sell year after year, although it was originally thought that they would last less than 1 year. One outstanding book that indicates the error that can be made in estimation was the best-selling paperback *Catch 22.* Offered to several publishers, it finally was recommended for publication by an assistant editor at Simon and Schuster. In recent years it has sold over 5 million copies, and estimates are that it should maintain a selling pace of several hundred thousand per year for many years to come.

New
Products
Strategy

For an individual company there are three major *sources* of new products. They are inventions, product improvement, and the acquisition of new companies.

The most profitable source of new products is through invention. This road is particularly powerful if the invention is substantially different from other products. An example of this type of product would be the Polaroid Land Camera. This product with its 1-minute (and less) developing time for a picture was a revolutionary development that resulted in the rapid growth and success of a single company. This product departed completely from all previously produced photographic equipment.

The success of a new invention such as the Polaroid camera is due to the fact that it met a consumer need. The firm holding the invention faced little competition and for many years received, in effect, monopoly profits. Some indication of the impact of an invention on company sales and profits can be gleaned from the fact that Polaroid's sales in 1950 were $6.4 million dollars; they increased to $369 million dollars in 1967. Profits increased from $794,000 (1950) to $109 million dollars in 1967.[3]

In the food industry one can cite numerous examples of products that represent inventions or new developments. For instance, Kleenex was the only major brand in its field from 1924 to about 1955.[4] Coca-Cola was first produced in 1886 and was virtually unopposed until 1935.[5]

Other inventions may affect only the package or some ingredient in a product. One firm may have a patent on a cap for a tube of toothpaste. This difference, although not substantial, can appeal to a sizable fraction of the consumers.

Thus inventions in many cases can become an important source of profits. However, as will be noted later, the impact of inventions on marketing is in a state of decline.

Product Improvement

The most likely sources of new products are changes and improvements that can be made in the firm's product line. This may include package changes, or changes such as the addition of a dry gas as an ingredient to a major brand of gasoline. Detergents with bleaches or enzymes added are another type of product ingredient change than can increase the sales volume of the present line of products.

In terms of package design, one can see an endless array of changes. The cigarette companies producing the hard package in preference to the soft pack, the soda producers introducing the pull-tab aluminum container, and the endless package changes found in women's cosmetics are just a few examples of the most widely appealing means of developing and introducing new product improvements.

Acquisitions

Many companies look at acquisitions as a means of expanding their product offerings. In recent years this road has been followed so widely that it has become a center of controversy among those entrusted with antitrust enforcement. Coca-Cola, for instance, in 1960 acquired the Minute Maid Corporation, one of the largest processors of frozen orange juice. In 1964 Coca-Cola added Duncan Foods Company, a major producer and processor of coffee and tea. Procter & Gamble, a major soap company, acquired Spic and Span in 1945, W. T. Young Foods (manufacturer of peanuts and peanut butter), Clorox Chemical

[3]*Moody's Industrial Manual,* July 1968, p. 1415.

[4]M. J. O'Conner, *Basic Patterns of New Product Strategy,* in T. L. Berg and A. Shuchman, ed., *Product Strategy and Management* (New York: Holt, Rinehart and Winston, Inc., 1963), p. 110.

[5]*Ibid.*

Company (later forced to divest itself of this firm), and J. A. Folger and The Colgate-Palmolive Company, a major competitor of Procter & Gamble has followed a similar path by acquiring the Wildroot Company, manufacturers of hair tonic, the Sterno Company in 1959, producers of canned heat and food service equipment, Reefer-Galler, a major producer of moth control products, and several other firms. Gillette over the years has acquired the Papermate Pen Company and Toni, one of the original developers of the home permanent kit.

In all these cases it was the intention of the firm to expand its line of products. In many cases, entrance into these fields opened up new opportunities for the firm.

Strategy Determination

The decision on where to concentrate the firm's resources among these three broad choices as a source for new products is of course a serious one. The decision is made on the basis of several conditions. One must remember that the three options open to management, *inventions, product improvements,* and *acquisitions,* vary in their impact. Inventions are becoming a limited source of new products in the marketing field for the simple reason that firms are finding it more and more difficult to

1. *Protect products completely from competition.* This is brought about by our technology, which is so vast that many competing firms can produce the same product without infringing on a firm's patents. For example, the Xerox Company owns worldwide Xerography patents for many years. Xerography is an electrostatic dry process of graphic reproduction. In spite of these patents, the firm has encountered severe competition in recent years from several large companies, each of which has designed and developed copy machines that do not infringe on the Xerox patents. One machine, for instance, produced by Minnesota Mining and Manufacturing Company, was actually recommended for use for federal government offices by a government agency that tests the efficiency of each of these machines on the market. Thus firms are finding that many of their product advantages attributable to patents are not long lasting.

2. *Maintain patents exclusively.* Many firms have found that the federal government has applied pressures to force the sharing of patent rights with competitors. Although the reluctant firm may obtain royalties, it nevertheless voids the opportunity to market a product exclusively for many years.

As noted previously, acquisitions and mergers represent one of the burgeoning areas of development for the typical firm in today's market. Rarely a year goes by when the large American corporation does not succeed in acquiring a smaller firm in order to add an additional product to its line. Yet changes and additions to the products presently produced by a company are the most logical and widely used means of increasing the firm's offerings to the public. Whether a firm decides to simply add to its present product line or make a change in its present products depends very much on three major factors: the firm's *production* and *marketing facilities, competition,* and *consumer demand.*

The first consideration is the production and marketing facilities of the firm.[6] Firms, of course, are concerned with the costs of any product. In particular, they are concerned with any additional costs that would be incurred in the producing and marketing of a new product. Thus, when a firm adds a new product, it can be expected that the firm will either increase their production or marketing costs, or both. Naturally, the firm expects that any additional revenue they receive from selling the product will more than cover the additional costs incurred. One major determinant in making a choice of adding a new product is an opportunity for management to keep production or marketing costs at a minimum.

The opportunity to do this is directly related to the type of product and marketing facilities already available in the firm. Consider, for example, a manufacturer of phonograph records that maintains a distribution system consisting of 150 major wholesalers throughout the country. To service these outlets, the firm maintains several salesmen. Also, the firm maintains a large production facility in a large city (see Figure 10-4a). What would be the additional costs of producing a new record for its present market?

The marketing costs of the company would be minimal, since the same wholesalers would stock the record and the firm's salesmen would still call on the same wholesalers, whether they carried 99 to 100 of the company's records. Hence the marketing costs would remain practically the same. The production costs of the same firm would not be taxed either, since the company has enough production facilities to produce at least 99 records. It can be assumed, therefore, that production costs would only be increased by the actual material costs, perhaps some additional labor costs, and, of course, the shipping costs. In summary, when the firm already has a marketing force calling on the same industry wholesalers (or retailers) and enough production capacity to easily handle increases in volume, both the additional marketing and production costs would be minimal. In this situation it becomes logical for management to add to these product lines on a regular basis.

Figure 10-4b demonstrates another company situation that requires similar strategy, but for different reasons. In this figure one sees an aluminum fabricator with a costly and complicated production facility. This facility may require an initial cost of over $20 million. With such a high initial investment plus a high maintenance cost, the overall consideration on the part of management in terms of marketing is to keep the production facility operating as many hours as possible. This represents the overwhelming driving force of this type of company. In this case the firm is now willing to establish an additional sales force and channel its business through a number of marketing channels, feeling the increase in marketing costs will be substantially less than the gain that will accrue from using the full facilities of the production plant.

All possible new products that can be channeled through this costly production facility are given serious consideration. Management in this firm is constantly searching for new products that fit this facility. In a sense, this organization stresses

[6]For a more extensive treatment of this topic, see T. A. Staudt and D. A. Taylor, *A Managerial Introduction to Marketing,* 2nd ed. (Englewood Cliffs, N.J.: Prentice-Hall, Inc., 1970), Chap. 11.

a production-oriented approach, since management is concerned with the needs of the production facility, rather than the consumer need, as its overriding motivation.

Figure 10-4c indicates a company situation that is the opposite of the preceding situation. In this company the marketing force is the most powerful element in the firm's effort. This force gives rather broad coverage to an industry throughout the total U.S. market. In this instance, additional products will add little incremental costs to the firm's marketing costs, since the marketing channels are intensively covered. Most importantly, the new product is practically guaranteed some success

FIGURE 10-4   Production and Marketing Facilities Related to New Product Strategy

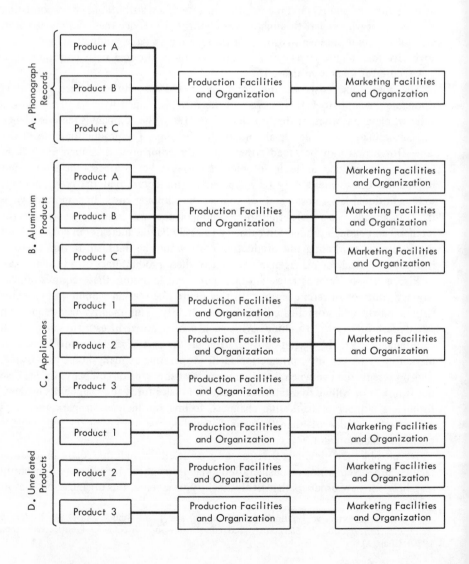

since the product will be presented to practically all possible buyers because of the strength of the marketing force.

In this situation, management's view is that the marketing force is so powerful that it is likely to overcome all production costs involved in producing additional new products for the company, even if the additional products require building more plant capacity. However, the new products must fit into the marketing organization's product mix. An example of this type of situation would be an appliance manufacturer with a strong marketing force. This firm may produce, in separate facilities, dishwashers, dryers, washing machines, and even small appliances in order to develop a line of products that will widen the firm's presentation to the buyer and increase the possibility of a sale.

The final form of new product strategy related to marketing and production facilities is shown in Figure 10-4d. This represents one of the most important phenomena of the 1960s — the corporate conglomerate. The corporate conglomerate usually is a large firm that as a policy acquires smaller firms in a variety of different businesses. This development is brought about by several factors. The first is the policy of the government to halt mergers among firms expanding in a similar field. The government, for example, has stopped large shoe manufacturers such as Genesco from purchasing other shoe firms. The government view has been supported by several court decisions which suggest that continued merging by firms in the same industry tends to lessen competiton. As a result of this policy, many firms have been forced to consider industries other than their own for expansion purposes. Since the government frowns on acquisitions in similar fields, the result is that the acquisitions made by the large company usually involve purchasing production and marketing facilities that remain separate and cannot be integrated with the firm's present line of products.

A typical example of a conglomerate is the W. R. Grace Company. Originally, W. R. Grace managed a steamship company. However, in recent years it has diversified into many fields and is considered one of the largest conglomerates in the world. Its products include chemicals, apparel, designing and architectural firms, and even hamburger stands in France. Within a firm such as this, each company operates in its own separate field. The opportunity to merge marketing forces with production facilities is usually slim. The question may be asked, if there are no savings in conglomerate acquisitions, why do firms follow such a route?

The answer is many-sided. One must first be aware of the fact that many of the conglomerates found that their original business became unprofitable. Thus Grace found this to be true of steamship lines. Textron, as another example, had the same experience in the textile field. Both firms were forced to look elsewhere.

Second, many firms have concluded that they bring to a merger the huge financial resources and top management talent that can take a relatively profitable firm and make it into a much better profit maker. The huge financial resources of the conglomerate serve also as a leveling device in some industries. For example, W. R. Grace purchased the John Meyer Company, an apparel producer, in an industry well known for its fluctuations. The fact that Grace stands behind this apparel firm gives its management less fear of making a wrong decision and of its ultimate consequences than if it were a single firm.

Competition

Many new products that appear on the market are produced in direct response to competition. In fact, some companies may be forced to introduce a product that they feel can never be profitable but, yet, must protect them against competition. A most recent example discussed earlier may be the decision by Ford to introduce a small car in direct competition with many of the less expensive imports.

In less dramatic fashion, many of the soap producers found that competitive products forced them to market new products. For instance, the introduction of the enzyme presoak Axion forced other competitors to market similar products. The introduction of the first fluoride toothpaste, Crest (Procter & Gamble), forced Colgate-Palmolive to rush out a similar toothpaste on the market.

Thus, although many products introduced in the market are carefully nurtured by the firm, in many cases competitive moves force many manufacturers to react in rapid order without the careful and considerate processes usually associated with new product introduction.

Consumer Demand

All decisions to introduce new products must ultimately reside in the belief that a market exists. Although marketing and production facilities and competition may force a company into such a move, the ultimate and overriding decision must be backed up by a belief that there is sufficient demand for the product among consumers. Along with overall consumer demand is the growing interest among firms in marketing segmentation (see Chapter 6), which has had an important impact on the increase of new products. For instance, the tendency of major oil companies to add winter additives to their gasoline in many northern sections of the United States is an example of catering to a segment of the market with a new product. The introduction of caffein-free freeze-dried coffee by Sanka is a similar example. Here General Foods has taken a product aimed at those who prefer caffein-free coffee and produced it in a form that would help them compete against the new freeze-dried competitive brands. In this case, General Foods was faced with two major pressures — one, the need to meet competition, and the other, the need to meet the needs of a segment of the coffee market.

Timing New Products

Marketing people are well aware that one of the key factors in the success of a new product is its timing. Mistakes in proper timing refer both to being too early as well as too late in introducing a new product.

An example of being too early was Chrysler's introduction of a compact car in 1953. It was the company's view that the American consumer was tired of large automobiles that were heavy gas consumers. The firm's view was proved wrong and, as a result of this action, its share of the automobile market declined from about 18 to 12 percent the following year. It is interesting to note that within 5 years the consumer reaction to a "compact" changed considerably, and the 1960s saw a gradual shift in interest on the part of a large segment of the consuming public to small cars, climaxed by the Ford introduction in 1969 of the Maverick.

Similarly, Columbia Broadcasting System's entrance into the television market with a line of black and white sets seems to be an example of being too late. The entrance of this firm, backed by the resources of the broadcasting unit, was doomed from the start, because one of the major problems of being late is that the new entrant must compete against already established firms that have dealt with and solved both their production and marketing problems.

There are numerous instances of firms being in the enviable position of being first with a product that has consumer acceptance simply because the timing was right.

The introduction of the stainless steel blade in the American market by Wilkinson, and later Schick, represents timing that resulted in substantial gains for two companies that held extremely small shares of the blade market before its introduction. The stainless blade had been around for several years, but in the opinion of the leader, Gillette, it had limited value because of the problem of maintaining quality for mass-production runs. It was evidently the view of Gillette's two competitors that the quality of the blade had reached the stage where the consumer would accept it. As a result, the shares of the market of both companies increased considerably in the 1960s.

The Importance of Being First

Proper timing in the introduction of new products is of crucial importance. Some of the reasons for being first are obvious — others less so.

The paramount reason for perfection in timing is the opportunity it presents to catch competitors by surprise. For example, Ford's introduction of the small Pinto automobile had given the firm at least a 1-year lead over major competitors in this market. With this lead time Ford had an opportunity to solve the many problems associated with the introduction of any technical product. It also allowed them a period of time in which they could monitor consumer reaction.

All the firms that will follow Ford's introduction of the Pinto will find that entering a market with an already established product places a special burden on the new entrant. Competitors under these conditions will have to solve many of both the technical and marketing problems that Ford has already experienced and solved.

In terms of the consumer, proper timing and being first have an additional benefit. It is the view of many marketing people that being first practically guarantees a large portion of the market to a company. There seems to be almost something magical in the consumer acceptance of those who produce and market a product first. Number one is usually hard to dislodge.

Other benefits can accrue to those who are first. If the market is sufficiently different, the first entrant can obtain higher-than-average profits. For instance, the introduction of the first ball-point pen in about 1948 resulted in sales to consumers at about $12 a pen. Today this same pen, vastly improved, can be purchased for as little as 10 cents.

The costs of introducing new products can be considerable. Usually, development of new products in large companies involves the following considerations.

New Product Costs

Product Research and Development Costs

At the initial stage the company is involved in spending monies for the basic research and development of a new product. This may include basic laboratory experimental work. Such procedures are common in the manufacturing of drugs.

Research in the business firm can be divided into two major categories, *direct* and *indirect*. Direct is the basic research indulged in by a firm with a deliberate goal in mind. Direct research is usually carried out in a firm by a group of technicians. It is somewhat on the order of the Manhattanville project during World War II, where theory had convinced scientists that it was possible to produce an atom bomb. Then government organized a group of prominent scientists and directed them to produce the first bomb. Much of the technological work on the first stages of our space program could be classified as direct research.

Many commercial firms develop new products in a similar way. However, they first determine that a need exists for the product before starting a direct research program. For example, a drug manufacturer may determine that there is a need for a serum to combat one strain of measles. His research and development department may inform him that the theoretical aspects of producing such a serum have been conquered and large investments in testing and developmental work should produce such a serum in the next 10 months. After approval, a group within the department may devote all its knowledge and time to producing such a product.

In contrast to a direct research effort, many firms conduct basic research with the hope of finding a process or product that can eventually be marketed. Here, again, the drug companies are examples, in that many on their staff conduct basic research without a clear consumer product in mind. This is usually referred to as indirect research. Food processing, electronics, space, and drug companies are among the many companies that support basic research, with the hope in mind that a project may culminate in a profitable commercial product.

Many research projects start out as basic research and are then transferred to direct research. The proportion of the huge Federal budget devoted to military and space exploration research has spurred the transfer of basic research projects for the military to the development of commercial products by manufacturers. Space food, solar batteries, and products using special metals are examples of such recent developments. Some of the firms doing basic research for the government develop abilities and techniques that can be used commercially. For instance, Magnavox Company, through working on several highly technical projects, was able to incorporate this ability into some of its new products — the completely transistorized electronic organ being one of these.

Marketing Research and Product Testing Costs

After a company seizes upon a product idea from research and development work, the product is usually tested through carefully controlled research studies. It is the purpose at this stage to determine the potential demand among consumers for these products.

At this point the firm may use systematic and formalized techniques for estimating the potential for the product under study. Formalized techniques may include actually producing the product and asking the consumer to try the product. This is a common first step in certain industries. For example, a firm planning the introduction of a new shaving cream may ask the consumer to use the product for several weeks and then return and subject the user to certain questions, with the intent of determining attitudes toward the product and perhaps making changes in the product.

The problem with this approach is that many firms find the costs of producing a sample product prohibitive. For instance, a major car company would have to invest millions in making even one sample car. The costs of producing a passenger airplane for testing could exceed tens of millions of dollars. In these cases companies may resort to consumer interviewing about a product that is in the planning stages. For instance, some auto companies ask for consumers' styling, color, and interior preferences in order to determine the design of a new model car.

Actual costs at the two stages of development (research and development and testing) can be considerable. Table 10-1 indicates that 111 new products in the food-processing industry incurred an average of $68,000 in research and development costs. Testing and research involved an additional expenditure of $26,000. However, the averages are deceiving in that costs for research and development on breakfast cereals averaged $122,000, while market research costs averaged $60,000.

Average Expenditures per Product for Research and Development and for Marketing Research, by Product Category TABLE 10-1

Product Category	Product Research and Development	Marketing Research[a]	No. of Products[b]	No. of Companies
Breakfast cereals — cold	$122,000	$60,000	21	6
Cake mixes	27,000	13,000	3	3
Frozen dinners and specialties	15,000	8,000	9	5
Margarine	65,000	17,000	10	4
Pet foods	91,000	37,000	13	7
All product categories (including those above)	$ 68,000	$26,000	111	19
Seven pioneering products	127,000	76,000	7	6

[a]Includes only expenses specifically charged to the individual products covered.
[b]Of the 127 distinctly new products analyzed in this report, there were 16 for which manufacturers were unable to provide data on preintroduction expenditures for product research and development or marketing research. Thus, this table reports results for a total of 111 distinctly new products only.

Source: R. D. Buzzell and R. E. M. Nourse, *Product Innovation in Food Processing* (Boston: Division of Research, Harvard University, 1967), p. 111.

Test Marketing Costs

After the product is approved for marketing, the company incurs what is identified as *product testing costs*. These costs are incurred when the firm is in a position to market the product in a limited area. Most manufacturers, where possible, attempt to gradually introduce a product rather than incur the expense and problem associated with a full-scale national marketing program. In addition, should the product fail, the risks to the company are less. Thus the manufacturer of the burgundy-flavored Tipalet cigar test marketed the product in the Boston area. This cigar was aimed at the youth market, which was estimated to be substantial in view of the "cancer scare" associated with cigarettes. It was the firm's view that Boston was the ideal area, since it contained a substantial number of colleges. It also afforded the company the opportunity to experiment with various youth-enticing promotions such as rock and roll concerts, giveaways, and tie-in record promotions.

Test marketing also involves sending the product back for further adjustments. Many adjustments are based on information derived from consumer surveys in the area where the product is being marketed.

Measuring the *actual costs* of *product testing* involves a calculation that should include (1) the gross profit from sales in the test market, (2) minus all direct costs involved in marketing the product.

Product Time Span

The work load involved in product testing may sometimes cover a considerable span of time. Although no averages are available, it seems reasonable to expect that from the first stages of research and development to the limited distribution stage usually involves from 2 to 3 years. Of the total time period, research and development is usually the most time-consuming part of new product development.

Aside from the cost problems, the length of time involved in distributing a new product depends on whether it is necessary to channel the product through all the outlined stages. How this can vary can be seen in Figure 10-5, where two products, pet foods and frozen dinners, are contrasted. In the former, one can observe that most pet food products go through all the stages of development. Thus all 13 began in the research and development stage. Of the 13, 10 actually went into product testing; of the remaining three, one went directly into distribution and two directly into test marketing. Of the 10 products in product testing, nine went into the test marketing stage. After completion of this stage, 12 of the 13 products were introduced on a regular basis.

In contrast, only seven of 10 frozen foods went though the research and development stage. The remaining three were entered into the product testing stage and test marketing, and one was actually introduced on a regular basis without any prior research activity.

One might ask under what conditions a firm would market a product without subjecting it to each of the formal stages in product development. In the case of frozen foods, one must conclude that the new product is probably quite similar to previous products, and the risk of failure is rather limited. Conversely, pet foods probably involve more technological and packaging complexity, and thus the stages of development and procedures are followed more carefully. One would also expect that the time period for development would be longer and the costs would be considerably higher in a firm selling pet foods than in one selling frozen foods.

Stages of Product Development **FIGURE 10-5**

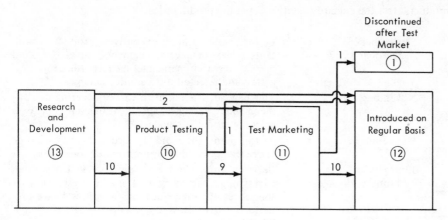

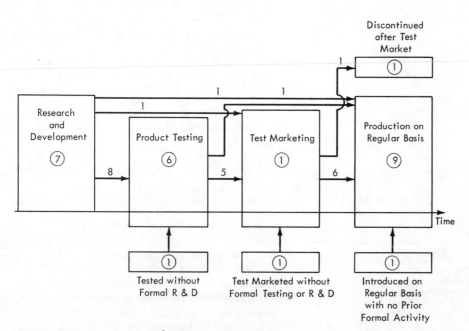

Source: R. D. Buzzell and R. E. M. Nourse, *Product Innovation in Food Processing* (Boston: Division of Research, Harvard University, 1967), pp. 104, 105.

From the discussion, one should not conclude that all products pass through these stages. As a matter of fact, most new product ideas never reach the formal stages of development. Although difficult to measure precisely, it would seem that no more than one in ten new product ideas ever reach the distribution stage. Most new product ideas are rejected before they ever reach the formal stages. Others, of course, may be rejected after the research and development or product testing stages.

However, one should not conclude that the time period in developing a product can be easily shortened. The following is an example of the time schedule for a new product, after the executive staff accepts the product idea.[7]

September– October 1962	Brainstorming among executives, product consultants, sales managers, engineers, advertising and market research personnel begins. Ideas are suggested and rejected until an idea emerges.
November 1962	The new idea is taken to the engineering department where sketches, specifications and, finally, a working model are made.
May–June 1963	At this point, the molds are ordered. The lead time for receiving molds is approximately one year.
June 1963– January 1964	Between June 1963 and January 1964, the sales, advertising, packaging and market research personnel resolve such questions as: How do we promote the toy? How do we display the toy? and, What is a realistic selling price for this item?
January 1964	By January 1964, the very expensive hand samples made out of the molds are available. These are the samples that are used for initial display of the item at the Toy Show.
January–February 1964	Final preparation for the Toy Show involves finalizing sales policies and price lists. The Toy Show is held in New York City usually within the first three weeks in March. During the ten days to two weeks that the show is open (for industry members only) the "new" toys for 1964 are shown.
March–June 1964	After the show, the salesmen begin their visits to distributors, discount houses, mail-order houses and variety chains, booking orders for September delivery.
June–August 1964	Some of the salesmen's attention is now shifted to the department stores, whose buyer's "open to buy" budgets are opened around July 1.
March–August 1964	While the salesmen have been booking orders, the packaging people have been working on developing the final packaging method.
July–August 1964	Production begins on Christmas products in July and shipments begin at the end of August.
October– November 1964	Production peaks around November 1 and is virtually complete by November 30.
December 1964	By the time December's toy sale boom has reached its peak a few weeks before Christmas, many of the toy factories have closed for the month.

---

[7] J. E. Ullman, *Product Innovation in Selected Industries* (Hempstead, N.Y.: Hofstra University Yearbook of Business, Hofstra University, 1966), pp. 19–20.

Previous to World War II, a large number of companies relied on the inventions of an individual, called by one source the "product champion."[8] The name "product champion," though it applies to the person who has had the foresight to invent or develop a new product, actually emanates from the strong desire on the part of an individual to promote his product until it is made available to the public. In some instances the inventor may actually start a company. In other cases, the product champion may sell his invention to another firm and collect royalties.

There are many examples of a product champion leading a company to success. As noted earlier, the most famous in recent years is the Polaroid Company, started by the invention of the Polaroid Land Camera. This camera was invented by the founder, Edwin H. Land. The inventor has been the motivating force behind the company and has assumed responsibility for both the marketing and continued research activities of the firm, indicated in the title he has acquired in recent years — Chairman, President and Director of Research.

Not all companies are such resounding successes. However, many have achieved success on a smaller scale. The following are three examples of product champions.[9]

1. A mechanic employed as a repairman in a mine noticed the inefficient use of labor in hauling ore cars. He invented a ball-bearing mine-car wheel of superior quality, and then proceeded to found one of the oldest companies in Colorado.

2. In his workshop a college dropout book salesman had trouble with his soldering iron. He made an iron for his own use and then started one of the largest companies in the Rocky Mountain area. By 1959 he employed 1,300 people and had a sales volume of approximately $18 million.

3. A mechanic tired of the physical effort required to remove nuts from truck wheels with the crude wrench available. He invented a special wrench and sold a local manufacturer on the idea of putting it on the market.

The product champion is a dying breed today for several reasons. Many new processes today require a great deal of technical education, usually not within the capabilities of one person. Thus it is more difficult for an individual to develop a highly technical product.

Second, and most importantly, the tremendous scientific data now available make it quite possible to form a group of technicians and proceed to develop a new product, within the present state of our technical competence. As noted earlier, many firms actually determine a need for a new product and then go out and produce it through the use of such scientific teams.

Most changes in present products are usually modest in nature. This is because management wants to maintain the basis for the product's success. It is highly unlikely, for instance, that Buick would make its newest model automobiles amphibious. If this happened, the firm might risk losing a good portion of its present market, a market that Buick has successfully nurtured over the years.

Similarly, one might consider the problem of a textbook publisher who is faced with the task of determining the type of change necessary to revise a book that has

---

[8]*New Product Development, Reducing the Risk* (Denver: Denver Research Institute, University of Denver, Dec. 1961), p. 3.

[9]*Ibid.,* p. 4.

sold successfully for many years. Should he change the present format drastically, or should he remain with the present book and simply update many of the passages and tables?

Most often, the publisher asks the author to revise the book within its present format, for if a book is being revised it usually indicates it appeals to a profitable segment of the market. To "develop a new product," it would be better, in marketing terms, to get another author to write another book.

Since most change in products is gradual, and firms rarely apply the "scientific lab" approach to new developments, the question arises as to where ideas for change come from?

Major Sources of Product Ideas

Where do firms get their major ideas for new products? The answer to this question depends on the firm, its internal structure, and the industry it competes in. If the firm has a strong market research staff, it may be that most of the ideas for product change or new products come from this source.

It is one of the major purposes of marketing research to feed back information to management concerning the status of the firm's products among consumers. By doing this it is implied that many of the things wrong with a product can be rectified by changing the product the next time. Thus, should a manufacturer learn from the research department that consumers would prefer an additional feature in his product, he will no doubt consider adding it next time. He may learn the same thing in an indirect manner through research, if the consumers indicate a preference for a competing product, particularly if it contains a feature that is not found in the firm's regular line. As noted in the chapter on research, the firm is constantly reevaluating its present product line. By continuing this process, the manufacturer will invariably find changes that have to be made.

Two other major sources of product change exist in the firm. They are the company staff and other channel members. Staff members usually include the sales force, which through constant contact with the customers develops ideas concerning possible changes that can be made. Many of the ideas for new products can come from this source. In addition, members of the firm's staff organization, through their own contacts and planning activities, develop product ideas. Some firms have been known to call meetings of executives and run all day "brainstorming" sessions on new product ideas. This is particularly useful in firms where the product can be made easily if someone can come up with a particularly good idea. The toy industry uses this approach.

Channel members such as wholesalers, retailers, and brokers are always useful sources for ideas on new products. Channel members are in close proximity to the final consumer and are thus more aware of the changing needs of the consumer. In addition, many of them are exposed to the manufacturer's competitors and have access to information concerning changes that are being considered by the firm's competitors. One usually finds that channel members have a great deal of background and knowledge in the field, and using them as a source of product ideas can prove valuable to the manufacturer.

Once the firm has decided to consider marketing a new product, it then undergoes a great deal of executive evaluation. This evaluation ordinarily takes the form of either informal or formal procedures, and in many cases a combination of both. By *informal* one refers to the usual top-level discussions that precede the decision to go ahead or reject a new product marketing plan. By *formal* one refers to the actual test marketing of new product concepts or the actual new products in selected markets.

Most major firms use a combination of both procedures. However, many firms do not engage in formal testing procedures for the various reasons discussed later. There exist many products on the market that never went into any sort of formal testing program.

Informal Evaluation Procedures

Practically all large firms engage in informal evaluating procedures before marketing a new product or service. This procedure may take several forms. For instance, it may involve nothing more than a discussion among the top executives of the firm who would be most concerned. Typically, one would find at such a meeting the president, marketing manager, controller, and production manager. In addition, the firm may also include the marketing research director, a representative of the firm's advertising agency, the product manager, and perhaps even an outside consultant.

The discussion usually follows several lines. But in totality, the firm's management is concerned with the profit potential of the new product, or, more accurately, the profit contribution the product will make to the firm's overall performance.

Most firms, before entertaining a new product, have certain criteria that must be met by all contemplated projects. For example, one major oil company insists that all new product ideas must return 20 percent by the second year on their investment. In addition, the firm insists that this return on investment must increase to a minimum of 30 percent by the fifth year. This knowledge then puts a constraint on any contemplated new product adventure on the part of its marketing staff.

Although we have considered that these procedures are informal, many concerns do develop certain checklists to guide management in its informal discussions preceding a new product decision. Figure 10-6 demonstrates a simple checklist used by a small manufacturer of new products and systems. Note that this simplified questionnaire contains most of the areas of vital interest to the firm contemplating entry into a market. In particular, one should note that the firm has set a minimum sales goal of $250,000. In addition, they must evaluate whether the product fits into the present production capabilities of the firm. It is noteworthy that the firm has established minimum price-weight ratios that must be met if the product is to be successful. The last question seems to indicate that the firm is particularly interested in highly specialized products rather than those that take them into direct competition with larger mass marketing firms.

FIGURE 10-6 Product Screening

CHECK LIST FOR NEW PRODUCTS OR SYSTEMS
Used by L. W. Benson Manufacturing Company

I. ITEM_____Product ☐ System ☐

II. MARKET

1. Are we now selling to this market?

    Yes ☐ No ☐ Market_____

2. If it is a new market to us, is potential at least $250,000 per year?

    New ☐ Present ☐ Market_____

3. Is item for an expanding market or a new market?

    Expanding ☐ New ☐ No ☐

4. Is size of market within our capability?

    Yes ☐ No ☐

5. Can the item be developed and marketed within a reasonable length of time?

    Projected time_____

6. Is it practical for us to sell to this market?

    Yes ☐ No ☐

7. Is it practical for us to manufacture – do we have types of machinery, know-how, ability to tool, etc.? Yes   No

8. How severe is competition – domestic – possible foreign?

    None ☐ Mild ☐ Substantial ☐ Severe ☐

    Domestic ☐ Possible Foreign ☐

III. PRODUCT

1. Projected price – would it be too high – how would it compare with competitive ways of accomplishing the same thing?

    Price high ☐ Competitive ☐ Low ☐

2. Weight price ratio – should be at least $1.50 per pound for sale and shipment nationally.

    _____per lb.

3. Is the item sufficiently specialized?

    Specialized ☐ Average ☐ Common ☐

    Date_____

    Signed_____

Source: *New Product Development, Reducing the Risk* (Denver: Denver Research Institute, University of Denver, December 1961), p. 42.

In the chapter on marketing information we discussed some of the techniques that have been developed and are now being used for testing new products. Here we should consider some of the problems and difficulties a firm encounters in conducting a testing program.

First, several points should be made. Most importantly, many firms studiously avoid involving themselves in any sort of a test marketing program. Both General Mills and Best Foods have marketed several products without the aid of any procedure even vaguely duplicating a test marketing program. General Mills, for instance, marketed an instant flour product nationally without first testing it in any major city.

Conversely, many firms will not market any product unless it is first tested in several cities or under home conditions. One can surely make the judgment that testing techniques have improved immensely in the past 10 years. Many firms have developed testing systems that practically guarantee a fair market evaluation for a company's contemplated new product. In spite of the sophistication, it is nevertheless true that the overwhelming majority of new products still fail; in spite of our growing knowledge in this area, the outlook is rather dim concerning any reduction in the failure rate.

Yet most major firms engage in some sort of test marketing of their product before going into a full-scale national marketing. The test may be in the form of selecting what are considered to be "typical" cities and offering the product in the outlets available to the company. Much of the testing is done in the consumer market, and hence is carried out through controlled conditions in stores. However, many firms prefer to do in-home testing, where the possible user of the product is given an opportunity to evaluate a product and then a questionnaire is administered at a later date.

One major difficulty in testing is that many products cannot be tested beforehand. For example, as noted earlier, it would be difficult for an auto maker to produce a car before introducing it, because of the tremendous cost. Once a manufacturer of this type of product engages in a tooling expense, he is almost forced to produce the product on a massive scale. This does not necessarily mean that little research goes into the development of such a product. As a matter of fact, the firm may spend years researching the product by studying the consumer through carefully controlled field surveys. From the results of these findings they may conclude that the new product will attain wide acceptance. However, it must be remembered that many new products cannot be produced in limited quantities for testing.

Testing, however, has several other major drawbacks. The severest problem with testing is that by putting a product in a test situation the firm informs its competitors of its intention. Once this occurs, the competitor is then in a position to perhaps introduce a similar product at the same time. Within the past several years, General Foods produced and tested a fruit-filled waffle (called Toast'em Popups) in several markets. This product could be heated in a toaster and was considered to be an important product with great potential. The actual test of this product, it was reported, cost General Foods over $600,000. The test seemed to indicate that it would gain wide consumer acceptance. A problem developed, however, when Kellogg's, a major competitor of General Foods, seemed to have come to the same conclusion and immediately introduced its own line of toasted waffles called Pop Tarts. Kellogg's did not test market the new product and immediately went into national distribution. The early entrance of Kellogg's into the industry earned them a first place standing in this large new market, whereas General Foods' entry seems destined to remain in second place. The belief among marketing people is that Kellogg's had no intention of producing such a product and only became aware of its possibilities when they first saw it being tested by General Foods.

Other problems are incurred when the competition becomes aware of the fact that a competitor is testing a product in a market. Some competitors may actually price cut their present product in order to reduce the opportunities of success for the product being tested. If the firm marketing the new product retaliates, it loses its opportunity to determine the potential sales of the new product.

The last drawback to test marketing is perhaps the most serious. It is sometimes referred to as the "laboratory effect." In establishing a testing program in some cities, those in charge of the program pay careful attention to the details involved in properly displaying the product under test in retail stores. One usually finds, in these tests, that displays are fully stocked, price tickets prominently displayed, and all decals and banners are positioned in an advantageous manner. In effect, this case is actually unreal, in the sense that when the product is actually marketed, it is doubtful that the product will receive anywhere near the same amount of attention from the retailer. It is doubtful that even the banners and displays will ever reach the point of sale in many stores. One should also remember that the executive in charge of the test may have a special interest in seeing to it that the test does come out favorably, simply because he may have been in on the planning of this product from its early development to the final test marketing stage.

Retailers' Attitudes Toward New Products

Retailers do not always welcome new products. There are several reasons for this. First, most retailers have limited space and hence they have to make room for any new products they buy. This involves either dropping a previously stocked product or reducing the space allocation for a product.

Second, most retailers find that many new products do not add significantly to their total volume, For example, when a major soap producer adds a new detergent, most retailers believe that the detergent simply takes sales from a competing product or the product already in the firm's line. Thus the net gain is usually negligible.

Finally, many retailers resent taking on new products that do not offer them higher margins of profit than they presently receive, since an accommodation must be made for the new entrant.

Manufacturers do not always find retailers resisting their new product offerings, however, For instance, most retailers pride themselves in featuring the latest merchandise, and thus many manufacturers find leading retailers in some cities welcome new products, in particular products that can create interest among consumers.

Manufacturers, of course, are well aware of some resistance on the part of many retailers to the introduction of new products. In the food industry there is a particular problem in that many chains insist that a new product pass the careful scrutiny of a buying committee. This committee usually meets once a week and discusses, in detail, all the ramifications of adding a new product to the firm's already crowded shelves. The buying committees are usually made up of top executives who have little direct contact with the manufacturer. This technique, supposedly, takes the decision away from the influence of a direct social contact (i.e., buyer–salesman relationship) and catapults it into a high-level objective decision-making process.

To obtain a favorable decision on the part of store management, manufacturers, through the use of brochures, stress the promotional plans for the new product and perhaps studies of its profitability, and attempt to influence the food buying committee. Nevertheless, they many times fail.

SUMMARY

Perhaps the biggest mistake a business can make is to market a new product that fails.

One should distinguish between additions to the present product line, improvements in the present product line, and distinctively new products.

The need to develop new products is governed by competition, consumer demand, and the present size of the marketing and production facilities of the firm.

New product costs can be considerable if we consider the costs of basic and marketing research. The time that elapses is also a cost factor. However, some products do not require all the introductory steps to be performed.

Since inventions are now a rather limited source of new product ideas, management must rely more on research and information flow procedures from all sources to develop a continuing program of new product development.

QUESTIONS

1. Why is the marketing of new products considered to be one of the riskiest parts of marketing?

*2. Why do you think the Campbell Soup Red Kettle line of products failed?

3. What dangers are encountered when a firm decides to add a new product to an already established line?

4. Why are firms so concerned with producing new products?

5. Relate the development of new products to the product life cycle.

6. Relate *permanence of a product* to the life cycle of a best-selling novel.

7. What is the major means of developing a new product?

8. Why are inventions becoming a more limited source of new products?

9. Show how a firm with an outstanding marketing facility could approach the development of new products.

10. Why is being first so important in introducing a new product?

*In-depth question.

11. Under what conditions would a firm *not* submit a product to all the stages in product development?

*12. How long does it take to develop the 1978 Chevrolets?

13. Since a retailer may gain additional sales from a new product offered by a manufacturer, why in some cases does the retailer resist the introduction of a new product?

*In-depth question.

Pricing the Product

11

SUMMARY KEY

Although customers are not always aware of the exact prices of products, price making in marketing plays an important role in the ultimate sale of a product. Involved in the many facets of making pricing decisions are various forces — the pricing organization, costs, demand, legal factors, and both the firm's objectives and the personal objectives of the executives making such decisions.

Pricing policies are set at the top, but the tendency is for large companies to allow the various divisions to set prices. However, price making must be made with the objectives of the firm clearly in mind. Sometimes the personal goals of executives may conflict with the overall company objectives.

Businessmen set prices based on their judgment of demand. Pricing in most areas of business is company controlled and not market controlled completely by supply and demand. Thus a firm is free to charge a penny or more per gallon of gasoline because of some differentiating factor, whereas in a purely competitive market the price is set by market forces.

The determinants of demand are usually considered to be the price of the product, the number of customers, the preferences of these customers, the level of family income, and the competitive products available. In determining the price of a product one must consider whether the demand is elastic or inelastic.

Demand is not the only consideration in determining price; a firm must also consider the role of supply, which is governed by the costs of manufacturing and distributing a product.

In considering costs, the manufacturer must take into consideration the types of costs — fixed, variable, and incremental. These costs are useful in determining the firm's break-even point. In addition, the firm can engage in marginal analysis by computing average and marginal costs and marginal revenue.

In setting the level of prices in a market the manufacturer has three choices, setting prices above the market, below the market, or with the market. Most manufacturers prefer to price with the market, since this avoids using price cutting, an easily matched factor, to distinguish one firm from another. It is far more useful to differentiate a firm on the basis of some other aspect.

233

Although it seems more sensible for the manufacturer to charge the same price to all customers, small firms find this a difficult policy to follow. In some industries a firm may exercise price leadership. This occurs especially when the products sold are standardized or substitutable. In establishing new products a firm can take the position of either engaging in skimming or penetration pricing.

In some instances manufacturers selling a line of products use price lining in order to clearly differentiate their products and the quality of each. In establishing a price for a product the firm must take into consideration the channel of distribution. Thus, the final retail price must take into consideration trade or functional discounts, quantity discounts, cash discounts, and seasonal discounts.

The legal aspects of pricing are governed by the role of the Robinson–Patman Act and resale price maintenance agreements in many states. As a general rule, the manufacturer must offer the same price to all buyers on the same level.

To establish the right price on the product is perhaps the most difficult decision management has to make. How does a firm establish a price on a product?

As will become obvious in this chapter, there is no one factor. Price making is concerned with many factors — a few are costs, demand, the firm's objectives, the retailer's influence, and many more.

It is the task of management to examine all these factors, weigh them carefully, and choose the price that will help the firm meet its goals.

Marketing and Pricing

Although economists think of pricing in terms of the demand in units for each level of prices, marketing takes into consideration many other factors. For instance, several studies have shown that consumers are not necessarily aware of prices or at least exact prices. In a study by *Progressive Grocer* magazine, among several thousand customers it was found that only 2 percent of the customers could recall the exact price of a shortening and only one third were within 5 percent of the right figure. Even for such a popular item as Ivory bar soap, only 17 percent could exactly recall price and again approximately one third were within the 5 percent range.[1]

Marketing executives are also well aware of the fact that many consumers relate quality with price. Over the years many companies have demonstrated the fact that higher prices in many instances result in higher sales. This is almost in direct contrast to an economist's view of the impact of price on sales. Companies such as Revlon have characterized themselves as firms that specialize in quality and carry merchandise priced well above the market.

In a study dealing with this relationship, Harold Leavitt noted that when he priced two brands, such as floor wax or razor blades, the subjects often chose the higher-priced products. For example, when faced with the choice between two brands of floor waxes, 57 percent of the subjects chose the higher-priced brands. In the case of razor blades, 30 percent chose the higher-priced brand. He concluded

---

[1] "How Much Do Customers Know About Retail Prices?" *Progressive Grocer*, Feb. 1964, pp. 104–6.

the study by saying, in effect, that the higher price may be an attracting factor rather than a repelling force for many different brands.[2]

Price making in marketing is composed of many different considerations. In some cases the right price is crucial to make a sale. In others, price may be only of casual importance. The product itself, the company selling it, or the service that accompanies the product may be the most important factor.

In this chapter will be discussed the many facets of making pricing decisions. The various forces involved will be covered — the organization, product demand, costs, legal factors, the firm's objectives, and personal objectives of those representing the firm.

The Pricing Organization

The study of price making in the large firm usually requires making a distinction in terms of those *who make pricing policy* and those *who carry out the actual price making* within the confines of the policy.

Several comments should be made, however, about the types of firms one is discussing. First, it must be recognized that there are firms who create national publicity and interest when they announce their prices for the coming year. Thus, when General Motors announces the new prices on its cars for the coming year, it is closely watched by several hundred other supplying firms, the federal government, and of course their competitors. This is understandable, since any action on the part of General Motors can affect the national economy. The same may be said for the major steel companies, oil companies, and many of the chemical and metal manufacturers. Thus in these firms the establishing of policy and prices must be made at the very top level and must by definition involve the president and most major officers.

In contrast, the smaller manufacturer is not faced with national pressures in setting his prices and thus may delegate many of the pricing options to his sales or marketing manager. However, in both large and small manufacturing firms the policies are set by top management. This cannot be delegated.

Although policies are practically always set at the top, the very large manufacturer does delegate more freely price-making decisions to the divisions of the firm. This is a logical routine since many of the divisions of these firms are in themselves large. Here firms such as General Electric, du Pont, and Union Carbide find that divisional managers and department heads can perform such functions. As noted by some authors ". . . product divisions of companies like G.E. or Union Carbide are, in the size of their operations, the equivalent of large companies. . . ."[3]

It is also noted that in a mixed line of products, such as that of General Foods, when a firm is engaged in distributing merchandise that is subject to short-run variations in competition, more direct participation is required by the sales force in pricing than in, for instance, General Motors, for which a total integrated pricing program for all car lines must be worked out well in advance of the model year.[4]

---

[2]"A Note on Some Experimental Findings About the Meaning of Price," *Journal of Business,* July 1954, p. 210.

[3]A. D. H. Kaplan, J. B. Dirlam, and R. F. Lanzillotti, *Pricing in Big Business* (Washington, D.C.: The Brookings Institution, 1958), p. 246.

[4]*Op. cit.,* p. 246.

The Firm's Objectives

All pricing policies and goals must be within the confines of the firm's overall objectives as discussed in Chapter 2. For instance, when a firm has an objective of improving its share of the market in the coming year, the firm will most probably be forced to take an aggressive stance in setting prices. On the other hand, if the firm has as its goal a profit improvement, the price makers may find that raising prices is a more reasonable act.

Many objectives of the firm may give direction to those entrusted with establishing prices. Although one would expect that the typical firm would attempt to establish the highest price possible, close examination of a firm's objectives may show that this is not possible. Consider some of the following objectives and their impact on price making.[5]

1. *The firm wants to sell all its products at a reasonable price.* There may be several reasons for this. One may simply be that this represents the view of management and is a long-term self-serving policy. The other is that the firm may be in an industry that requires public support, such as the American Telephone and Telegraph Company.

2. *The firm wants to avoid legal prosecution by the government.* Here one finds large firms with quasi-monopoly power setting their policy. One would think that General Motors with a reported share of the market of 44 percent would find itself in this position. Perhaps it may feel that the government would consider antitrust action, if its share increased much beyond 50 percent.

3. *The firm may be interested only in some fixed amount of profits, rather than all the profits it can make.* One will find many firms with this objective. It may result from the firm's inability to gauge a maximizing price policy and, in effect, represents what management considers to be a fair return on its investment. Or this policy may represent a fairly easy goal that can be understood by management at all levels.

As with the firm's overall objectives, it is management's task to make sure that all executives engaged in pricing are aware of these objectives.

Personal Goals of Executives

In examining the company goals one must also consider that each executive has his own personal goals. For instance, an executive could have as his personal goal the recognition of his talents by the industry. Although achievement of this goal may not necessarily be in conflict with a firm's goal of perhaps achieving a certain profitability, it could preclude the executive engaging in some sort of a "price war" with the rest of the industry. Should he take this stance, he may gain the animosity of many of the industry leaders, and thus fail to achieve his personal goal of recognition. Those aware of the growth of the discount store since the early 1950s are also familiar with the fact that these stores were considered to be unfriendly by the traditional retail organizations.

---

[5]D. V. Harper, *Price Policy and Procedure* (New York: Harcourt Brace Jovanovich, Inc., 1966), p. 32.

Personal goals of executives would perhaps involve some of the following:[6]

1. Elevation in the firm's hierarchy.
2. Greater monetary rewards.
3. Security of position and income.
4. Approbation of superiors, colleagues, and subordinates.
5. The respect (and possibly even fear) of executives in rival firms.
6. Association with a large and successful firm.
7. A position with distinction within the industry and perhaps holding an office in the trade association.

Examination of these personal goals would seem to indicate that they may sometimes conflict with the goals of the firm as indicated previously. For instance, the need to maintain a secure position and income would seem to indicate that the executive would refrain from engaging in any risky price-making policy. It would seem more likely that this same executive would play it safe, even if the opportunities to successfully carry this policy out are present.

Market prices exist when the seller has no control over the price he receives in the marketplace. In this context, most pricing engaged in cannot be considered market pricing. As a matter of fact, if businesses were engaged in purely competitive markets, where the price was set by the supply and demand entering the marketplace at any given time, there would be no need for a chapter on price making in marketing. Perhaps in some narrow segments of the vast U.S. market there may be examples of market pricing in action. There is some indication that certain agricultural products come to the marketplace and the farmer receives what is considered to be a price based on the free play of forces. Perhaps milk, strawberries, and fresh vegetables may come closest to this ideal. On the other hand, one must recognize that even in this purely competitive and rarified marketplace for agricultural products there have been successful attempts on the part of many cooperatives in charge of marketing such products to establish differences between their products and others coming into the marketplace. Clavo avocados would seem to represent a successful attempt to differentiate the product from others flowing into the marketplace.

In direct contrast to market pricing is the view widely held that businesses set their own prices based on, in effect, decisions made by the executives in that organization. Thus a marketing executive is free to set a price on his product and the consumer is free to either buy or ignore the product. In setting his price, of course, the business executive must take into consideration such forces as supply and demand, along with the many other things he does in order to influence the demand for his product and the value placed upon it by the consumer.

Although all these factors must be considered, in general the businessman establishes prices based on his opinion as to the ability of his product to differentiate itself from similar products. Thus the producer of Shell gasoline may set a price directly in competition with the refiners and distributors of Exxon

Market Pricing

---

[6]A. R. Oxenfeldt, *Executive Action in Marketing* (Belmont, Calif.: Wadsworth Publishing Company, Inc., 1966), p. 245.

gasoline, since it is his belief that the consumer does not differentiate between the two gasolines. On the other hand, the refiners of American gas may feel quite free to charge perhaps a cent or two more for their gasoline, since in their opinion the fact that their product does not contain lead differentiates it enough from Shell and Esso to command a premium price. Similarly, the manufacturer of Polaroid Land cameras no doubt feels that he is free to price his product on the basis of what the market will bear, since his patented product is clearly differentiated from other cameras on the market.

What we are saying here in effect is that businessmen are free to set prices based on their judgments. Although the marketplace is the final influencer of the success of this judgment, they can ignore the marketplace if their product is sufficiently differentiated from their competition.

Demand   One of the most crucial aspects in setting prices is determining the demand for a product or a line of products. Demand refers to the various quantities of a good that buyers will take off the market at the many alternative prices available to the seller. It follows from this concept that the higher the price, the smaller the quantity of product sold. As the price increases, the quantity sold will decrease. In effect, as the price rises some buyers will drop out. In other cases some buyers will buy less than they had anticipated. From this one can safely reason that price and quantity are inversely related.

This does not mean that for all price rises for all products less will be sold. For it has been noted in the sale of some products that the higher the price, the more alluring the product becomes, and the firm may actually sell more. This example has been repeated many times in the cosmetic industry, where price may indicate quality and a certain ability to be more effective. However, this happening is relatively unusual. For the normal run of products the quantity taken at a given price decreases as the price rises.

TABLE 11-1   Demand Schedule for Sailboats of the Abe Company

Price ($)	Quantity Taken
1,000	40
900	50
800	60
700	70
600	80
500	90

The demand for a product can be seen in Table 11-1. Here one sees that the higher the price for a product, the lower the quantity taken. Thus, when setting a price of $1,000 for a sailboat, a firm can expect to sell approximately 40 boats. Should the price be set at $700, the firm may expect to sell at least 70 boats.

The demand for boats can perhaps be better illustrated in Figure 11-1, where the data in the demand schedule are put into graphic form and in effect become a demand curve. By simply drawing a line from the price to the demand curve and then continuing it vertically to the axis, the quantity that will be taken can be determined. Thus at a price of $700 (P4), 70 (Q4) boats will be sold.

Demand Curve for Sailboats of the Abe Company   FIGURE 11-1

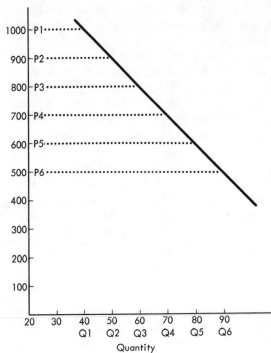

Determinants of Demand

What determines demand or the price quantity relationships is shown in Table 11-1. No doubt such a list would be rather extensive. In addition, it is also clear that any attempt to list determinants would be futile, since firms recognize that many influences have not even been recognized or detected at this point. The most obvious support for this view is found almost daily in the department stores, where ads that are repeated fail on many occasions to produce a similar consumer response. One may offer several valid reasons. Yet many of these results do not fall into any easy-to-understand pattern. In fact, on numerous occasions the response the second year may be substantially greater than to the previous year's ad.

The determinants of demand, however, can be attributed to several of the following factors:

1. Price of the product.
2. Number of potential customers in the area.
3. Preferences of customers.
4. Level of family income.
5. Competitive products available.

Many of these determinants were discussed in the chapters on the consumer. The role of each would seem to be important in developing a demand schedule for most products. In the sale of a product that has appeal to a narrow segment of the market these factors would play a particularly important role.

One could see, for instance, that in the marketing of the Rolls-Royce automobile, which sells for upward of $30,000, the number of purchasers in an area would be rather limited. In fact, it is safe to assume that most of the dealerships would be located either in the Middle Atlantic States or the Pacific Coast area, where the average per capita income is the highest. It would be a relatively simple task for this company to determine the number of families with incomes of over $50,000 per year that reside in these areas. These would more than likely represent the strongest potential customers for the firm's product. Should the firm determine that the general tendencies among these families is to purchase expensive boats in preference to expensive cars, then the firm would make an adjustment in the demand schedule for their automobile. In addition, the firm may find that other expensive competitive models are making an appearance in the American markets, which could also force the company to reconsider its estimates of demand.

In addition to these factors, the price would also be an important consideration, particularly when there have been changes. For instance, if the firm found that the recent reevaluations of the American dollar warranted a reduction in the price of the Rolls-Royce, this could be a favorable development.

Price Elasticity

In discussing demand one must appreciate the term *price elasticity,* which measures the responsiveness of the quantity sold to price changes. In more specific terms we usually state that the demand for a product is elastic if the total revenue derived increases at the same rate as a price reduction. Thus, if we reduce the price on shoes by 1 percent and if the total revenue increases by 1 percent, we can say that the price of the shoes is *elastic.* If however, we reduce the price by the same 1 percent, and the demand for the product either decreases or does not increase by the full 1 percent, we call this situation *inelastic demand.* In essence, therefore, the more sensitive the quantity demanded is to price changes, the more elastic is the demand for the offering.

However, when we discuss individual products for a company, the demand in many cases can be elastic, whereas the total demand for the generic product may be inelastic. A good example of this situation can be found in the gasoline industry, where the demand for automobile gasoline is relatively inelastic for some very obvious reasons. Since there are so many automobiles on the road and gas tanks can only hold a certain amount of gasoline at any given time, the demand for gasoline in the total United States tends to be fairly stable and only rises as the number of cars purchased and maintained on the road increases. However, as any gasoline service station operator can tell you, any dramatic downward changes in his pump price for either low-test or high-test gasoline will cause an immediate increase in demand for his brand of gasoline. This situation is usually referred to as *brand elasticity.* Hence in many marketing situations the firm finds that, although they cannot increase overall demand for their product, a carefully planned change in pricing can cause a substantial increase in volume, provided all other factors stay the same.

As one can see, management is often faced with an important decision of when and how much a price change shall be made. This decision may be made for a new product, an established product, or a product that is adding an attribute, such as a change in warranty policy. But if management is to have a complete picture, they should know what volume changes will occur when they make a change in the price of the product.

Understanding the concept of demand is only one side of the total picture in the marketplace. One must also recognize that, aside from a demand schedule, there exists a supply schedule. This supply schedule is directly related to the price–quantity relationship discussed previously. It differs from the demand schedule in that it slopes upward and to the right, since the higher the price the more willing manufacturers are to supply additional goods. The supply function is shown in Figure 11-2.

Supply and Costs

The Supply Function   **FIGURE 11-2**

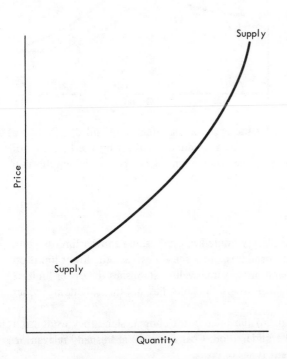

In Figure 11-3 one can see that when we put the demand and supply function together there exists a point where equilibrium is reached. At the point of intersection, one can see that the equilibrium is reached where the quantity and price that sellers are willing to offer are equal to the quantity and price that buyers are willing to accept. In essence, what this shows is that at prices set below the equilibrium point a shortage would exist, simply because the suppliers would not be willing to produce enough goods to supply the market demand. Conversely, at higher than equilibrium prices the customers would take a smaller quantity and thus supply would exceed demand.

FIGURE 11-3   Price Equilibrium

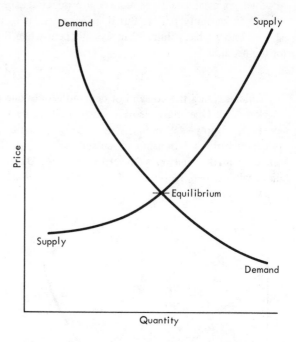

The supply curve is governed by the costs of manufacturing and distributing a product, and not simply the demand for a product. That is why the firm cannot supply large amounts of goods at prices that seem to fall below the equilibrium price.

Costs

The role of costs in pricing is mainly limited to establishing a lower limit beyond which the firm will not price its products.[7] In a sense costs set the lower limits on the price of a product, and demand or consumer value establishes the upper limit. It is the job of management to establish where the point lies and then, by doing so, set prices.

Although costs may not relate to the price point chosen, since they establish a floor for pricing, they should be understood. Cost concepts are usually relevant in terms of (1) time and (2) different types of costs.

In terms of time the marketing executive is usually *not* concerned with historical cost data, since what has happened in the past is usually not relevant in a changing dynamic market. In the case of a new product or a drastically changed product, the historical analysis is not even available. Current costs all suffer from the same problem, since they are still historical, in the sense that after they are collected they

---

[7]Harper, *op. cit.,* p. 53.

then become past information. This is not to deny that in any firm costs tend to stabilize. However, in most cases the dynamics of marketing competition seem to make *past* and *current* information limited in its use toward establishing the best kind of relevant cost information, that is, *future costs.* Thus the manufacturer is always concerned with the future direction of costs, a figure that can help him establish the floor level of prices that he may establish.

Types of Costs

Mostly, executives are concerned with three major types of costs: (1) fixed, (2) variable, and (3) incremental. *Fixed* costs are usually referred to as overhead costs. These costs are usually considered to be costs that do not vary with the firm's output. Generally identified as making up these costs are contractual payments, such as interest, rent, and associated property taxes, and executive and clerical wages.

Variable costs, as implied by the name, refer to those costs that vary with output. Examples include direct labor costs, materials, and utilities used in the production of the product.

A type of variable costs are *incremental* costs. Incremental costs are those that are incurred when the firm changes its production level and thus increases the firm's output by adding a new product to the line.

Break-even Analysis

How many of a new product must we sell if we are to make a profit? is a question often asked of the marketing department by management. Although in planning a new product sales management first develops a planned volume of sales, it is important to remember that estimates of demand are at the least precarious.

To gain some insight into the level that must be attained, management can construct a break-even point. The *break-even point* represents the point on a break-even chart where the total revenue (or sales) equals the total costs of producing the product, the total cost being the *variable* and *fixed* costs.

To understand the workings of the break-even analysis one must recall that fixed costs and variable costs play different roles in profits analysis. Fixed costs may remain the same whether a manufacturer sells 10,000 units or 15,000. Thus, if one prices a product at $10 and the fixed costs are $20,000, the firm must produce and sell 2,000 items to break even with fixed costs. However, fixed costs do not represent total costs, since for every product a firm produces they incur additional costs of labor, materials, sales commissions, power usage, and so on. This cost as noted earlier is called variable cost and by definition varies with the production of each item. Thus, if the product has a variable cost of 50 percent on each item produced, the firm must plan to sell 4,000 units, which represents the break-even point. Any sales above this point will increase the profits substantially. Figure 11-4 demonstrates this fact. Here one sees that fixed costs remain at $20,000 throughout the production estimates. At 2,000 units, one should note that only fixed costs are covered, and at 4,000 units (or $40,000 in revenue) the total costs curve and total revenue curve meet, and this represents the break-even point. In effect, this represents the point where management can rightfully expect to make a profit.

FIGURE 11-4   Break-even Point

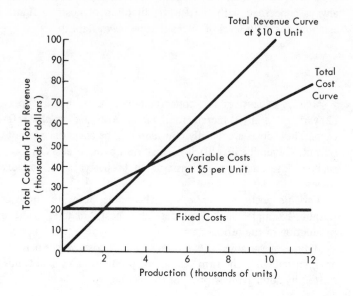

Marginal Analysis

Aside from estimating break-even points, a firm may consider the use of marginal analysis in determining the best price for its product. To understand this concept, one should consider the following definitions:

Average costs are derived by dividing total costs by the number of units of the product sold. Thus a company producing 5,000 items at a cost of $10,000 incurs an average unit cost of $2.

Marginal cost is the additional cost incurred in the production of one additional unit. It represents the change in total costs involved in producing this additional unit. Thus, when the firm produces 5,001 units at a cost of $10,005, the marginal cost is $5.

Marginal revenue is the change in total revenue (or receipts) that results from the sale of an additional unit of a product. When the firm sells 5,000 units and gains revenue of $20,000, all revenues above this sum, if they sell more than the 5,000 units, are considered to be marginal revenue.

Table 11-2 illustrates the use of this type of analysis. In essence, this table brings together cost and revenue measurements that are the counterparts of our earlier mentioned supply and demand. First one should note that total costs include both variable and fixed costs. This table also indicates how costs will change under various assumptions of output. For instance, it is indicated that when the output increases from 1,000 to 3,000 units the total costs will rise from $4,500 to $8,000.

Column 2 indicates the changes in costs from each increase in production. For instance, a shift from 3,000 to 4,000 units would involve an increase in costs, or a marginal cost of $1 ($1,000 ÷ 1,000) per unit. Average costs per unit are computed in column 3 by simply dividing the output into the total cost.

Marginal Analysis **TABLE 11-2.**

Output[a]	1 Total Costs	2 Marginal (Unit) Costs	3 Average Costs	4 Price Obtainable	5 Total Revenue	6 Marginal Revenue
1,000	$ 4,500	$ —	$4.50	$6.00	$ 6,000	$ —
2,000	6,500	2.00	3.25	5.00	10,000	4,000
3,000	8,000	1.50	2.66	4.00	12,000	2,000
4,000	9,000	1.00	2.25	3.00	12,000	0
5,000	10,000	1.00	2.00	2.00	10,000	-2,000
6,000	11,000	1.00	1.8333	1.00	6,000	-4,000
7,000	14,000	3.00	2.00	0.80	5,600	-400

[a]For convenience, we shall assume that output and sales are always equal.
Source: Adapted from A. R. Oxenfeldt, *Executive Action in Marketing* (Belmont, Calif.: Wadsworth Publishing Company, Inc., 1966) p. 276.

The manufacturer also has revenue estimates. Based on his estimate of the price obtainable (column 4), the firm can determine the increases in total revenue that can occur. This is seen in column 5. In the last column one can see the changes that occur in marginal revenue. This column is obtained from data collected in column 5.

One can now see that if the firm decided to increase its output from 3,000 to 4,000 units the increase in marginal revenue would be zero. In addition, the firm can see that this additional volume of output incurs shifts in marginal costs of $1 a unit or $1,000 in total costs. Thus by increasing the output the firm would actually end up with a net revenue of minus $1,000. (3,000 units = $8,000 in costs and $12,000 in revenue; 4,000 units = $9,000 in costs and $12,000 in revenue.)[8]

Here one can see that a change in output or prices results in changes in both costs and revenues for the executive. As long as the marginal revenue gains exceed the rise in costs, the move can be considered a major possibility. However, when the costs rise more rapidly than the revenue potential, then the businessman will not make the change.

Level of Prices

In setting the level of prices in a firm, the manufacturer must choose among three types of alternatives: pricing with, below, or above the competition.

The choice of policy reflects the type of product a firm carries and implies the need to be well aware of the consumers' and competitors' reactions at all times.

Pricing with the Market

Most manufacturers follow the course of pricing with the market; that is they set prices at the same level as competitors. This does not necessarily mean that the

[8]Oxenfeldt, *op. cit.*, p. 277.

manufacturer will set his prices exactly as his competitor's. It does mean, however, that he will maintain a price that is well within the price of some of his competitors. For instance, although the Ford's new Pinto automobile was marketed originally as a direct competitor of the German-made Volkswagen, the prices differed slightly, $1,919 and $1,899, respectively. It is obviously Ford's contention that a $20 price differential means little to the consumer, and the Pinto is priced within the zone of its competition.

There are several reasons why manufacturers prefer to price with the market. The first and foremost is that most manufacturers do not care to use price as a major weapon, since it is the easiest way for a competitor to retaliate. It also can lead to endless price cutting and losses to both parties. This latter situation can become difficult in industries with a high-labor-content product, where most manufacturers have the same cost structure.

In addition, most manufacturers find ample room to differentiate their product from competition by other means than pricing. For example, an automobile manufacturer can offer servicing facilities, more appealing styling, and more accessories, rather than relying on lower prices.

Another aspect of pricing with the market is that it completely avoids the need to make the enormous effort necessary to find out what the consumer will pay or the impact of a slightly different policy. By pricing in this way, the manufacturer assumes that his competition has done much of this work for him, and he can assume that they have made correct estimates. This is a particularly profitable policy for a manufacturer who runs a more efficient operation and perhaps has lower costs. In the automobile industry materials and services, as costs as a percentage of sales, vary substantially when one compares General Motors with either Ford or Chrysler. For example, in 1969 General Motors' costs of materials and services approximated 40 percent (related to sales), whereas Ford and Chrysler's percentages were 55.1 and 58.5 percent.[9] Thus, if General Motors can maintain a profitable price policy that is followed by its major competitors, its total profit picture will be substantially greater because the firm is a relatively low-cost producer in the auto industry.

Pricing above the Market

Ordinarily, a firm does not have the option to price its product above the market. Assuming it does so, it would probably find that its sales would decline substantially. Nevertheless, there do exist firms that price above the market. Some engage in this pricing activity simply because they are a high-cost producer and have little choice.

Most other firms, however, price above the market deliberately and for good reason. One of the major reasons for pricing above the market is that the firm's product is sufficiently differentiated in the mind of the consumer to entitle the company to command a higher price. Magnavox and Sony both sell television sets, but in the mind of the consumer they both sell a quality product and thus can

---

[9]*The Automobile Industry – The Road Ahead* (New York: Oppenheimer and Company, 1971), p. 16.

command a price above the other major manufacturers. The ability to differentiate a firm's product can help it maintain a policy of pricing above the market.

There are cases, moreover, where pricing above the market can actually increase volume and maintain profits. Although such instances are rare, they nevertheless exist. In the cosmetic industry, for instance, many major firms have discovered that the consumer sometimes relates quality with price. As a result, several companies price new products above the market, so as to appeal to this market. Alberto Culver, for instance, has followed this policy for many years, and the management many times prices its new products above the going market price. Revlon has also followed this policy to a great extent.

Pricing below the Market

The most aggressive policy a firm can pursue is to price below the market. This policy is particularly successful when the firm has lower costs than most other firms in the industry, and when the demand is such that following a lower price policy will substantially increase the firm's share of the market. In cases where demand is not too elastic, this policy will really result in a notable success. Both the Volkswagen and the Japanese imported automobiles would seem to be excellent examples of companies pricing below the market and doing so to a great extent because they have a lower cost structure than the American car makers.

Pursuing such a policy, however, can be fraught with danger. The most important is that competitors may freely choose or be forced to follow such a policy. By matching the prices of a firm, competitors could most certainly lessen the impact of such a policy. The second danger, always a possibility when a firm prices below the market, is the implication to the consumer that the product is of a lesser quality than its competition.

Varying Prices

A major decision that most manufacturers must make is whether they should establish a one-price policy for all customers or vary the prices. As noted later in this chapter, the firm must adhere to the legal limitations of the Robinson–Patman Act, which restrict the use of discounts to customers on the same level. However, it is an open secret that in many industries the law is not followed, particularly by small manufacturers. One major industry that varies prices to the retailer is the garment industry. This sort of practice occurs mainly in industries where there exist hundreds (and in the case of apparel, thousands) of firms. The very size of such firms make them fair game for the large buyer.

In contrast, in industries where only a relatively few firms control most of the industry, customers are offered the same prices, and only minor variations would occur. These larger firms are of course more liable to inquiries by the government, since their very size makes them tempting targets. In addition, most of the laws concerning restrictions on discounts have developed over the years as a result of complaints and suits filed against the large corporations.

As a policy, it is of course more desirable to maintain one price, since a firm can plan more easily the projected revenue to be derived from any action they may make. A one-price policy also avoids the possibility that a customer may learn of a lower price that occurred during another transaction with a competitor. Avoided, also, is the fact that price negotiation is time consuming and thus costs more; as a procedure it relies heavily on sales managers or salesmen who are of a higher caliber and thus more costly; salesmen will tend to emphasize lower prices in order to obtain a sale; and, finally, the central organization loses control over prices.[10]

The one-price policy has almost the opposite effect of the varying price policy. For instance, the maintenance of this policy eliminates the salesman from engaging in price bargaining. It may also result in the salesman emphasizing product qualities with less emphasis on price. It clearly avoids the problem of one customer believing another customer gets preferential treatment.

Its major disadvantage, of course, is that it does shut out the firm from making sales where a little flexibility could accomplish this. It is usually slow to adjust to changing conditions in the marketplace. All in all, however, it would seem to represent a growing trend among companies in most industries.

Price Leadership

Many firms are not involved in establishing the level of prices because through competition or choice they prefer to follow the pricing policies of the leading company in their industry.

Price leadership is particularly important in industries where the products are standardized and substitutable for each other. In this type of industry, firms realize that any reduction in price will usually result in direct retaliation by competition, since a great number of buyers will shift from one supplier to another if the price differential is substantial.[11]

The leader of the industry may vary. However, in most major raw material industries one firm tends to dominate. Table 11-3 shows the dates of price changes of the three major aluminum firms in the industry. Note that Alcoa, the largest firm, led the "big three" on five occasions during price increases, and tied once in a total of nine listed changes during those years.

The acceptance of price leadership in the steel, copper, tin can, farm equipment, and oil production is a natural result of the history of these industries, in which violent price fluctuations combined with cutthroat competition resulted in forced consolidation of competitors.[12]

These experiences have resulted in most of the management of these industries taking care to consider all price changes before announcing such decisions publicly. This avoids the charge of "cutthroat" competition and puts the industry on notice of a carefully thought out price change.

The acceptance of the role of price leader does not always fall to the largest firm in the industry. For instance, it is well recognized in banking circles that nationwide policy changes on interest rates can only become effective if the major New York

---

[10] Harper, *op. cit.,* p. 174.

[11] Jules Backman, *Pricing: Policies and Practices* (New York: The Conference Board, Inc., 1961), p. 50.

[12] Kaplan, Dirlam, and Lanzillotti, *op. cit.,* p. 271.

banks go along with the increase or decrease in the rates. Although California's Bank of America is the country's largest bank, a change by these banks has much greater importance. Thus, in March, 1971, Chase Manhattan Bank reduced its prime rate over the protests and in many cases cynical comments of other bankers throughout the United States. Nevertheless, within 1 week all major banks had followed Chase's lead.

Timing of Changes in Prices of 99 Percent Plus Primary Aluminum Ingot (30 Pounds), Three Leading Companies, 1950-1956   TABLE 11-3

Price ($)	Alcoa	Reynolds Metals	Kaiser Aluminum
0.175	May 22, 1950	May 23, 1950	May 25, 1950
0.19	Sept. 25, 1950	Sept. 29, 1950	Sept. 28, 1950
0.20	Aug. 4, 1952	Aug. 4, 1952	Aug. 4, 1952
0.205	Jan. 23, 1953	Jan. 23, 1953	Jan. 22, 1953
0.215	July 15, 1953	July 20, 1953	July 20, 1953
0.222	Aug. 5, 1954	Aug. 6, 1954	Aug. 6, 1954
0.232	Jan. 13, 1955	Jan. 10, 1955	Jan. 12, 1955
0.244	Aug. 1, 1955	Aug. 6, 1955	Aug. 2, 1955
0.259	Mar. 29, 1956	Mar. 27, 1956	Mar. 26, 1956

Source: Jules Backman, *Pricing: Policies and Practices* (New York: The Conference Board, Inc., 1961), p. 51.

It should be remembered, however, that price leadership is followed as a principle in basic industries where the products are not differentiated. In industries where the products are differentiated, either in reality or in the view of the consumer, price leadership is not as important an influence in terms of establishing prices.

Pricing New Products

In establishing new products, the firm has several choices in terms of its policies. Thus in 1947 Milton Reynolds developed the ball-point pen that was ballyhooed as being able to write under water; the pen was sold at prices ranging from $12.50 to $17.50 in many of the major department stores. This pen is now being duplicated by the Bic Pen Corporation for less than 30 cents and there is little doubt that today's pen is more reliable. The policy followed in the early development of the product is known as *skimming* the market.

Skimming, as a policy, is an attempt to charge relatively high prices at the early developmental stages in introducing a new product. This early developmental stage usually coincides with heavy promotional expenditures. Basically, the firm attempts to recover all its development and research costs (if any) at an early stage. In cases when the product has a high level of obsolescence, it represents a preferred method of pricing. Typical of this policy was the development of color television during the late 1950s when the segment of the market that was interested in obtaining this relatively new product paid a premium price. This premium price helped the manufacturer recover much of his early investment in designing and producing the first sets. After several years passed, the price of color television sets declined and the major manufacturers adjusted their prices accordingly.

New books represent a skimming policy in action on a very profitable basis. When a new novel or general topic book appears, it is priced at perhaps $5 or $10. Those interested in reading a well-advertised book are quite willing to pay the retail price for the initial printing. However, if and when the book makes the bestseller list, within a relatively short period of time it appears as a paperback and sells for a fraction of its original hardcover price.

The marketing of drugs represents an attempt on the part of the manufacturer to recover his research costs during the original introduction stage of the product. In addition, the firms are concerned about obsolescence, since new developments in this industry are constantly replacing established drug products.

As a general policy, skimming represents a safe way of introducing a new product, since it is always easier for a firm to reduce prices if necessary than to raise them. In addition, many firms take this approach since they have no way to measure the possible demand for a new product. This is particularly true when the product is so new that it can be said that it has little or no competition presently on the market.

Several illustrations of skimming can be found among products when there were no substitutes available. For instance, when du Pont introduced cellophane in 1924, it was sold at $2.65 a pound. Twenty-one price reductions later, it was selling at 40 cents a pound in 1939. Penicillin had a similar history. When introduced in 1945, bulk prices per billion units were approximately $6,000. By 1955, the price quoted by one producer was $34.50.[13]

Penetration pricing refers to the firm's attempt to establish a very low price that will result in the attainment of a large volume. In this case, however, management believes that demand is elastic; that is, a low price will increase sales proportionately over a high price. In addition, it is also management's view that a low price will result in large production savings as a direct result of mass production.

Although this can be a rather regular policy for most any firm, it does not necessarily mean that it is chosen because of the above factors being present. It is more likely that concurrent with the management view that the product will sell in large quantities management may be aware that adequate substitutes exist for their product. In effect, they are almost forced to establish a penetration pricing policy. Detergents are usually handled in this manner.[14]

Price Lining

By price lining one refers to the policy on the part of manufacturers to offer their products to the public in a limited number of price lines. For instance, a manufacturer of men's ties may establish retail price lines of $3.00 and $5.00 for his nationally advertised product sold in men's wear stores. This policy has several purposes. First, it establishes price points that in the view of the manufacturer are appealing to the consumer. Second, it avoids confusion at the retail level. For instance, should a manufacturer establish a price line for ties at $3.00, and $3.25, and $3.50, the salesperson may be hard pressed to explain any difference to the

---

[13]Backman, *op. cit.*, p. 48.

[14]Backman, *op. cit.*, p. 46.

consumer. As a matter of fact, the different prices may be due simply to fluctuating labor or material costs incurred in the production of such ties. In effect, the manufacturer incurring such costs simply establishes a policy of placing higher-cost products in the nearest price line. He may, for example, decide to price a tie in the $5.00 price line if its costs exclude it from the $3.00 price line.

The manufacturer many times uses price lining to indicate quality to the consumer. In the tie example the lower price would indicate a lower-quality tie than the $5 or $10 tie. The point is that the quality is indicated clearly, whereas should the manufacturer maintain pricing steps ($3.00, $3.25, etc.) between each of these price points, the consumer may not see such a clear distinction. However, by establishing substantial price differences between each line, the consumer can more clearly recognize differences.

One must be aware, however, that much of the manufacturer's price lining policies are strongly influenced by the retailer. Many retail stores establish price lines and manufacturers must adhere to their policy. For example, a store selling ties may accept two or three major prices, such as $3, $5, and $10. Since most stores have preset margin goals, it is obvious that manufacturers selling to these stores are also faced with preset prices that they can charge the retailer.

For example, many retail firms purchase products based on some preconceived price line for their store. Thus a variety chain may establish a policy of selling toys that do not exceed $5.00 at retail. If a manufacturer, for example, should produce a toy item that would cost him approximately $4.00 to produce and distribute, he would find that this variety chain would be unwilling to purchase the product from him. He would also find that a product that retails at $5.00 at the variety chain would have to cost the variety chain $3.00 (40 percent off the list price). In addition, he may also find the variety chain demanding a 5 percent quantity discount, since they may make an initial commitment for several thousand, and an additional 2 percent discount for cash. Thus the manufacturer must reconcile himself to the fact that the variety chain will pay him somewhere in the vicinity of $2.80 per item.

Of course, the manufacturer does not have to sell to the variety chain with its rigid price lines. However, he may be also aware that if he is interested in producing and selling tens of thousands of toys he will find these outlets a desirable alternative to selling to thousands of smaller stores throughout the United States. What happens, therefore, is that many manufacturers produce products that fit into the pricing policies of the large chain stores; and, in effect, these stores control the pricing policies of many manufacturers.

Many manufacturers attempt to cover as many price lines in the sale of their product as possible. They do this with the belief that each of these price lines may represent a separate mass segment of the market. In Figure 11-5 one can see the suit price lines sold by Hart Schaffner and Marx to their thousands of retail store customers around the country. The range of retail prices stretches from a low of $60 to a high of $300.

Automobile Pricing

The many factors that manufacturers must take into consideration and their effect on the dealers' pricing can be seen in the pricing of the automobile.

FIGURE 11-5   Retail Suit Prices

		$50	75	100	125	150	175	200	250	300
Hickey – Freeman									▓	▓
Walter – Morton									▓	▓
Gilbert & Lodge									▓	▓
Society Brand Clothes						▓	▓	▓		
Graham & Gunn, Ltd.						▓	▓	▓		
Hart Schaffner & Marx						▓	▓	▓		
Sterling & Hunt						▓	▓	▓		
Austin Reed of Regent Street				▓						
Johnny Carson				▓						
M. Wile		▓	▓							
Craigmore		▓								

Source: Hart Schaffner and Marx (Chicago), *Annual Report, 1970,* p. 10.

Early in 1971 the new Ford minicar, the Pinto, had an advertised showroom price of $1,919. It was the intention of Ford to compete directly with the best-selling imports, the Volkswagen and Japanese automobiles. The wholesale price of the Pinto to the dealer was $1,502. The dealer, however, pays the Ford Company $1,538. The $36 or 2 percent of the retail price is a rebate or a forced savings for the dealer.

At the retail level the Pinto has a 17 percent markup on the retail price, which approximates $1,810 ($1,502 = 83 percent). Added to this retail price is $109 for the federal excise tax, making the price $1,919. The Pinto retail price makes it the lowest-priced Ford car made in the United States. The fact that Ford was striving to market Pinto at the lowest price possible caused them to add a lower than average markup (17 percent) to the wholesale price of the car.

In contrast, consider a Ford LTD, a much larger car. The wholesale price of this car is $2,512, but with the 2 percent rebate the dealer pays $2,579. This car carries a 25 percent markup on the retail price and thus sells for $3,349. Add to this $186 in federal excise tax plus $40 for a dealer preparation charge and the showroom price now becomes $3,575.

This sticker price is merely the list price of the automobile, and few sales are made at this figure. Most large dealers discount the price of these cars, depending on the competitive situation and the time of year. In addition, most buyers of automobiles purchase optional equipment, which carries a much larger markup to the dealer. In the case of the Pinto, however, one can see that the low markup of the car in relationship to the larger cars indicates that the buyer will not receive very much of a discount. In the case of the Pinto the dealer has a markup of $310, whereas in the larger Ford his markup approximates $800. Here, again, one sees the urgency of the *competition* for the small-car market dictating Ford's choice of a lower markup for the lower-priced car.

The example of automobile pricing gives us some insight in the complex discount system that a manufacturer must build into his pricing system.

A pricing system as developed by a manufacturer starts with a list price. Although there are several list prices, most definitions refer to the list price to the retailer. The retailer expects to receive a discount from this list price. In a sense the list price is the manufacturer's suggested *retail* price for his product. Thus a toy manufacturer may feature a list price on his product of $1.00. It is his intention that this product should be sold to the ultimate consumer for this price. The retailer in turn pays him a price of perhaps 60 cents for this toy; this discount from the list price represents one form of discount commonly called a *trade* or *functional* discount.

The following are most of the major discounts the manufacturer must take into consideration in establishing a pricing schedule.

Trade or functional discounts are a reduction or discount from the list price, which in a sense is payment for functions performed. Thus in the toy example the discount from the list price of 40 percent is in effect a recognition on the part of the manufacturer that the retailer should receive payment for services rendered. These same discounts are paid to wholesalers. The amounts vary by industry and are related to an extent by the operating expenses of each industry.

Distribution of the Consumer Food Dollar (Retail Store Purchases)   **TABLE 11-4**

	Meat *1963*	*Cereals* *1963*
Farm value	$0.59	$0.22
Food manufacturing	0.11	0.48
Purchased transportation	0.03	0.05
Wholesale costs	0.06	0.07
Retail costs	0.21	0.18
Total	$1.00	$1.00

Source: Arthur D. Little, Inc., estimates. Appears in G. H. Marple and H. B. Wissmann, eds., *Grocery Manufacturing in the United States* (New York: Praeger Publishers, Inc., 1965), p. 274.

The need for functional discounts can be seen in Table 11-4, where the distribution costs are illustrated for meat and cereal products selling to the ultimate consumer for $1.00. In the case of a meat product, one can see that the packing firm has several decisions to make on discounts. The first involves establishing a pricing system that takes into consideration retailing costs of 21 cents, wholesaling costs of 6 cents, and the manufacturer's transportation costs of 3 cents. In the case of meat, the meat-processing firm pays the farmer 59 cents and resells the product for 70 cents plus the transportation charge.

The cereal manufacturer faces a similar problem in that he must establish a discount system from list price that takes into consideration the retailer, wholesaler, and transportation costs. One should note, however, that in the case of cereal the farmer only accounts for 22 cents of the total distribution cost, whereas in meat almost 60 percent of the total cost was accounted for by the farmer. The striking difference between the role of the manufacturer in both products can be better understood if one remembers that a great deal of cereal selling relies greatly on the ability of the manufacturer to advertise and promote a product and brand name. Thus 48 cents of each dollar spent on cereal is accounted for by the value added by manufacturers.

The point of this discussion is that each product varies in terms of its cost and functions performed. The manufacturer in establishing a functional discount system must therefore take these differences and needs into consideration.

Quantity discounts are offered to customers to encourage them to buy in large quantities. By selling in large quantities the seller incurs certain savings, and thus passes some of them on to the buyer.

Cash discounts are offered to the buyer to encourage him to pay his bill promptly. Most channel members extend credit to buyers, and the discount system attempts to encourage them to pay bills before they are due. Terms such as "2/10 net 30" mean that the buyer can deduct 2 percent from the face of the bill if he makes payment within 10 days. If he so chooses, he may pay the bill without taking the discount within 30 days.

Seasonal discounts are offered to buyers if they purchase merchandise out of season. For instance, boating manufacturers may offer a retailer an additional 10 percent discount off the list price of a boat if he purchases several boats in the winter season when boating is at its lowest level.

Government Impact on Pricing

Since World War II, the federal government began to play an important role in the pricing of basic industrial products. The government's role has been in the form of direct pressure on many of our basic industries. The reasons for this intervention are many. One is the belief on the part of the President's economic advisors that price increases in basic materials have a broad effect on all segments of the U.S. economy. It is their view that a price increase in steel will affect many of the major industries, such as automobiles, appliances, and housing. Additionally, it is the government's belief that basic industries are perhaps more monopolistic than consumer goods industries; hence they are in a better position to maintain control over their prices. A vivid example of this was brought out in 1965 when the copper industry threatened to raise prices at a time when the administration was interested in combating inflation. To avoid this happening, the then Defense Secretary McNamara threatened to unload 200,000 tons of government stockpiled copper. This threat caused the copper companies to rescind their planned price increases. During the same year, the government carried out the same plan in the aluminum industry with similar results.[15]

The aggressiveness of the government in the basic industries has caused a shift in the pricing policies of many of these firms. It has been noted that previous to the government policy change in this area the steel companies usually announced

---

[15] J. Backman, "Conclusion: The New Framework for Pricing," in E. Marting, ed., *Creative Pricing* (New York: The American Management Association, Inc., 1968), p. 215.

across-the-board price increases for all products. Now, however, they tend to raise prices on only selected products. In addition, the increases tend to be less than in the past.[16]

The government's role in the consumer goods industry has not been as direct. Its power resides in its ability to enforce antitrust legislation and bring to court important cases to help implement these laws.

Legal Restraints on Pricing

In establishing prices the manufacturer is particularly aware of the fact that all aspects of the pricing strategy may be challenged by the government, backed up by a whole network of laws and court decisions.

Quantity discounts can be interpreted in terms of an important court case that involved the Morton Salt Company, which was decided in 1948. Up to that time Morton offered its customers a choice of noncumulative discounts or cumulative discounts. Noncumulative discounts referred to "one-shot" discounts, where the selling firm offered a discount to a buyer for making a sizable purchase. This type of discount has usually been permissible, provided the discount is related to actual cost savings and naturally is offered to all customers.

Cumulative discounts allowed the purchaser to accumulate all his purchases over a period of time and qualify for a special discount. Since the settlement of the Morton Salt case, cumulative discounts have been questioned by the FTC. Morton's discount schedule was based on[17]

	Price per Case ($)
1. Less-than-carload purchases of salt at one time	1.60
2. Carload purchases at one time	1.50
3. Purchases of at least 5,000 cases during the course of a year.	1.40
4. Purchases of 50,000 or more cases per year	1.35

The FTC in this case pointed out several things. The first was that only five buyers in the United States could qualify for the largest discount. In effect, the government was saying that by offering cumulative discounts they were favoring the large buyer, who was allowed to accumulate his orders and get credit for them. Thus a firm that purchased 5,000 cases every month was given a special discount over the firm that purchased 5,000 cases perhaps only twice a year. It was the government's contention that there was no cost saving to the seller, since they both purchased in the same quantity, and there was no commitment on the part of the buyer to purchase any set amount.

Nevertheless, under the Robinson–Patman Act quantity discounts would be legal if the firm can demonstrate that cost savings were incurred by selling in larger quantities. Demonstrating this is rather difficult, for it requires that a firm keep

---

[16]*Ibid.*

[17]P. G. Peterson, "Quantity Discounts and the Morton Salt Case," *Journal of Business,* April 1952, p. 110.

extremely accurate records of all of its marketing costs. However, even if the costs are available, it becomes questionable as to how much of the saving can be applied to the larger purchaser.

The difficulties of accomplishing this are seen in the case where a firm producing 1 million tires a year and selling them at $10 was asked by a large retailer to produce an additional 500,000 and sell them to the firm for $8.

In the ensuing argument the firm showed that marketing cost savings were obvious in that the firm did not have to pay a sales commission, made only large full-carload deliveries, and could operate the plant without adding additional space. The increases in costs were only for materials and some extra production workers. The point was that the $8 per tire was a very profitable order.

The government's contention in this dispute was that the $8 price was only possible because the firm already had orders for 1 million tires from a variety of retailers. Furthermore, it was the government's view that those retailers who placed the orders for these tires should also share in the production cost savings. Hence the government allowed only direct savings in marketing costs and not production-cost savings, since all orders must share in the latter, because without one, the other's cost per unit would be increased.

Price Fixing

The Sherman Act has had its greatest impact in the area of price fixing, that is, situations where companies agree to fix prices at a certain level, or agreements between buyer and seller to fix resale prices.

The decision to price fix, aside from its moral and ethical considerations, can be costly to the firm. At one point it was thought that the Sherman Act was ineffective in that its criminal penalties call for a fine of $50,000 and/or a 1-year prison sentence. This view has changed, however, on the basis of the 1961 electrical equipment case where 29 producers of electrical equipment and 44 of their employees were charged with fixing prices. The net result of the proceedings was that firms were fined $11.8 million and the executives a total of $137,500. Twenty-three executives received a 30-day suspended jail sentence. In addition, a large number of treble damage suits were filed by former customers of these companies. Although no exact figure has been determined, it is reported that General Electric by 1964 had paid $173 million in claims![18] This case would seem to clearly indicate that price fixing among manufacturers is clearly in violation of the Sherman Act and can prove costly.

Resale Price Maintenance

One of the leading forms of legislation that tends to influence some manufacturers are the Fair Trade laws. In essence, these laws allow the manufacturer and retailer to circumvent the antitrust laws and enter into price agreements that establish a set retail price throughout the state. Since agreements of this type are banned by the antitrust laws, legislation had to be passed in order to nullify certain sections of the present law.

---

[18]Harper, *op. cit.,* pp. 96–97.

The first Fair Trade law was passed in California in the early 1930s. During the depression the California legislature under pressure from small retailers passed an amendment called the nonsigners clause. In effect, this clause made it mandatory for all retailers to agree to a minimum retail price on a branded product once a manufacturer signed an agreement with one retailer in the state. This became effective upon a public announcement to the trade.

Subsequently the Congress in response to unfavorable Supreme Court rulings on the nonsigner's clause passed the Miller-Tydings Amendment[19] in 1937 and the McGuire Amendment[20] in 1951. However, the impact of these amendments was weakened by antagonistic views toward nonsigner clauses by the various state supreme courts. As a result, even when the law is still in effect the onus of enforcing the clause falls upon the manufacturer.

The little enforcement that is maintained presently is in the cosmetic and drug industries. For example, Revlon maintains retail prices in New York State by vigorously enforcing the state Fair Trade Act. To accomplish this the firm must obtain a court order against all violators of the law. Revlon, however, is one of the few firms that would expend such an effort and incur such a cost.

Why would a manufacturer as a matter of policy attempt to maintain retail prices? In the case of Revlon one can assume that by doing this they curry the favor of retailers who favor lines that shield them from price competition. This usually results in retailers recommending Revlon and giving it a primary space allocation in the store.

As noted earlier, Revlon has one other view that may have ranked just as important in choosing this strategy. It is the view of management that the consumer associates quality with the price level in selecting cosmetics. It is their belief that the demand for cosmetics does not follow the usual relationship of lower prices resulting in higher volume. Price cutting would be particularly harmful to Revlon in the firm's view, since most discounters would feature their product since it has gained such wide acceptance among consumers.

SUMMARY

Establishing the most profitable price for a firm's product represents a decision that involves many considerations. Some of the more important ones are:

1. The cost of producing the product, which includes fixed and variable costs, and break-even analysis. Incremental costs are also a consideration, particularly when a firm is looking for additional business.

2. The objective of the firm as stated by management. Here the objective of the executive may be a consideration.

3. The firm's ability to correctly forecast demand.

4. The pricing policy of the firm, which considers the level of prices in relationship to competition. Thus policies of pricing below, above or with the market are a consideration.

---

[19] Amended the Sherman Antitrust Act.
[20] Amended the Federal Trade Commission Act.

Other pricing considerations are also relevant. For instance, in pricing new products the firm wanting to recover full costs of development may establish a skimming policy. Its choice could include a policy of penetration pricing.

The retailer can strongly influence the discount policy of the firm, when the retailer is powerful. Whatever the policy, the firm must consider the laws that affect pricing policies. The Robinson–Patman Act, the Sherman Act, and the Resale Price Maintenance Acts are of particular significance.

QUESTIONS

1. The higher the price for a product, the less the firm will sell. Comment.

*2. Demonstrate how the personal goals of the executive can conflict with the firm's objectives in making pricing decisions.

3. What are the major determinants of the demand for a product?

4. Define price elasticity and discuss its role in establishing a price for a product.

5. Relate fixed, variable, and incremental costs to making pricing decisions.

6. Why is it so often stated that a manufacturer has little use for historical cost information?

7. In Table 11-2 indicate the implications of raising the output from 5,000 to 6,000 units.

8. What steps have to be taken to carry out a policy of pricing above the market?

9. Why do manufacturers prefer to price with the competition?

10. Why do some firms find it difficult to follow a policy of varying their prices to their customers?

11. In what types of industry is price leadership most likely to occur?

12. Under what conditions would a firm engage in penetration pricing?

*13. Illustrate the use of price lining in a retail store.

14. Why would a manufacturer want to maintain fair trade prices for his product, particularly in view of the fact that the lower the price, the more he will sell?

*In-depth questions.

Communicating with the Customer

12

SUMMARY KEY

All the efforts put forth by a company to communicate its product and service to the public are called promotion. Promotion includes advertising, personal selling, publicity, and activities that are loosely referred to as involving sales promotion. The latter includes such activities as store displays, trade show exhibits, contests, and other similar activities.

Firms vary in the usage of each promotional technique. As a general rule, when the product is nontechnical, firms tend to spend more on advertising. In firms where the cost of contacting an individual customer is high and the potential return to the company is also high the firm would tend to rely on personal selling.

One of the problems with promotional activities is that it is difficult to measure or estimate their future impact. To overcome this, many firms rely on experiments and testing.

Advertising does not guarantee success nor does it indicate that a firm will eventually monopolize an industry. It is, however, a major means used by most firms to communicate with their markets.

The fastest growing media for advertising is television. Since 1950 all other media shares of the advertising dollar have declined. Newspaper advertising has been especially hard hit. As a result, newspapers have been forced to rely on local advertising of retailers more and more. Magazine advertising has also been decreasing with the resultant closing of mass magazines and the offering of regional advertising opportunities to national advertisers.

Strong criticism has been launched against advertising. In recent years the consumerism movement has called attention to several instances of misleading advertising in all media.

One of the most important parts of the firm's total mix is the planned strategy that goes into the firm's means of communicating its products and services to the consumer. All these efforts are called *promotion.*

Before discussing the makeup of the firm's total promotional mix, several comments can be made concerning the promotional mix that seem relevant to its role in the firm, particularly when the marketing concept represents the firm's philosophy.

The first is that whatever the firm does in the form of communicating and attempting to persuade the consumer to buy the firm's product or use the firm's services must be coordinated with the total firm strategy. To offer a simple example, if the firm defines its target customer as being a "well-heeled" executive, then they would certainly consider advertising the product in the *Wall Street Journal.* The general theme of the ad would also have to tie in with this concept of the firm's market.

Second, many firms survive today simply on the basis of their strong emphasis on promotion. However, at this point one should point out that although our tendency is to equate promotion with advertising it is not the latter that is always emphasized in firms. For instance, many firms stress personal selling as their major means of promotion. This is particularly true of those companies selling in the industrial field to users of basic products such as steel, copper, textiles, and other similar products. In addition, there exist many firms that engage in little selling or advertising, but rely on publicity or word-of-mouth advertising. An example of the use of different degrees of advertising would be in the motion picture industry, where word-of-mouth advertising is the most important vehicle for developing a success, as witnessed by the recent growth of low-budget pictures produced by unknown firms in direct competition with many of Hollywood's major studios. The promotion of a world's heavyweight fight would seem to be an example of promotion that places more stress on obtaining free publicity in the newspapers, arranging television interviews, and developing a "grudge fight" image for the event. Followers of baseball are well aware of the use of publicity in the development of the New York Mets baseball franchise, which has become the envy of baseball owners in the major leagues. Here, again, publicity and promotional devices (such as banner day, when the fans parade in the ballpark with their homemade banners espousing their love of the Mets) have helped them to attract not only the largest crowds seen at ballparks in many years, but have endeared them in particular to young fans.

Types of Promotion

When one considers that promotion represents an attempt on the part of management to persuade consumers to purchase a product or service, it is obvious that many activities fall under this definition. However, one usually recognizes four major types of promotion that would include all these activities.

The first and most obvious is the paid form of nonpersonal presentation called *advertising.* Advertising of this type always has a sponsor and more than likely is presented in mass communication media, such as television, radio, magazines, or newspapers. It may even be seen on billboards as one travels by auto.

The second activity that makes up the promotion mix is *personal selling,* which involves direct personal contact with the thought of persuading one to purchase the firm's goods and services. Personal selling need not be a direct person-to-person contact, but can be in the form of group selling, such as an auctioneer or the device engaged in by a number of companies of running house parties and selling the company products to the assembled group.

The third form of promotional activities engaged in by companies is what is termed as *publicity,* which refers to *free* news items that appear in communication media. These items are not paid for and thus do not qualify as advertising. Yet they are an important aspect of the firm's promotional efforts.

The last form of promotional activities is what is loosely referred to as sales promotion activities. These are activities other than advertising, personal selling, and publicity that help to stimulate sales. Although more will be said about these activities in Chapter 14, it is important to recognize that these activities do exist. Included under this definition are such diverse activities as store displays and trade-show exhibits, contests, coupons, and plant tours.

Decision Alternatives

The purpose of all promotional activities, of course, is to increase sales. The choice of which of the four types of promotional activities to spend most of the company's money on is of paramount importance and is constantly being reviewed.

Table 12-1 shows the tremendous variance one finds among firms' choices of advertising ratios as measured against outlays for personal selling. For example, firms producing food products seem to spend an average of $12 for advertising for every $1 outlay for personal selling. The converse of this ratio is found in the industrial equipment field, where the ratios are reversed 11 to 1.

Ratio of Advertising Outlays to Personal Selling Outlays   TABLE 12-1

Product Class	Ratio	Product Class	Ratio
Food products	12:1	Bulk seed	1:3
Lawn seed	4:1	Women's apparel	1:3
Grocery products	2:1	Paint	1:3
Malt beverages	2:1	Insulation	1:3.5
Lawn mowers	1:1	Kitchenware	1:4
Cellulose tape	1:1	Auto equipment	1:5
Furnaces	1:1.5	Control devices	1:6
Feed	1:1.5	Farm machinery	1:6
Roofing	1:2	Bakery flour	1:7
Electrical supplies	1:2	Industrial equipment	1:11
Bedding	1:3	Paper specialties	1:11

Source: P. J. Robinson and Bert Stidsen, *Personal Selling in a Modern Perspective* (Boston: Allyn and Bacon, Inc., 1967), p. 16.

Why is the emphasis reversed for these two types of goods? Why does it vary for most goods listed in the table? The answer to these questions, although not applicable in all cases, can be generally theorized by considering the product-market and the firm's outlook approach.

In the *Product-Market approach,* one usually indicates that where a product is practically nontechnical, low cost, and requires little shopping time on the part of the consumer, the firm selling the product tends to emphasize a nonpersonal or advertising approach in marketing the product. Thus a firm selling toothpaste would tend to spend most of its monies on advertising and little on personal selling. Conversely, a firm selling an item such as diesel engines would tend to emphasize personal selling (perhaps using sales engineers), and would do little advertising. What little advertising that would be done would probably be in the form of direct-mail advertising. All in all most theory would seem to agree that Figure 12-1 would tend to summarize the difference between industrial goods, which are sold in most cases on the basis of technical knowledge, and consumer goods, for which emotional factors are usually emphasized. In this figure one can see that as personal selling grows in stature in the industrial field the importance of advertising declines considerably. The opposite effect takes place in the sale of consumer goods.

FIGURE 12-1   Promotional Mixes for Consumer and Industrial Goods

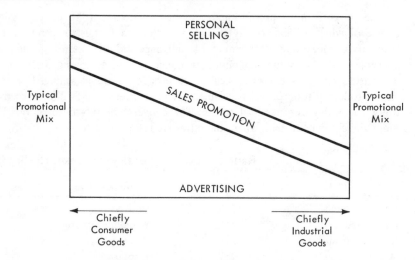

Source: P. J. Robinson and Bert Stidsen, *Personal Selling in a Modern Perspective* (Boston: Allyn and Bacon, Inc., 1967), p. 57.

The *Firm's Outlook approach* recognizes the firm's emphasis on cost values related to the potential return. In markets where the cost of contacting a customer on an individual basis is high in relation to the firm's ability to realize a substantial return, the firm would tend to emphasize the nonpersonal approach to promotion. Usually the characteristics of such a market are its homogeneity, with its markets dispersed over large areas.

On the other hand, markets for industrial products are characterized by relatively small groups of potential customers, where the expected conversion of the customer to a sale results in a large return to the company.[1] These customers may be found in only a few major areas of the country.

---

[1] P. J. Robinson and B. Stidsen, *Personal Selling in a Modern Perspective* (Boston: Allyn and Bacon, Inc., 1967), pp. 56–57.

Sales promotion outlays are among the most risky for management if one is interested in getting an adequate return on an investment. The problem with sales promotion is that nobody can tell you what the return from any given outlay will be. Many of the reasons for failure in any sales promotion expenditure cannot be reconstructed in terms of determining any rational behavior on the part of the consumer. On the other hand, there exist some segments of sales promotion that can be analyzed from a perfectly rational point of view. However, even these rational factors are in a sense uncontrollable in that their occurrence can cause distortions in the results. For instance, an advertised promotion of air conditioners or fans will be much more successful if the weather is unseasonably hot. The ratio of sales of soft drinks to coffee during a given season at a ballpark is directly related to the average temperature. The relationship of these factors to the sale of the product is reasonably determined.

On the other hand, much of the results of sales promotion are due to factors that are either so whimsical as to be unmeasurable, or so complex that we do not have the research abilities at this point in time to determine why they occur. A buyer for a major department store once cited the fact that during November of each year he ran a sale on English-made shoes for $7.99. The ad had been quite successful (the store accepted mail and phone orders), and thus the sales promotion manager decided to continue the same one-page ad year after year. One year, however, they received orders for well over $100,000 worth of shoes (practically double any previous experience) in spite of the fact that they had run the same ad in previous years. Unfortunately, they were unable to fill most of the orders since the shoes were purchased directly from England and were unavailable. Study of why the increase in sales occurred was unavailing. It is interesting to note that the following November the drawing power of the ad reverted to the normal amount of sales incurred during the previous years.

One could come up with some logical explanations. Perhaps the competitors were not competing as strongly during that one week. Although an examination of the ads did not show this, it could have been that their in-store displays were more enticing. Perhaps many consumers were under strong financial pressure during this particular year and hence were more prone to look for bargains. Perhaps the ad was run opposite a news story in the newspaper that attracted a large readership. Although these explanations all sound logical, the fact is that management was unable to isolate a reason that would help them repeat the performance. Perhaps a reason could have been uncovered if the firm engaged in detailed research. However, the cost of uncovering these data would be prohibitive in relation to the total dollars of profit involved.

The truth is that few firms are able to accurately predict the result of any sales promotion campaign. They are aware that the sales promotion activities they engage in will produce needed sales volume, but the overall impact can only be looked at historically; that is, more money expended will usually result in more sales.

Nevertheless, one should not get the impression that firms spend money on sales promotion without some sort of controls. One major guide of companies is the use of *pretesting* of all marketing campaigns, which includes all related sales promotion activities. For example, the mail-order division of a major publisher, before commissioning the writing of a book aimed at a trade (that is, businessmen), will many times send out a pretest mailing to a sampling of prospective users of the book. The results of the mailing of promotional literature will determine whether or not they will ask a potential author to write the book. If the returns from the mailing fail to get a response that the company considers to be promising, they may try another mailing piece or perhaps change the original price. If at this point they get a better-than-average return, they may commission the writing of the book.

Large advertisers in many instances will measure the impact of a new promotion or advertising campaign by simply running the effort in one city or major marketing area. If it is successful, then they may increase the campaign in other areas of the country until eventually it is nationwide. In some cases the campaign is measured against similar cities where the promotional campaign is not being run. In this way the firm can eliminate such variables as an unexpected increase or decrease in the demand for the product due to seasonal changes in consumer demand.

Most measuring devices used by large firms are historical in nature. That is, the firms measure what happens after they engage in several promotional activities. For instance, firms using coupons to promote their products can use the services of the Nielsen Company to evaluate the impact of the couponing on the sale of the product. The consumer uses a coupon to obtain a discount from a retailer, who is then compensated by the manufacturer who issued the coupon.

The evaluation of coupons is relatively simple since the company codes them in terms of (1) product description, (2) area code, (3) face value of the coupon, and (4) where a direct mailing is made, income by neighborhood.[2]

Product description is important, since most manufacturers that use couponing use them on several products. The code tells them what product the coupon is being redeemed for at the retail store. The area code indicates to management the weaknesses in their market coverage, and conversely the areas that seem to be most likely to redeem the coupons. The face value of the coupons indicates to management the impact of off-price deals on the redemption of coupons. For example, management may find that a 5-cents-off deal may be every bit as effective as an 8-cents-off offer. Conversely, management may find that the mailing of a 5-cent coupon may result in a substantially lower redemption rate than a higher coupon offering. In this case the coupon offers the manufacturer the type of control that can aid greatly in making decisions.

Role of Advertising

One is certainly aware in our society that advertising is a big business. Once one has scarcely started his day he is affected by advertising of all kinds. The most obvious place of all is the television set where billions of dollars are spent annually by American firms in order to sell their products. If one were to put on the radio, one would also be subjected to similar claims on behalf of products. Should one sit down in the morning and skim the morning newspaper, one would find similar attempts to persuade on practically every page of the newspaper. Should one go to the mail box, one might find advertising from manufacturers in the form of offers,

---

[2] A. C. Nielsen, Jr., "The Impact of Retail Coupons," *Journal of Marketing*, Oct. 1965, p. 12.

or perhaps coupons that offer discounts on products that are sold in the local grocery store. Stepping outside one may find billboards and signs on stores. Even a ride on mass transportation is usually not free from advertising, and here one may find posters inside or on the outside of the vehicle. No wonder when we examine advertising statistics we find that marketing firms spend about $85 per capita for media advertising in the United States versus $20 in Great Britain or West Germany and about $10 in France.[3]

These huge outlays for the various media give some indication of the hundreds of alternatives in terms of the strategy that may be employed. Some firms may make a choice of not advertising at all. Few firms selling consumer products to a nationwide market have made such a choice. In some way most firms manage to advertise the product to the consumer. Nevertheless, a large number of companies do not spend much money on advertising their product simply because brand recognition is not an important factor in motivating the consumer. Typically, products found in the local hardware store are not advertised extensively. For instance, hammers, nails, thumbtacks, and screwdrivers are not advertised to any substantial degree. On the other hand, one finds products in this same outlet that may have an elaborate advertising program behind them. Elmer's Glue, Rubbermaid products,and Scotch tapes are typically heavily advertised products.

As will be shown later, many firms spend considerable sums of money on advertising. Some may run as high as 30 to 40 percent of sales. However, most firms engage in modest advertising efforts and their choices of media and amount of expenditures are carefully considered and related to their market.

Advertising in the Marketing Mix

Advertising is usually only one aspect in the total marketing mix. In some firms it is among the most important of activities. In others it is of little importance and interest. In any case it has been recognized as an important force in developing and maintaining a market for a company. Nevertheless, there is good evidence that advertising alone cannot create a market nor maintain this same market without the rest of the marketing mix playing its part. In effect, what we are saying is that the ogre of the advertising monster is not true unless one understands that the other aspects of the marketing mix are just as important.

In Table 12-2 are shown 11 major industry classifications. Also shown are the concentration ratios based on the top four firms in the industry. When these ratios are compared to advertising as a percentage of sales ratios, it becomes obvious that the ratios are not related to industry concentration. As a matter of fact, in only three of the eleven industries does the advertising ratio exceed 2.5 percent.

This does not mean, of course, that advertising does not result in some sort of monopolistic tendencies. It would seem that if the listed soap companies were forced to stop advertising, one would assume that their share of the market would decrease considerably. What it does show, however, is that advertising alone cannot sustain a monopoly. It takes other factors in conjunction with advertising to accomplish such goals.

---

[3]*Proceedings, 14th Annual Conference,* Advertising Research Foundation, Oct. 15, 1948 (New York), p. 45.

TABLE 12-2 Concentration Ratios and Advertising Ratios Contrasted in 11 Industries

	Concentration Ratio (Percentage of Sales by Four Largest Companies)	Advertising (as a Percentage of Sales)
Motor vehicles	88.1[a]	0.9
Cereals	83.0	4.8
Other tobacco (cigarettes)	77.0	5.4
Tires and tubes	74.0	1.9
Sugar	65.1	0.3
Hats	63.2	2.1
Soaps	63.0	7.9
Distilled liquors	60.0	2.4
Motorcycles and bicycles	58.0	1.1
Cigars	54.0	2.4
Carpets	51.4	2.1

[a]1954

Source: Jules Backman, *Advertising and Competition* (New York: New York University Press, 1967), p. 92

For instance, one can see that the highest concentration ratios and one of the lowest advertising to sales ratios occur in the automobile industry. Although there are many reasons for this situation, one would certainly have to admit that the marketing efforts of several of the major automobile manufacturers are an important reason for their position. One of the major reasons for the success of General Motors is their ability to select and maintain top auto dealers in most of the major markets. The dealer is one of the key elements in the maintenance of a position in the automobile industry, because the manufacturer relies on the dealer to engage in aggressive selling and to service the automobile after it has been sold. In addition, many dealers must be able to supply parts to independent garages that repair the manufacturers' cars, but are not part of the franchise system. Setting up a dealership costs a great deal of money, and this ability to entice dealers into carrying their product is an important step in marketing automobiles. Many observers believe that this may be the most important part of the automobile marketing mix.

The results of a company's attempt to "cash in" on its advertising abilities and marketing abilities can be seen in Table 12-3. Campbell Soup, a company that has dominated the wet soup (canned) market, decided to enter and compete in the dry (dehydrated) soup market. Previous to its entry, Campbell was reported to have held 90 percent of the wet soup market. As a matter of fact, even today very few stores could risk customer ire by not carrying Campbell Soup products. After 4 years in the dehydrated market, and seeing its share drop in half from 16 to 8 percent, Campbell reported that it was dropping from the market after spending over $10 million on advertising.[4]

Two generalizations can be drawn from this observation. One would seem to be that spending a lot on advertising does not necessarily guarantee a firm a profitable

---

[4]Backman, *op. cit.,* p. 110.

Share of the Market for Dry Soup (%)　　TABLE 12-3

	1962	1963	1964	1965
Lipton	47	50	56	57
Knorr	25	22	14	12
Campbell	16	14	9	8
Wyler's	7	10	13	16

Source: Frank Biancamano, "Campbell Soup Co. Keeps Simmering Along," *Printers' Ink,* Nov. 25, 1966, p. 9, and P. J. Kelly, "Campbell Soup's Cup Runneth Over," *Printers' Ink,* Sept. 10, 1965, p. 21.

market. Second, although advertising is important in terms of some products, a firm marketing well-advertised and successful products in one market is not necessarily guaranteed success in other markets, using the same approach.

Advertising Expenditure Trends

Many major firms selling products to the American consumer engage in advertising as a means of persuasion. Advertising in 1970 for all media was slightly under $20 billion.

The figures in Table 12-4 indicate clearly that a strong trend toward television advertising has been developing in the past 20 years. For instance, in 1950 approximately 3 percent of all advertising went into television, whereas most recently about 18 percent of the advertising monies go into television.

Total Advertising Expenditures by Media: 1950–1972　　TABLE 12-4

	1950	1960	1972
Magazines	9.2%	7.6%	6.2%
Newspapers	39.7	30.8	30.3
Radio	11.6	5.8	6.7
Television	3.3	13.6	17.6

Source: *Advertising Age.* Prepared by McCann-Erickson, Inc.

Clearly, television advertising has the responsibility of carrying a firm's message to the public in many organizations. It is also clear that manufacturing firms have decided that since television has the ability to reach millions of people during one show it will continue to outdistance its rivals — newspapers and magazines. How important television is can be seen in recent years when politicians running for higher office have practically avoided the tedious job of meeting the public on a personal basis and have substituted a professionally handled television campaign that avoids the necessity of mingling with small groups. In his book on the presidential campaign of 1968, Joe McGinniss[5] gave the public a close look at how

---

[5] *The Selling of the President, 1968* (New York: Trident Press, 1969).

President Richard Nixon ran a television-oriented campaign, which deliberately avoided the usual practices followed in previous campaigns. It is widely believed that one of the factors responsible for Nixon's previous loss in 1964 to President Kennedy was his poor showing on television in comparison to his opponent.

It is not uncommon today for a political figure running for the Senate or a governorship to appoint an advertising agency to handle the forthcoming campaign. In any case, it is quite obvious that campaigning has changed from 1948 when Harry Truman won the presidency on the basis of a nationwide whistle-stop campaign. Most of the change is directly attributable to television.

Other Media

The growth of expenditures for television advertising has caused a decline in the share of advertising for the other major media. Magazines, newspapers, and radio have all experienced a decline in their share of advertising monies.

Particularly hard hit by the growth of television advertising have been the newspapers. Since 1950, newspapers' share of the total advertising expenditures has declined steadily and sharply. Since this trend developed, several changes in newspapers have occurred. The first has been the decline of the big city newspaper. Many cities that previously supported several daily newspapers have experienced the closing of many of these papers, to such a point that many of the major cities in the United States have only one or two daily newspapers. For example, New York City has only two major morning newspapers and only one evening paper.

Ironically, however, the number of newspapers in the United States has declined only slightly in the past several years simply because the suburban population movement spurred the development of many local suburban newspapers. However, many of these papers are small and do not have the impact that the big city papers have.

It is interesting to note that of the total advertising expenditures in newspapers, only about 20 percent are composed of national advertising. These are ads placed by companies with national distribution of their products. The balance of the advertising in the newspaper comes from local advertising placed by local retailers. This ratio of local to national has changed in the direction of more local-supported advertising in newspapers, indicating that the newspapers have lost some support from national manufacturers, who prefer television as the most efficient way of reaching many of their markets.

During this same period, the most dramatic decline for the use of advertising has occurred in the magazine industry. During this period, the large mass market magazine has simply gone out of business or has been forced to change its format to reach a segment or specialized market. The magazine format has several major failings in the view of the national product promoter. The first is probably the fact that the marketer can reach many more people through television more quickly than he can in a magazine. Second, magazine ads must be produced many months before the magazine appears on the newsstand. Third, there is a lot of wasted circulation in the use of magazines that sell to a mass market. In contrast, firms using television can run a commercial in any area of the country they desire.

Naturally, magazines have attempted to overcome this handicap and in some ways they have achieved this. For instance, many mass circulation magazines offer advertisers opportunities to place ads in certain regions only where the magazine is circulated. More importantly, many newer magazines and even some of the formerly larger magazines have turned to specializing in markets in order to attract advertising from manufacturers interested in these markets. Nevertheless, the advertising dollars going into magazines have declined considerably.

Perhaps the most interesting change in expenditures has taken place in radio. When looked at over the years, radio has lost its share of advertising dollars. Specifically, its share has declined from a high of 10.6 percent in 1950 to its present-day share of 6.7 percent. It is noteworthy, however, that in the past 10 years radio's share of the advertising dollar has increased, a phenomenon not experienced by other media, except of course television.

The reasons for the growth in radio advertising are many. Perhaps the increase in the number of radios, and particularly the availability of cheap portable transistor radios and auto radios, has spurred the development of this market. The increase in the number of local stations and the growth of the FM stations have increased advertiser interest in an inexpensive way of reaching a specialized market. More importantly, the character of local radio has changed. It is now directed specifically at the resident of the area and offers him programs that he is interested in. In other words, the radio as a media has become more specialized and aims at segments of the market. Listeners, therefore, can listen to classical music stations, popular and rock, news stations, discussion programs, or whatever type of listening they prefer. This has increased the interest in radio and perhaps more than anything else accounts for the increase in its share of advertising expenditures.

Criticism of Advertising

In recent years advertising has undergone a great deal of criticism. Perhaps some of this criticism is directly attributable to the growth of the consumer movement, as outlined in Chapter 4. On the other hand, one can certainly say that there is a growing recognition on the part of consumers that advertising is telling only the producer's side of the story. One can certainly cite numerous instances where this occurs. As an example, up until 1963 Anacin consisted of three ingredients — aspirin, caffeine, and phenacetin. In the advertising, the firm referred to the product as consisting of a "combination of ingredients." During that year, however, medical reports appeared that indicated that phenacetin might damage the kidneys, with the result that Anacin dropped the ingredient and thus became a two-ingredient product. The firm, however, continued to advertise the product as consisting of "a combination of ingredients," although the consumer was totally unaware that the number of ingredients had been lowered by one. This fact, of course, was not publicized.[6]

If the makers of Anacin were asked to reply to this statement, they might point out that in their view the product is still more effective than other pain killers on the market. In addition, they may indicate that their competitors would point this information out to the American public if they thought it important.

Another criticism falls into the category of "the half truth." For instance, Clorox has been described as "the most effective household disinfectant of its

---

[6]C. D. Edwards, "Advertising and Competition," *Business Horizons*, Feb. 1968, p. 73ff.

kind" by Procter & Gamble. In its advertising, Clorox makes the statement that no other bleach makes clothes cleaner and whiter. The Consumers Union makes the statement that this is true, but that many other bleaches (which also contain sodium hypochlorate in a 5¼ percent solution) give results as clean and white.[7] The statement, of course, implies that Clorox does a superior job, when in fact it probably cleans clothes no whiter than most of its competing brands. Although the firm of Procter & Gamble in this case is not telling an untruth, by implication it is telling what we may call a "half truth." This example reminds one of the airline to New Orleans that advertised "fastest to New Orleans." The slogan was truthful in that no other airline flew to New Orleans faster. However, since this airline was the only chartered airline that could fly the New Orleans run, it was also true that the airline was the "slowest to New Orleans!"

Little criticism is made of advertising that is found in classified pages of newspapers and magazines. Nor is advertising to industrial buyers subject to this type of criticism. Even advertising by local retail firms is usually free of the major criticisms launched by those who resent advertising. Although the local Better Business Bureau or the State's Attorney General may take action against certain disreputable retailers who intend to defraud the public, in reality little major criticism is made of retail advertising, since it is considered to be informational with a strong emphasis on price.

Much of the advertising that is presented on television passes the scrutiny of the Federal Trade Commission and in only a few instances has the government concluded that there is a definite action on the part of the company to make completely false statements about a product. On the other hand, one author noted that television does offer the firm an opportunity to demonstrate its product in such a manner that some of the cues offered the viewer may be considered to be questionable.[8] Cited are such examples as the recent use of lemon fresh odors as an indication that the product has the freshness and cleanliness of lemons, a characteristic that has nothing to do with the cleaning power of the soap product. Similar attributes are claimed for soap products that have a strong ammonia smell. Here again the strength of the smell has little to do with the product's cleaning superiority.

Color was also used to deceive the public according to this same paper. For example, the demonstration by Chevron that the exhaust from its gasoline would not make a plastic balloon as black as competitive gasolines was cited by the Federal Trade Commission as an attempt to mislead the public. The Commission noted that the cleanliness of a car's exhaust does not indicate lack of pollutants; in fact, some pollutants are colorless and fairly odorless, they observed.[9]

---

[7] *Ibid.* p. 72ff.

[8] Dorothy Cohen, "Behavioral Criteria for Determining Deception in Consumer Advertising," paper presented at the Fall American Marketing Association Conference, Sept. 1, 1971, Minneapolis, Minn.

[9] *Ibid.*

Communicating with the customer includes the following promotional activities:

1. Advertising (television, radio, newspapers).
2. Personal selling.
3. Publicity, or free news items.
4. Sales promotion activities (store displays, trade shows, contests, coupons, etc.).

The emphasis on each of these activities varies by industry and firm. A firm selling an industrial product is more likely to spend money on personal selling rather than advertising. A cigarette company would do the opposite.

The ability to measure and estimate sales that will occur as a result of sales promotion outlays is limited to testing and historically based estimates.

Advertising is perhaps the largest segment of the marketing mix. Television and newspaper advertising take the largest share. However, television is rapidly growing, whereas newspaper advertising is declining in terms of these same shares.

Advertising, since it is in direct contact with the public, has been under a great deal of criticism in recent years. This may be due to the growth of consumerism.

QUESTIONS

1. According to Table 12-1 what types of firms are more likely to spend most of their money on personal selling? Why?

*2. How would one go about measuring the results of a new display designed for supermarkets by a major beer company?

3. Why has television advertising usage by manufacturers gained at the expense of other media?

4. What has been the effect of this trend on newspapers?

5. What effect has this trend had on magazines?

*6. Discuss a recent commercial or ad you have seen from the point of view of the misleading information it offers.

7. Why do automobile companies have such a low advertising to sales ratio and yet maintain such a high level of concentration in the industry?

8. Would a manufacturer of chewing gum rely more on advertising or personal selling? Why?

*9. Contrast the Revlon Company and Avon, both producers and marketers of cosmetics, and their reliance on personal selling and advertising. Do they differ? Why?

*In-depth questions.

Developing an Advertising Strategy

13

SUMMARY KEY

An important step in using advertising is to first choose the theme. Corollary decisions that have to be made include determining the amount of money to be spent and carefully evaluating the effect that has taken place.

Advertising is used in different ways, depending on the product life cycle. At its introduction management overspends with little hope of recovering its monies in the short run; the outlook is definitely long run. As the product gains acceptance, the advertising expenditures and sales growth level out. As the cycle draws to a close, the firm is more reluctant to invest its monies into the product.

It is difficult to establish advertising budgets in any scientific way simply because of the difficulty of estimating the return that will accrue to a particular advertising program. Nevertheless, advertising budgets have to be made and firms ordinarily rely on one of three methods – the historical, goal, or subjective approaches.

In all cases the firm should experiment particularly in allocating dollars to product lines. Thus records of the impact of increasing advertising expenditures on each product or product line should be noted.

In organizing a large firm, most firms maintain a corporate advertising department at central headquarters rather than a separate department for each division. Some maintain an office in both places.

Most major firms employ the services of advertising agencies in order to produce the necessary commercials. The role of the advertising agency has been growing in that many agencies now help the client plan their total marketing program. The advertising agency has several departments – the media, research, creative, and account management departments. Agencies earn most of their fees from commissions (usually 15 percent) received from the medium where they place their advertising.

Obvious problems exist when a firm tries to measure the results of its advertising. In some cases firms attempt to pretest an advertising campaign. Testing can be classified into two major groups, *artificial* tests, which use order of merit and paired comparison devices, and *real-condition* tests.

The variance among the many products in terms of the amount of money spent on advertising is due to many factors. Certainly, the type of product and its

technology play a role, as does the motivation of the buyer. The size of each
purchase also plays a role.

273
*Developing
an Advertising
Strategy*

technology play a role, as does the motivation of the buyer. The size of each
purchase also plays a role.

There are many legal restraints on advertising. The major laws that affect
advertising are the Federal Trade Commission Act, Wheeler-Lea amendment, and
the Robinson-Patman Act.

If one carefully examines the advertising appearing in a media, he will become
aware that the ads usually carry a distinct theme. Reflecting on this, one should be
aware that the firm that produced the advertising had many choices of themes to
select from. A manufacturer of a detergent could emphasize many product
attributes in his advertising. He could emphasize its price, its cleaning ingredients,
its packaging, or perhaps its smell. He might also consider its ecological attributes or
perhaps call attention to a free gift enclosed in each box. Other soap manufacturers
may note that the product is guaranteed. No doubt, this list of advertising themes is
incomplete.

In making a choice the firm may use the service of its advertising agency, its own
advertising department, and, if available, its own or independent research services.
In effect, the theme of the advertising has been carefully thought out and selected
from a group of alternatives.

The choice of a theme is not the only decision management must make. The
amount of money to be spent is obviously an important corollary to an advertising
program. The amount to be spent looms vital in the final selection of the media to
be used.

The final step in any management procedure is to be able to evaluate, through
controls, what has happened. In accomplishing this, management uses research
procedures as an aid to evaluating the decisions made previously.

Developing a Strategy

Advertising, since it is totally controllable by the firm, sets out to accomplish
specific things. Some of these objectives may be stated specifically in these terms:

1. Call to the attention of the public the introduction of a new product.
2. Uncover new prospects for the firm's salesforce.
3. Develop a brand image for the firm's products.
4. Develop goodwill for the company.
5. Steer consumers to the proper retail outlet.
6. Create continuous interest in the product on the part of both middlemen
and consumers.

Although this list has hardly scratched the surface, it is sufficient to indicate that
the task of advertising can be manifold. Each objective requires special study and
perhaps the selection of different media in order to accomplish its task.

Advertising Cycle

It may be recalled from an earlier chapter that products usually go through a life
cycle, whether the time period is 50 days or 10 years. For many products a life
cycle of advertising can also be detected. Figure 13-1 indicates how this life cycle of

FIGURE 13-1   Product Life Cycle and Advertising Expenditures

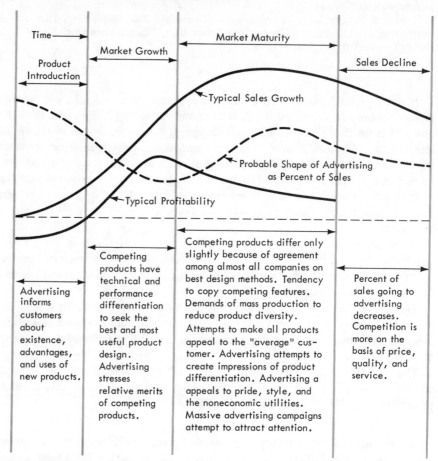

Source: J. W. Forrester, "Advertising: A Problem in Industrial Dynamics," *Harvard Business Review,* March–April 1959, p. 108.

advertising follows the product life cycle. This figure indicates that at the beginning of the product life cycle advertising expenditure increases should exceed sales increases. During the introductory stage the goal of advertising is to inform potential customers that the product now exists and of the merits of the product. Depending on the product and the industry, it is at this stage that advertising expenditures are made all out of proportion to the possible immediate gain. A firm introducing a new product may spend millions from coast-to-coast without any possible hope of recovering this expenditure in the short run. At this stage, it is obviously the long-run gains that excite management to the extent that they will expend such huge sums of money. For example, the day Rheingold decided to introduce its first nonfattening beer, Gablingers, in the eastern part of the United States, they spent a reported 1 million dollars in order to reach 60 million people in one day.

Thus the main task of advertising at this stage is to acquaint the market with the new product, spelling out the details of its uses, but mostly informing people of its existence.

If the product has been carefully tested and properly designed, it then enters the second stage of development, the *market growth* period of development. During this period, advertising as a percentage of sales reaches its lowest point for two reasons: (1) the product is growing in sales at a rate that usually exceeds management's estimates, which indicates that the product has strong market acceptance; (2) the saturation level of the product is usually far off, and thus advertising efforts receive above-average response. During this period of time, the advertising effort includes mainly the comparison of the merits of the product with competing products. At this stage the consumer is now well aware of the availability of this product and others like it, and is now in a position where the relative merits of the products enter more fully in making a product choice.

At some point in time both the product and the advertising growth rate level out and enter what one calls the *maturity stage.* Although sales and expenditures for advertising tend to expand during this period, they expand at a much less rapid rate than during the previous period. At this stage, the firm is hard pressed to differentiate its product from competitors. This has come about because competitors now copy many of the key features of the leading product in the industry. At some point one might say "all products look alike." All products at this stage may be aimed at the mass market, and hence product diversity is difficult to maintain, since costs must be kept minimal to meet the demands of this massive market. Since all products are basically similar, the advertising then takes on the task of creating an image for the product, rather than dwelling on actual product differentiation. At this stage, most advertising monies are spent, and in advertising some products the campaign may reach national importance, relying on millions of dollars of expenditures in order to keep the product ahead. For the first time, however, the firm will usually find that the saturation level has been reached and that increases in sales are hard to come by.

Depending on the product, the market maturity stage may last for many years. For instance, automobiles have been in this stage for many years. Conversely, a new record or book may maintain this same period for no more than 1 month. In any case, at some point in the life cycle of a product a period of declining sales sets in, and management becomes less and less interested in investing money in advertising. The actual dollars of advertising at this stage decline sharply. Most products start to lose money, and many firms may abandon such products. Advertising at this stage in the product cycle may place great stress on price. The decline of advertising expenditures at this stage indicates strongly that management does not expect to receive a productive return on its promotional expenditures. In all likelihood the sales decline of the product will continue. Its actual decline may take years, but eventually it will cease to be profitable, at least in the mass markets.

Setting advertising budgets is not a science. In fact, it was reported in one study that few companies have a formula that is useful for establishing advertising expenditures.[1]

**Setting
Advertising
Budgets**

---

[1]D. L. Hurwood, "How Companies Set Advertising Budgets," *The Conference Board Record,* March 1968, p. 34.

It is not surprising to learn that most budgeting for advertising is subjective and gives one the impression of being unscientific. Estimating for advertising runs into many difficult problems. First and foremost, it is almost impossible to determine consumer reaction in advance. For any given dollar of investment, management has only the slimmest of chances of determining the exact response they will get from the consumer target.

Second, the economy's stage in the business cycle is a strong influence on the consumer response for certain types of goods. During the 1970 recession, for example, automobile sales of all major firms declined in spite of the advertising expenditure. However, one should also note that during such a downturn most firms cut back on their advertising expenditures. This supports the belief that most firms consider that advertising expenditures are most productive when the economy is progressing.

Third, the artistic effort in the advertising may be responsible for the success of an advertising campaign. If the quality of these efforts is particularly creative and efficient, a response to an advertising campaign may be greater than at any similar period of time. The importance of the creativity of advertising can be seen in the interest among large firms in the "small creative advertising shops." Many of these firms have grown in the past 10 years and have strongly influenced not only the advertising themes, but also the marketing programs for many firms. One particular agency, for instance, influenced American Motors to offer air conditioning on one of its model cars as standard equipment. This same agency, it was suggested, also influenced the design of the new Gremlin model car produced for the first time by the company.

Finally, it is practically impossible to measure the influence of one advertising effort on the sales of a product to such a degree that management can find advertising measurement useful in decision making. For example, it is quite obvious that if General Motors did not run any advertising in this coming year, they would still sell many cars. The problem really is how many cars would General Motors not have sold if they didn't advertise. Although later in this section we shall discuss advertising measurement and testing, its value at this point in time is rather limited, and much more effective when one measures the results of an individual theme or a part of the firm's campaign.

Basis for Setting Budgets

Advertising budgets are set on the basis of three major techniques, usually referred to as the historical, goal, and subjective approaches. The *historical* approach refers to the firm establishing a set ratio of sales as the determining factor in the setting of an advertising budget. For example, in a company that previously has maintained an advertising to sales ratio of 3 percent, the firm projects sales for the coming year of $50 million. The advertising budget will be approximately $1.5 million. This ratio has been established in the past, historically, as the firm's best and most productive ratio.

Firms using the historical approach are among the most numerous. However, management in many of these same firms finds that the establishment of a historical figure is much too rigid and reduces the opportunity of remaining flexible. Flexibility is an important ingredient for those companies in industries where advertising is an important tool of management. As a result, many of these firms use the advertising *goal* approach to establish budgets. The goal approach is much more flexible in that it does not predetermine the size of the advertising budget.

As implied in its name, the goal method goes about establishing first the basic objectives that the firm's advertising program will attempt to accomplish. As an example, the firm may decide to introduce two new products during the year, expand into a new marketing area, and introduce its present line of products in several new marketing channels. Knowing this, the company then sets out to design an advertising and total sales promotion program to accomplish these goals. At this point the company's advertising department may actually determine the media, types of advertising, and the total costs of accomplishing this program during the coming year. This plan then becomes the firm's budget after review by a top committee.

The last method, referred to as the *subjective* approach, is used mainly in companies where advertising is not the major means of reaching the public. For instance, a company in the industrial field that depends heavily on its sales force may find this approach entirely suitable. In this case the firm will establish its budget for the sales force first, and then consider its advertising budget. This latter budget will be determined on the basis of the executive's experience and judgment. In most cases not much work goes into making this determination.

Product Line Budgets

Although the preceding methods relate to the overall company budgets, much the same methods may be used in setting budgets for the various divisions of the firm.

Once the budget is established, the firm still must allot its budgeted monies to each of its divisions. This allocation problem is usually solved on the basis of past performance of each division and perhaps the future plans.

On the other hand, the firm must at some point decide which divisions will benefit the most from increased funds. It would be unusual were a firm to decide to allot advertising funds equally to each division.

Should a firm pursue this allocation in a systematic manner, they might develop an experimental procedure as illustrated in Table 13-1 for the ABC company and its four divisions A, B, C, and D.

Table 13-1 shows that in the first month (T_1) the budget for division A is 20 percent higher, B is normal, C is down 20 percent, and D is normal. In the following months similar changes are made.

In Table 13-2 one sees the results. The indications are that division A reacts dramatically when the budget is varied. Thus during the first month, when the advertising budget was increased by 20 percent, the net revenue of the division increased by 22 percent. Conversely, in month T_3, when advertising was reduced by 20 percent, sales in this division decreased by 19 percent.

Division D, on the other hand, reacted much differently. In fact, the net revenue of this division did not seem to be affected in any way by an increase or decrease in

TABLE 13-1   Experimental Schedule of Advertising Budgets for ABC Company

| Division | Monthly Periods | | | |
	T_1	T_2	T_3	T_4
A	Up 20%	Normal	Down 20%	Normal
B	Normal	Up 20%	Normal	Down 20%
C	Down 20%	Normal	Up 20%	Normal
D	Normal	Down 20%	Normal	Up 20%

Source: Adapted from J. L. Simon, *The Management of Advertising* (Englewood Cliffs, N.J.: Prentice-Hall, Inc., 1971), p. 138.

TABLE 13-2   Net Revenue Results of Experimental Variation in ABC Company

| Division | % | | | |
	T_1	T_2	T_3	T_4
A	+22	+2	-19	-2
B	+2	+10	-3	-9
C	-7	-1	+8	-1
D	+1	-2	-2	+2

Source: J. L. Simon, *The Management of Advertising* (Englewood Cliffs, N.J.: Prentice-Hall, Inc., 1971), p. 139.

the advertising budget. One could assume therefore from this experiment that the firm can safely shift funds from division D to division A, and expect favorable results.

Organization of the Advertising Function

In the typical corporation one finds a main corporate office and separate offices for each of its major divisions. The latter may actually be separate companies, such as in a conglomerate, or they may simply be large divisions of a large firm, such as a specialized steel division of a large steel company.

In organizing an advertising department, the divisionalized firm has several options. One, of course, is simply to maintain an advertising department at the corporate headquarters. This department would be in charge of developing the total advertising program for all divisions of the firm. In addition, it would take on the added task of maintaining the firm's overall corporate image.

The other choice for the firm is to maintain a corporate advertising staff and also to see to it that each division has its own advertising department.

It would seem, based on a survey conducted by the National Industrial Conference Board, that most major companies maintain an advertising department at the corporate level only. Of 166 divisionalized firms, 73 maintain this arrangement. Forty maintain advertising departments at the divisional level only, and the balance of 53 maintain advertising departments at both the corporate and divisional levels.[2]

---

[2]*Advertising, Sales Promotion, and Public Relations – Organizational Alternatives,* Experiences in Marketing Management 16 (New York: National Industrial Conference Board, 1968), p. 3.

The reason for maintaining advertising departments at the corporate level only seems obvious. First, since top executives who make the major decisions are at corporate headquarters, it does not seem illogical that the head of advertising, who manages a function that is of paramount importance, should be located at the same place. Additionally, it would also seem that corporate headquarters is the most logical place for the advertising department to coordinate the corporate image. Thus, when a firm wants to maintain one image in the mind of the consumer for all of its various divisions, it would seem that the advertising department is best located at the central headquarters.

In spite of the logical explanations for maintaining a corporate advertising department, there are many objections to its maintenance in a divisionalized firm. One of the most telling complaints is that the corporate advertising department is almost always hard pressed to maintain sufficient knowledge about each division's particular communication problems so as to prepare meaningful advertising. This is particularly true in firms that handle more than one product line, and particularly so in firms where the product lines are not related in any way. Thus for a conglomerate firm such as W. R. Grace, with its various divisions selling everything from plastics to shopping bags, the maintenance of a single corporate advertising department would seem to be an almost impossible assignment.

In addition, the maintenance of only a corporate advertising office in a divisional firm involves the problem of maintaining communication with each division. Thus, although many firms still maintain a single corporate advertising department by hiring specialists in each area of the company's business, it is still an awesome task to maintain communications with all divisions. In addition, if all other functions are maintained at the divisional level, such as planning and product management, it would make coordination of all these efforts extremely difficult.

In the overwhelming majority of cases, the advertising manager reports directly to the marketing head or sales manager. The reason for this is that advertising under today's marketing concept must be totally integrated with the rest of the effort of the firm. Thus, since the marketing head is charged with the coordination responsibility, it is only natural that he have advertising directly under him.

In respect to the other major communication functions, that is, sales promotion and public relations, both of these departments usually report directly to the advertising manager, and develop programs and plans through his office. Again, the organizational choice depends on the relative importance of advertising and the need to coordinate other communication functions.

In some firms the advertising director is also in charge of the sales function and does not have a separate department. In firms where sales promotion represents an enormous part of the firm's outlay, the department may be separate and may report directly to the marketing head. However, it is more likely that in most firms such departments report directly to the advertising manager.

Advertising Agency

Most major firms use the services of an advertising agency in producing the necessary advertising materials. Ordinarily, an advertising agency helps the manufacturer produce the necessary artwork, filmed production, and copy to launch his advertising campaign throughout the year. In addition, the agency helps the manufacturer to select the proper media for presentation of the campaign. Thus a typical advertising agency will actually produce the television commercials that appear on the home screen. In addition, they will select the programs they will be shown on. Ordinarily, the advertising agency will produce the copy and artwork found in most newspaper and magazine ads. Here again they will select the newspapers and magazines in which this ad will be shown.

The important role played by advertising agencies can be seen in Table 13-3, where the billings of the top 30 agencies are shown. One can see that the total amount of advertising carried by these agencies is considerable and represents a substantial proportion of the advertising one sees in the various media.

In the past 10 years the role of the advertising agency has been undergoing great change. Most major agencies have taken an active role in the marketing decisions that must be made by each firm. This role has been expanded due to the development of the marketing concept, which holds that advertising must be integrated with all other facets of the total marketing mix. Thus the advertising agency has been asked not only to carefully plan campaigns and produce the necessary services, but also to act in the role of a consultant and help the company make the necessary decisions concerning the product strategy.

Many major manufacturers have started to listen to the counseling of advertising agencies because of a recognition that they have depth of experience through their handling of thousands of products. In addition, and most importantly from the manufacturer's point of view, many advertising agencies maintain sophisticated research departments that can be of great assistance to the manufacturer.

Advertising Agency Organization

To understand these changes, one has to be familiar with the organization of the advertising agency. Typically, one finds several divisions within the large advertising agency. Most agencies contain a media planning department, research, account management, and creative services.

The *media department* makes the choices of the media that are to be used to convey the client's message. The question asked on all occasions is shall we advertise in magazines, newspapers, radio, or television, use direct mail, or is there some other medium we might use? Once the media department chooses certain media, the next problem becomes how much shall we spend on each and which ones shall we choose? In the area of magazines one might ask, shall we advertise in a women's magazine, a mass magazine, a sports or perhaps a news magazine? All these decisions are made by the media department and are based on past experiences and, most importantly, information obtained from the firm's media research department.

The *research department* represents a major department in many of the large advertising agencies. The above-mentioned media research department may spend all of its monies on determining the media that is to be used for the client's products. One large advertising agency in New York boasts a research staff of 40 people engaged in media research. On this same staff are approximately 35 additional people engaged in supplying technical services to their clients and other divisions of the agency.

TABLE 13-3 Billings of 30 Agencies in the over $25,000,000 Group (add 000,000)

1972 Billing Rank World	1972 Billing Rank U.S.		World Billing 1972	World Billing 1971	U.S. Billing 1972	U.S. Billing 1971
1	1	J. Walter Thompson Co.	$767.0	$779.0	$393.0	$421.0
2	8	McCann-Erickson	625.0	593.9	207.7	232.9
3	2	Young & Rubicam	563.5	503.5	357.7	317.3
4	4	Leo Burnett Co.	471.2	423.6	313.4	300.3
5	6	Ted Bates & Co.	457.8	424.8	252.8	244.8
6	9	Ogilvy & Mather International	399.2	315.2	200.0	180.0
7	3	Batten, Barton, Durstine & Osborn	370.1	331.5	323.2	296.1
8	5	Doyle Dane Bernbach	323.0	280.3	259.1	234.9
9	7	Grey Advertising	314.0	256.0	247.0	195.0
10	17	SSC&B	269.4	239.8	134.7	122.6
11	10	Foote, Cone & Belding Communications	266.5	235.0	194.3	174.5
12	11	D'Arcy-MacManus & Masius	231.0	245.0	181.0	185.0
13	16	Benton & Bowles	225.7	198.5	160.2	141.3
14	13	Needham, Harper & Steers	205.9	155.6	171.5	139.0
15	12	Dancer-Fitzgerald-Sample	183.0	170.0	178.0	164.9
16	21	Compton Advertising	177.3	174.8	102.3	101.0
17	27	Norman, Craig & Kummel	168.9	163.4	67.7	68.2
18	14	William Esty Co.	165.0	151.0	165.0	151.0
19	15	N. W. Ayer & Son	163.0	148.3	163.0	148.3
20	20	Kenyon & Eckhardt Advertising	126.7	117.7	107.0	99.3
21	18	Wells, Rich, Greene	118.3	110.0	112.4	104.6
22	22	Ketchum, MacLeod & Grove	116.3	107.1	99.8	94.1
23	19	Campbell-Ewald Co.	112.0	121.8	112.0	119.8
24	25	Marsteller Inc.	99.8	90.0	81.9	73.8
25	23	Clinton E. Frank Inc.	86.8	79.2	86.8	79.2
26	24	Cunningham & Walsh	85.2	77.3	85.2	77.3
27	26	Campbell-Mithun	76.0	75.0	76.0	75.0
28	28	Ross Roy Inc.	60.3	49.5	60.3	49.5
29	29	Bozell & Jacobs	60.1	53.8	60.1	53.8
30	30	Gardner Advertising	59.0	59.6	57.7	58.6

Source: *Advertising Age*, Feb. 26, 1973, p. 30.

The next major division of the advertising agency is the *creative department*. This division includes all the production activities required in creating all the commercial artwork and copy needed to produce the advertising message. Television, the major user of such services, has caused many of the agencies to establish separate divisions within the agency to handle commercials for this media.

The last major division or activity is that of *account management*. This department handles the relationship between the agency and the client. It is its function to make sure that the plans of the client are in line with the advertising plans being turned out by the agency.

Agency Fees

For the services they perform, most advertising agencies derive income from two major sources, commissions and direct client payments.

About two thirds of agency services are paid for by the medium they place advertising with. For instance, should a large agency buy television time for an automobile advertiser for $1 million, the agency would receive a 15 percent commission from the television network, $150,000. In the actual workings the television network will bill the agency for $850,000, while the agency will bill the client for $1 million.

The balance of the agency's income is derived from billing clients for services provided over and above the placing of advertising. For instance, the agency may be asked by the client to conduct a research study, or the client may request special drawings for further promotional work; or the agency may offer to produce the client's television commercials. All these services may be charged for by the advertising agency.

On the other hand, many of the particularly large agencies are reluctant to make special charges for many of these services, particularly to large accounts. The agencies may be satisfied with receiving the 15 percent discount as payment for all the services they perform for a client. However, there is a general movement in the advertising field for the agency to receive additional compensation for its efforts, since the agency is providing many more services to the client than in former years.

Problems in Measuring Advertising

One executive was quoted as saying "we know 50 percent of our advertising is productive, the only problem is that we don't know which 50 percent." This represents a fair appraisal of the present ability of management to estimate precisely the contribution of advertising to the company's sales and profits. There are some serious problems that must be overcome if a firm is to measure advertising. They are

1. Many advertising efforts cannot be measured in terms of sales. The role of advertising includes also the ability to develop a product image in addition to creating sales.

2. Many advertising efforts are long term in nature and thus cannot be measured in the immediate future. Many firms attempt advertising programs that will pay off in sales only after a long period of time has elapsed.

3. Many advertising efforts have been influenced by previous advertising promotional efforts. For example, should General Motors attempt to measure an

advertising campaign on behalf of its Buick automobile, it would have to discount all the previous advertising done and determine that it had no effect on the present advertising. Additionally, it is difficult to determine the impact other forms of advertising have had on the consumer. For instance, even if one could measure the impact of a television commercial on the sales of Buick, it would be difficult to be accurate, because the consumer is also exposed to newspaper advertising, billboards, radio commercials, and so on. It would, therefore, be unrealistic to indicate that increased sales were solely due to the television advertising.

4. Sales measurement is usually limited to products that the consumer reacts to immediately. Thus one might get an immediate reaction to an offer to sell a $10 camera. It is unlikely that one will get many immediate reactions to an advertised tour of the Orient, since such a purchase implies a considerable amount of planning and the cooperation of other individuals.

5. Since sales cannot be used as a guide in the advertising of items that require a period of gestation, other measuring devices are used. Many of these devices are not always related to sales. For example, one may substitute the ability to recall your advertising, or the number of people who remembered a number of important incidents in your television commercial, or a change in attitude toward your product once they were exposed to the commercial. In all these cases, favorable responses do not necessarily mean that the firm will sell more merchandise.

In spite of these problems, firms still engage in advertising research and testing.

Advertising Testing

In an earlier chapter we discussed marketing research. Marketing research is used to develop plans and strategy for the future of the business. In effect, marketing research feeds back information to management concerning changes and new developments in its markets. In many cases marketing research may establish the effectiveness of the products being sold and the programs that are presenting these products. In many cases information gained from marketing studies will indicate the type of media to be used.

In most large companies the preceding description of marketing research is separated from what is now being called "testing." Advertising testing has as its goal to measure the advertising program in total or some specific elements of that program.[3]

Advertisers are interested in testing advertising both before and after it has been run in various media. *Pretesting* of advertising involves the testing of the message in the advertisement in terms of the illustrations, the words, and the print impact.

The "after" testing procedures are much more sophisticated and costly since the number of variables and coordination required are much more complex. At this stage one has run the advertising, set up a meaningful schedule, and assigned various monies to each of the media. This type of research involves a great deal of time, sophisticated methods, and is costly.

The main concern with testing is that (aside from using a valid measurement device) it be relevant to the firm's problem. For example, if the firm is launching a new product, the test must determine whether or not people are aware of this new

[3]C. H. Sandage and Vernon Fryburger, *Advertising Theory and Practice,* 7th ed. (Homewood, Ill.: Richard D. Irwin, Inc., 1967), p. 551.

product. One may also measure in this case whether or not the parties being reached are good prospects for buying the newly launched product. If a cigarette company is engaged in trying to switch people to their brand of cigarette, then the measure must be some test that can measure change in brand shares.

One can divide advertising tests into *two major groups,* those that are *artificial* (i.e., consumer opinions or recall tests are staged) and those that are tested under *real conditions.* In the first grouping, one has opinion, attitude, and recall tests. In the latter, we have controlled experiments.[4]

TABLE 13-4 **Opinions of 25 Respondents Concerning the Relative Merit of Eight Advertisements**

Respondents	A	B	C	D	E	F	G	H
				Advertisements				
1	1	5	7	8	3	4	2	6
2	4	7	6	3	2	1	5	8
3	1	8	5	3	4	2	7	6
4	6	4	2	1	5	3	8	7
5	2	7	4	6	3	5	1	8
6	5	8	3	2	4	1	7	6
7	2	7	6	5	4	1	8	3
8	7	6	5	4	1	2	3	8
9	2	5	7	8	6	1	4	3
10	4	6	8	5	1	2	3	7
11	3	2	1	4	7	5	6	8
12	5	7	6	2	4	3	1	8
13	3	8	7	1	6	2	5	4
14	4	7	8	5	3	2	6	1
15	2	4	8	6	3	1	5	7
16	4	3	6	1	8	7	2	5
17	1	3	7	6	4	2	5	8
18	1	2	8	3	6	4	7	5
19	6	7	2	5	1	3	4	8
20	5	8	7	2	6	1	3	4
21	4	1	2	7	8	5	3	6
22	1	6	3	5	7	2	8	4
23	5	7	3	4	2	1	6	8
24	5	2	7	4	3	1	6	8
25	4	8	6	1	7	2	3	5
Total	87	138	134	104	106	63	118	150
Average	3.48	5.52	5.36	4.16	4.24	2.52	4.72	6.00
Rank	2	7	6	3	4	1	5	8

Source: C. H. Sandage and Vernon Fryburger, *Advertising Theory and Practice,* 7th ed. (Homewood, Ill.: Richard D. Irwin, Inc., 1967), p. 570.

----

[4]*Ibid.,* Chaps. 25–27.

Most advertising testing in the artificial groups is conducted before the advertising is run. In some cases respondents are asked to rate two advertisements and choose the best one. Although many techniques and means of measurement are used, two of the most popular are the order of merit and the paired comparisons method.

The *order of merit* system is a group method for ranking a number of advertisements. The relative standings of each advertisement are tabulated and the ad with the lowest score is considered to be the most highly thought of by the consumer. This technique is illustrated in Table 13-4. It can be noted that the respondents have ranked ad F first and ad H last. The problem with this technique is obvious; most people end up guessing when they start making comparisons among eight different advertisements. At best, most of their answers are vague evaluations.

To avoid this problem, many firms are switching to *paired comparison tests.* This technique consists of comparing the eight ads, but on an individual basis. Thus each individual ad and the scores are kept. Table 13-5 illustrates this technique. Thus one finds that ad A was ranked a winner four times; the winner, however, is ad C, which won seven times and thereby ranked first.

This technique also suffers from problems. The most important is that when a large number of ads are to be compared the various combinations can be endless.

Individual Score Card in Paired Comparison Test   **TABLE 13-5**

	A	B	C	D	E	F	G	H
A	—							
B	A	—						
C	C	C	—					
D	A	B	C	—				
E	E	E	C	E	—			
F	A	B	C	D	E	—		
G	G	G	C	G	G	G	—	
H	A	B	C	D	E	H	G	—

Source: C. H. Sandage and Vernon Fryburger, *Advertising Theory and Practice,* 7th ed. (Homewood, Ill.: Richard D. Irwin, Inc., 1967), p. 570.

For instance, even in making the comparison among the eight ads, 28 comparison tests had to be made.

Several other tests are available for ranking ads in terms of the consumer reaction to proposed ads. One of the most interesting in recent years is the testing of television commercials conducted in studios, particularly in New York City. In this artificial situation a few hundred individuals are invited into a studio and asked to indicate their brand preferences for products before viewing a series of commercials (sometimes tied in with filmed entertainment). At the conclusion of the commercials, the viewers are asked to indicate their preferences again for the same products. Any change attributable to the commercials is duly noted and, when measured against standards, a judgment is made as to how effective the commercial will be. Significant attitude change toward the advertised product would seem to indicate a strong commercial, whereas negative or no change would seem to indicate the opposite.

This latter measurement device suffers from many shortcomings. One, of course, is the artificiality of the technique. People involved in this test are asked to vote on products that may not hold any interest for them, and the circumstances under which the measurement is taken are far removed from a real-life situation. Nevertheless, a number of manufacturing firms have made decisions on commercials after conducting in-studio tests.

Other research firms have attempted to reduce the artificiality of the in-studio test by subjecting consumers to commercials in their home environment. By using this technique, some feel the research firm can find it easier to get cooperation and can pick out more easily those that will cooperate. Again, however, the showing of planned commercials in the home is still an artificial situation.

Another type of advertising test is the *recall test.* It is the view of those conducting these tests that recall tests can determine how effective the advertising is on the basis of whether or not a person can recall seeing an advertisement. The theory underlying this technique is that if more people recall a commercial or ad it follows that they are more likely to purchase the product. One of the longest established rating services is the Starch Ratings produced by the Daniel Starch organization. This organization tests the recall of readers of magazine advertisements. Each ad in the magazine is rated according to whether they were "Noted" (percentage of readers who indicated they saw the ad), "Seen-Associated" (percentage of readers who indicated they had read any part of the ad), and "Read Most" (the percentage who indicated they had read over 50 percent of the reading matter in the ad).

Other variations of recall tests exist, for instance, tests that tell those who are interviewed the advertising slogan and ask them to identify the company and product. In all cases the major criticism leveled at this type of research is that the recall ability does not necessarily indicate that the consumer will purchase the product.

Real-Conditions Testing

To overcome the criticism of artificiality and questionable assumptions concerning the saleability of a product, many research people have developed experimental or controlled research techniques.

In this sort of test, two groups are usually used, those that are exposed to the advertising variable and those that are not. Comparisons between the two groups result in an evaluation of the impact of the variable on the person exposed. One of the longest established techniques is the *"split run"* studies in which a newspaper or magazine alternates the running of two ads in a specific issue. By keying replies to the ads, it can be concluded that differences in responses are due solely to the impact of the ad.

In more recent years many firms have developed control techniques for testing that involve elaborate statistical models and preparation. In one case a large firm decided to determine whether or not the injection of supporting radio spot advertising would help sell a product that was heavily advertised on television. To

287
*Developing
an Advertising
Strategy*

make this determination, the firm took a measurement of retail sales in two similar cities. Then, after a few weeks passed, they injected the radio commercials in one of the cities, but not in the other. By comparing the results in each city as measured against their first measurement, they were able to determine that the radio spots did not seem to increase the sales of the product. At that point they decided to stick with their previous television format.

Many of these experimental design techniques are entering a stage where they are relatively more complicated than anything done previously. With the aid of the computer, many firms find that a great deal of statistical manipulation can be carried out and more analysis can be developed to solve problems. Nevertheless, most of the advertising testing performed today is of the less complex design discussed.

Table 13-6 indicates the advertising outlays per dollar of sales among different groups of products. As an avid watcher of television, one can guess that cigarettes, beer, toilet preparations, and soaps would be expected to rank in the first 10 biggest spenders in relation to sales. Cigarette advertising has been recently banned from television by the FCC.

Advertising Decision Making

Advertising Sales Ratio   **TABLE 13-6**

		Advertising Outlays per Dollar of Sales, 1967 to 1968
1.	Perfume, cosmetics, and other toilet preparations	10.75
2.	Soap, detergents	10.89
3.	Drugs	9.54
4.	Beer and malt	5.96
5.	Watches and clocks	4.89
6.	Tobacco	6.04
7.	Wines, brandy	4.44
8.	Confectionery	3.25
9.	Cutlery, handtools, hardware	3.85
10.	Grain-mill products	3.43
11.	Photographic equipment	2.56
12.	Distilled liquor	2.53
13.	Appliances	2.42
14.	Bakery products	2.37
15.	Hotels	2.13
16.	Tires and tubes	2.10
17.	Radio and television	2.00
18.	Paints	1.66
19.	Dairy products	1.58
20.	Footwear	1.61
21.	Household furniture	1.14

Source: *Advertising Age,* Jan. 25, 1971, p. 77.

Several general conclusions can be drawn from this table. The first is that impulse products are those that receive the highest advertising support. This would certainly be true of cigarettes, drug preparations, liquor, and soaps and detergents. The second factor is that the firms at the top of the list invariably have developed strong brand interest among consumers. The same items are good examples of this view. For example, when brand loyalty is a minor factor one finds little advertising support per dollar of sales. Apparel, for example, is not even on the list.

One comment concerning this list that does not appear in this analysis is the view that in industries where there is little relationship between the material cost of the product and the final selling price one will usually find a substantial proportion of this retail price supported by large advertising outlays. Soaps and toilet preparations are typical of this view. One cosmetic firm recently admitted that the material product costs of its lipstick were less than 10 cents, although the product was sold all over the country for over $1. The huge difference between the material cost of the product and the retail price was principally due to large promotional expenditures on the part of the manufacturer. It is not unusual for a cosmetic manufacturer to spend over 20 percent of his sales dollar on advertising. This fact is reflected in the table, where it can be noted that the top companies engaged in selling toilet preparations spend more than 10 times the amount spent by the companies with the lowest advertising sales ratio listed in the table.

In a sense the table represents management's view of the importance of advertising in the total mix. Those products at the top of the list, of course, are examples for which advertising is the most important part of the mix. Those at the bottom of the list, or those which do not appear on the list, because they are small advertisers, find advertising to play a minor role. Most products that are advertised fall somewhere in the middle. Management determines the amount of advertising according to the nature of the product and in a theoretical manner, which may be called marginal analysis.

The nature of the product is depicted in Figure 13-2. Here one sees that in marketing an industrial product advertising plays a minor role in the marketing mix. Conversely, in the sale of a grocery product or, in particular, a mail-order product, advertising is an important factor in marketing.

This figure, of course represents a simplification. It is a fact that many companies in the industrial field have developed sophisticated advertising programs and have managed to successfully market such products. However, this is ordinarily the exception rather than the rule.

Why does advertising play such a minor role in industrial advertising and a more important role in the marketing of consumer products? One answer lies in the buying motivation of the industrial buyer and the quantity that he consumes. In addition, the type of product plays an important role. For example, much of the purchasing in the industrial field may be technical. Thus No. 3 wheat can be purchased in many markets and should meet the same standards all over. Here the product is very difficult to differentiate and advertising will then play a minor role. Steel, for example, can be bought on a technical basis, and again differentiation is minor. When industrial products are bought on a technical basis, buyers are usually more interested in delivery and the reliability of the company. Finally, purchases in the industrial field are usually large and the firms concentrate geographically. As a

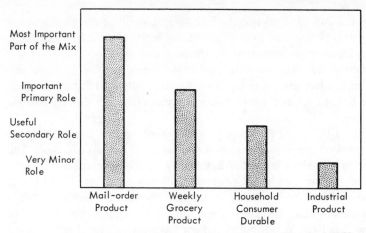

Source: Gordon Medcalf, *Marketing and the Brand Manager* (Elmsford, N.Y.: Pergamon Press, Inc., 1967), p. 139.

result, the manufacturer of industrial products need only locate a few customers and need not concern himself with reaching massive markets. Advertising, therefore, is used sparingly.

The buyer of consumer products buys in smaller quantities and does not rely on technical purchases as such. Factors such as the image of the product and emotional motives are more important to the consumer than to the industrial purchasing agent. These values can be explored and enhanced through advertising, especially to mass markets.

The power at the federal level to restrain advertising is derived from three major acts. They are

Legal Restraints on Advertising

1. The Federal Trade Commission Act (1914).
2. The Wheeler–Lea Act (1938), amending the FTC Act.
3. The Robinson–Patman Act (1936).

The Federal Trade Commission has within its power the ability to prohibit "unfair or deceptive acts or practices" by firms. This clause would, of course, give the Commission the power to examine cases of false advertising. This power does not mean that "puffery" is forbidden on the part of the seller, but it does include half truths, misleading statements, or falsehoods.

A "half truth" would be illustrated by the bread manufacturer who advertised each slice of his bread had less calories than the competitors. The statement was true since he had cut the bread slices thinner!

A misleading statement could be the cheese manufacturer who advertised his product as "Swiss cheese," but manufactured the product in Finland. His point would be that the cheese had a certain taste and contained holes that most Americans associate with Swiss cheese.

289

A falsehood would be the drug manufacturer who indicated his product could cure the common cold.

The Wheeler-Lea Act strengthened the FTC by specifically spelling out some of the merchandise areas where this type of advertising tends to prevail. Specifically, the act identifies food, drugs, cosmetics, and therapeutic devices.

Until the Wheeler-Lea Act, the FTC could take action only when there was evidence that such advertising was injurious to competition. This act made it possible for the FTC to act in cases where a practice was unfair or deceptive to the public.

In addition, the FTC gained enforcement power. Now the FTC's orders are final 60 days after served on the advertiser, unless the advertiser appeals to a court. The FTC can also get an immediate injunction against any advertising practice.

The Robinson-Patman Act (1936) restrains advertising in the sense that it restricts the manufacturer from offering competitive allowances to retailers, unless it is on a proportional basis. In effect, the manufacturer must offer cooperative advertising allowances to all his customers and not just a few.

Other Restraints

Several other restraints exist in the form of acts and government agencies. In the drug industry, the Federal Food and Drug Administration (a branch of the Department of Health, Education, and Welfare) controls the labeling and the establishing of standards for many drug products. It has been particularly interested in establishing the safety of drugs and chemicals. An important part of its task is to curb illegal drugs, and weed out medical quacks and false therapeutic claims.

In many areas of drug and food production the government establishes standards that must be adhered to. Labeling of these products must conform to government standards for their ratings. For instance, the government has established minimum content standards for aspirin. This requires that all producers of aspirin must meet these requirements if they are to indicate that their product is aspirin.

Other governmental decisions also have an impact on advertising to some extent. For instance, the Federal Communications Commission reviews the quality of the advertising when reviewing television and radio station licenses for renewal.

The Post Office Department has the power to act against mail fraud in advertising. In addition, it has the power to establish standards for publications in terms of the types of materials that may be judged to be obscene.

SUMMARY

In developing an advertising strategy the firm is faced with many considerations and choices. Some of these considerations are

1. The position of the product in the product life cycle. At different levels the need for advertising varies.
2. The type of product sold. As a general rule, the convenience product attracts more advertising effort than the shopping goods or industrial product.

In terms of the organization of the advertising department,

    1. Most companies maintain central advertising departments. This causes problems in firms with many divisions. Thus some firms have decentralized their advertising departments or maintain both central and divisional departments.

    2. Most manufacturers use an advertising agency to support their office efforts.

    3. Advertising budgets are set on the basis of one of three techniques — historical, goal, or subjective approaches. The historical is the most widely used.

QUESTIONS

*1. Describe the choice of advertising themes available to the manufacturer of furniture.

  2. At what stage of the product life cycle will a manufacturer be more likely to spend most of his advertising money? When will he spend the least?

  3. Why is it so difficult to measure the impact advertising will have on sales?

  4. Distinguish between the three major techniques used to set advertising budgets.

  5. What advantages and disadvantages accrue to the firm using the historical approach to advertising budget making?

  6. A company marketing several lines of different products maintains an advertising department in each division of the firm. In order to save money they are considering centralizing the advertising department at corporate headquarters. Under what conditions would you recommend that they take this step?

  7. Why do most major advertisers use advertising agencies?

  8. What types of artificial testing techniques are used to measure the impact of advertising? What are their shortcomings?

  9. In examining Table 13-6, would you say that a general pattern is discernible?

10. What role does the motivation of the buyer play in determining the amount of advertising money that will be expended?

*In-depth question.

Sales Promotion
and Personal Selling

14

SUMMARY KEY

Sales promotion activities can best be thought of as bridging the gap between advertising and selling. Most sales promotion activities involve work at the retail level. Sales promotion activities range from conferences to the issuing of trading stamps.

Two types of sales promotion activities are usually identified as those that are passive or *indirect* and those that are *direct* in their impact on sales. Direct activities in this area include consumer premiums and coupons. Indirect include publicity and public relations.

Cents off, bonus packs, and premiums are widely used promotional devices, particularly in food stores. Offering free samples is another direct promotion that can have an immediate effect on sales.

Cooperative advertising is one of the major direct promotional tools used by a manufacturer. It is particularly useful to the manufacturer in that it not only calls attention to his product but also tells the potential consumer where the product can be purchased. Point-of-purchase materials also rank high on the list of preferred promotional activities on the part of the manufacturer.

The most effective indirect techniques include trade shows, where both consumers and retailers are made aware of the industry products, free publicity in the form of planted stories in the general media concerning the firm's activities or new products, and general sales promotion activities as found in the cosmetic industry.

The role of the salesman is undergoing a great change in our society. In effect, he must be better trained and more knowledgeable than in previous eras. The insurance salesman is an example of this change. All sales compensation plans have advantages and disadvantages. The major types are the straight salary, straight commission, and a combination plan that uses both.

Training and hiring salespeople are costly. To keep this expense within reason and to enable the firm to hire the best salespeople, firms engage in pretesting of potential applicants, establishing current reports as a means of watching their behavior, and what are known as post tests. These involve using quantitative measurements, such as sales salaries related to expenses or a measurement of sales volume. Qualitatively, the salesman can be judged by the types of firms he sells to or, more directly, the number of customer complaints that develop.

Although in a number of companies advertising takes precedence over other means of communicating with the customer, it sometimes is relegated to a secondary position behind the firm's sales promotion and personal selling activities.

Sales promotion activities can best be thought of as bridging the gap between advertising and selling. Most sales promotion activities involve work at the retail level, described as the most important three feet in marketing.

Personal selling, of course, involves a direct approach to selling the product. Many firms use personal selling as their major device for selling the product. All the other potential activities play a lesser role. An extreme example of the role of personal selling can be seen in the operation of the Avon Cosmetics Company, which is represented by over 450,000 salespeople throughout the world. Although most of these people are part-time workers, the emphasis of the firm on direct selling is obvious. Other cosmetic firms place a much greater emphasis on advertising and sales promotion activities, such as point-of-purchase displays.

Sales Promotion

As noted, sales promotion activities are aimed at the point of sale. Although more will be said about these activities, it is sufficient now to note that most are concerned with stimulating the retailer to sell the product or the consumer to buy the product.

Why does the manufacturer engage in such activities? The answer lies in the contrasts between the retailer and the manufacturer. As will be noted later, the retailer is not concerned directly with the sale of a manufacturer's product. He is not concerned, for instance, with the sale of the ABC pen, but is more interested in the sale of all pens in his store. His lack of concern in the ABC stems from *his* view that if the pen doesn't sell he can get another that will. Thus he may very well treat each pen alike; and in most cases the manufacturer can expect little emphasis on his particular product.

On the other hand, the manufacturer of ABC pens is only interested in the role of his pen product, and understandably he may resort to sales promotion activities to enhance its role.

This does not say that the store does not engage in sales promotion activities. They do in the form of direct mailing, contests, and storewide campaigns. For instance, a major store recently featured merchandise from Italy in all the store's departments. In this promotion they gained the cooperation of the major Italian airline and the Italian government. All week the store featured products and foods from this country. During another season the store featured a similar program, this time showing products from Finland.

Most of the store's activities in this area are retail oriented; that is, they attempt to bring customers into the store. They are not product oriented, and hence the manufacturer feels obliged to engage in activities that serve his own purpose.

Table 14-1 lists most of the activities falling under our definition of sales promotion. The extent of these activities can be seen from this list. Some, of

TABLE 14-1 Examples of Sales Promotion Materials and Activities

Catalogs	Price lists
Conferences and conventions	Product publicity
Consumer literature	Promotional literature, brochures
Contests for prospects or distributors	Prototype and use-test exhibits, facilities
Coupons	Sales and product bulletins
Customer seminars	Sales training materials
Direct mail	Salesmen's contests, awards, incentives
Displays	
Distributor services	Salesmen's selling aids
Distributor training materials	Sampling
Exhibits	Service and maintenance manuals
Giveaways	Slides
Mats and other materials for retailer ads	Speakers' bureau
Merchandising	Special-purpose advertising
Movies	Specification data sheets
Plant tours	Trade-show exhibits
Point-of-purchase materials	Trading stamps
Presentation devices (flip charts, other	Training materials for maintenance and user personnel

Source: *Advertising, Sales Promotion, and Public Relations — Organizational Alternatives,* Experiences in Marketing Management 16 (New York: National Industrial Conference Board, 1968), p. 91.

course, are widely used, such as coupons. Others are not as widely used by most firms. The variety of choices listed in this exhibit does indicate that there are many approaches to spurring the sale of the firm's product through means other than advertising and personal selling.

Types of Promotional Activities

Although all sales promotion activities have as their goal the stimulating of sales, they vary in their impact and approach. Here one can distinguish between two types of sales promotion activities, those that are passive (indirect) and those that are direct.

Passive activities are those that are not directly concerned with immediate sales. In a sense they are indirect. Specific examples are speakers bureaus, where an investment firm such as Merrill, Lynch, Pierce, Fenner, & Smith, Inc., supplies speakers to clubs to explain the workings of the stock market and investment activities. Although direct sales may result from such work, the firm feels that this work calls attention to the public that the firm exists. In this way they hope that this knowledge will eventually result in future sales.

Publicity and public relations activities also fall into this grouping. The purpose of both is to call attention to the products or activities of the firm in a favorable manner, thereby creating goodwill and, hopefully, sales in the future. Some public relations activities are particularly indirect, such as calling to the attention of the press a talk given by a company top executive or introducing to the press some facet of the business that is news and casts favorable light on the firm.

Direct activities are mainly concerned with increasing sales almost immediately. They include offering the consumer premiums, coupons, or in some cases cents off on the purchase of a company product. In measuring the impact of such activities, management usually measures sales.

In some industries direct sales promotion activities are an important means of increasing sales at the retail level. In a study of such activities, Alfred Gross noted that cents-off promotions were used as a major tactic by firms selling food, drink, and household (cleaning, laundry, etc.) and personal (bar soap, dentifrices, and shampoo) products. In this same study he found that other forms of direct promotion were less of a factor, but nonetheless an important part of the programs of many of these companies. For instance, in Table 14-2 it was shown that cents-off promotions were used on the average of once a year for each company brand. Coupons (included in the package or advertised in media) were used an average of 0.51 per brand. Other activities, such as the offering of a premium, refund offers, and bonus packs (usually where the firm offers a free product with the purchase of another), were used much less.

Direct
Promotional
Activities

Use of Promotion Tactics (1967 to 1968 Average):   **TABLE 14-2**
Average Number of Promotions per Brand per Year

Promotion	All Categories	Food and Drink	Household	Personal
Cents off	0.985	0.66	1.52	1.55
Bonus pack	0.13	0.13	0.13	0
Coupons (all)	0.51	0.56	0.39	0.58
Refund offers	0.19	0.26	0.04	0.16
Premiums (all)	0.33	0.35	0.30	0.21

Source: Alfred Gross, *A Descriptive Study of the Use of "Cents-Off" Promotions By Manufacturers of Grocery Store Products* (Teaneck, N.J.: Consumer Research Institute, Inc., Nov. 1969), p. 17.

When analyzed by product category, a slightly different picture emerges. In the case of cents off it becomes clear that the firms selling household and personal-need products use cents off as a major tactic. As indicated in the table, they are used over one and one half times per brand during the year. Cents off seems to be less of a weapon in the food and drink categories.

In Table 14-3 one sees that these promotional activities were maintained over long periods of time. Most of these activities lasted for over 2 months and, when broken down by types of products, one finds some of the offers lasting well over 3 months.

TABLE 14-3 Use of Promotion Tactics (1967 to 1968 Average): Average Number of Months per Promotion

Promotion	All Categories	Food and Drink	Household	Personal
Cents off	2.46	3.17	1.83	2.02
Bonus pack	2.52	2.16	3.15	0
Coupons (all)	2.23	2.35	1.73	1.07
Refund offers	2.32	2.00	7.40	2.00
Premiums (all)	3.56	3.85	3.00	2.00

Source: Alfred Gross, *A Descriptive Study of the Use of "Cents-Off" Promotions By Manufacturers of Grocery Store Products* (Teaneck, N.J.: Consumer Research Institute, Inc., Nov. 1969), p. 20.

The length of time involved and the amount of usage are further verified in Table 14-4, where one sees the sales impact from these activities as measured by annual sales volume. Here one finds that cents off seems to be the most important promotional activity in terms of increasing sales by about 27 percent over the period studied. Other activities accounted for important increases also. Although one may question the exactness of these figures, they do represent an important part of the firm's sales plans.

TABLE 14-4 Sales Impact from Promotion Tactics (1967 to 1968 Average): Estimated Percentage of Annual Sales from Use of Each Tactic

Promotion	All Categories	Food and Drink	Household	Personal
Cents off	27	31	26	21
Bonus pack	18	19	17	0
Premiums (all)	14	12	15	14
Coupons (all)	13	13	3	12
Refund offers	13	12	12	65

Source: Alfred Gross, *A Descriptive Study of the Use of "Cents-Off" Promotions By Manufacturers of Grocery Store Products* (Teaneck, N.J.: Consumer Research Institute, Inc., Nov. 1969), p. 23.

Other Direct Activities

Perhaps the four largest sales promotion activities that can be classified as direct are retail couponing, sampling, cooperative advertising, and in-store displays. The latter is usually referred to as point-of-purchase displays.

Retail Coupons

As noted previously, a major stimulant of consumers at the retail level are retail coupons. These coupons usually offer the consumer a price reduction when redeemed in the retail store for the manufacturer's product. The retailer, in turn, receives a premium from the manufacturer when the coupons are returned, averaging about 3 cents per coupon. A typical coupon may offer the consumer 5 cents off the retail price when he purchases Crest toothpaste. These coupons are widely used in the food industry. Every year billions are issued by the manufacturers. Of the 20 leading manufacturers in the food industry, 14 are among the top 20 couponers.[1]

The decision to use a coupon depends on the needs of the firm. It represents a natural means of introducing new products. The coupon usually helps the firm to overcome resistance on the part of the consumer by offering him an incentive to try the product. The coupon used in this manner usually offers the consumer a substantial reduction in price over the shelf price of a competing product.

Another major use of the coupon is to act as a *pull-push* force on the retailer to stock a product that may be either just introduced in the area or one that has not had much retail support previously. The theory is that retailers (particularly small outlets) will succumb to the pressure of coupon-bearing consumers who insist that the store carry the product. This type of promotion has another effect in that the company salesman finds it easier to sell the product, since the coupon has already stirred up interest.

Finally, coupons can be used as a means of reducing inventories. In cases when the firm finds that it has oversold or overproduced the product, the firm can use coupons to help reduce inventory. When the firm is changing the product package or making a price adjustment, coupons are also a valuable means of accomplishing this without running into retailer resistance.

Although using coupons for the purposes described is a strategy employed by many firms, there exist many drawbacks to this type of promotion. One major problem is the recognition on the part of many manufacturers that the coupons are not being redeemed for their products, particularly in the small grocery store. Thus a customer receiving a coupon for, let us say, Crest toothpaste is allowed by the merchant to receive the same reduction on Colgate toothpaste. Since the merchant need only send in the coupon to Crest (Procter & Gamble) and receive payment, he can accommodate the consumer in this way. Naturally, this is a violation of the agreement on the part of the retailer, yet he may find he is under pressure from a good customer to do this. How many times this type of transaction takes place is anybody's guess. However, many companies believe that it is enough of a problem to print on their coupons that they must be used only on their products and "any other use is fraud. . . ." Or in the case of Q-Tips (a cotton swab) the coupon states, "This coupon is redeemable only by retail dealers handling Q-Tips Cotton Swabs. Invoices proving the purchase of sufficient stock of Q-Tips Cotton Swabs to cover coupons presented for redemption must be shown upon request."

Another problem related to coupons is that based on the number of people who actually use the coupons the distribution costs can be substantial per redeemed coupon. Many offered coupons are not redeemed and, although statistics are not available, it would seem that the number of redeemed coupons would be small in comparison to those offered to the public.

It must be remembered, however, that coupons are offered to the public in a variety of ways. Many large firms offer coupons as part of their advertisements in

---

[1]A. C. Nielsen, Jr., "The Impact of Retail Coupons," *Journal of Marketing,* Oct. 1965, p. 11.

both magazines and newspapers. Thus, the reader may simply tear the coupon out of the advertisement and redeem it for the product at the local grocery store. The low redemption rate of these coupons is due solely to the fact that these media are read for other reasons and are used, in many cases, by all members of the family. In fact, tearing out coupons from a newspaper may interfere with the reading of the paper by members of the family. As a result, the tearing out of the coupon may be left until every member of the family has read the paper. The result of all this is that many interested parties forget to save the coupon before throwing the paper out. The same problem holds true for the coupon inserted in the magazine.

Perhaps the most effective couponing technique is for a company to send a consumer a variety of coupons through the mail. The problem here is that it is a costly means of distributing coupons. It has become so costly that most firms tend to mail several coupons in order to take advantage of the initial cost of the mailing. As a consequence of this high cost, several large firms have combined with other types of promotional firms in order to reduce their mailing costs. One large soap manufacturer recently included with his coupons a certificate that entitled a consumer to subscribe to a national magazine at a reduced price. The national magazine in return paid for a substantial portion of the mailing cost.

The last problem associated with using coupons is that the consumer, once offered the price reduction, may not respond favorably to paying the regular price when the promotion ends. Although one can only speculate on this happening, since no hard evidence is available, it would seem that consumers would react in this fashion.

Sampling

Closely related to the use of coupons is a technique usually referred to as sampling. Samplings are nothing more than giveaways by manufacturers in order to get customers to try their product. This product is usually new, but in many instances may be an old product with a new feature.

The use of sampling is particularly followed in the soap industry and among producers of household personal products. It was recently noted by Lever Brothers, one of the world's major soap manufacturers, that sampling was so intensive in a recent year that the free samples had the same effect on sales as if the housewife had stopped doing laundry for 3 weeks.

Samples of the product are distributed in a variety of ways. The most prevalent are through mass mailings, advertising, door drops, and handouts.

Mass mailings include the insertion of coupons that offer the customer an opportunity to obtain either a free product or obtain sharp discounts on the item being promoted.

Advertisements placed in the media many times offer the consumer free samples of a product by having the consumer simply send a request to the firm. One firm ran a series of ads in *Parade* magazine over a period of time offering the consumer 19 products worth $18 for $3.75.[2]

Handouts, usually in food stores, are familiar means of getting the products in the hands of the consumer at the point of sale. General Foods recently used this

---

[2]*Advertising Age*, Sept. 20, 1971, p. 8.

tactic to introduce its new iced-coffee powder mix in several areas of the country. Welcome Wagon accomplishes the same thing for many firms by distributing free products to new homeowners.

The door drop is widely used by soap companies. Ordinarily, the soap firm pays an organization to distribute the product to each apartment or house dweller in an area. In recent years the door drop has become a little more sophisticated in that the distributor is sometimes asked to ring the bell and perhaps inform the housewife of the free package. In some cases, when nobody answers the door, the distributor is instructed not to leave a free sample. In other cases, the distributor is actually urged to present a low-keyed sales pitch to the housewife. The latter two methods are particularly expensive and resorted to only when the firm feels the product will not reach the party it is intended for.

Cooperative Advertising

Aside from selling merchandise through direct advertising of goods to the ultimate consumer, the manufacturer many times makes the choice of offering advertising allowances to all retailers who will advertise the manufacturer's product. This allowance is called cooperative advertising. Its intent, from the manufacturer's view, is to indicate to the consumer where he can purchase the product. For example, a manufacturer of cameras may offer Macy's $500 or perhaps half the cost of an ad in order to entice them to run ads displaying his camera. Once the ad is placed, Macy's sends the manufacturer a tearsheet of the advertisement as it appeared in the newspaper and a bill for the manufacturer's share of the cost of the cooperative advertisement.

Cooperative advertising is an important source of funds for the retail firm. Table 14-5 indicates that a substantial number of departments in department stores receive cooperative allowances. These range on the average from a low of 7 percent to a high of 100 percent.

Lines of Merchandise for Which Cooperative Advertising Was Used and the Percentage Paid by Cooperative Funds for 44 Pennsylvania Department Stores[a] **TABLE 14-5**

Number	Line of Merchandise	Percentage of Department Advertising Paid by Co-op	Low and High Percentage Paid by Co-op Advertising
21	Major appliances	62	31–100
22	Small appliances	47	5–90
16	Housewares	39	1–65
18	Radio, phonograph, TV	50	30–75
5	Records and instruments	30	10–50
11	Furniture and bedding	36	5–75
18	Mattresses and springs	38	5–75
3	Lamps and shades	27	5–50
9	Rugs and carpets	29	5–75
6	Other floor coverings	56	50–75
9	Draperies and curtains	22	5–5

TABLE 14-5 (cont.)

Number	Line of Merchandise	Percentage of Department Advertising Paid by Co-op	Low and High Percentage Paid by Co-op Advertising
7	China and glassware	26	1-5
3	Gift shop	31	10-50
8	Toys and games	36	2-85
2	Luggage	27½	5-50
4	Small leather goods	32½	10-50
2	Candy	55	10-100
6	Silverware and jewelry	54	2-100
3	Clocks and watches	23	10-50
9	Costume jewelry	36	10-75
8	Women's coats and suits	24½	2-50
16	Women's dresses	30	2-50
32	Underwear, slips, robes	41	5-50
34	Corsets and brassieres	52	5-100
8	House dresses, aprons, etc.	15	3-33
35	Hosiery	52	5-80
19	Women's shoes	37	5-100
12	Blouses, skirts, sportswear	27	3.7-50
5	Millinery	100	100
5	Girl's wear	37	10-50
12	Infants' wear	31	3-50
9	Men's clothing	24	1-50
8	Children's shoes	36	5-100
9	Men's furnishings and hats	34	5.7-50
7	Boys' wear	28	1.3-50
3	Men's shoes	7	2-10
10	Piece goods and domestics	25	2-75
14	Notions	40	10-50
3	Books and stationery	27	15-50
4	Soaps and cleaners	50	50
22	Drugs and toiletries	52	50-75

[a]44 stores checked at least 1 type of merchandise.
Source: *Advertising Allowances,* Hearings before the Select Committee on Small Business, U.S. Senate, Eighty-eighth Congress, First Session, on Competitive and Antitrust Aspects of Joint Advertising Programs by Retailers, and the Nature and Purpose of Advertising Allowances Given to Retailers by Manufacturers and Wholesalers (Washington, D.C.: Government Printing Office, 1964).

Much of the advertising monies for cooperative ads accrue to the larger firms simply because these arrangements are based on the size of the purchases a retailer will make. Advertising allowances are common practice in both the department store and food fields.

The manufacturer has several important purposes in developing a cooperative advertising program. The major purpose would seem to be to help the dealer sell more merchandise. However, when one examines that motive, it would seem to be misleading, since the manufacturer need not have the retailer promote his product, for as we have already noted he can go directly to the consumer and advertise, create demand, and thus sell his product.

A more important reason for the manufacturer to use cooperative advertising is to gain patronage identification for his product. By patronage identification, one refers to the consumer's ability to find a store where he can purchase the product. By advertising a product for the manufacturer, Macy's indicates where it may be purchased. One should not overlook the fact that by advertising the product Macy's implies also their approval of the product and the manufacturer who is marketing this product. This is particularly useful to a manufacturer of a new product or a manufacturer that is not well known.

The size of the manufacturer's cooperative program with retailers seems to depend on two major factors: (1) what the law allows, and (2) the control the manufacturer has over the outlet he sells through and the type of product he is selling through this outlet.

The law is fairly clear on the point of advertising allowances. There is no restriction on the size of the advertising allowance as long as it is offered proportionately to all retailers. If a manufacturer offers a cooperative advertising allowance to a large chain, it must also offer the same deal to a smaller chain on a proportionate basis.

The control the manufacturer has over the outlet he sells to is indeed the major deciding point for a manufacturer contemplating a cooperative advertising program. For example, manufacturers of food products have no opportunity to control the number of outlets in the food field, nor where or how their products are displayed in the food store. In other words, the food manufacturer has little control over the outlet he is selling to. Consequently, one finds that food manufacturers engage in a great deal of cooperative advertising programs in order to improve their position in the food store and create demand among consumers.

Point-of-Purchase Displays

Although a manufacturer may spend millions of dollars on advertising his product, he is well aware that the product must still be purchased in a retail store. It is extremely crucial to him then that the customer's attention be drawn to his product while she is shopping. This is particularly true in the case of a product that falls into the convenience category. Take, for example, the housewife who shops in a supermarket. Upon entering, she is faced with a dazzling display of merchandise all competing for her favor. It is the job of point-of-purchase displays and advertising to gain her attention, and thereby make a sale. To accomplish this, manufacturers design displays and advertising materials that they believe, in addition to the product's package, will accomplish their goals.

Many manufacturers are of the opinion that their product can only be sold if the retailer uses their display. As a result, one finds, for example, a hosiery manufacturer who will only sell to retailers who use his fixture, which displays his product effectively. In some cases the manufacturer will sell the fixture to the retailer at an attractive price; in other cases he may actually give the retailer the fixture. One finds a similar situation in the men's shirt field, where some of the major brand manufacturers offer a retailer a fixture that has proved its ability to attract the customer.

Perhaps the greatest array of point-of-purchase displays can be found in the supermarket. Here manufacturers of convenience products are pitted against one another without the influence of any sales person. Food manufacturers know that in this environment an impressive display that may reinforce either an advertising campaign or some useful promotional theme can increase the sales of a product. In recognition of this opinion, many manufacturers employ missionary salesmen to set up displays of their products in attractive ways in many of the food stores.

Aside from its obvious abilities, there are other reasons for a manufacturer to engage in experimenting and developing good point-of-purchase materials for his product. Perhaps the most commanding is the fact that displays can act as a sort of substitute for a retail salesman. It is a general consensus that the retail salesperson has too many products to concern himself with and finds it difficult to call attention to only a few. In other instances many manufacturers complain that retail salespeople are not doing the type of selling that should be done. In view of this, it is obviously to the firm's advantage to attempt to overcome these selling deficiencies by attempting to attract the customer and at the same time call to the attention of the consumer the product's major attributes.

Good point-of-purchase displays can also serve as a reminder to a shopper of something she had planned to buy but had forgotten. This type of occurrence is particularly applicable to the food shopper. It has been demonstrated in numerous studies that most food shoppers buy more items than their shopping list calls for. In addition, many shoppers do not use shopping lists.

Indirect Promotional Activities

Indirect activities are the most numerous of the firm's promotional program. As seen in Table 14-1, speakers' bureaus, plant tours, exhibits, movies, brochures, consumer literature, and catalogs are just a few of these activities. Among these many activities, trade shows and free publicity represent two of the typical activities engaged in by many firms.

Trade Shows

Although not strictly an indirect activity, as we shall see, trade shows represent an opportunity for many manufacturers to influence both the dealer and the consumers of his products. For example, the boating industry usually runs several national boating shows throughout the year. Although the area may differ, the show itself contains the same elements. In one particular national show held annually in New York City, the industry sets aside the first few days of the show for the dealers to examine carefully the boats being offered to the public by the major manufacturers. During this period of time while the displays are being set up for the consumer aspect of the show, retailers freely enter the show and examine the newest lines with the manufacturer's representatives, who man the display booths. In addition, many manufacturers take this opportunity to attempt to add additional retailers for their products. Although in most cases the sales to retailers are minimal at the show, the manufacturer may find substantial orders being placed by retailers after the show has closed down.

After the first few days of the show, the public is then allowed to view the boats that are being displayed. In some cases the retailers assist the manufacturers in manning the booths, and some find this a useful means for obtaining leads and new customers.

In analyzing this show, one is prone to play down the direct sales, since in proportion to the large crowds entering the show they are minimal. Nevertheless, they act as a major force for creating interest in boating as a leisure-time activity and whetting the appetites of those who are already committed to boating.

Trade shows exist in most major industries. In some industries, such as apparel, they have become a marketplace where sales are made, usually to retailers or other types of buyers. However, many of these shows represent a sort of publicity force for the industry they represent.

Free Publicity

Firms are constantly looking for sources of free publicity for the products they sell. Much of this publicity may appear in fashion pages or home entertainment pages of the newspapers. Some occurs through mention on radio or television programs. In all cases, the firm looks favorably upon free publicity.

When a favorable discussion of the company's product appears in a newspaper, it is particularly welcome. It is the view of the manufacturer that this type of editorial publicity is more believable to the consumer than paid advertising. As a result, it represents an excellent means of aiding sales in an indirect manner.

Many types of products are distributed with a strong assist from free publicity. The most obvious product is a new novel or other book released by a publisher. Most publishers attempt to get the author interviewed on radio and television shows that feature interesting guests. Publicity of this sort helps publicize and promote the book. Many authors on a visit to New York City may be subjected to 20 or 30 radio, television, and press interviews within a two-day span.

In a similar vein, manufacturers of apparel and furniture have recognized the value of gratuitous mention of their product in the fashion pages of magazines and, particularly, newspapers. Much of the information that appears in the fashion pages of newspapers is concerned with products carried by the large stores. Many of these stories that appear about the availability of products are well read by the readership and represent strong positive publicity for the manufacturer.

The question many manufacturers ask themselves is what is the basis for choosing items that appear in the newspapers? The answer seems to lie in the amount of advertising the newspaper receives from the store they are writing about.[3] Although there is little guarantee that the manufacturer's product will be

---

[3] S. A. Shaw, "Store Press Publicists and Their Work on the Women's Pages," *Journal of Retailing,* Vol. 32, Winter 1956–1957, p. 168.

mentioned, most manufacturers can be fairly sure that the store that uses the most newspaper advertising will receive most of the publicity on the women's pages. The same can probably be said of many of the fashion magazines.

Although one characterizes free publicity as not costing anything, most firms would affirm that such publicity may cost just as much as any given ad expenditure on any particular day. This seeming contradiction is brought about simply because firms have staffs that direct these efforts in the area of public relations and free publicity for the firm. These staffs may supply the editors in charge of fashion and news columns with information that can be used in their newspapers or magazines. A continuous program of this type costs money, and in some cases the use of the term free publicity is misleading.

Sales Promotion Program

In some industries sales promotion programs are perhaps the most important aspect of the total marketing mix of the firm. The type of firm that indulges extensively in sales promotion usually follows the philosophy that the consumer must be strongly influenced at the point of purchase. Perhaps the best example of a sales promotion program in action can be found in the cosmetic industry.

The typical cosmetic firm is concerned with the middle-income or middle-class customer, since it is their view that this customer has the necessary means and time to indulge herself in cosmetic purchases. In addition, it is the view of these firms that the cosmetic consumer has a parallel interest in fashion. Following this philosophy, the cosmetic firms take a strong interest in the department store, which is a fashion leader and is attractive to the middle-class consumer.

The importance of this market to the cosmetic firms can be gathered from the sales promotion activities that the firms pursue in their relationships with the department stores. Aside from their generous contributions to the cooperative advertising funds, they also engage in the following:

1. Supply and pay for customer mailer inserts in monthly store bills.
2. Contribute to the salaries of cosmetic demonstrators.
3. Supply the personnel and train such demonstrators for the store.
4. Offer the customer accompanying gifts with each purchase during various times of the year.
5. Pay for alterations and fixture costs in setting up their cosmetic counter in the stores.
6. Run makeup clinics for teenagers and other groups under the store's auspices.

Several of these activities are indulged in by many other industries. However, a few are peculiar to the cosmetic industry. Paying for the salary of the demonstrator is characteristically followed by many of the top firms. It stems from the view that a good cosmetician can sell the product, whereas the typical department store salesperson would perhaps lose a lot of valuable business. It is also the view of the firm that knowledgeability by the salesperson can increase the average sale substantially.

The offering of free gifts during certain times of the year has also become standard procedure in promoting cosmetics in large stores. These gifts are usually other cosmetics in the line, and in many cases their value exceeds the price of the purchase. They have been found, however, to stimulate sales by introducing a customer to the firm's line.

A clear indication of the marketing view of the cosmetic firm that department store space is perhaps the most important ingredient in the success of the firm is the fact that many cosmetic firms actually pay for alteration and fixture costs in setting up their departments. It was reported by one trade paper that the cosmetic companies were paying $50,000 to some major New York City stores for this privilege.[4] Although this is a costly procedure, the option to the major cosmetic firm is to be stationed away from the traffic.

The most expensive form of persuading the consumer to buy is personal selling. Perhaps no other form of communication has changed as drastically in the past 20 years as selling. This has been brought about by the growth and interest in the marketing concept in which the salesman is an active participant in developing new products and approaches to marketing the company's product.

Previous to this era, the salesman had the image of a backslapping happy-go-lucky type, the implication being that he had little training for the job, except a superficial exterior useful for persuading people. Although that type has not disappeared from the scene, it has become quite obvious that the selling requirements of companies vary considerably and certainly have become more demanding in terms of needing to attract a higher-type salesman.

The changing types of salesmen are best illustrated by the insurance salesman of today and yesterday. In previous years the insurance salesman sold insurance. He was told by his company that if he made 10 calls (for illustration purposes) he would make one sale; if he made 20 calls, he would make at least two sales. Thus insurance salesmen were encouraged to take a quantified approach to selling and were encouraged to uncover leads and make calls. They also developed an image as tenacious pushers who rarely took a "no" answer from a potential customer as final. Most insurance salesmen considered that most everybody was a potential consumer of the product and hence were not reluctant to make "cold calls," that is, among customers who did not give any previous indication that they were interested in buying insurance. Many of the salesmen used scare techniques and played hard on the housewife by pointing at cases where people had died without life insurance.

In the automobile insurance field most of the companies sold through brokers who solicited little business but waited for people to call them, since most people purchased insurance when they bought an automobile.

The contrast between the former practices and those of today are startling. Today's top insurance salesmen are no longer salesmen. They act as financial advisors in that they advise clients not on buying a policy, but attempt to help them plan their estates. For example, many of them advise clients on setting up a retirement program by using life insurance and annuity policies as a vital part of the

Personal Selling

---

[4]*Women's Wear Daily,* Sept. 10, 1971, p. 33.

total program. Many insurance agents combine with people who are knowledgeable as tax experts or financial advisors to offer their clients professional approaches to their problems. Other insurance men sell mutual funds as a hedge against inflation and in order to round out some financial program. In any case, a top insurance salesman today should have a thorough knowledge of the income and estate tax laws. To aid today's salesmen, many insurance companies have established departments to plan insurance portfolios for their salesmen's clients.

In the auto insurance field one finds new approaches to selling such insurance in terms of changing channels and the type of salesmen needed. One of the most dramatic was to take a great deal of auto insurance selling out of the broker's office and put it where the customers are — in the retail store. One of the pioneers in this technique is Sears, Roebuck's Allstate division, which started selling auto insurance right over the counter in Sears stores. This type of selling requires a knowledgeable salesman who concentrates all his efforts on one type of insurance. By specializing, he is not cluttered by numerous details and the wide knowledge needed by the broker who carries all types of insurance. By specializing, Sears felt that they could do a better job, a feeling that has been borne out by the fact that Allstate is one of America's largest auto insurance companies.

As a general rule, salesmen can be classified into two general areas, those who engage in order taking, and those who engage in hard selling.

One may find examples of order-taking salesmen in retail stores, where the firm advertises regularly and salesmen in the store have to write up orders received in the mail, over the telephone, or from customers who walk into the store to buy the advertised product. The salesman in this situation rarely needs to offer the customer information and simply sees to it that the product is paid for and delivered. In retailing, a great number of sales transactions are of this nature and reflect consumer interest in presold merchandise or convenience goods.

In the manufacturing firm, sales representatives selling to wholesalers or retailers can also be order takers. For example, many of the leading soap companies, such as Procter & Gamble, employ salesmen who sell to the small grocers in most areas of the United States. These salesmen are selling some of the most heavily advertised products in America, such as Crest, Ajax, Salvo, and Ivory Soap. Since this merchandise is presold and few grocers would risk not carrying the merchandise, many of these salesmen would, therefore, fall into the order-taking category.

On the other hand, the sale of Procter & Gamble products to the large food chains may require an actual presentation of the product to the firm's buying committee, particularly, when introducing a new product. Here the manufacturer must present his product to a committee that consists of top merchandising and operating executives of the firm. In this presentation the firm must convince the company of the superiority of their product. The presentation must be sophisticated, because a decision by this committee to carry the product will result in dropping other products carried by the firm. This usually takes place because the typical supermarket chain store is filled with products and so is its available space. Even the checkout counters of most supermarkets are crowded with merchandise. Thus Procter & Gamble when introducing a new product must convince the retail firm that their product will produce more dollars of profit per square foot of space over similar products.

One other type of selling should be introduced, and that is the selling of technically produced products. One finds this type of selling mainly in the industrial field where producers of such products sell their wares to other producers of finished products. For example, United States Steel may sell its product to a manufacturer of machinery where tolerance limits are crucial in the production of this machine. Here the firm may engage a salesman who is an engineer to work with a company engineer to make a sale.

In recent years the companies that produce electronic data-processing equipment and systems have engaged in a great deal of preparation before they attempt to sell their product to companies. For example, International Business Machines Company (IBM) may spend months and sometimes years in studying an industry before a salesman approaches these firms with an offer to sell electronic data-processing equipment. IBM may employ dozens of research people and technicians to prepare manuals and systems that will complement their equipment. For example, before selling the retail industry equipment, IBM developed manuals (called Impact Manuals) that explained and illustrated the potential benefits from their equipment. In these manuals, one finds some of the most advanced systems programs offered to date in this industry.

In a sense, therefore, the IBM salesman comes equipped with presold data that will help him greatly in breaking down any barriers that he may encounter. It is the belief of many observers that the edge that IBM now holds in this industry is due to this preparation work on behalf of the sales department.

Nevertheless, there exist many forms of hard selling today. The most obvious place the consumer runs into this type of selling is in the automobile showroom, where salesmen are trained to pressure the buyer to buy; this is in spite of the fact that the consumer can purchase the exact same auto from another distributor. High-pressure salesmen are also found in the apparel industry, where the product life cycle is short and the risk of failure great. In fact, most high-pressure selling is found in industries where differentiation is lacking, or where advertising is not the main force in selling the product.

Compensating Salesmen

Salesmen are usually compensated in one of three ways: straight salary, commission, or a combination of both.

Straight salary is not a widely used method of compensating salesmen. This is because the salesman has little incentive to produce more sales since his salary does not increase proportionately. On the other hand, many firms use this technique, particularly in industries where the salesman has to perform functions other than selling. For example, a cosmetic salesman for a large manufacturer may be charged with the important task of arranging to build elaborate and attractive displays in major department stores throughout his territory. It is the firm's feeling that these heavily advertised items are presold through advertising and thus the maximum benefit is derived if the retail firm properly displays all the merchandise and has it available at all times for the customer. Hence the firms would like the salesman to engage in extensive nonselling functions, and thus a commission on sales would seem to be most inappropriate. In the above-mentioned Procter & Gamble situation, where the salesman is selling presold merchandise to small grocers, here again the firm is interested in the salesman covering a great number of stores rather than doing a selling job, since it is the firm's view that these products are presold and the salesman is simply an order taker who will receive orders based on the number of calls he can complete in a day.

Commission plans are much preferred by most companies for several reasons, the most obvious being that they offer the salesman an incentive to sell more. In addition, the firm also finds that it can control the cost of sales easier by using a commission plan. A firm with a 6 percent commission plan can be assured that its selling cost will approximate 6 percent of sales. Some firms tie in the commission plan with a bonus arrangement by which the salesman is given a certain percentage of business over and above the set sales quota. In any case, the salesman's compensation is closely tied in with his ability to sell.

The major problem with using a sales commission plan is that the salesman will spend all his time selling and will not perform the necessary nonselling work required on most jobs. Thus, if a cosmetic salesman were on a commission basis, it is highly unlikely that he would engage in setting up displays or handling customer's complaints. It is just as unlikely that a salesman for a brewery would spend much of his time setting up displays in supermarkets if he was on a commission. Nevertheless, the commission plan is the most widely used compensation plan in the sales field.

The plan that seems to offer the best of both plans and at the same time neutralizes the negative aspects of each is the combination commission and salary plan. In this plan the salesman is given a guaranteed salary and a lower commission rate for each sale. Typically, a salesman may receive a base salary (let us say $100 per week) and a commission on all sales of 3 percent. In some cases the firm may maintain a 6 percent commission rate, but subtract the base salary from all commissions earned during the year. However, a true combination plan usually guarantees the salesman a salary. Thus the firm feels that the salesman is adequately compensated for all nonselling work and will be more likely to engage in many of these activities. In addition, the firm also feels that the commission offered will motivate him to increase his sales.

The drawbacks to such a plan are many. Again, the salesman, in view of the fact that he is offered a commission, may still emphasize the selling side of his work in order to earn more money. On the other hand, many firms have found that when the salary guarantee is substantial the salesman may lose most of his incentive to sell more than is absolutely necessary. In this case, it is the task of management to establish a salary that is not high enough to present the salesman with these choices.

Controlling the Sales Force

Selling expenses in the marketing organization can be considerable. Thus it is particularly important that management establish controls over the quality of the selling job and its cost. To do this requires many different approaches and control applications. These controls can be described as pretesting, current reporting, and post-testing.

Pretesting

309

*Sales
Promotion
and Personal
Selling*

Before hiring a salesman, the firm pretests the applicant and thereby attempts to weed out those that will not prove to be good salesmen. In theory, this is an important function in controlling the quality of salespeople. Many firms, for example, will check the previous record of the sales applicant. When a record of success is indicated, they may feel that he offers exceptional promise and will tend to hire the applicant.

In recent years many firms have resorted to testing applicants in order to better understand the individual and predict some sort of probability of success for the applicant. Many of these more recent techniques include psychological testing; many companies will not hire anybody on the sales level who does not measure up to the standards of the psychological test. More and more marketing firms are using the services of outside testing firms to aid them in making this decision.

On the surface this type of testing seems to be much more accurate and sophisticated than simply using an executive's judgment or a resumé check based on previous history. However, when one examines both the record of psychological testing and some of the problems, one is not so impressed. One of the assumptions of psychological testing is that somehow we know the ingredients that make up a good salesman for our product. Implied also in such testing is that all salesmen must have these characteristics, regardless of the type of product they are selling. Thus an insurance salesman should have the same characteristics as a car salesman. Even if one does distinguish in terms of the characteristics for selling in each of these industries, one is still faced with explaining the successes of one salesman versus another. All in all, most firms will readily admit that they cannot spot with any definitiveness those who will be successful and those who will not. Thus firms using tests find that many people are rejected who might otherwise have been successful salesmen. One might also add that many people have an aversion to testing and do not do as well as others. Nonetheless, it is clear that more and more firms are using tests to select potential salespersons.

Current Reports

Once the salesman is hired, the firm continues to control his behavior through the use of sales reports and field evaluations by upper management personnel. Typically, a salesman will be asked to file reports on some sort of a regular basis so that management has a clear picture of his whereabouts and efforts. For instance, a field salesman may fill out a report on a daily basis with the sales manager, indicating his whereabouts, whom he called on, when he should follow up, and any other pertinent information. In this manner management can measure the effectiveness of the sales calls as well as the number.

All sales reports are supplemented by a periodic field evaluation by either the sales manager or a district supervisor. These evaluations usually include traveling with the salesman while he makes calls. In some cases the firm may find that the salesman requires further or supplementary training in order to round out his potential.

Most well-run companies evaluate sales productivity after the selling period has ended. In these post tests, the company usually resorts to measuring *quantitatively* the results of the sales effort and also applies some *qualitative* measurements.

The quantitative measurements usually include a measurement of the sales expenses per salesman versus the sales volume produced. Thus the firm may measure the overall sales ratio of the firm against some national figure that is available.

The interpretation of this ratio requires careful study. For example, should a company spend 7 percent of its sales volume on selling, it may be high in comparison to either previous years or comparable figures of other companies. This could mean that the firm has too many salesmen, or that those they have are not operating efficiently. Conversely, when the firm finds that its sales expenditures are well below the national average, it could mean that the firm is not expanding enough effort in this area. Thus it may have too few salesmen covering too large a territory.

The most widely used control on the sales force is the establishing of sales quotas and the determination as to whether or not the sales force and individual salesmen exceeded the quotas. Thus a salesman allotted a quota of sales of $100,000 annually for a territory such as the state of Arizona would be under pressure to fulfill that quota. As noted earlier, many firms use quota goals as the basis of compensation.

Quotas are established on the basis of past records and what one might call "educated guesses," that is, based on the firm's previous experience and their forecast of the next year. Forecasting in some firms certainly does not involve a guessing procedure; however, in others they simply may look at economic forecasts and realistically infer their own industry's and firm's participation in this growth. In other firms, forecasting may include the use of mathematical models, special surveys, and statistical techniques aimed at deriving a meaningful figure. Many of these techniques were discussed in Chapter 3.

Aside from these quantitative methods, the firm can look at other measurements in order to control the quantity and quality of their sales effort. For example, one firm examines customer complaints carefully and tries to relate them to a salesman's territory. A salesman who receives a high proportion of customer complaints may be doing an unsatisfactory job and hence may be in need of further training or other assistance.

SUMMARY

Sales promotion and personal selling are two useful means of promoting a company's products to the public. There are literally dozens of sales promotion activities, most of which are aimed at the retailer or his employees.

For convenience purposes one can divide sales promotion activities into two major groupings:

1. Direct-activities, which have as their goal an immediate increase in sales. Included here are coupons, samplings, cooperative advertising, and point-of-purchase displays.

2. Indirect-activities, which have as their goal attaining goodwill or some longer-range sales goal. Here one finds such diverse activities as trade shows and free publicity.

Several things can be said about personal selling. The first is that the salesman's job is changing in that he is forced to take a much more important role in developing new approaches to the marketing of the firm's product. The insurance salesman is an excellent example of this change.

Second, no one compensation program can adequately accomplish everything wanted. Here one must experiment and select the plan that helps the salesman and the company achieve their goals.

QUESTIONS

1. In what ways does couponing help the sale of new products?

2. Why are most sales promotion activities aimed at the retail firm?

3. Why doesn't a firm engage in direct activities only, in preference to indirect promotional efforts?

4. What is cooperative advertising?

5. Why is cooperative advertising of great interest to the manufacturer?

6. What advantages accrue to the retailer engaging in a cooperative advertising program?

7. What role do point-of-purchase display materials play in the supermarket?

*8. A major boating firm declined to display its wares at the annual boating show in New York City in 1973. Support its decision with logical arguments.

9. Most salesmen prefer a straight commission form of compensation. True or false? Discuss.

10. How does a firm control the quality of its salesmen?

*11. A detail man is a salesman who represents a drug company. Ordinarily, it is his major task to call on doctors and get them to prescribe his drugs. How has the role of the detail man changed in the past 20 years?

*In-depth questions.

Physical Distribution Mix:
An Introduction

15

SUMMARY KEY

Physical distribution in marketing is concerned with the movement of the manufacturer's goods to the place where they can be sold to the ultimate seller or directly to the consumer.

Today physical distribution is an integral part of the total marketing mix and stands alongside of promotion, pricing, and the product with equal status.

The definition of physical distribution has been broadened, therefore; it is not only concerned with flow to the ultimate consumer, but also with different types of available channels for accomplishing this goal.

Population shifts, new products, and a changing transportation network have caused manufacturers to continually shift and reevaluate their physical distribution mix.

The management of the physical distribution mix can be a positive force, and if used efficiently, distribution can become a major differentiation factor.

Part of the manufacturer's task of maintaining an efficient physical distribution system is to motivate and somehow control the middlemen, the wholesaler and retailer. The wholesaler has had particular problems in fitting into the system because of the growth of the large retailers, who prefer to buy directly from the manufacturer. Conversely, the proliferation of product lines has helped the wholesaler, since it is more likely that retailers will need fast delivery.

In selling retailers, manufacturers may follow a pushing or a pulling policy. Each has different implications for the manufacturer and the retailer. Aside from a policy of this sort, manufacturers can resort to other techniques, such as training salespeople, offering faster delivery, offering a lower price, or perhaps cooperative advertising. The list is endless.

In establishing an overall channel policy, the manufacturer has three choices — to follow the dictates of the seller, to establish a leadership position, or to establish a balanced relationship.

In his choice of channels the manufacturer can choose to sell directly to the consumer, through a wholesaler to a retailer, or directly to a retailer. His selection depends very much on the type of product he sells and the volume that can be generated through each of these channels.

Physical distribution in marketing is concerned with *the movement of the manufacturer's goods to the place where they can be sold to the ultimate seller or directly to the consumer.* One aspect of physical distribution is the logistics problems connected with the sale, that is, the most profitable mode of transportation to the place or person of sale. At one period of time the physical distribution function was only the concern of those interested in cost-cutting procedures in shipping both finished goods and raw materials from one place to another, without any direct relationship with the marketing departments. In recent years, however, a change in attitude has occurred that has integrated the distribution of the product with the marketing mix. In effect, the physical distribution mix is an integral part of the total marketing mix and stands alongside of promotion, pricing, and the product with equal status. Although more will be added later, it might be pertinent to point out that the reason for this shift in interest is due to the recognition that how we distribute the product can affect all our other policies. For example, a logistics decision to warehouse a product in five areas of the country could affect the firm's pricing policy, particularly if the firm previously shipped all finished goods from one central warehouse. Additionally, this same move would require that the production facilities create more inventory in order to keep the warehouses properly stocked. This move would also affect the sales force, since their customers would not have to wait as long for delivery. It is obvious that such a change would cause a complete reshuffling of the decisions that make up the marketing mix.

It seems obvious then that a much broader definition of physical distribution is needed in order to encompass the integration of this important function of the marketing mix. With this in mind, *physical distribution is concerned not only with the workings of the flow of goods and services from the producer to the ultimate consumer, but is also concerned with the different types of available channels for accomplishing this goal.* As defined, then, our study of physical distribution will concern itself with examining the channel institutions, that is, wholesaling and retailing, and the distribution alternatives involved in choosing between balancing costs and services. In this latter area will be discussed costs incurred in carrying inventories related to modes of transportation and warehouse choices. In effect, a broad view of physical distribution has been established that recognizes the impact of the movement of goods and services on the total marketing program.

Pressure for Change

Firms are always in a state of change in terms of their choices as to channels and alternative means available for accomplishing their primary task of selling goods and services. The Magnavox Company is a good example of a firm that is constantly looking for new and better ways of accomplishing this same goal. Magnavox for most of its history has sold its basic product, television sets, through department stores and fine specialty stores who are interested in complete control over the price of a product. By accomplishing this type of channel arrangement, Magnavox has had to sell directly to retailers and thus establish its own warehousing system. In contrast, most of the other major manufacturers of television sets sell through distributors who are free to sell to discounters or any other outlet that can carry television sets.

As a result of this policy, one finds Magnavox in a small number of outlets in any given city, whereas competitive products can be found in most any outlet in the same town. What Magnavox is attempting to accomplish through this policy will be discussed in more detail later. However, pursuing this policy, that is, establishing a small number of price-protected outlets, has caused Magnavox to look for additional outlets for its products that will accomplish the same thing, without interfering with its present channel arrangements. To accomplish this, Magnavox entered into arrangements with the Singer Company to sell its products in the Singer Sewing Machine Centers, although this plan was subsequently discontinued. In addition, Magnavox signed an agreement to supply Montgomery Ward with its sets under the Ward private-brand label.

Reason for Shifting of Distribution

The constant shifting and reevaluating of the firm's channels of distribution are due in the main to the changing consumer depicted in Chapter 6. In particular, shifting population can cause huge gaps in the manufacturer's market and cause him to react. The intense population shift after World War II caused many manufacturers to establish outlets that were quicker in following this shift; also, these outlets seemed to comprehend the importance of such shifts in the market. As a result, many manufacturers were forced to consider selling their products in the highway discount stores that became popular after World War II. Previously, many of these same manufacturers had been dealing exclusively with the more traditional stores, that is, department stores and variety stores, which had a commanding position in the downtown areas of most American cities. However, many of these stores were slow to expand to the suburbs and, perhaps more importantly, did not quite fathom what the suburban shopper wanted. Hence manufacturers selling through the traditional channels were faced with this change and many were slow in adjusting to the market. The choices were clear; manufacturers could either stick with their traditional outlets, drop the traditional outlet and switch to the new discount stores, or try to sell to both outlets.

Aside from population shifts, other factors can account for the continuing pressure on firms to restudy their present distribution system. New products and changes in transportation systems simply add to the need to examine a firm's distribution policies.

New products have had an important impact on management's attitude toward physical distribution. For instance, the proliferation of products has caused inventory growth at both the factory and distribution level. As a result, both the manufacturer and distributor are more concerned with maintaining an efficient and adequate flow of merchandise. For example, the manufacturer of breakfast cereal has been faced with a proliferation of new products. As a direct result, warehouses and wholesalers have been forced to carry much larger inventories in order to maintain a flow of products to the retailers. The retailers on the other hand have also been faced with maintaining larger inventories, since the consumer is looking for a wide assortment. In some instances the retailer has reacted to this proliferation by pressuring the manufacturer to keep the inventory levels at the retail stores to a minimum. To accomplish this, the manufacturer must maintain large stocks in company warehouses and, in so doing, must maintain an efficient communication system that will accomplish this.

The shifting interest in alternative transportation methods has also caused manufacturers to reconsider many of their old distribution methods. The federal highway program and the development of large airplanes (e.g., Boeing 747) have caused a total reevaluation of transportation in terms of helping the company get its products to market faster and at a lower cost.

The costs incurred in transportation are many times invisible costs in the sense that they do not appear on a bill of lading. For example, the time it takes to transport merchandise from one point to another is an important factor to the customer of a manufacturer, since he must base his inventory on how long it takes to replenish his stock. Higher stocks result in higher costs to all middlemen.

From the marketing point, one can view physical distribution (logistics) as a passive force supplying the goods to the firm within the constraints of the marketing objectives. That view, however, is changing, and there is a growing belief that physical distribution can be used as a strong *positive* force in helping the company achieve its marketing goals. It has been said that it is a particularly powerful tool in marketing goods that are substitutable or sensitive to price changes.[1] The development of superior logistics systems can be a major differentiation factor for the firm. In essence, it can affect the services the firm offers to its customers and as a result improve its profit potential.

Customer Services

Retailers have always been aware of the fact that superior customer services can give one firm a decided advantage over another. The services retailers offer indicate this view. Delivery services are a standard among traditional retailers. Charge accounts and installment accounts have been used as a device to attract consumers who do not have the money to buy. The care with which the retailer chooses a store location is an indication of his understanding of the importance of offering convenience as a service. The adjustment in the hours the stores are open is again an indication of the importance of such services to the consumer. The growing importance of telephone shopping and catalog selling would also seem to emphasize the importance of this view.

The firm's ability to supply its customers with needed stocks is an important factor in developing a substantial market. A superior physical distribution program can do this for the manufacturer who is selling to a large market. Thus a firm with a good inventory control system supported by computer equipment can gain a distinct advantage over its competitors, if it can offer fast and accurate service.

The advantage of this capability to the firm is obvious. Many purchasing agents or buyers for firms find that prices among many firms are about the same. As a result, many decisions are made on the basis of the ability of the supplier to make

[1]D. J. Bowersox, E. W. Smykay, and B. J. LaLonde, *Physical Distribution Management* (New York: Macmillan Publishing Co., Inc., 1968), pp. 24–25.

fast and accurate deliveries. Deliveries to an industrial manufacturer are almost always crucial. For instance, a manufacturer of machinery may rely very much on a supplier who can deliver a small part for the machinery since the equipment cannot be completed without this part. In the consumer field a retailer may deal only with a firm that can guarantee quick delivery on products such as drugs and prescription goods.

In the case of the manufacturer of machinery, the failure to deliver the item on time may result in disaster for the firm in that the total manufacturing facility may be shut down. Thus a buyer of the product for this company will put great stress on the seller's delivery capability. In the case of the retailer who expects fast delivery of drugs and prescriptions, poor delivery may not be as crucial; however, it can result in lost sales.

Quick delivery can also result in lower costs to the recipient, since it will not be necessary to carry large stocks of merchandise, which will, in effect, reduce the financial needs of the buyer. Although more will be said about this later, the value of fast delivery is reflected in faster turnover and allows the recipient to plan his materials-handling function much more efficiently.

Profit Potential

With the increasing competitive nature of marketing, many business firms have started to recognize that many marketing opportunities exist if one can reduce the time and cost of delivering products to the consumer or middleman. Thus the Avon Company has devised a physical distribution system that will allow their thousands of door-to-door cosmetic salesmen an opportunity to deliver the ordered merchandise within the span of a few hours where necessary. Should a firm try to compete with the Avon Company, they would have to invest millions of dollars to establish warehouses and communication systems immediately. At this stage, potential competition for Avon would seem to be almost nil, since their system would be costly to duplicate and their know-how would be almost insurmountable. How profitable this system can be can be seen from the fact that Avon sells more cosmetics than any other firm in the country.

Many firms have determined that the establishment of a warehouse in the right marketing areas of the country can give their firm a distinct cost and time advantage over many competitors. Thus a book publisher found that by setting up a major distribution warehouse in California he could handle last-minute orders from college book stores and could send out review copies for teachers more quickly. As a result, the firm found that its market penetration in this section of the country increased tremendously over a period of 5 years.

Controlling Middlemen
It is the manufacturer's task to control or in some way motivate middlemen to sell his products. As noted later, this task is extremely difficult, since the middlemen may have conflicting policies and problems. Nevertheless, the manufacturer must somehow motivate both middlemen to accomplish his goals. In the sections and chapters that follow we shall discuss each of the major middlemen, retailers and wholesalers. In the last chapter we shall discuss the important task of

rounding out the physical distribution mix, that is, controlling inventories and facing the organizational problems encountered in getting the goods to market.

Channel Control Resistance

Aside from some of the obvious problems that the manufacturer faces in attempting to control the retailer and wholesaler, such as competition and the disinterest of consumers in his product, the manufacturer has come to recognize conflicts in philosophy and general outlook on the part of the middlemen he deals with. This is particularly true in his dealings with retailers.

Looked at superficially, the retailer, wholesaler, and manufacturer have the same goal, to make profits. That is, usually the more they sell, the more money they will make. Thus the retailer selling more of the firm's product will make more money. However, one has to understand that retailers, wholesalers, and manufacturers have an entirely different outlook on what to sell, and what constitutes a long-run profit. These differences will be discussed in the next few chapters. Nevertheless, they exist and the manufacturer must be aware of their existence.

Wholesaler Problems

The role of the wholesaler has been complicated by the growth of the large retailer. The development of the large retailer has resulted in a need to deal directly with the manufacturer and thus bypass the wholesaler. This trend has become particularly noticeable in the past 10 years, which have seen the growth of large discount chains throughout all areas of the country. The merger movement in retailing has also taken customers away from the wholesalers in many lines of products.

Large retail firms prefer to place orders directly with manufacturers, simply because they believe they can get lower prices. These price savings can be passed along to the consumer, or simply added to the margin the retailer gets.

On the other hand, the proliferation of product lines that need to be carried by the retailer has helped rather than hindered the growth of wholesaling. Thus retailers have to carry more products than ever before, and must order many of these products well in advance from manufacturers. This poses serious problems for the retailer for two reasons. First, to buy directly from many manufacturers, they must order certain minimum quantities. For example, one toothpaste manufacturer insists on a minimum retail order of 144 (a gross) tubes of toothpaste. Multiplying this order by thousands of products, one can see that the inventory requirements for a single drug department in a department store can be tremendous. This can place great pressure on even large retailers to carry excessive inventories. The ordering of 144 tubes may represent an inventory supply that meets consumer demand for many weeks. Additionally, many retailers dealing directly with manufacturers may find that the manufacturers require at least 1-month lead time to deliver merchandise.

It is therefore not surprising to see that many large retailers deal with both manufacturers and wholesalers. Many drug wholesalers service the drug departments in large retail stores. Since the retailer can get same-day service on many of the convenience products sold in this department, they find they can reduce the size of their inventories and need not worry about such long lead times in placing orders. In effect, the retailer transfers the inventory problem to the wholesaler.

Overall Strategy for Selling Retailers

Most manufacturers are in the position of trying to persuade retailers to carry their products. True, there are a few situations in our economy where the retailers try to persuade the manufacturer to let them carry his line. In most cases, however, the manufacturer tries to persuade the retailer to carry his product line and to sell it. The retailer is ordinarily not as concerned with the individual product as he is more concerned with a whole category of products. Thus the retailer may not be concerned with whether or not the Papermate pen is selling in his store; he is more concerned with whether he is getting his share of the pen market. In most situations the retailer has a wide selection of merchandise to choose from and the manufacturer is placed in the position of negotiating his product through the distribution system to the ultimate consumer. This policy is usually referred to as the *pushing policy*.

In a number of instances, some manufacturers have managed to maintain a *pulling policy*. In carrying out this policy, the manufacturer turns his attention to the ultimate consumer, through sales promotion and advertising techniques, to create demand for his product. If the system is working properly, the manufacturer can expect that the consumer will put enough pressure on the retailer to force him to carry his product. This policy is followed by several major food and soap manufacturers. For instance, it is doubtful that one can find a supermarket where Campbell's soups are not carried, or a drugstore or supermarket where Colgate toothpaste is not stocked. One would also doubt that one could find a major drugstore without Gillette blades, Revlon cosmetics, or baby products by Johnson & Johnson.

Most of these companies that engage in pull policies spend a great deal of money on television advertising. In a very direct way they persuade the potential consumer that their product is superior to their competitor's product and turn this persuasion into action. A wise retailer aware of this influence will of course stock the manufacturer's product. He will continue stocking the product even in cases when it doesn't meet some of the company buying norms discussed below. In a sense, therefore, the manufacturer has forced the retailer to stock his product simply to accommodate the consumer.

In firms carrying out such a policy one finds that the retailer receives less of a gross margin (the difference between the selling price and the price the retailer paid for the product) than he would under conditions where the manufacturer had to convince the retailer to buy his product and there was not particularly strong consumer demand.

The *pushing policy* is in direct contrast to the pull strategy. In carrying out this policy the manufacturer must offer the retailer a legitimate incentive to purchase his product. In addition, the manufacturer must develop a means of getting the sales people in the retail store to present his product properly.

The manufacturer has many different ways of gaining the interest of the retailer and his staff in his product. One of the most obvious is to offer the retailer a lower price than he can get from other sources. The problem with a price allowance is that it can be easily matched by competitors. As a result, many manufacturers try to rely on other techniques, such as developing new products, offering advertising programs and cooperative allowances, or developing a particular image for their product that cannot be easily duplicated by competitors.

Manufacturers may consider other ways of selling retailers. For example, they may hire and train sales personnel in order to help the retailer improve his ability to sell the manufacturer's product. Thus a retailer of apparel may receive some good technical information on washing instructions for products from the manufacturer. Another may be a situation where the manufacturer can promise quicker delivery to the retailer than any other manufacturer. Or a manufacturer may offer a retailer a reduced price in other lines of products as an incentive to buy his new product. Or the reputation of the manufacturer may far exceed the reputation of similar firms in the industry. In any case, it has always seemed clear that most retailers have literally dozens of reasons for accepting or rejecting a manufacturer's product.

Table 15-1 lists some of the reasons food chains offer for buying a manufacturer's new product. Careful examination of the list tells a great deal about the food chain's decision-making process. Although the first rank, "usefulness of the product," comes as no surprise, it is interesting to note that the second-ranking item refers to the fact that the new item does not duplicate an existing item. Since food chains usually carry wide assortments of food products, the item that is

Food Chain's Evaluation of Factors Affecting the Choice of a New Product   TABLE 15-1

	Rank
Usefulness of product	1
Does not duplicate an existing item	2
Product profitability	3
Advertising support	4
Gross margin	5
Appearance of package	6
Quality of package	7
Retail price	8
Good experience with manufacturer's other products	9
Reputation of supplier	10
Test market results	11
Introductory allowance	12
Advertising allowance	13
Amount of shelf space occupied	14
Deals offered	15
In-store merchandising support	16
Competitor's action on new item	17
Item well-presented by salesman	18

Source: *The Selection and Introduction of New Items, A Study of Retailer Attitudes,* The Food Trade Marketing Council Report to the Industry, No. 5 (New York: Family Circle Magazine, Sept. 1964), p. 13.

different will no doubt rate higher with the buyers. Thus a firm selling coffee will find that the typical chain may be handling six or seven different brands. In order to interest the chain, the product will have to be somewhat different. Aside from the duplication of inventories that the chain will want to avoid, it also means that, since space in the supermarket is at a premium, if the food chain buys an additional coffee item they will more than likely have to reduce the space allotted to the present items. Thus the new item *must* produce additional profits that warrant such action.

Channel Control Policies

Although manufacturers can establish channel policies for their firm, they usually find that their policies must be based on a realistic appraisal of their relationships with the channel members and their competitors. Many of these policies are governed strictly by the balance of power between the buyer and the seller. For instance, a small manufacturer may use an agent or broker simply because he does not have the finances necessary to establish his own sales force. On the other hand, he may find that most large retailers interested in his product may not want to deal with a middleman but prefer to deal directly with his firm. Here the manufacturer may choose to deal with large accounts directly and may establish a sales force for the smaller accounts.

In essence, a manufacturer may have a choice of three policies: either *follow the dictates of the seller, establish a leadership position,* or establish a sort of in-between policy called a *balanced relationship.*

One finds the followers in fields made up of a large number of sellers. The boys' apparel field would be an example where the size of the firm is extremely small in comparison to firms in many other industries. Toy manufacturers would also seem to follow the same patterns. One finds in these industries that much of the price setting and terms are established by the retailer. For instance, one finds when a retailer establishes a toy price line of $1 the manufacturer must produce a product that sells for 60 cents to the retailer. This enables the retailer to price the product at this price line and also receive the markup he has established as the norm for his store.

The women's apparel field represents an industry that deals directly with the retailer and is dependent on the whims of the retailer. In this situation it is the retailer who carries the power and is in a position to dictate many of the terms. Here again we have an industry where the firms are small and numerous.

At the other extreme and in a leadership position, one finds firms such as Magnavox establishing franchises among retailers. Only retailers who meet certain requirements are allowed to carry the Magnavox line. The pressure and control that Magnavox can put on retailers can be seen from a recent Federal Trade Commission charge to the effect that Magnavox has allegedly:

1. Limited reimbursement for cooperative advertising to those ads which bear the established price.

2. Prohibited dealers from using trading stamps in conjunction with sales of Magnavox products.

3. Refused to offer franchises to dealers who also own discount houses.
4. Paid rewards to dealers who report other dealers for cutting prices.
5. Levied fines on dealers who cut prices.

Many of the franchises that have developed in recent years represent attempts on the part of the manufacturer or seller of the franchise to control a certain amount of the market. Thus franchise holders of Midas Mufflers, Aamco Transmissions, and McDonald's Hamburgers are all subject to strict control by the franchiser. This control extends to forcing the franchisee to buy his product, selecting his store location, choosing the promotions he runs, and setting the prices he pays for the products used in his operation.

The automobile industry seems to be one where the manufacturer has strong control over the distributors or retailer. Although following World War II manufacturers had almost despotic control over the dealers, the late 1950s saw an increase in both dealer resistance to manufacturer pressure and increasing interest on the part of the federal government in this controversy. Such pressure has reduced the power of the automobile companies, but nevertheless many still have strong control over their automobile franchises.

On the other hand, most manufacturers exist in a competitive environment where control over the outlet that distributes their product is not possible. This situation exists in industries where the manufacturers are numerous. Under these competitive conditions it is practically impossible for the small manufacturer to control the retailer or wholesaler. In this type of industry the very large retailers establish the terms and relationships.

In a competitive industry where the manufacturer is outnumbered, firms are always looking for opportunities to control the middlemen, the task that is usually not possible under normal conditions. A few firms, however, are able to mount a strong consumer campaign that can force retailers to regard their products as a needed product to ensure the success of their stores. In recent years many producers in this type of industry have taken a further step by purchasing retail outlets, thus avoiding the need of competing for retailers. A recent example is the Hart, Schaffner and Marx clothing firm, which has purchased over 200 men's apparel stores, and thereby built a market for their men's clothing. Many major shoe manufacturers have purchased hundreds of shoe outlets to handle their output. Typically, this move not only avoids competition, but many times closes out marketing opportunities to competitors.

Products and Channel Selection

Although competition and the control manufacturers have over their distributors are important in establishing channels of distribution, the type of product being sold may have some effect on the channel selected.

The choices of channels are noted in Figure 15-1. If one considers that the types of goods sold can be classified into convenience, shopping, and specialty goods, then the type of channel in some cases may be dictated by each of these goods. However, one should be aware that firms in many cases use more than one channel to reach the ultimate consumer. However, one can make the generalization that the greater the risk of obsolescence, the *shorter* the channel of distribution. Hence, firms selling high-fashion dresses in practically all cases *sell directly* to the retailer. On the other hand, firms selling standard convenience *products* almost always sell most of their output through wholesalers. However, one cannot generalize on the sale of these three classifications of products.

FIGURE 15-1   Channel Distribution and Products

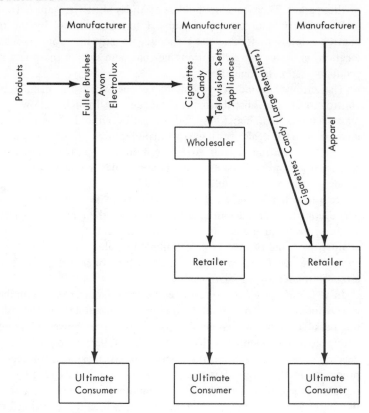

Direct to the Consumer

Products sold directly to the ultimate consumer include Fuller brushes, Electrolux and Kirby vacuum cleaners, and Avon cosmetics. Most products sold in this way are either shopping or specialty goods. Here the consumer is looking for variety; thus opportunities to present product features are plentiful. The sale of vacuum cleaners through door-to-door selling has become almost institutionalized since this product lends itself to easy demonstration with strong emphasis on product features. In addition, the price of the product makes it possible to pay a salesman a high commission.

Fuller Brush, with its wide variety of brushes produced for the dozens of needs of the typical household, has developed into a specialty good. Thus a typical Fuller salesman may offer hair brushes, brushes for cleaning the garage, and brushes to help with dishwashing.

Convenience goods are sold through wholesalers in the main. Cigarettes and candy bars are sold in most cases in this manner with one exception, when the buyer orders in huge quantities. Thus the American Tobacco Company will sell cigarettes in large quantities directly to Kroger Supermarkets. However, to distribute the product to the thousands of small grocery and candy stores they must rely on wholesalers. Since their product is a branded convenience good, they are concerned with gaining a wide distribution for it, a necessary prerequisite for a convenience product.

On the other hand, shopping goods are many times sold through wholesalers' support. By definition, shopping goods do not require a wide distribution and thus one might assume they do not need wholesalers. However, manufacturers of television sets and appliances find wholesalers (distributors) are necessary in order to supply the necessary technical support to sell such items. For example, the buyer of a color television set requires installation and repair service to consummate the sale. Thus a distributor of RCA's television sets also services the sets.

Direct to the Retailer

Most apparel, which is classified as shopping or specialty goods, is sold directly to the retailer. Apparel, by its seasonal nature, requires a shorter channel of distribution. It is a general rule that the riskier the style, the more likely it will be sold directly. High-fashion dresses are therefore always sold directly, whereas on occasion less fashionable apparel (or staples) may be sold through middlemen.

SUMMARY

Previously, physical distribution concerned itself with the choice of channels of distribution and the finding of the cheapest way of shipping goods to the customer.

This attitude has changed in many respects. First is the recognition on the part of manufacturers that the proper choice of channel members, that is, wholesalers and retailers, can be perhaps more important than any sales promotion or product policies a firm may develop.

Second is the recognition that the logistics part of the physical distribution effort can be an important advantage to the marketer of a product. Thus a firm that through careful selection of warehouses and inventory size can deliver goods faster to a market than a competitor may end up with a sizable advantage.

Manufacturing firms spend a great deal of time in attempting to control the channel members through the development of policies. Here one finds the pull strategy that forces the retailer to carry a manufacturer's product. On the other hand, many manufacturers may find that they must adjust their firms to the demands of a large retailer or wholesaler.

*1. How does the broad definition of physical distribution more closely reflect what is meant by the marketing concept?

2. What major types of decisions are made by those in charge of the physical distribution mix?

3. How have population changes affected the physical distribution mix of the manufacturer?

*4. Give three examples of how the physical distribution mix can be used as a positive marketing force by a furniture manufacturer.

5. What forces are working to make the wholesaler an integral part of the manufacturer's strategy?

6. A manufacturer of toys is pursuing a pushing policy. How does this policy affect his total marketing mix?

7. In what ways does the strategy of pursuing a pulling policy affect the retail customer?

8. An easy but avoided way of getting the retailer to buy your product is to offer the lowest price. What other alternatives does a manufacturer have?

9. In what type of an industry can a manufacturer establish a policy of controlling the retailer?

10. Under what conditions would a manufacturer prefer to sell directly to the consumer?

11. Give an example where a manufacturer would sell through a wholesaler and at the same time would sell directly to a retailer in some markets.

12. Is a staple product more or less likely to pass through a wholesaler? Explain.

*In-depth questions.

The Wholesaling Channel

16

SUMMARY KEY

Wholesalers and retailers perform economic functions; otherwise they would not exist. When one institution is circumvented, the remaining institutions must assume the functions of the eliminated institution. This is referred to as the *transfer principle.*

Wholesalers perform functions for retailers and manufacturers. For the retailers the major functions they perform include anticipating needs, offering credit, delivering goods, breaking down large shipments, and several lesser functions, such as acting as a buying representative for small retailers.

For the manufacturer they perform a selling function, carry inventory, reduce the need for credit, and provide valuable market information.

Aside from the functions performed by a wholesaler, the manufacturer must consider certain variables in making a decision concerning the need for a wholesaler. These variables include the finances that are available to the firm, the requirements of the product they are selling, the location of the retailers, the life cycle of the product, and retailers' preferences.

There is little evidence that the wholesaler has declined. However, he has been forced to change. In the grocery field one finds voluntary cooperative wholesalers; in drugs there has developed a specialty wholesaler who will deliver prescription products quickly; and there are several other kinds of specialty wholesalers.

In spite of their need for cooperation, the wholesaler has many conflicts with the manufacturer. Some include the demand that he receive exclusive territories, the demand that the wholesaler service and carry out the product guarantees of the manufacturer, and the need to perform services at the retail level for which he is not compensated. The manufacturer's major complaint concerning wholesalers is that their salesmen take the line of least resistance and thus rarely push his products.

The typical wholesale organization is substantially larger than the average retail firm although it has less than 20 employees. In terms of its operating statistics, the larger the firm, the lower its expenses as a ratio of sales; it operates on slender margins, and payroll accounts for over 50 percent of its total expenses. Lacking very much automation, this latter figure is understandable.

The largest wholesalers are the merchant wholesalers who account for close to 50 percent of all volume. Others include merchandise agents, such as brokers, commission merchants, and selling agents; manufacturers' sales outlets; service wholesalers, which include rack merchandisers; and limited function wholesalers.

All wholesalers and retailers exist in our economy because they perform economic functions, that is, functions which service the needs of other institutions and the ultimate consumer of the product or service. Thus, should a retailer prefer to buy directly from a manufacturer and circumvent a wholesaler, someone has to assume the task of maintaining a supply of goods at all times that can be ordered. The shifting of functions from manufacturing to retailers and in some cases to the ultimate consumer has given rise to what is sometimes called the *transfer principle,* which states that when one marketing institution circumvents another in the exchange of goods the remaining institutions involved in the exchange must assume the functions of the eliminated institution. Some examples should make this clearer.

Let us say, for example, that John Jones, a potential customer for a suit, decided to take advantage of the generous offer of a friend and buy the suit directly from a manufacturer. Ordinarily, he purchases his suits at a retail store; hence by making a purchase directly from the manufacturer he hopes to save money. However, the transfer principle indicates that by his doing so either he or the manufacturer will end up performing many of the functions of the retailer and thus someone will incur additional costs. In the case of the consumer, costs may be additional out-of-pocket expenditures or they may be costs involved in risk or extra energy expenditures.

The first cost that John Jones will incur is that of travel. Since most retailers are conveniently located, and a major factor in their success is their ability to choose profitable locations, it may be assumed that John Jones will have to travel to an inconvenient location in order to purchase his suit in the manufacturer's showroom. In addition, since most retail firms locate in shopping areas, he will be unable to do any other retail shopping in this area during that one trip. Since manufacturers are not concerned with the convenience of the ultimate buyer of their product in locating their plants, one can visualize Mr. Jones traveling to an inconvenient site and perhaps climbing up a few staircases in order to select his suit. In addition, he will probably have to complete this shopping trip at an off hour since a suit manufacturer's showroom may be closed after working hours.

Once Mr. Jones arrives at the showroom, he will find a rather limited selection of suits, since most manufacturers of apparel specialize in selling a certain style. He will also be limited in terms of the colors. Thus, typically, Mr. Jones may find hundreds of suits in three colors and one style sitting on a rack awaiting shipment to retailers. Once he does select his suit he must pay cash for it, since the manufacturer would not offer a customer buying a small quantity of suits credit. In addition, Mr. Jones will find that he has to take the suit to his own tailor to be altered. Finally, Mr. Jones will have to take the suit home with him since the manufacturer does not supply delivery services except to his regular retail customers.

The reader should carefully note the many functions that Mr. Jones has to perform and the many costs (i.e., out-of-pocket expenses and effort) he has to incur in order to make this purchase below the retail price. It is not inconceivable that Mr. Jones may decide that the effort and the actual saving may not warrant his going to purchase the suit from a manufacturer.

In any case, in this example we see the transfer principle applied to a situation. Retailers ordinarily perform functions for the consumer, the most obvious being offering wide selections of merchandise, credit, delivery, and convenient location. Those going around the retailer must either assume the functions performed by the retailer or shift them to the manufacturer. In this case our Mr. Jones assumed all these functions, and it then became his decision to determine whether the savings he received by buying directly from the manufacturer offset the costs and effort he incurred by assuming many of the functions of the retailer.

The transfer principle applies to dealings between various marketing institutions also. For instance, suppose that a retailer decides to deal directly with a manufacturer rather than a wholesaler carrying the manufacturer's product lines. The retailer will most probably have to deal at a greater distance than he would should he chose to buy the item directly from the wholesaler. Thus the buyer for the retailer may have to write a letter or make a long-distance call in order to inform the manufacturer of his interest in buying direct. In addition, the retailer may find that even though he places an order directly he will have to make purchases in larger quantities for a variety of reasons. For example, many manufacturers insist that all buyers buy in certain established standard minimum orders. Thus a retailer buying cleanser directly from Lever Brothers may discover that the minimum order that can be placed is 1 gross (144). In addition, the retailer may discover that he must place all orders with the manufacturer 3 weeks in advance so as to receive the merchandise when he needs the item. This comes about because it takes the manufacturer 3 weeks to process an order from a retailer. In addition, the retailer may find that all problems concerned with the merchandise are now handled over a longer distance, since the wholesaler is no longer involved.

Small retailers may find even more problems in that they cannot sell a gross of most products profitably. They may also find that credit terms from manufacturers are much more inflexible than those offered by wholesalers.

Functions Performed for Retailers by Wholesalers

Although we shall discuss in greater detail the various types of wholesalers and the different functions they perform, all perform at least one or more of the following necessary functions for their retail customers.

Anticipate needs. The major function to be performed by the wholesaler is his ability to anticipate the needs of his customers, the retailers. This necessarily involves maintaining adequate stocks of merchandise in order to quickly refill requests. This represents the wholesaler's major function in that in most cases proper performance of this function determines whether or not he will remain in business. In effect, retailers dealing with a wholesaler who carries large stocks transfer most of the risks involved with holding inventories to the wholesaler.

The wholesaler involved in carrying large stocks must therefore be able to anticipate the needs of the retailers, which are ultimately dependent on the whims of the consumer.

Offer credit. A major function performed by some wholesalers revolves around their granting credit to retailers, who ordinarily do not possess the necessary capital to pay for goods not already sold. One finds, for instance, that wholesalers that deal with small retailers often offer generous credit terms. It is not unusual for a wholesaler selling to small retailers to allow credit terms to exceed the normal 30 days. In this case the wholesaler is actually supplying the capital necessary to run the retailer's business. One can therefore expect the wholesaler's price to reflect this function performed.

Deliver goods. Most wholesalers perform the delivery function. This is particularly true of wholesalers that distribute hard goods, such as appliances, television sets, washers, and dryers. Many wholesalers deliver the product directly to the consumer once the sale is made by the retailer. For example, the Simmons Mattress Company makes many deliveries directly from their local warehouses to the consumer on behalf of the store selling the merchandise. In this case, the mattress company acts as the warehouse for the retailer and also extends credit by billing the retailer at a later date. Many firms that sell television sets perform similar functions for the retailer.

Breaking down function. An important and growing function performed by wholesalers is the breaking down of large orders. In these cases the wholesaler who places large orders with the manufacturer breaks down the orders when they arrive into smaller shipments and delivers them to retailers. Naturally, small retailers are great users of this service. However, in recent years, with the growth of branch stores, this service has become more important, particularly when the wholesaler is able to break down a shipment and deliver to each of the large retailer's branches.

By buying in this way, that is, purchasing large quantities and then delivering smaller quantities to each store, the wholesaler can take advantage of quantity discounts and lower transportation charges. Through careful planning he can pass on some of these discounts to his retail customers.

Other services. The wholesaler performs other services for the retailer. One is that in effect he acts as the buying representative for the retailer. Wholesalers servicing small retail accounts are especially useful in this way, in that they perform a function for a retailer, who has neither the staff nor opportunity to search the markets for merchandise. In addition, many wholesalers specialize in handling imported goods, and thus retailers using them as a source of supply avail themselves of an international search organization. For example, a toy wholesaler may carry many varieties of toys produced in Japan and Hong Kong, areas much too far away for the small retailer.

A rather specialized service in the toy field is performed by a number of large wholesalers who develop Christmas toy catalogs that can be distributed to consumers on behalf of small retailers. These catalogs contain toys from all over the world and can be supplied on almost a daily basis to the retailers. In effect, the retailer is given a catalog that is competitive with stores many times his size at very little cost.

Wholesalers also serve as active information sources for retailers. The wholesaler's salesmen, for example, can provide information as to what is selling and what competitors are doing. In effect, many of the salesmen actually bring market information directly to the retailer, making it many times unnecessary for him to go into the market to obtain merchandising and marketing information. In addition, the wholesaler can provide the retailer with information as to how he can better manage his business. In particular, many wholesalers show the retailer how to control his inventories and maintain records. This service is performed mainly for small retailers.

It is a fact that in many cases the retailer, and particularly the large retailer, can circumvent the wholesaler and deal directly with the manufacturer. However, as will be pointed out later, the retailer or the manufacturer will have to perform many of the functions of the wholesaler and thereby incur additional costs. The problem of the retailer is, in effect, to balance the savings in price versus the additional costs that will incur when he deals with the manufacturer directly. The fact that wholesalers exist in our society is ample proof that many retailers believe that the wholesaler can perform many of these functions more efficiently and thus to the advantage of the retailer.

Functions Performed by the Wholesaler for the Manufacturer

The wholesaler does not perform functions only for the retailer. Perhaps just as important, he performs functions for the manufacturer. Again, these functions are needed economic functions and he receives compensation for his performance. Some of the more important functions are as follows:

Selling function. Many wholesalers provide a sales force for the manufacturer. That is, their salesmen represent the manufacturer throughout the prescribed territory. In some cases the wholesaler may provide the only selling services for the manufacturer. For instance, many manufacturers of appliances distribute their products by using wholesalers and their own sales force. In many cases the manufacturer deals directly with large retailers through his own sales force, while reaching the smaller retail firms through the use of wholesalers. Thus a manufacturer of toys may sell directly to the retail giants in his territory. However, he may find it inefficient and uneconomic to sell to the literally thousands of small outlets that carry toys. For instance, one may find toys in small candy stores, in drug stores, and even in small grocery stores.

To sell his product to these outlets would be uneconomical because of the small size of orders that are placed. In this case he may need the services of a wholesaler, who finds it economical to deal directly with many small retailers. Although more will be said on this subject later, suffice it to note that many of these wholesalers carry other lines of merchandise that can be sold to the small retailers at the same time.

Carrying of inventories. One of the most useful functions the wholesaler performs on behalf of the manufacturer is the carrying of inventories in anticipation of the needs of retailers. This is referred to as a capital-saving function. In this way the manufacturer usually finds that it is not necessary to carry huge inventories or to build a warehouse, since it is the wholesaler who takes this risk. Obviously, if the manufacturer would perform this function, there would be little need for the wholesaler, particularly in cases where the retailer can wait a reasonable period of time for his merchandise.

If operating properly, the manufacturer can control his production and plan his shipments to coordinate with the needs of the wholesale outlets. Since the wholesaler takes title to the goods he buys, he further reduces the manufacturer's capital requirements by paying for the merchandise within a reasonable period of time.

Reduce need for credit. Another major capital-saving function the wholesaler may perform for the manufacturer is to reduce his need for the financing of credit among many retailers. Thus the large producer may find that in the absence of a wholesaler he may have to sell to hundreds of retailers and thus is forced to extend credit to these same outlets. By selling through wholesalers, the manufacturer finds that it is the wholesaler who will carry the account, and thus the manufacturers need only establish the wholesaler's credit rather than that of hundreds of small accounts.

Provide market information. The wholesaler has always been a major source of market information to the manufacturer. The diverse accounts and experiences of the wholesaler obviously make him an excellent source of product ideas and consumer information for the manufacturer. Most manufacturers use the wholesaler (and one might add the retailer also) as a source of information to adjust their product lines to the needs of the consumer. Although the wholesaler does not usually make a conscious effort to acquire such information, through sheer day in and day out contacts they, and particularly their salesmen, acquire a great deal of knowledge and background on most any product they handle.

Decision Variables

Aside from the functions performed by wholesalers, the manufacturer has to consider many variables and many combinations of variables before making a decision concerning whether or not he shall deal directly with the retailer or shall employ the services of a wholesaler. Although there are many variables to be considered, it is a fact that in some industries one variable may take precedence over others. Some of the major variables that enter into making this decision are discussed next.

One major variable that must be considered by a firm is the finances that are available to management. Thus, if a firm chooses to use its own warehouses for stocking inventory, the cost will be very high. Their option of using a wholesaler to accomplish the same purpose may be made on the basis of availability of capital to build the warehousing system throughout the United States. As a result, one usually finds that small manufacturers rely greatly on the wholesaler.

Warehousing of inventory is not the only aspect of channel management that demands a strong financial position. For instance, the establishment of a sales force to deal directly with the retailer also requires a substantial capital investment. Firms choosing to use the wholesaler and his sales force can accomplish the same thing and eliminate the needed investment.

Making a decision as to whether or not to use the wholesaler, a manufacturer also has to consider the requirements of the product he is selling. Some products can be marketed better to the retailer if the manufacturer uses his own sales force directly under his control. Conversely, other products manage to sell themselves and only need the wholesaler to distribute them. Thus the producer of Winston cigarettes is mainly concerned with getting his product to the candy store, super-market, and vending machines. Through his advertising and promotional work (pull policy) he guarantees that people will recognize his product and will purchase it as long as it is available. Thus most cigarette companies distribute their products through wholesalers.

Conversely, manufacturers of greeting cards have found that sales through wholesalers must be reinforced by direct contact with their own company salesmen. Most major greeting card companies maintain their own sales force, which deals directly with even the smallest retail firms. In most instances they take orders directly from the retailer, set up displays of greeting cards within the stores, and generally aid the sales of their product through direct action. It is obviously the feeling of these manufacturers that the product will not sell as well if they simply sit back and rely on the sales force of the wholesaler.

In many instances the manufacturer is unable to reach the retailer, because the outlet for his product may be located in scattered or rural areas. Thus some manufacturers use wholesalers to reach the scattered market, but deal directly with retailers located in large urban areas. For example, manufacturers of grocery products use wholesalers in areas where the small rural grocery store is the major outlet. In this instance the large manufacturer of canned food products usually finds that it is uneconomical for him to either solicit or deliver directly to this type of outlet.

Product life cycle may have an important bearing on a manufacturer's decision to sell direct to a retailer or through wholesale channels. In most cases where the product life cycle is relatively short, or where the risk is great, the manufacturer will tend to avoid using wholesalers or any middlemen. Thus apparel manufacturers who sell fashion merchandise will more than likely deal directly with the retailer, since he is handling a product that has a relatively short season in which the risk of loss is great. On the other hand, the manufacturer of such stable products as underwear, slacks, or dungarees would find that the wholesalers will be willing to carry such products, since most of these items are neither seasonal nor is a great fashion risk involved. As a general rule, when fashion risk is high, short and speedy channels of distribution are maintained.

Although many manufacturers ordinarily consider using a wholesaler, it is not uncommon to find the same manufacturers dealing directly with retailers, simply because of the retailer preference. Thus many large retailers prefer dealing directly with manufacturers in order to obtain a lower price and particularly in many cases to obtain services not available from wholesalers. Here one finds large supermarkets buying candy directly from candy manufacturers. On the other hand, most candy manufacturers also deal with wholesalers who handle their small accounts. However, even if a candy manufacturer were willing to sell his total output to the wholesaler, many large supermarket chains would prefer to deal directly.

The growth of large retail firms outlined previously has been a constant threat to the existence of the wholesaler. As noted, however, the retailer must perform the functions of the wholesaler or transfer them to the manufacturer. It is a fact that many of the former types of wholesale organizations have gone by the wayside with the development of larger retail chains and less need for a wholesale organization.

On the other hand, there is also evidence that the wholesaler is not declining. In a real sense the wholesaler has changed to meet present-day needs. For example, due to the wide diversification of lines carried in many retail stores, the wholesaler has tended to specialize more in order to meet the needs of the retailer who cannot maintain adequate stocks nor reorder directly from manufacturers who require several weeks of lead time. The growing diversification in the shoe field has afforded a new wholesaler an opportunity to service many of the chains that cannot possibly carry all styles, sizes, and colors.[1]

In general, the wholesaler who has survived has had to become more aggressive and less apt to simply sit around. For instance, many grocery wholesalers who have lost their previous role dealing with the independent grocer have formed *voluntary cooperatives.*

The voluntary chain or cooperative is formed usually upon the initiative of the wholesaler. The retailers that join agree to purchase most of their merchandise from only this wholesaler. The cooperative has been particularly effective in the grocery field where independent grocers join the organization. Their benefits usually consist of lower prices, since the wholesaler can make much larger purchases than previously; the availability of executives to help plan a layout and even find property; and, most of all, participation in a local cooperative advertising program that will attract customers to the cooperative store. In a sense the cooperative presents one image to the public in terms of the merchandise offered and the construction and appearance of the store.

In line with this aggressive behavior, many wholesalers are at the point where they have developed services that are simply not available to retailers from any other source. For instance, in the toy industry, as noted earlier, a number of wholesalers have developed toy catalogs that are distributed to the public at Christmas time by member retailers. The wholesaler will fill all orders placed by retailers for toys listed in this catalog. This allows the small retailer of toys, and even the store that carries toys as a sideline, an opportunity to use a catalog that he could never produce, because of the great expense and necessary inventory that has to stand behind the catalog.

Each city has its example of wholesalers that have specialized and offered special services that enable them to perform a service at a profit. For example, a specialty wholesaler has evolved who will deliver prescription items to the druggist within hours of receiving such an order. This wholesaler has grown because of the growing proliferation of prescription drugs, making it most unprofitable for the average druggist to carry slow-moving items.[2]

---

[1] E. H. Lewis, *Marketing Channels: Structure and Strategy* (New York: McGraw-Hill Book Company, 1968), p. 18.

[2] *Ibid.,* p. 20.

The wholesaler, like all middlemen institutions, has conflicts with the manufacturer. Some are real and others are related to the manufacturer's view that a wholesaler should spend all his time promoting the manufacturer's product. In reality, many wholesalers carry many different products and thus are unable to devote the time and energy to a product as a manufacturer might like them to. Even in cases where the wholesaler may carry only a line of products produced by one manufacturer (such as a distributor of RCA products), the wholesaler must perform many duties not necessarily involved in the direct selling of the product.

Conflicts with the manufacturer arise in many areas. One major area of dispute is the wholesaler's desire to maintain an exclusive territory. In the case of some products a large exclusive territory is tantamount to receiving monopoly profits. For example, should RCA appoint a wholesaler for all its products and allow him to carry its products exclusively in the states of New York, New Jersey, and Connecticut, the wholesaler would no doubt be inundated with orders and would find this arrangement quite profitable. This would occur since RCA has hundreds of retail outlets in these areas, and the appointment of a wholesaler automatically brings with it an enormous amount of business without any effort on the part of the wholesaler. Thus RCA's decision in establishing wholesaler territories is to determine the balance between the amount of services required by the firm's retail customers versus the amount of business required by a wholesaler in order to profitably maintain a service and supply organization.

Another area of conflict lies in the wholesaler's obligation in many product areas of maintaining and guaranteeing the manufacturer's warranties and guarantees. In most arrangements of this sort the manufacturer reimburses the wholesaler for performing services. However, the wholesaler may not be reimbursed for many other services that he performs which he considers to be additional work. Such things as training store personnel, setting up displays, informing retailers of product and price changes, and the myriad of routine activities, such as returns that must be processed. Most wholesalers feel that they are not adequately compensated for carrying out these necessary functions.

In the sale of certain other types of merchandise the wholesaler must actually service the product and in most cases will receive compensation from the manufacturer for his work. For example, car dealers must service new cars on behalf of the manufacturer. Upon performing this service, they are reimbursed by the manufacturer. Most car dealers feel that the reimbursement by the manufacturer is not adequate to compensate them for the actual work performed. They feel that the rates set are minimal, and if any complications ensue, the dealer will actually lose money. In the industrial field most distributors are required to handle routine servicing problems with the manufacturer's product. In performing many of these functions few middlemen feel that the compensation received is adequate.

One major complaint made by manufacturers against wholesalers is that the manufacturer feels that the wholesaler's salesmen take the line of least resistance. That is, the wholesaler who carries a number of lines will act as an order taker and will not push any product, even if it has superior qualities. Most wholesalers will deny this. They are quick to point out, however, that they carry many lines of products and thus to spend time on selling one product is not possible. They usually make the added point that a product competing with so many other routine products in a channel should be either presold or the manufacturer should offer the wholesaler an incentive to promote the product.

Characteristics of Wholesalers

To better understand the role of the wholesaler and his relationship to the manufacturer, one should recognize the size and operating characteristics of the wholesaler.

Several contrasting statements can be made about the wholesaler and retailer in terms of the manufacturer's view of them. First, the typical wholesale firm is much larger than the typical retail firm. As will be noted in Chapter 17, many retail firms may average well under $600 a week in sales volume. In contrast, one can see in Table 16-1 that about 40 percent of the wholesale establishments range in size from a volume of $200,000 to a volume of about $1,000,000. The number of establishments in these groups seems to be about equal to those with a sales volume below $200,000.

TABLE 16-1   Sales Size of Wholesale Establishments – United States: 1967

	Establishment		Sales	
Sales Size of Establishment	*Number*	*Percentage of Total*	*Amount in millions of dollars*	*Percentage of Total*
United States, total	311,464	100.0	459,476	100.0
Establishments operated entire year with annual sales ($) of				
20,000,000 or more	2,663	0.9	138,612	30.2
10,000,000 to 19,999,999	3,993	1.3	54,126	11.8
5,000,000 to 9,999,999	8,564	2.7	58,843	12.8
1,000,000 to 4,999,999	59,977	19.3	125,572	27.3
500,000 to 999,999	49,611	15.9	35,189	7.7
200,000 to 499,999	73,643	23.6	23,944	5.2
Less than 200,000	105,200	33.8	10,170	2.2
Establishments not operated entire year	7,873	2.5	13,020	2.8

Source: U.S. Department of Commerce, Bureau of the Census, *U.S. Census of Business*, 1967.

It should also be noted that the typical wholesale organization has less than 20 employees. However, firms with over 50 employees, although they represent about 3 percent of all establishments, account for over 25 percent of total wholesale sales. Several other characteristics of wholesalers are also noteworthy. For instance, Table 16-2 seems to indicate that the larger a wholesale firm is, the lower its expense ratio. Thus the more sales volume a merchant wholesaler generates, the greater his profit and the lower his expense ratio. Although this same thing holds for retailing, it is recognized that after certain levels the expenses and profits of the large firms do not decline.

This fact, that is, declining operating expenses as sales volume increases, is important in the business practice of wholesalers, who are constantly striving to increase their sales volume by carrying more product lines.

When measured against other forms of distributors in the marketing system, the wholesaler operates on rather slender margins. Since the wholesaler must establish prices that must cover his operating expenses plus his profits, Table 16-3 seems to indicate that wholesalers maintain markups well below those of a retail organization or, for that matter, the manufacturer. Thus one finds operating expenses running at a rate from a low of 1.9 percent for import agents to a high of 14.4 percent for wholesale merchant distributors. It is noted that 12 of the 16 firms listed had operating expenses below 10 percent. In comparison, the typical department store has an expense ratio that exceeds 33 percent of sales.

One should also note that payroll expenses account for well over 50 percent of the total costs of operating the average wholesale business. For instance, merchant wholesalers who sell groceries, confectionery, and meats experienced operating expenses of 13.5 percent (see Table 16-2) in 1967. About 54 percent of the total operating expenses were accounted for by the payroll expenses.

Merchant Wholesaler Operating and Payroll Expenses by Sales Size — United States: 1967   **TABLE 16-2**

Sales Size of Establishment	Operating Expenses as Percentage of Sales	Payroll as Percentage of Sales
United States, total	13.5	7.4
Establishment operated entire year		
with annual sales ($) of	13.5	7.5
10,000,000 or more	8.1	3.3
5,000,000 to 9,999,000	11.4	6.2
2,000,000 to 4,999,000	13.9	7.7
1,000,000 to 1,999,000	16.6	9.3
500,000 to 999,000	18.9	10.7
300,000 to 499,000	20.9	12.0
200,000 to 299,000	21.7	12.3
100,000 to 199,000	23.1	12.8
Less than $100,000	24.7	13.1
Establishment not operated entire year	13.1	6.8

Source: U.S. Department of Commerce, Bureau of the Census, *U.S. Census of Business,* 1967.

The high payroll cost is understandable in wholesaling, in that the industry does not lend itself to automation to as great an extent as say manufacturing. For example, the wholesaler must employ people to search out merchandise and to handle the mountains of paperwork associated with ordering, distributing, and billing customers. The fact that many wholesalers deal with small firms means that they must constantly break down large orders into smaller lots, a task that requires a great deal of labor input.

TABLE 16-3 Operating Expenses — Wholesalers

Type of Operation and Kind of Business	Establishments (number)	Sales ($1,000)	Operating Expenses Including Payroll Amount ($1,000)	Operating Expenses Including Payroll Percentage of Sales
Wholesale trade, total	311,464	459,475,967	(x)	(x)
Merchant wholesalers, total	212,993	206,055,065	27,772,069	13.5
Wholesale merchants, distributors	204,783	181,775,733	26,123,778	14.4
Importers	5,171	10,353,989	1,061,734	10.3
Exporters	2,272	9,507,734	386,441	4.1
Terminal grain elevators	767	4,417,609	200,116	4.5
Manufacturers' sales branches, sales offices, total	30,679	157,096,541	11,304,285	7.2
Manufacturers' sales branches — with stock	16,709	67,174,649	7,582,469	11.3
Manufacturers' sales offices — without stock	13,970	89,921,892	3,721,816	4.1
Merchandise agents, brokers, total	26,462	61,347,022	2,479,147	4.0
Auction companies	1,594	4,792,386	137,589	2.9
Merchandise brokers for buyers or sellers	4,373	14,030,462	449,909	3.2
Commission merchants	5,425	14,068,048	479,485	3.4
Import agents	270	1,790,666	39,993	2.2
Export agents	548	3,372,043	62,997	1.9
Manufacturers' agents	12,106	15,256,996	980,534	6.4
Selling agents	1,891	6,889,890	287,448	4.2
Purchasing agents, resident buyers	255	1,146,545	41,192	3.6
Assemblers of farm products, total	11,101	10,155,511	870,030	8.6
Country grain elevators	6,477	5,590,708	394,225	7.1
Other assemblers of farm products	4,624	4,564,803	475,805	10.4

Source: U.S. Department of Commerce, Bureau of the Census, *1967 Census of Business, Wholesale Trade.*

Table 16-4 shows the relative status of all types of wholesalers. Note should be made that the most numerous by far is the merchant wholesaler, who accounts for close to 50 percent of the total wholesale volume in the United States. Combined with manufacturers' sales branches, merchant wholesalers account for over three quarters of all establishments and sales. Although there are numerous wholesalers, one must remember that only a few categories are of major importance. In the following section, a brief discussion will be presented so that one can begin to understand the role each plays in the distribution of merchandise. Two major groupings, assemblers of farm products and petroleum bulk stations, will not be discussed since they are not of major interest in this book. Other subclassifications will be overlooked since their specialty is of little import to the study of wholesaling.

Wholesale Trade — Type of Operation and Kind of Business, 1967   TABLE 16-4

Type of Operation and Kind of Business	Establishments	Sales in Millions of Dollars
Wholesale trade, total	311,464	459,476
Merchant wholesalers	212,993	206,055
Manufacturers' sales branches, offices	30,679	157,097
Petroleum bulk stations, terminals	30,229	24,822
Merchandise agents, brokers	26,462	61,347
Farm products assemblers	11,101	10,156
Kind of Business		
Motor vehicles, automotive equip.	31,214	46,122
Drugs, chemicals, allied products	11,543	27,795
Piece goods, notions, apparel	11,400	21,280
Groceries and related products	40,055	74,458
Farm products — raw materials	14,962	38,148
Electrical goods	16,730	32,115
Hardware, plumbing, heating equipment, supplies	13,497	12,055
Machinery, equipment, supplies	52,431	50,432
Metals and minerals	7,891	33,704
Petroleum, petroleum products	34,484	33,373
Scrap, waste materials	7,927	4,626
Tobacco, tobacco products	2,597	6,048
Beer, wine, distilled alcoholic beverages	7,309	14,164
Paper, paper products	9,586	12,783
Furniture, home furnishings	8,023	7,723
Lumber, construction materials	13,622	16,390
Other miscellaneous products	28,193	28,737

Source: U.S. Department of Commerce, Bureau of the Census, *U.S. Census of Business,* 1967.

Table 16-4 also indicates the various kinds of businesses wholesalers engage in. The most numerous seem to be in groceries; machinery, equipment, supplies; petroleum; and motor vehicles equipment.

The largest in terms of sales volume is groceries, as might be expected, since food represents the largest area of consumer expenditures.

Merchandise Agents

The U.S. Census in 1967 listed 26,000 merchandise agents. This group accounts for approximately 12 percent of the total wholesale sales in that year. Under this grouping one finds brokers, commission merchants, purchasing agents, selling agents, manufacturers' agents, auction companies, and export–import agents.

Merchandise agents as a general rule

1. Buy and sell merchandise for others.
2. Engage in this activity in both domestic and foreign markets.
3. Rarely take title to goods or warehouse goods.
4. Receive compensation in the form of a commission on each transaction.

Although it is difficult to classify each broker, since they perform overlapping functions and many have their own way of operating, still a number seem to operate in a general pattern.

For instance, the *broker,* whether it be in marketing or real estate, serves the function of bringing the buyer and seller together. In practically all cases the broker represents the seller and receives a commission as compensation. Many brokers work on a free-lance basis, preferring to move from company to company rather than engage in a long-term agreement with one firm.

In direct contrast is the *manufacturer's agent* who acts on behalf of a manufacturer. In effect, this agent is a company salesman. Although he will not carry a directly competing product, the manufacturer's agent usually carries a number of noncompeting but yet allied lines of merchandise. Since they act as salesmen for many companies, the manufacturer's agent is the most numerous of merchandise agents.

Commission merchants operate in a similar manner as brokers. Typically, they represent sellers and operate on a commission. Unlike the broker, the commission merchant may actually take possession of the goods in his own warehouse. On occasion he may even sort and grade the merchandise. However, the buyer of the merchandise does not know who the manufacturer of the merchandise is, and deals only with the commission merchant. Like brokers, the commission merchants may work for many different manufacturers. Commission merchants are used mainly in the food, textile, and lumber industries.

The *selling agent* is also an independent business entrepreneur. Selling agents usually contract with the seller to sell his entire output on a commission basis. Their contracts usually cover long periods of time. The selling agent is usually found in the textile industry. In effect, the selling agent acts as the sales department of the producer. In many cases they act as partners in the firm, in that they influence prices, production schedules, and the terms of sale.

As a general rule, all these agents are used by firms that have limited resources.

Classified as wholesale organizations are manufacturers' sales offices and branches. The former acts as a headquarters away from the company plants for the firm's sales force. As a general rule, they do not carry stocks. When necessary the firm may carry stocks in its own warehouse or, more than likely, have a local wholesaler carry the inventory. The sales force in this office may help stimulate sales in the assigned area.

Sales *branches* differ in that in some cases they may carry stocks and, most importantly in the case of mechanical goods, they may be charged with the task of servicing these products.

Sales branches and offices are usually found in the grocery, metals, electrical, and chemical fields.

Manufacturers' Sales Outlets

The most numerous and important wholesale outlets are the merchant wholesalers. These outlets are independent businessmen and are distinguished by the fact that they take title to the merchandise they sell. In addition, they usually store merchandise (with the exception of the drop shipper) and perform all the services required of these types of outlets. Thus they usually provide financing, delivery services, and assemble and sort merchandise.

It is customary to divide merchant wholesalers into two major groups — service and limited function wholesalers.

Merchant Wholesalers

Service Wholesalers

Approximately nine out of ten merchant wholesalers can be classified as service wholesalers. The four major types in this grouping are the wholesale merchants or distributors, rack merchandisers, export-import merchants, and terminal grain elevators.

The most numerous of the full-service wholesalers are the wholesale merchants and distributors. These outlets sell to practically all marketing organizations, such as retailers, institutions, and industrial and other commercial enterprises. Typically, a wholesaler of this type may sell apparel to small stores; others may supply newspapers, magazines, paperbacks, and tobacco products to candy stores; still others supply houseware items to other stores. Some may serve more than one market. For instance, a plumbing supply firm may sell to plumbers and to retail homeowners.

A more recent type of wholesaler is the rack merchandiser. This wholesaler developed in recent years, aided by the advent of scrambled merchandising in the food supermarkets. Many operators of supermarkets found that they were being forced to carry many nonfood items, such as phonograph records, apparel, housewares, and toys. Rather than establish a buying organization for nonfoods, some of these supermarkets use the services of a rack merchandiser to supply the merchandise and change the displays. The rack jobber for performing these services receives payment for merchandise that is sold after the store deducts a commission on each sale. The inventory is the merchandiser's, and the store only pays for each item sold. Ordinarily, the rack merchandiser services the smaller supermarkets, since the large chains prefer to buy directly from the manufacturers.

Export-import wholesalers specialize, as their name implies, in selling foreign goods in the domestic market. These firms sell practically all products available in the domestic markets, such as apparel (e.g., gloves), toys, electronic supplies, jewelry, auto supplies, and hundreds of other products. Their appeal is mainly to the smaller- or medium-sized stores that would find direct dealing with foreign countries impractical. In addition, many of these firms sell to large department stores, because they maintain large stocks of merchandise and manage to maintain a superior knowledge of many of these markets.

The last type of service merchant is the terminal grain elevator active in the farm industry. These elevators buy from other assembly points but do not deal directly with the farmer. Most of the major terminal elevators are located in the large midwestern cities. Their customers include distilleries, milling companies, manufacturers of food products, and most any firm needing grain for further processing. Companies of this type lease or own storage elevators in most of these major terminal markets.

Limited
Function
Wholesalers

Although of much less importance than service wholesalers, limited function wholesalers nevertheless perform functions and in most cases maintain stocks of merchandise for their customers. Four major types exist: cash-and-carry wholesalers, drop shippers, truck wholesalers, and mail-order wholesalers.

The *cash-and-carry* wholesaler operates as the name implies on a noncredit basis. In addition, it is customary in dealing with this type of wholesaler to pick up the merchandise at his place of business. Traditionally, these firms service small retailers who are constantly in need of fill-in items. Larger stores use these wholesalers to fill in temporary out-of-stock conditions. For example, large department stores use cash-and-carry drug wholesalers to keep them in stock on many of the hundreds and perhaps thousands of drug items carried in the cosmetic and drug department of the store. Many of these firms flourish in the grocery field.

In direct contrast to the cash-and-carry wholesalers are the *desk jobbers* or *drop shippers.* Drop shippers do not maintain warehouses nor do they carry inventories. They do, however, take title to the goods and are responsible for billing a customer and collecting payment. All orders to the manufacturer are shipped directly to the drop shipper's customer. Most of these firms operate in the lumber, building materials, and coal industries, where the costs of hauling and transportation are high in comparison to the final price of the product.

Truck wholesalers usually perform the functions of full-service organizations. However, although they maintain a warehouse, they operate by selling and making deliveries directly from a truck. Ordinarily, the truck wholesalers handle nationally advertised food specialties such as potato chips, bakery products, fruits, vegetables, and numerous other like items.

Their appeal to the manufacturer is great since they, in effect, supply him with an aggressive means of obtaining business, since many of these firms call on retailers on a daily basis. Their appeal to the retailer is that they carry items that require quick turnover since they deteriorate rapidly. Thus through rapid delivery and careful display they can add to the retailer's profits without the necessary attention he would have to devote to accomplish the same thing.

Mail-order wholesalers, as the name implies, do not engage in any personal selling. They are also not of any paramount importance in any one line of merchandise. Nevertheless, they do exist in many fields. They operate in many different ways. For example, some use missionary salesmen to leave catalogs and instruct retail firms or other wholesalers on how to order merchandise through their catalogs. Many of these firms are found in the printing and stationery fields.

SUMMARY

Wholesalers, like all marketing institutions, perform functions. Since wholesalers are middlemen, they perform functions for both the manufacturer and the retailer. For retailers they perform the following major functions:

1. Anticipate needs.
2. Offer credit.
3. Deliver goods.
4. Perform breaking down function.

For manufacturers they perform the following functions:

1. Selling.
2. Carry inventories.
3. Reduce need for manufacturers' credit.
4. Provide market information.

In terms of their operating characteristics, wholesalers are larger than retailers, their payroll represents one half of their expenses, and the larger the firm, the lower the expense ratios.

Merchant wholesalers' and manufacturers' sales branches represent three quarters of all the wholesale volume.

QUESTIONS

1. The number of wholesalers is declining because they no longer perform economic functions. Discuss.

2. Wholesalers perform functions *mainly* for the manufacturer. Discuss.

*3. What would be the most important two functions a wholesaler would perform for a manufacturer of refrigerators?

4. Discuss the importance of the transfer principle as a consideration in developing a marketing strategy for a manufacturer.

5. What functions provided to a retailer are of greater interest to a small retailer? Why?

6. In what way does the financial position of the manufacturing firm determine the need for a wholesaler?

*In-depth question.

7. How has the wholesaler adjusted to changes in the needs of his customers?

8. Has the number of wholesalers declined? Why or why not?

9. One of the major areas of conflict between the wholesaler and manufacturer is the demand on the part of the former for an exclusive territory. Present the manufacturer's point of view.

10. Since large-volume wholesalers have lower expenses than lower-volume firms, it is understandable that wholesalers attempt to carry a wide variety of lines whenever possible. True or false? Discuss.

*11. A toy manufacturer wants to sell his low-priced toys in supermarkets, toy stores, and variety stores. What types of wholesalers would you recommend he use?

12. Why would a manufacturer use a selling agent rather than his own sales force?

*In-depth question.

The Retail Channel

17

SUMMARY KEY

The retailer is of great interest to the manufacturer because he represents the last link in the chain that ends with the ultimate consumer.

In terms of conflicts of interest the manufacturers and retailers have differences that range from product attitudes to obtaining exclusives, private branding, and product change.

Retailing is one of the most competitive industries in the United States. The reason for its competitiveness is that entry into retailing is easy, and many small retail firms can exist without earning profits.

In spite of the competitiveness, there is evidence that many retailers earn profits comparable to manufacturing. They accomplish this by differentiating themselves in terms of the merchandise they carry, the services they offer, or the locations they select.

Retailing is filled with contrasts. For example, almost one out of three retail stores produces an annual volume of less than $30,000. Over 80 percent of the retail stores in the United States are single-unit operators. In contrast, one can find that chain department stores account for over 80 percent of the sales of all department stores.

The major types of stores that are of interest to manufacturers are the specialty stores, which include those selling women's apparel, handbags, phonograph records, and the like; the department stores, which have a strong metropolitan following; chains, which include supermarkets, drug chains, and large apparel chains; discount stores, which historically date from the end of World War II; and franchise firms and vending machines.

To encourage the retailer to buy his product, the manufacturer may rely on advertising and other allowances, exclusive or selective distribution territorial rights, and other fringe services such as training or inventory count systems.

In selling to the retailer the manufacturer may deal with the owner in the case of a small firm, a central buying organization in the case of a large chain, where he may encounter a buying committee, or an independent buying organization representing retailers from all over the country.

The retailer is of central interest to the manufacturer, because he represents the last chain in the link before selling to the ultimate consumer. Practically all manufacturers selling to the ultimate consumer must move their product through the variety of retail outlets. In essence, therefore, the manufacturer is faced with making decisions as to the type of outlets he will sell through. This encompasses the problem of gaining the cooperation of the chosen channel of distribution.

In this chapter we shall discuss the retail channel from the point of view of the size and number of retailers, since this is an important determinate in the manufacturer's decisions as to which outlets he will select to sell his merchandise. As a background for this analysis, we shall discuss retail competition. Finally, we shall present a section on how the retailer makes buying decisions.

Before entering into this discussion, we need to be aware of the fact that retailers may have a different outlook on the sale of a product than a manufacturer. Many of these conflicts come about because of internal organizational differences and differences in product attitudes. Some of these conflicts will be presented next.

Conflicts with Retailers

One of the major conflicts a manufacturer may have with a retailer is the difference in attitude toward products sold by the manufacturer. A manufacturer spends most of his working day thinking about various strategies for promoting his product. He is, as noted in this book, concerned with developing meaningful strategies for establishing new markets for his products. He is constantly surveying these markets with the thought in mind of developing additional means of increasing the sale of his product.

For instance, his firm may be organized by product lines and he may have executives charged with doing nothing more than concentrating on a product sold and marketed by his firm. Thus General Foods has a product manager in charge of Yuban coffee only. The specialization and interest in only a few products by the manufacturer is well demonstrated by the cosmetic executive who spent a whole year for a major cosmetic manufacturer writing and rewriting the company information and advertising that was to appear on the packages holding the firm's famous lipstick.

Conversely, as noted earlier, the retailer is not product oriented in the sense that he is deeply concerned with the manufacturer's product. Although a retailer is interested in selling a line of products, he is usually not too involved with individual products. For example, although a retailer hopes that his stationery department sells its share of the pen market, he is not too concerned with the sale of the pen manufactured by the ABC Company. His reasons are many. First, he carries so many products that his major concern by necessity has to be with the overall problem of selling pens. Second, if he finds that the ABC pen does not sell, his reordering system is such that the pen will automatically not be reordered. Thus the retailer concentrates mainly on a number of lines of a product, which is in direct conflict with the manufacturer, who is interested in selling only his product.

Another major area of conflict is the retailers' growing interest in obtaining exclusives. A retailer as part of his strategy is always trying to obtain an exclusive product for his store. His reasons are obvious. Once he has obtained a product on an exclusive basis the customer must deal with him. As a result he may expect to benefit from less competition by gaining higher prices than he would ordinarily expect to receive. Another indication of this growing interest in exclusives is the developing strategy among retailers to establish private-brand merchandise. Private-brand merchandise is by definition merchandise that can only be purchased from one retail organization. As noted in Chapter 9, some private-brands have become so powerful as to overshadow many of the national brands promoted by manufacturers.

Private branding is in conflict with most of the interests of the manufacturer, particularly those that promote nationally branded products. By private branding the retailer is free to choose and change his source of supply whenever he feels he can make better arrangements.

It is not to the manufacturer's interest in most cases to allow his retailers an opportunity to become the exclusive distributor of his line in an area. This is only feasible when the market is rather limited. Thus Rolls-Royce can have an exclusive dealer arrangement since there are only a relatively few people in any large city that can afford a $24,000 minimum starting price. Conversely, it is not to General Electric's interest to offer exclusive franchises for its television sets since they are aiming at selling a mass market and require massive exposure. Thus the conflict; on the one hand, the retailer wants exclusive lines of products; on the other hand, the mass-selling manufacturer prefers as many retail outlets as warranted.

Other conflict areas also exist. For instance, the retailer as a general rule resents product change. The manufacturer, on the other hand, uses product change as a weapon to attract customers. The manufacturer's reasons are obvious, and in many industries product change is the accepted mode of doing business. It is accepted and expected by both manufacturers and consumers. Although the retailer in many cases is forced to accept product change, many resent its use for reasons that may not seem too obvious to the uninitiated.

One major reason among retailers for resisting product change is the fact that most retailers have the unchanged model still in stock. In some cases the number in stock may be considerable and will require particular skill if the retailer is to sell them before taking on the newly changed product. Again, if the retailer were only concerned with one product, he could manage this problem with greater skill; however, most retail firms stock thousands of products. In addition, in cases when the retailer handles products that require servicing, he is faced with the practical problem of carrying spare parts, which eventually develop vast inventory requirements involving a considerable investment.

One interesting area that causes conflict among retailers and manufacturers is the drive of the retailer to obtain the lowest price versus the manufacturer's need to sell at the highest price. Should the manufacturer sell a product that is in great demand by the consuming public, particularly when he holds a virtual monopoly (Polaroid cameras for example), the product will most likely be sold at a price that is favorable to the manufacturer. Conversely (and this is true for most goods sold), when the manufacturer is just one of many, one can expect that he will be more competitive in his pricing and will be more prone to offer concessions to retailers.

Finally, although more will be said about this aspect later, many of the retailers are not as profit oriented as the manufacturer. In fact, it is well known that many retailers operate without profit, a situation that simply cannot exist for long in a manufacturing firm.

Profile
of the
Retailer

Retailing is one of the most competitive industries in the United States. The reasons for its competitiveness lie in the fact that entry into retailing is easy and that many firms can exist without the need of profits.

Entry is easy in retailing since it takes little capital to start a retail business. In the retail firm little money is invested in fixed assets, in comparison to a manufacturing firm. Most of the investment in a retail firm is in the inventories, which in effect are liquid assets. This is particularly applicable to firms that sell on a cash basis. In the typical retail firm, expenditures for cash registers and fixtures are minor in comparison to the inventory investment. In addition, the inventory can be purchased on a credit basis if necessary. With the proper turnover of merchandise, it is quite possible that a retailer will have the cash necessary to pay for his inventory well before the inventory has to be paid for. It is common knowledge that many retailers can start a store for an investment of less than $5,000.

In contrast, one starting a manufacturing firm would find it much more difficult and costly. Typically, a manufacturer would need equipment that in some instances could exceed millions of dollars of investment. A manufacturer needs tools and capital equipment. He also finds it necessary to hire workers, buy raw materials, and wait before he receives payment for his goods. It is no secret that the capital needed for almost any manufacturing enterprise easily exceeds $100,000.

This is not to say that many retailers do not invest a great deal of money in their stores. What it does mean, however, is that an enterprising entrepreneur can start a retail store practically on a shoestring. One economist noted a number of years ago that the average investment in manufacturing exceeds $12,000 per worker, which is about two and one half times the investment in retail firms per worker.[1]

In addition to the ease of entry, one must bear in mind that many retail firms exist without earning economic profits. This is particularly the case among small retail firms. This comes about simply because the operators of many small firms are satisfied to earn a living in a retail firm and are not concerned with earning a return on their investment, which one usually identifies as profits. Many of these people running small stores are unable to earn wages in other occupations. Others are independent and enjoy being in business for themselves and thus prefer working in their own stores. In other cases, the retail store provides employment for the whole family. Thus in the "momma and poppa" grocery store the family may receive wages. When the wages they earn in the store equal what they could earn working for somebody, one might conclude that their earnings include no profits. However, should the store's earnings greatly exceed the wages they could receive elsewhere, then the difference can be classified as profits or a return on the investment in the business. The point is that many small firms earn no profits, and the owners simply earn wages that they could get elsewhere working for some other enterprise.

What this means in effect is that entry into retailing is easy, and one finds that not only will firms enter the field because of low capital requirements, but also

---

[1] Jules Backman, "Why Wages Are Lower in Retailing," *The Southern Economic Journal,* Vol. 23, Jan. 1957, pp. 295–305.

many entrants into retailing do not have to earn profits as they do in most manufacturing businesses.

One might expect therefore that in retailing, when compared to manufacturing, the concentration of firms (i.e., firms controlling substantial fractions of their industry) is low. Referring back to Table 4-3, one can recall several instances where manufacturing firms have achieved high levels of concentration. The ratios range from a high of 86 percent for four chewing gum firms to a low of 5 percent for the top four manufacturers of fur goods. The average would seem to be somewhere around 40 or 50 percent.

In direct contrast, in Table 17-1 one should note that the four largest food chains (the largest retail business in the country) account for 16 percent of the total sales of food in the United States. In addition, the top four giants in the general

Total Sales of the Four Largest Firms in Three Retail Fields, 1970   TABLE 17-1

	Millions of Dollars
Food stores	
Great Atlantic & Pacific Tea Company	5,664
Safeway Stores	1,798
Kroger Stores	3,735
Acme Markets, Inc.	1,798
Total four largest	12,995
Total all food stores	81,466
Percentage	16%
Variety stores	
F. W. Woolworth	2,527
S. S. Kresge	2,558
W. T. Grant	1,254
J. J. Newberry	414
Total four largest	6,853
Total all variety stores	7,056
Percentage	97%
General merchandise stores	
Sears, Roebuck	9,262
Montgomery Ward	2,226
J. C. Penney	4,150
Federated Department Stores	2,091
Total four largest	17,729
Total all general merchandise stores	62,867
Percentage	28%

Source: Various annual reports and the Bureau of the Census.

merchandise industry account for 28 percent of this group of merchandise. Variety chains represent the highest ratio of concentration at 97 percent. One should be careful in jumping to any conclusions about variety chains, since their type of merchandise is also sold in the general merchandise stores, and if they are lumped into this category, their percentage of concentration would drop substantially.

Differentiation

In spite of such competition there is some evidence that many retail firms have maintained profits that are comparable to many of the largest manufacturing firms.[2] Why the paradox? In an industry with easy entry and vigorous competition one still finds profits in many retail firms as high or higher than manufacturing organizations.

The answer lies in the retailer's ability to differentiate his firm from the rest of his competitors. At the forefront of this attempt is the retailer's constant struggle to carry merchandise exclusively. In this endeavor he may search the world markets, in addition to constantly imploring the domestic manufacturers to sell their merchandise exclusively to his firm, in his area. In addition, the retailer may attempt to establish and then differentiate the services he offers the consumer. He may specialize in free delivery or in making available exceptional and knowledgeable sales personnel. Thus the local drugstore may attempt to differentiate itself from competing drugstores by offering a free delivery service. The supermarket may offer its customers free delivery to the car.

Retail stores can also differentiate their firms by wisely choosing locations or in some cases gaining extrance into a shopping center that excludes the firm's major competitors. This is a very common occurrence in shopping centers featuring large department stores, where the department store's major competitor may be deliberately excluded. The shopper looking for department store merchandise may find her options limited if she chooses to shop only in a shopping center.

Thus the retail firm's ability to earn profits over and above the average for the industry depends on the ability of the firm to differentiate itself from competition and of course to manage its business in an efficient manner.

Quantifying Retailing

Retailing is filled with paradoxes, and manufacturers are well aware of this. Although retail sales in a recent year exceeded $351 billion, many of the 1,700,000 retail stores are extremely small. Table 17-2 indicates that almost one third of these stores produce an annual sales volume of less than $30,000. This would mean that the typical store in this group produced about $100 per day in sales volume over the year. Additionally, about one quarter of the retail firms had no paid employees and almost half of all retail stores have no more than one employee. In addition, one may also note that over 80 percent of the total number of retail stores in the United States are single-unit operators.

In essence, therefore, one must conclude that the manufacturer is faced with a retail distribution system that contains hundreds of thousands of very small organizations. It is the task of the manufacturer to reach these organizations in selling many of his products.

On the other hand, manufacturers that are *not* necessarily interested in selling to every last vestige of a market may find that by limiting the firm's sales to multiunit operators they can cover the market in some categories. Thus one sees in Table 17-3 that department store chains with over 11 stores account for over 80 percent of the

[2] David Rachman, *Retail Strategy and Structure* (Englewood Cliffs, N.J.: Prentice-Hall, Inc., 1969), pp. 41–43.

Sales	$351,633[a]
Establishments (add 000)	1,763
Establishments operated entire year	1,671
Annual sales ($)	
Less than 30,000	583
30,000 to 49,999	227
50,000 to 99,999	323
100,000 to 299,999	359
300,000 to 499,999	74
500,000 to 999,999	55
1,000,000 or more	50
Single units	1,543
Multiunits	220

[a]1969 (billions)

Sources: *Survey of Current Business; U.S. Census of Business, 1967*, Vol. I.

sales in that category. Similarly, variety stores with over 11 units account for almost 80 percent of variety store sales.

From this same figure however one can see that a great deal of merchandise, such as furniture, jewelry, and drugs still is sold through single-unit stores.

Geographic Areas

Table 17-4 indicates that manufacturers can use retail sales as a guideline in establishing sales quotas and market targets for various areas of the country. Thus one can see that the Middle Atlantic states and the East North Central states account for almost 40 percent of total retail sales in the United States.

In addition, the manufacturer is sure to note that many metropolitan areas account for substantial sales volume, ranging from the New York metropolitan statistical area with over $15 billion in sales to the 38th ranked Sacramento, California, with just over $1 billion in retail sales volume.

All these markets represent different challenges to the manufacturer who is faced with the task of gaining his share of many of these markets.

Types of Retail Outlets

One of the most numerous types of retail stores is the specialty shop found in downtown business districts, shopping centers, and neighborhood business districts. This store specializes in the sale of many major categories of merchandise. Typically, one will find specialty stores selling women's apparel, handbags, phonograph records, stationery, or the like. Ordinarily, these stores are small, consisting of one unit (chains of these stores will be discussed later), and appeal to a relatively narrow segment of the market, a segment that is particularly interested in high fashion and large assortments of merchandise. In addition, most customers of these stores have above-average incomes. In recent years the specialty store in the apparel field has put even a greater accent on fashion, and one sees the boutique flavor throughout many shopping areas. Stores of this type will continue to grow as consumers' interests in variety and fashion continue to increase.

349

TABLE 17-3 Retail Trade — Sales of Multiunit Organizations, by Kind of Business: 1970 to 1971[a]

Kind of Business	1970	1971	Percentage[b] 1970	Percentage[b] 1971
Total sales	117,245	125,607	31.2	30.7
Durable goods stores[c]	8,617	8,455	7.5	6.4
Tire, battery, accessory dealers	1,827	1,955	32.8	30.7
Furniture and appliance group	1,508	1,600	8.5	8.6
Nondurable goods stores[c]	108,628	117,152	41.6	42.3
Apparel group[c]	5,475	5,741	27.6	27.6
Men's and boys' wear stores[d]	819	750	17.7	15.9
Women's apparel, accessory stores[e]	1,875	2,123	24.7	25.9
Shoe stores	1,473	1,498	42.1	42.4
Drug and proprietary stores	4,358	4,693	32.5	34.2
Eating and drinking places	2,859	2,716	9.6	8.7
Food group[c]	44,072	45,954	51.2	51.5
Grocery stores	43,183	45,235	54.1	54.5
General merchandise group, including nonstores[c]	46,102	52,092	75.2	76.5
Department stores, excluding mail-order sales	31,893	36,544	85.5	87.0
Variety stores	5,417	5,398	77.8	77.4

[a]In millions of dollars. Data based on sales of organizations operating 11 or more retail stores in 1967. Quarterly data are not adjusted for seasonal variation or trading day differences.
[b]Multiunit sales as percent of all retail sales.
[c]Includes data not shown separately.
[d]Comprises men's and boys' clothing, furnishings stores, and custom tailors.
[e]Comprises women's ready-to-wear, other apparel, accessory, specialty shops, and furriers.
Source: Adapted from *Statistical Abstract of the United States* (Washington, D.C.: Government Printing Office, 1972), p. 740.

Divisions and States as a Percentage of Total Retail Sales: 1958 to 1967   TABLE 17-4

Division and State	Percentage Change in Sales 1963 to 1967	Percentage Change in Sales 1958 to 1967	Percentage of U.S. Total Retail Sales		
			1958	1963	1967
New England	25.6	52.2	6.23	6.18	6.11
Maine	24.1	37.4	0.51	0.49	0.47
New Hampshire	33.8	67.6	0.35	0.36	0.38
Vermont	32.4	59.8	0.22	0.22	0.23
Massachusetts	23.4	46.9	3.12	3.04	2.95
Rhode Island	22.7	48.8	0.46	0.46	0.45
Connecticut	28.4	62.5	1.55	1.61	1.63
Middle Atlantic	23.4	43.5	20.23	19.22	18.68
New York	21.3	39.9	10.38	9.82	9.38
New Jersey	25.4	56.2	3.63	3.71	3.66
Pennsylvania	25.8	42.0	6.15	5.70	5.64
East North Central	27.7	53.2	21.13	20.73	20.83
Ohio	26.3	50.0	5.42	5.28	5.25
Indiana	28.6	60.9	2.58	2.65	2.68
Illinois	26.7	50.5	6.38	6.22	6.21
Michigan	30.0	58.6	4.44	4.44	4.55
Wisconsin	27.9	48.9	2.22	2.12	2.14
West North Central	26.3	46.0	9.12	8.60	8.57
Minnesota	31.7	50.4	1.98	1.86	1.93
Iowa	29.1	49.0	1.68	1.59	1.62
Missouri	27.2	46.8	2.57	2.43	2.44
North Dakota	14.9	31.1	0.38	0.36	0.32
South Dakota	17.4	33.2	0.39	0.36	0.33
Nebraska	21.9	47.8	0.86	0.86	0.82
Kansas	21.5	40.8	1.22	1.16	1.11
South Atlantic	32.2	67.8	12.77	13.25	13.79
Delaware	28.7	57.3	0.29	0.29	0.30
Maryland	37.0	74.5	1.66	1.74	1.87
District of Columbia	13.1	22.9	0.65	0.58	0.52
Virginia	28.4	65.3	1.86	1.96	1.98
West Virginia	18.4	31.1	0.80	0.73	0.68
North Carolina	33.6	73.3	1.92	2.04	2.14
South Carolina	36.6	77.7	0.87	0.93	1.00
Georgia	35.1	75.0	1.76	1.87	1.99
Florida	35.1	76.0	2.91	3.12	3.31
East South Central	28.8	61.9	4.92	5.06	5.13
Kentucky	25.5	54.3	1.29	1.30	1.28
Tennessee	31.8	65.1	1.60	1.64	1.70
Alabama	26.6	60.5	1.28	1.33	1.33
Mississippi	31.8	70.3	0.74	0.78	0.81
West South Central	30.5	55.0	8.85	8.60	8.83
Arkansas	27.7	64.9	0.77	0.81	0.82
Louisiana	40.4	61.9	1.47	1.39	1.53
Oklahoma	25.8	51.9	1.20	1.19	1.18
Texas	29.4	52.4	5.39	5.21	5.30

TABLE 17-4   (cont.)

Division and State	Percentage Change in Sales 1963 to 1967	Percentage Change in Sales 1958 to 1967	Percentage of U.S. Total Retail Sales		
			1958	1963	1967
Mountain	20.3	54.1	3.97	4.16	3.94
Montana	17.7	31.7	0.43	0.40	0.37
Idaho	21.3	40.5	0.41	0.39	0.37
Wyoming	6.8	25.0	0.21	0.20	0.17
Colorado	23.9	55.8	1.05	1.08	1.06
New Mexico	16.5	39.7	0.49	0.48	0.44
Arizona	22.6	75.0	0.70	0.83	0.80
Utah	15.6	50.6	0.46	0.50	0.45
Nevada	26.4	119.1	0.20	0.29	0.29
Pacific	26.4	67.0	13.13	14.19	14.12
Washington	35.2	59.9	1.71	1.66	1.76
Oregon	24.9	56.6	1.07	1.10	1.08
California	24.6	67.9	9.96	11.01	10.80
Alaska	41.5	99.5	0.10	0.12	0.13
Hawaii	44.2	107.5	0.26	0.31	0.35

Source: *U.S. Census of Business.*

Department Stores

One major retail outlet in terms of its drawing power and wide appeal is the department store. The typical department store carries a wide variety of apparel for both men and women of all ages, home furnishings, housewares, stationery, cosmetics, and hundreds of other major classifications of merchandise.

These stores are distinguished by their departmentalization of each major category of merchandise and their control and coordination by top management. Thus the typical department in a department store maintains complete records and has a manager who bears responsibility for its success.

The typical customer of most department stores is a middle-class housewife with above-average income. Most customers of the department store are female.

The department store is a major power in the distribution field. There are several reasons for this. First and foremost, the department store is usually big. Some department stores have sales volumes in the downtown area alone of over $100 million. Several have sales volumes exceeding $200 million if one includes their branch stores, usually located in the same area.

Second, they spend more money on advertising and promotion than practically any other retail type of outlet in the United States. The wide use of advertising has resulted in a tremendous ability to attract a constant stream of customers to their outlets. As a result, department stores are openly solicited by shopping-center promoters and offered the most favorable rental terms, since they are an almost irreplaceable attraction to any shopping area.

Third, department stores cater to middle-class fashion needs and hence are leaders in the apparel industry. With the power to attract the female by selling fashion, they automatically have become leaders in several other allied areas, such as fashion accessories and, of course, children's wear, which results from attracting the housewife.

The department store strategy has changed, however, over the past 25 years. Previous to this era the department store had a secure place in the retailing complex of the city. Typically, the large department store was located in the major downtown business district. In most cases it was immediately adjacent to the major transportation arteries. A store such as Macy's in New York City was located near two or three subway lines and had buses from all over the city stop at its door. J. L. Hudson's in Detroit, with its huge downtown store, resides in the key location in the business district. In a sense, many of these stores had a monopoly, since land for competitors was simply not available at almost any price.

During the early 1950s, however, a trend started developing in the major cities that affected these almost perfect locations. The populace started moving to the suburban areas of the cities (see Chapter 7). It is axiomatic in retailing that population movements are always accompanied by retail development, and many of the department stores had to develop branch outlets in these suburban areas. Movement into these new areas made the department store more vulnerable to competition. It also made the location aspect less reliable, particularly since the suburbanite relies more on automobile travel, which allows more options in terms of choosing shopping areas, than the in-city shopper who may rely more on public transportation.

Additionally, the government highway program has kept the location value of store sites in an ever-changing flux and has tended to undermine even the most seemingly secure store locations.

In addition to all this, the department store has been faced with a direct assault upon its competitive position by the most recent innovator in retailing competition, the discounter. This store has taken away many of the department stores' traditional lines of products and has managed to outsell these outlets on the basis of price competition and convenience. More will be said about these outlets later.

Finally, due to the growing number of branch stores, the department store has found it much more difficult to maintain efficient control over its inventory and management organization in each of the outlets.

In spite of all these problems, it is still a fair statement to say that the department store remains one of the most influential of retailing institutions. It is still almost a principle of fashion apparel manufacturing to first get a major department store to buy your line if you want to catapult your newest line of fashion nationally.

Chain Stores

Although not a mutually exclusive type, the chain store should be recognized as an important force in American retailing. The chain store is particularly powerful in the grocery, variety, drugs, shoes, and low-priced apparel fields.

Chain stores are tightly controlled at a central office. Thus practically all buying, advertising, and merchandising plans are made at the central office. Store managers who manage each of the firm's units are usually relegated to the job of simply reordering merchandise from central headquarters. Few engage in making choices, or setting prices or policy.

The chains survive simply because by centrally locating all buying and management functions they can acquire purchasing power, as well as top executive talent, which they can spread over many stores.

To establish a chain operation the firm must concentrate on selling staple types of merchandise, and limit their offerings of fashion merchandise severely. In effect, the chains concentrate on selling merchandise that appeals to mass markets rather than small segments of the market. Thus the chain will emphasize merchandise that sells in large quantities, since the firm recognizes little risk is attached to the sale of this type of merchandise.

The largest chain organizations in the country are represented by the supermarket food chains such as A&P, Safeway, Kroger, Food Fair, and Grand Union. These chains carry practically all nationally advertised food products. In addition, they put strong emphasis on their own private brands of merchandise. A&P, for example, carries its own private brands, such as Jane Parker baked goods, Ann Page jellies, and Bokar coffee.

The supermarket developed during the early 1930s as a large self-service, checkout, food operation with ample parking. It is characterized by relatively low markup and fast turnover, and has changed little since then, except in terms of its location. In recent years these stores have located outside of the cities as free-standing highway units or in shopping centers.

Other chains include such diverse groups as the J. C. Penney stores, which specialize mainly in selling apparel, but in recent years have tended to go the way of Sears, Roebuck by developing a mail-order catalog and hard-goods lines such as appliances and auto supplies. Smaller chains include National Shoe Stores, Cunningham Drug Stores, and People's Drug Stores.

Discount Stores

Probably the most important development in the past 20 years is the growth of the discount store. These stores have created particular problems for the traditional type of retail firms.

The discount store as we know it today started immediately after World War II when several merchants saw an opportunity to sell appliances at a minimum markup to the millions of goods-starved families, starting after the troops returned home. Many of these firms were started by returning veterans, others by those in different fields of retailing. But all had the same goal in mind, to sell appliances at a discount. Since the service guarantees on practically all appliances were handled by the manufacturer, the customer did not have to concern himself with the reputation of the retailer. This was particularly helpful to retailers starting out on limited capital. Although these stores began as sellers of appliances, they soon added many other products, such as toys, cameras, luggage, housewares, and, much later, apparel. Firms that started in this manner later became huge operations, and many are well established even today. Such names as E. J. Korvette, Masters, Polk's, and Two Guys are particularly well known.

During the late 1950s and the 1960s another type of discounter appeared, the apparel discounter. They started in the New England states with an emphasis on low-priced apparel items. During this period they spread out over the country. Many of these firms started in abandoned textile mills, and not until recent years did they carry the appliances and hard goods emphasized in the postwar discount development. Many of these firms attained considerable sales volumes, and practically every major metropolitan area was surrounded with them. Some of the better-known firms are Zayres, Shoppers Fair, Kings, Spartans, and the Atlantic Thrift Centers.

In more recent years many of the large traditional retail stores have moved into the discount field and have established separate divisions whose purpose it is to regain some of their lost sales and compete directly with these firms. Thus the variety store Kresge has established the K Mart and Jupiter stores, and F. W. Woolworth the Woolco Stores. J. C. Penney has established the Treasure Island stores in a similar manner. The importance attached to this type of outlet can be seen in the fact that Kresge has opened 385 K Mart stores between 1962 and 1970.[3] Other department stores have also joined in the movement, and one finds both Federated Department Stores and May Department Stores proceeding along the same line with the Gold Circle and Venture Stores, respectively.

Aside from carrying mainly staple merchandise, most of this variety of discount house tends to

1. Sell merchandise below traditional margins.
2. Offer the customer a limited number of services.
3. Offer a self-service or self-selection selling arrangement.
4. Stay open for long hours and perhaps on Sunday.
5. Place less reliance on statistical control systems.

Although the varieties of discount stores are enormous, one thing is certain, and that is that manufacturers must consider them in their choice of outlets. Many of these discount chains have now exceeded the sales volume of many of the largest traditional organizations.

Franchise Firms

During the past 10 years the franchise firm has developed as a serious competitor to all kinds of retail firms. A franchise is a license to sell a firm's goods or services in a given area under a contractual arrangement. Franchises today number in the thousands. Some idea as to the extent of their development can be seen in Table 17-5. The contractual arrangements may vary greatly. Some firms charge the franchisee a fee for their services, others a fee based on gross sales; others sell the franchise holder all the products he uses in his business. The concept is the same, however. All franchisers provide a complete management training program. They also offer expert advice in selecting sites and, if necessary, constructing a store.

Franchising is not particularly new. For example, the Howard Johnson restaurant chain has been around for some time. However, the change in franchising is the tremendous number that have developed during the past 10 years. There are many reasons for this growth. First is the general prosperity throughout the 1960s that has enabled individuals to accumulate the necessary capital to invest in

---

[3]"How Kresge Became the Top Discounter," *Business Week,* Oct. 24, 1970, p. 62.

business. Second is the recognition that small retailers can gain buying advantages by joining together and concentrating their purchasing power. Finally, there is a growing belief among business promoters that by systematizing a retail operation, one can produce profitable stores.

TABLE 17-5 Selected Franchise Groups, 1969

Franchise Groups	*Franchise Outlets*
Franchise outlets, total	540,000
Auto and truck dealers	27,780
Gasoline service stations	244,100
Soft drink bottlers	4,000
Tire suppliers	100,000
Car wash	15,000
Auto parts suppliers and repairs	11,000
Motels, hotels	4,000
Convenience grocery stores	21,000
Drive-in food, drink, ice cream	32,000
Coin-op laundry and dry cleaning	18,000
Water conditioner service	3,000

Source: *Industry Week,* June 29, 1970, p. 27.

Vending Machines

Vending machines account for approximately 2 percent of all retail sales in the United States. Although overall they have not made much of an impact, they do account for the sale of about one out of five candy bars, cigarettes, and soda pop.

In recent years, because of the development of larger and more sophisticated machines and the availability of change-making devices, vending machines have moved into selling other types of merchandise. For instance, many firms now maintain employee or public cafeterias by using only vending machines that sell hot and cold meals. Other retail outlets, such as gasoline stations, use vending machines as major dispensers of products used by the highway traveler.

Although vending is growing as a business, it still suffers from many serious limitations. First, it is costly, in that most vending machines require a great deal of maintenance and labor to replenish them. Second, the machines are limited in terms of carrying assortments of merchandise. This accounts for the fact that they have been mainly successful in the food and convenience goods field. Finally, since machines that will change more than a $1 bill have not been perfected, the merchandise or even food one can offer in these machines is rather limited.

Nevertheless, vending machines can be an important outlet in a number of convenience goods fields.

Motivating
the Retailer

To increase the possibility that a retailer will purchase a product (assuming the manufacturer engages in a push policy), the manufacturer resorts to many techniques.

The most widely used technique revolves around the use of cooperative advertising money. Cooperative advertising was discussed in Chapter 14. Although most cooperative advertising expenditures are given for newspaper display ads, it is important to recognize that not all monies are spent in this way. Many of the ways in which retailers can obtain allowances from manufacturers are listed next.[4] Many of these payments, in effect, help to increase the sales volume or profits of the retail firm.

1. Cooperative advertising allowances.
2. Payments for interior displays including floor fixtures, self-extenders, dump displays, "A" locations, extra facings, aisle displays, overhead banners, general promotional cooperation, and so on.
3. Payments for window display space — plus installation costs.
4. Push money for salespeople.
5. Contests for buyers, salespeople, and others.
6. Allowances for a variety of warehousing functions.
7. Payments for seasonal inventories.
8. Demonstrators.
9. Label allowances.
10. Coupon-handling allowances.
11. Free goods.
12. Guaranteed sales.
13. Local research work done through retailer.
14. Delivery costs to individual stores of large retailers.
15. Payments for mailing to store lists.
16. Liberal return privileges.
17. Contributions to favorite charities of store personnel.
18. Contributions of infinite variety to special store anniversaries and to store openings. (The great hoopla at the opening of giant new stores is largely financed by manufacturers, brokers, sales agents, and wholesalers.)
19. Payments for use of special fixtures owned by the store.
20. Payments for store improvements — including painting.
21. An infinite variety of promotional and merchandising allowances.
22. Payment of part of salary of retail salespeople.
23. Trade deals of innumerable types.
24. Time spent in actual selling on retail floor by manufacturers' salesmen.
25. Inventory adjustments of many types.
26. Transportation allowances.

Exclusive or Selective Distribution

Manufacturers can use other important techniques for gaining the cooperation of the retailer. For instance, the manufacturer can offer the retailer an exclusive or protected territory. Thus the department stores and specialty retailers that sell Magnavox are selected by the company, and although they do not usually have the franchise exclusively, they know that the number of sellers is restricted by Magnavox.

---

[4]Hearing before the Antitrust Subcommittee (Subcommittee Number 5) of the Committee on the Judiciary, House of Representatives, Eighty-seventh Congress, First Session, Aug. 30, 1961 (Serial No. 19), *Functional Discounts.*

It is interesting to observe that the policy followed by Magnavox represents a selective or restricted policy on their part. In contrast, the Radio Corporation of America follows a policy of offering their television sets to almost any retailer who will carry them. This is referred to as an *intensive* distribution policy. Although both firms sell the same product (and one might add for many years Magnavox purchased their television tubes from RCA), the approach to selling the retailer is entirely different and the marketing policies indicate these differing philosophies.

Magnavox takes the approach of selling its products on a more or less restricted basis in order to gain the favor of the retailer. Should a retailer take on the Magnavox line, he is automatically protected from price competition on this line, since one of the restrictions he must adhere to is to maintain prices. As a matter of fact, retailers commonly run sales during the year only when Magnavox approves. By maintaining retail prices Magnavox can almost guarantee the retailer a profit on the sale of each item in the line. This of course is a great incentive to the retailer to sell the line. Most importantly from Magnavox's point of view, the retailer will urge his salespeople to sell the Magnavox set over any other he may have in stock. Thus, although the retailer may carry many different lines of products, he will prominently display the Magnavox product, and one can be assured that all customers entering the store without any predisposition toward a brand will be introduced to the Magnavox set. This of course gives Magnavox a major edge if this happens.

In contrast, RCA does not offer exclusive distributorships for its product. As a matter of fact, most RCA television sets can be found in all stores. This is in direct opposition to the Magnavox policy. Why the different approaches?

Magnavox, through its limited distribution policy, attempts to sell to a quality segment of the market that is willing to pay slightly higher prices for sets sold in quality outlets. Through this sytem of distribution they gain the help of the selling force of each of the outlets. On the negative side though, by pursuing this system of distribution they limit their market and cannot compete in terms of total sales against firms that sell their products to almost any retail outlet in the market. Thus a system that restricts distribution to only a few outlets is doomed to sell only a fraction of the total market.

By contrast, RCA is aiming at a larger mass market. By attempting to place their product in as many outlets as possible, RCA, if successful, will gain a substantial fraction of the television market. Their reasoning is that the more outlets a firm has, the higher the probability they will make a sale. Included in this theory is the view that many people shopping for television sets will only shop in a few stores. Thus, if the probability is that RCA sets will be found in most of these few stores they shop in, they will be more likely to consummate a sale.

The television set statistics seem to support this view. RCA outsells Magnavox by 5 to 1. In addition, General Electric and Zenith with similar mass marketing policies as RCA also hold substantial leads over Magnavox. In spite of this lead, Magnavox maintains its policy of limited distribution, because through this policy it maintains the support of a substantial group of retailers who maintain a quality and high price level for their product.

Manufacturers engage in many other activities that are aimed at attracting the retailer. For instance, many firms maintain training programs for the retailer. That is, they help inform retail salespeople as to the various selling points of their product. Other firms offer the salespeople special commissions on the sale of their product. This was once a common practice in the bedding field. Other firms spend a great deal of money and effort on point-of-sale display materials. Many of the major breweries hire missionary salesmen whose job it is to set up displays and banners in supermarkets to help move their product.

Finally, there are many firms that maintain inventory counts for the retailer, set up displays, and will actually maintain all the records for the retailer in exchange for his business. Perhaps the ultimate in retailer treatment is the Revlon Company, which not only keeps track of large retailer stocks, but actually maintains lists of trained cosmetic personnel that can be hired to fill in any vacancies. In addition, when the store is a large purchaser of cosmetics, Revlon offers allowances to help pay the salary of the cosmeticians.

Retail Buying

Manufacturers selling to retailers are faced with many organizational differences. In many firms, particularly in small firms, the manufacturer must deal with the owner-manager of the business. In dealing with large chains the manufacturer must sell to a centralized organizational arrangement that may include a company buying committee. In the case of general merchandise and specialty stores, the manufacturer may find himself dealing with buying organizations that are either owned by the company or act as a market representative. In other cases the manufacturer finds the retailer sends his buyers directly to the manufacturer to select the merchandise.

Although these various organizational arrangements will be discussed, it must be remembered that most manufacturers deal with various organizations and not usually just one. Thus a manufacturer of food products may deal directly with a large central buying group representing a national chain; in other market areas he may supplement this effort by using wholesalers.

Owner Management

The owner-manager arrangement is usually found in the small retail firm. Here the owner purchases the merchandise and with his employees engages in the sale of it. As this type of buying arrangement allows the owner little time in the marketplace, great reliance is placed on wholesalers or, in the case of fashion merchandise, buying representatives located in the major markets. In addition, many of these small retailers may place orders directly with salesmen representing manufacturers.

Even large manufacturers may deal directly with the small retailer when the volume of business warrants it. For instance, the Colgate Company maintains a separate sales staff that calls on small retailers only. The larger accounts, such as food chains, are handled by a special sales staff.

Central Buying Organization

The large retail firm and particularly the chain store engage in buying centrally. There are many advantages to central buying, the most obvious of which are the economies of scale that accrue to the firm. By purchasing merchandise centrally, the firm can qualify for discounts that are unavailable to smaller competitors. In addition, chains find that centralizing the paperwork and distribution helps them maintain better control over individual stores.

Although this may seem to be reason enough for the chain to centralize their buying organization, several problems do exist in this type of decision-making organization. For example, centralized buying usually results in buying for a store whose customers are totally unfamiliar to the buyer in the central office. In addition, the huge amount of central paper work may cause delays, errors, and, in particular, duplication, since a great deal of the centralizing procedures are performed again once the merchandise is shipped to the store.

The manufacturer in dealing with large firms that buy centrally is faced with different organizational approaches to decision making. For example, many of the food chains make buying decisions on the basis of a committee recommendation. This committee with a food chain is made up of all levels of management. Table 17-6 shows a typical buying committee. As can be seen from this listing, most of the members of the committee are in top executive positions. Although no two committees operate in the same manner, most firms follow the same procedures. As a general rule, the committee concerns itself with new products only. However, the

TABLE 17-6   Job Titles Represented on Buying Committees

Job Title	*By Store (%)*
Merchandising Manager	59
Advertising Manager	44
Sales Manager	30
Branch/Division Head	23
Purchasing Director	21
Overall Department Supervisor	21
Overall Department Merchandising Manager	20
Store Supervisor/District Manager	20
General/Operating Manager	17
Executive Officer	9
Sales Promotion Manager	3
Warehouse/Transportation Manager	3
Store Manager	2
Accountant	2
Personnel	1

Source: H. L. Gordon, "How Important Is the Chain Store Buying Committee?" *Journal of Marketing,* Vol. 25, Jan. 1961.

committee usually receives data concerning the turnover and sales of the present product lines.

As a matter of procedure, all products are screened prior to their presentation to the food committee by a food chain executive, usually called the buyer. The buyer listens to and evaluates the presentation by the manufacturer's representatives or salesmen. As part of his duties he collects all the necessary information and acts as the manufacturer's salesman at the meeting by presenting the information. On the basis of the information presented the committee makes its decision.

One problem that a manufacturer of a new product faces revolves around the basic weakness of the committee buying technique; that is, the manufacturer rarely gets to present his case to the group. He is obviously dependent on the food chain buyer to present his product favorably. This often acts as an immovable obstacle to many manufacturer, who feel that an unenthusiastic buyer will rarely sway a committee favorably.

In selling to department stores or apparel specialty stores the manufacturer may be faced with a number of different problems. In many cases he must deal directly with the store buyer, whether it be a large department store chain or a medium-sized specialty store. Practically all major department stores maintain buying staffs for each major store. Thus Gimbel Brothers in Pittsburgh maintains apparel buying staffs at its main store, as does Gimbel's, New York and Philadelphia. In these cases the manufacturer deals directly with the buyer. The reason for the seeming duplication of effort in the case of Gimbel's is that many of the fashion products they sell vary by area, and thus a skilled buyer is needed to maintain the proper merchandise mix in each area.

However, not all products sold are so subject to fashion, and thus one finds that most department stores supplement their local buying staffs with buying organizations located in major marketing areas.

In the case of apparel, most likely the buying organization representing the retailer will be located in New York. In addition, offices in California and perhaps in a number of foreign countries may be maintained.

In terms of ownership these offices may vary considerably. Many are independent buying offices that will represent a firm in the marketplace. They supply current information to member stores, and perhaps make purchases on behalf of the store in the marketplace. Member stores usually pay a fee based on their sales volume. The size of the buying organization and staff varies from the very small to the gigantic firm, such as Frederick Atkins in New York, which has member firms with a total sales volume over $1 billion.

Other buying organizations situated in markets are store-owned buying organizations where the stores actually run and control the buying organizations. In store-owned buying organizations, independent stores may be invited to join as well as chains. The largest among these is the Associated Merchandising Corporation.

Similar in structure are the chain-owned buying organizations. Here the corporate chain maintains buying organizations that cater to the needs of the chain stores. Such buying organizations are located in New York City for Gimbel's, Macy's, Allied Stores, and Associated Dry Goods.

From the manufacturer's point of view these firms represent large markets for their merchandise. Although the buyers in the central office do not always make the final decisions, the manufacturer knows that they are in a position to favorably present their offerings to the buyers in the individual stores. Thus a manufacturer of ladies' apparel may encourage the central office buyer for Macy's to distribute and publicize his offering to the Macy's store buyers in New York, Atlanta, Kansas City, and San Francisco, areas where Macy's maintains large stores.

Manufacturers are also aware of the fact that many of these buying organizations are trusted with the task of developing a constant supply of private brands, that is, brands that can only be found in the cooperating stores under the buying organization's or the store's name. The purpose of developing these brands is obviously to undercut the impact of national brands that can be found in most competing stores.

SUMMARY

The retailer remains the last link in the chain of distribution to the ultimate consumer. Therefore, he is extremely important to the manufacturer in that he must motivate the retailer to sell his product. The problem with the retailer lies in two complex areas. First, the retailer and the manufacturer do not have similar ways of looking at the same thing. Thus the manufacturer is product-oriented, whereas the retailer is oriented toward looking at the total number of products sold in his store. To overcome this conflict, the manufacturer engages in cooperative advertising, sales promotion techniques, price reductions, and exclusive arrangements.

The second area that represents a problem for the manufacturer is the fact that retailing represents a diverse group of stores. Some are so small that the economic costs of reaching them far exceed the potential gain. Others are so huge that many manufacturers find it difficult to present their case directly and must work through intermediaries.

In all cases the manufacturer must constantly stay on top of his retail distribution problems, since for many firms they represent the difference between growth and stagnation.

QUESTIONS

1. Why do some retailers resent product changes by the manufacturer?

2. How can a manufacturer overcome the resentment toward product change by a retailer?

*3. Given the fact that the average retail firm is small and has few employees, what problems would a firm such as Procter & Gamble have in selling to food stores?

*4. Contrast the marketing strategy necessary to sell to drug wholesalers versus directly to retail drugstores.

5. What incentives can a canned food manufacturer offer retail food stores other than price?

6. How can a retail firm with sales of under $30,000 annually exist?

7. One manufacturer considers that the department store is the most important outlet in retailing. Support this view.

*In-depth questions.

8. Contrast the buying organization of the chain store with that of an independent department store.

*9. What problems does a manufacturer encounter in trying to sell to both discount stores and traditional types of outlets?

10. According to Table 17-3 both drug and furniture store chains have a small percentage of the total sales in their groups. Why?

11. Why is the level of concentration so much lower in retailing than in manufacturing?

12. What is the major attraction of the apparel specialty store to the consumer?

*In-depth question.

Physical Distribution

18

SUMMARY KEY

Physical distribution is concerned with getting the product to the right place, at the right time, and at the lowest cost.

Physical distribution is costly; one estimate indicates it runs to about 22 percent of sales. About 30 percent of this figure is for inbound and outbound transportation costs. The cost of a lost sale is an additional cost to a manufacturer that cannot be measured.

In planning a physical distribution network there are two considerations: the system that is necessary to accomplish the job, and the information that is necessary to monitor the system. The size of the planning depends on whether the firm needs a full distribution system, where the firm sells directly to the consumer, as in the case of Avon Cosmetics; a partial system, where the manufacturer sells to retailers or through wholesalers or maintains area warehouses; or a one-step system, where the manufacturer sells to only one middleman, who in turn sells to the consumer.

To monitor such systems the firms rely on historical or past data to plan their facilities. In addition, current data are necessary in order to make adjustments in the present system.

The demands of the customer being serviced by the supplier determine the type of system that must be designed. Naturally, the supplier must limit his service to his capabilities. These demands include the financial investment necessary to support the inventories, the necessary marketing services, the amount of inventory maintenance, warehousing, and transportation. The actual level of service is determined by the product being sold and the competitive environment.

One major problem in maintaining a physical distribution system is the control of the costs and size of inventories. Several costs are involved — ordering costs, which are those costs attached to placing an order, and carrying costs, the cost of physical storage of the inventory plus the cost of the money tied up in inventory. These costs can be as high as 20 percent of the cost of the inventory. As noted earlier, an unmeasurable cost can be the cost of a lost sale.

A key to the maintenance of proper inventory levels is the establishing of proper order quantities based on the needs of customers. The quantity ordered must meet the fluctuations of demand, which involve a forecast of the sales, an estimate of the lead time, and the maintenance of a safety or buffer stock.

Firms use warehouses for many reasons. The most basic is the need to maintain stocks for the firm's customers; other reasons are the need to maintain warehouse stocks because trucking deliveries at peak times of the year are much slower, the opportunity to buy products at a discount, to help ripen and condition products, or to make full-carload deliveries by consolidating shipments out of a warehouse.

Since transportation costs are among the highest costs in the physical distribution system, the addition of warehouses lowers the distance that must be traveled between the factories and customers. In general, costs tend to decrease as distance decreases.

Aside from a central warehouse system, many firms favor using decentralized warehouses. Their choice of either system depends on the type of product sold and the way their customers buy.

To properly select a warehouse location, a detailed analysis involving transportation cost, warehouse maintenance costs, and inventory carrying costs for each location must be made; in addition, the firm can also measure the cost of using public warehouses rather than building their own.

Modes of transportation are trucks, which are the cheapest, railroads, which can carry larger and more diversified materials, air, which is the fastest in most cases but is severely limited in terms of capacity and the lack of air terminals in many smaller markets, and water and pipelines, which are used usually by specialized industries. Several coordinated systems of transportation serve the manufacturer, such as piggyback, fishyback, and rail–water.

Among the major modes of transportation, the railroad has grown the slowest. Trucking has continued to grow at a fast rate. Air transportation, practically unknown in 1950, has increased substantially in recent years.

As noted in Chapter 15, there has been an increasing interest and use in the physical distribution function as a marketing tool. Its development and growth, though recent, have been spectacular.

By physical distribution, marketing people refer to the process or system involved in moving goods from the factory to the ultimate consumer. Physical distribution always existed as a function; however, it was usually referred to in terms of the costs incurred in transporting goods. It was treated in a sense as an inevitable cost that all firms incurred, and it was implied that there was little a firm could do about this cost.

Today, however, all this thinking has changed, and there is general recognition on the part of firms that the proper performance of the physical distribution function can enhance sales and profits.

Although physical distribution is concerned with the physical handling of goods, its problem is much deeper than the simple carrying of merchandise from the factory to its point of destination. Physical distribution is just as concerned with getting the product to the *right place* at the *right time* and at the *lowest cost.* It then becomes clear that physical distribution involves expertise in terms of transportation, warehousing, and handling costs.

Cost of Physical Distribution

The cost of physical distribution can be enormous. Any examination shows clearly why marketing people are becoming increasingly interested in the proper utilization of this function. Although various estimates have been made of the cost of physical distribution, one study of 270 American corporations seems to indicate that an average of close to 22 percent of sales constitutes the cost of physical distribution.

Table 18-1 breaks these costs down into functions. Examination of this table seems to indicate that transportation both outbound and inbound accounts for approximately 30 percent of the total physical distribution cost. Inventory carrying costs would also seem to be substantial. Although more will be said about this later, it should be mentioned that many costs cannot be tabulated; yet they exist. For instance, should the system be out of stock on an item, it could result in a lost sale. This would in effect be a cost; however, it would represent a figure that at best could only be estimated.

TABLE 18-1 Physical Distribution Costs by Function

Functional Activity		*Percentage of Sales*
Administration		2.4
Transportation		
Inbound	2.1	
Outbound	4.3	6.4
Receiving and shipping		1.7
Packaging		2.6
Warehousing		
In plant	2.1	
Field	1.6	3.7
Inventory carrying costs		
Interest	2.2	
Taxes, insurance, obsolescence	1.6	3.8
Order processing		1.2
Total		21.8

Source: American Trucking Association, Washington, D.C., 1962.

Planning the
Physical
Distribution
Network

As noted in Chapter 3, one of the major management tasks is to plan. The physical distribution system requires intensive planning in many firms, since it involves a complex network of plants, warehouses, and inventory levels.

The planning of the physical distribution flow requires planning in two major areas: (1) the planning of the system, and (2) the communication (information) flow through the system. Although these will be discussed separately, they are obviously related and planned at the same time.[1]

Planning of the System

The planning of the system requires a complex of decisions that usually involves huge expenditures. The system usually includes the planning of the firm's

[1] B. J. LaLonde and J. F. Grashof, "The Role of Information Systems in Physical Distribution Management," in D. J. Bowersox, B. J. LaLonde, and E. W. Smykay, eds., *Readings in Physical Distribution Management* (New York: Macmillan Publishing Co., Inc., 1969), pp. 194–95.

production plants and distribution centers. This involves actually determining the size and design of each of these facilities. In addition, the inventory assortments and locations must be established within each of these facilities. Finally, the firm must establish a transportation system that attempts to minimize these costs.[2]

The size of the planning task is determined by many factors, but in particular it depends on the firm's system of distribution. In effect, one must decide whether the firm is involved in a *full distribution, partial,* or *one step* system. A *full distribution system,* which is entered into by only a few companies, involves the actual production and distribution to the *ultimate consumer,* the family unit. Firms such as Fuller Brush and Avon Cosmetics engage in this type of system.

The *partial system* is the one engaged in by most firms. That is, they sell through an intermediary of some sort. Typically, a firm such as RCA sells its products through distributors, who in turn sell to retailers. Or a food processor may sell directly to large retail food chains. In some cases, this same firm may use the services of food brokers, who obtain orders from small grocery stores and relay them to the processor, who ships the merchandise directly to the retailer. A *one-step* system implies that the manufacturer turns over his production to one intermediary, such as a wholesaler or retailer, on a direct basis. This system is typically followed in the apparel industry, where the manufacturer in most cases sells directly to the retailer and does not engage any intermediary nor does he maintain warehouses to stock his merchandise. Although the one-step system is simply a form of the partial distribution system, it implies that the firm using such a system is rather small and not too strong financially. Although RCA engages in a rather simple distribution system for their television sets, they do maintain large inventories at company warehouses and in their plants.

Using a full distribution system involves a complexity of decisions. For instance, the Avon Cosmetic Company must maintain a complex system of warehouses throughout the United States in order to accommodate their thousands of salespeople who sell directly to the consumer. Thus the firm must establish warehouses in each major area in order to guarantee that once their salespeople make a sale the customer is guaranteed delivery within a few days. Thus Avon must establish stock levels and distribution locations in each market where the volume of business warrants such locations. To expedite the flow of goods to each of these facilities, Avon must carefully choose its production sites in order to minimize transportation costs and time factors.

How does Avon plan the locations and level of inventories that are to be maintained in each location? The answer lies in two information sources: historical and current data.[3] By developing information *from the past,* the firm can make a judgment as to what institutions and stock flow requirements are necessary to keep the system providing a necessary level of service. Thus a study of last year's data may indicate that the firm requires additional warehouses in several major marketing areas of the country. Or it may indicate that inventory levels at several points can be reduced substantially because of a drop in demand for a given area.

Information Systems

---

[2]*Ibid.,* p. 194.
[3]*Ibid.*

Current data allow management an opportunity to monitor the present system and make judgments as to whether or not the system is operating well and the costs that may be incurred if one were to make a change. For instance, although management may consider a change in plans based on the historical information developed in the first stage, it is to be remembered that one of the considerations in making a forecast of the future is that the past is an indication of the future. This does not always hold up, and the monitoring of the current situation may change all this.

In effect, the current information system allows management to adjust the system and, in addition, measure whether or not the system is meeting the company goals and objectives. One major objective of the firm may be to establish a desirable service goal. This represents the type of information flow management needs in order to make that judgment.

Customer Service Determinants

A system of physical distribution is designed to service the customer. Nevertheless, the producer *cannot* give the customer all that he wants. In the case of Avon, the consumer perhaps would like to have the cosmetics as soon as they place the order. In reality, to accomplish this would result in an astronomical increase in costs, since Avon would have to move its warehouses even closer to the point of sale. Thus the producer is always making decisions that compromise perfect service. However, one should be aware of the demands of the producer's customers to understand the goals that the producer should attempt to reach. Some of the more important follow.[4]

Financial Investment

The customer of the producer would prefer to carry merchandise on consignment (i.e., carry without payment until sold). By doing this, the buyer reduces his risk and investment in the business. Some buyers look to the supplier to aid in the financing of the inventory when consignment terms are not available. It is not unusual for a small retailer of appliances to have his whole inventory financed by the producer through a bank or some other financial institution.

Marketing Services

The buyer expects to meet a producer's sales representative who is knowledgeable and who takes a particular interest in the buyer's operating problems. As a matter of fact, suppliers sometimes look for a salesman who seems to be on their side in obtaining concessions from the company office.

The buyer also expects to be liberally supplied with point-of-purchase sales aids and promotional techniques that will aid him in selling the product. He looks to the producer for advertising monies. Finally, he expects to be kept informed about competition and any major changes that are expected in the market.

---

[4]Adapted from J. L. Heskett, R. M. Ivie, and N. A. Glaskowsky, Jr., *Business Logistics* (New York: The Ronald Press Company, 1964), p. 156.

The customer's needs in the area of physical distribution involve three major elements of customer service: inventory maintenance, warehousing, and transportation.

Inventory maintenance and warehousing. In this case the customers want the supplier to maintain as much of the inventory as possible. In many cases the buyer or customer prefers to have the supplier maintain his own warehouse. Although the buyer may be willing to maintain a warehouse, he prefers to keep his warehouse size to a minimum, operating at capacity at all times. In addition, the buyer prefers to have the supplier make deliveries directly to his customers. For example, as noted previously, a large retail department store prefers to have a mattress producer ship the product directly to the consumer's home once the order is placed with the retailer. In this way the retailer avoids double handling, and need only carry floor samples to do business.

Additionally, the supplier may be obligated when dealing with the retailer to actually take inventory and write up an order. This is commonplace in the food field, where many missionary salesmen representing large food producers actually stock the shelves of the food store after establishing the fact that the retailer needs more merchandise. It is not unusual for a cosmetic manufacturer to take a stock count in department stores on a regular basis, write up an order, and actually submit the order for the store buyer's signature.

To maintain low inventories, the producer will find the retailer will prefer to place orders more frequently rather than large orders on a regular basis. The retailer or wholesaler will also place orders only when the stocks are dangerously low where possible, again in order to keep the firm's inventory at a minimum level.

Transportation. In dealing with the mode of transportation, the customer prefers to name the carrier in order to consolidate shipments for his benefit. In addition, by so naming one carrier, the customer hopes to obtain concessions and special services. He naturally expects the supplier to file for all claims and handle disputes concerning damaged goods.

All the preceding represents a sort of *utopian* standard of the customer for the producer. Nevertheless, the producer must take into consideration his customers when he designs and plans his physical distribution system.

The next logical question has to be what determines the actual service the customer gets? What are the determinants of this service? The answer lies in the many factors considered next. The two major criteria seem to be the *product* itself and the *competitive* environment.

**Service
Determinants**

Product

The service support that is necessary for the product depends on a number of product factors. The most obvious is whether or not the customer can substitute one product in stock for another. Thus, in a shopping situation where the consumer regards products as similar, not having the exact product is not tantamount to losing a sale.[5] Hence the customer may be quite willing to substitute and the producer need not concern himself with maintaining an almost perfect in-stock position in each outlet that he sells through. A producer of a variety of candies may find that the customer, not finding his favorite candy, may be quite willing to accept a substitute candy product. A customer in a men's wear store may be willing to accept a dark gray suit when he cannot find a dark blue suit in his size. Under these conditions the supplier is not under tremendous pressure to make immediate deliveries.

Tied in with the product itself is the demand for the product, which determines the type of physical distribution service that needs to be maintained. For instance, the demand for Christmas cards is mainly limited to the period directly before Christmas. The same may be said for toys. Thus the distribution system must make deliveries well in advance of these periods, since lateness may actually result in a total loss of business. The most obvious example is represented by the distribution system that supplies daily newspapers to stores. By definition, the system must deliver daily newspapers before the consumer is ready for his daily purchase. In contrast, the delivery of an automobile may have a comfortable lead time of from 1 to 2 months without causing any particular problem in dealing with the consumer demand.

The price and expense associated with the product may also determine the ability of the firm to establish a high level of customer service. For example, the newspaper rarely warrants the use of a major distribution system. Firms involved in making newspaper deliveries invariably handle other products used by the store. These delivery systems may also deliver cigarettes, candies, and magazines on a daily basis. Conversely, toys, because of the weight and price relationships, can be stored in warehouses awaiting delivery during Christmas time.

Competition

Competition is an important factor in determining the physical distribution service level for a manufacturer supplier. A supplier dealing in industries where the competitors strive to service the buyer instantaneously must eventually meet this competition. This is particularly true when the supplier is servicing a retailer directly. For instance, an apparel manufacturer must meet the needs of his customers (retailers) and particularly service his needs for fast-selling merchandise quickly. Failure to do this consistently will result in the retailer ordering from other sources during the next season.

As a general rule, when the manufacturer deals with a wholesaler, he can expect to space his deliveries much farther apart than if he is in a position of dealing directly with the retailer. In the case of dealing with retailers who are in the habit of ordering in small quantities, the manufacturer may be forced to enter into establishing warehouses to accommodate them. As a general rule, suppliers dealing directly with retailers usually establish a much higher level of delivery service than if they were dealing with wholesalers only.

The constant battle among manufacturers to provide outstanding services in

---

[5] *Ibid.,* pp. 158–61.

competitive industries would seem to represent a strong incentive to maintain a high level of service.

An important aspect of the firm's distribution policy is its ability to control its inventories. These inventories may be accumulated in warehouses or within the firm's plant where production is maintained.

The problem with inventory control is that in many industries mistakes can be costly. More important, however, is the fact that fluctuations in supply and demand cause the firm severe problems in maintaining inventory balance. Thus a firm may find that in total dollars its inventory is adequate. However, it may discover that although its dollars are in balance the firm is out of items that the firm's customers want. In this case, the inventory balance may not be adequately maintained, although the firm may have a large inventory.

Additionally, even when the firm manages to maintain a balanced inventory, it may find that its inventories are too high in total. Also, the firm may find that its inventories at each warehouse may be too high in some places and much too low at other sites. Thus customers of the firm may have many different experiences in each of the marketing areas of the firm.

Overall, therefore, the purpose of an adequate inventory control system is to avoid stockouts and to maintain profitable inventory balance.

**Inventory
Control**

Costs of Inventory

Although there are no exact records on the costs of maintaining an inventory, in Table 18-2 estimates are presented that indicate that these costs can reach over 20 percent of inventory value on the average. Although the cost will surely vary by industry, these costs can be substantial. In addition, these costs vary by the size of the inventory.

Most inventory costs can be divided into two major categories — ordering costs and carrying costs. *Ordering costs* represent those costs that are attached to placing an order. It should be observed that the costs of placing an order are independent of the size of the order. That is, it usually costs a manufacturer just as much in terms of processing costs to place a $100 order as a $10 order with a supplier. Included in this cost are record keeping and handling of the paper work associated with each order.

The *carrying costs* are the costs of physical storage of inventory plus the cost of the money tied up in inventory. The physical costs include the costs of physical facilities, taxes, insurance, inventory depreciation, obsolescence, and shrinkage.

The money tied up in inventory represents what is sometimes referred to as opportunity costs, that is, the opportunity to use the money elsewhere. For instance, should the manufacturer maintain an inventory that is estimated to be $100,000 more than is necessary, his additional costs result not only in the total dollars wasted, but the amount of money he could earn by using the money in other ways (or taking advantage of other opportunities). In many cases, the inventories that he does maintain are financed, and he is presently paying interest on the size of the inventory to the banks (indicated as interest on capital invested).

Thus the manufacturer incurs a double cost in that he is paying the bank interest on the oversized inventory and is foregoing other opportunities.

TABLE 18-2   Estimates of Inventory Carrying Costs

Author	*Publication*	*Estimate of Carrying Costs as a Percentage of Inventory Value*
L. P. Alford and John R. Bangs (eds.)	*Production Handbook* (The Ronald Press Company, 1955), p. 397	25
Dean S. Ammer	*Materials Management* (Richard D. Irwin, Inc., 1962), p. 137	20–25
John B. Holbrook	*Managing the Materials Function* (American Management Association, Inc., 1959), p. 67	24
John F. Magee	"The Logistics of Distribution" *Harvard Business Review,* July – August 1960, p. 99	20–35
Benjamin Melnitsky	*Management of Industrial Inventory* (Conover-Mast Publications, Inc., 1951), p. 115	25
W. Evert Welch	*Scientific Inventory Control* (Management Publishing Corpora- tion, 1956), p. 63	25
Thomson M. Whitin	*The Theory of Inventory Manage- ment* (Princeton University Press, 1957), p. 220	25

Source: R. S. Foster, "What Does It Cost to Carry Inventory?" (Washington, D.C.: The National Association of Wholesalers, no date), p. 3.

Unmeasurable Costs

In spite of the fact that one can identify many costs, it is also true that one cannot actually measure all inventory costs. A major unmeasurable cost to the firm is the loss of a sale that cannot be made because the firm is out of stock at a particular time. This cost can be severe in that the firm may not only lose a sale, but it may also lose a customer for all time. Thus a phonograph record manufacturer may find that being out of stock at a particular time may result in a complete loss of sales for a particular best-selling record. This is brought about because the selling period for many records is particularly short. A manufacturer of apparel may find that large customers finding him consistently out of stock during crucial periods will approach other apparel manufacturers to fill their needs during the next season. Thus the cost of being out of stock can actually result in the demise of a business.

In essence, therefore, the manufacturer must carefully weigh the opportunities of making sales and maintaining a high level of customer service against the costs of carrying inventories that are too high and too costly.

Although it is not the purpose of this book to delve into the intricacies and formulas involved in developing economic order quantities, it is desirable to understand some of the problems associated with developing these statistics.

The quantity ordered must be sufficient to meet the fluctuations of demand. This includes not only covering the sales during a certain sales period, but the lead time, that is, the time it takes to process an order and receive delivery from a vendor. In addition, the manufacturer in establishing a scientific system of inventory control must maintain a buffer or safety stock at all times in order to avoid being out of stock. This buffer stock must take into consideration fluctuations in demand and also the lead time necessary to obtain shipments of the merchandise.

It is obviously to the advantage of the manufacturer to place large orders and establish a production system that will avoid being out of stock. In fact, the tendency among manufacturers is to place large orders rather than series of small orders. In firms where the manufacturer maintains a system of warehouses, the tendency is to allow the warehouses to place large orders. The problem can be seen in Figure 18-1. When the order quantity is 34 units and the depletion of the

**Effect of Reorder Quantity on Average Inventory on Hand,   FIGURE 18-1
Assuming Constant Depletion (Demand)**

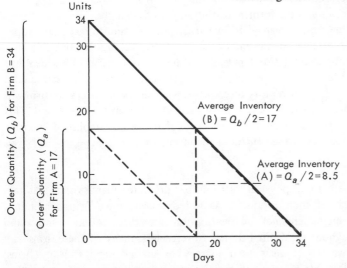

Source: J. L. Heskett, R. M. Ivie, and N. A. Glaskowsky, Jr., *Business Logistics* (New York: The Ronald Press Company, 1964), p. 278.

inventory is constant, the average inventory is 17 units over the 34 selling days. In contrast, when the firm orders only 17 units and the depletion or rate of sale is constant, the average inventory over this period is only 8.5 units over the 17 days. In effect, the firm ordering 17 items at regular intervals need only carry an inventory half the size of the firm ordering twice as many units on a regular basis. As noted previously, the costs of carrying large orders can be considerable, and the firm is tempted to place smaller orders and thus reduce the average inventory.

Forecasting and Inventory Management

Most of the preceding discussion concerning inventory control on the part of the manufacturer revolves around an important ability, that is, the ability to properly forecast the needs of the firm's customers and maintain a proper inventory balance.

In the forecasting of demand for products, firms adopt sophisticated statistical methods in order to automatically replenish inventories. In addition, the development of the computer and the availability of personnel who know how to use the computer has activated the use of these systems.

Most forecasting starts with a review of the past. Many firms stop right there and use the past 12 months as an indicator of the future. In many cases, they may take a company forecast of sales increases and apply it to major product groups. Thus a firm with a sales forecast of 5 percent for the coming year may apply part of the increase to its forecasted inventory level over the next 12 months. This may be done without resorting to any high-level statistical manipulation.

More probably, however, firms use one of the more sophisticated techniques available, which avoids the problems of just using the previous 12 months as a guide to the future. This avoids some of the obvious problems. For example, the previous 12 months may contain unusual fluctuations that are not expected to occur again. This complication can be avoided and the fluctuations eliminated by using two forecasting techniques now available – *trend analysis* and *exponential smoothing*. Both techniques rely heavily on demand in the past, with the latter putting greater weight on later periods and the former treating all periods equally.

The ability of the firm to manage its inventory properly and to make the proper forecasts is usually reflected in the end of the year statistical reports. In Table 18-3 one sees that the important ratio of net sales to inventory consists of a wide range of averages. Thus the successful retailer of building materials may maintain a sales ratio of $15 to each $1 of inventory investment, whereas the unsuccessful firm will establish a sales inventory ratio of $5.20 for each $1 of inventory investment. This demonstrates the wide range of inventory ratios that can be established by firms with different approaches to the control of the inventory function.

Warehouse Distribution

As part of their total physical distribution program, many firms maintain distribution points for their products. As noted earlier, some firms maintain a wholesaler as a major channel of distribution for their product and avoid warehousing throughout the United States. Nevertheless, many of these firms may still maintain a warehouse near their factory or in key regions. Many firms, however, find it desirable to maintain their own warehouse, and without question for most products, firms must maintain some warehousing capacity, whether they or wholesalers manage to perform this function.

Warehouses are needed for several reasons. The first is to maintain basic stocks for the firm's customers. By basic stocks one refers to those items in the producer's lines for which there is an established continuous demand. The Revlon Company can expect that consumers will purchase lipsticks on a daily basis. This fact pressures Revlon to maintain a continuous supply of lipsticks to its retail customers through a system of wholesalers and branch warehouses throughout the United

Ratio of Net Sales to Inventory in Various Types of Businesses   TABLE 18-3

Ratio of Net Sales to Inventory
(Net Sales per $1.00 of Inventory)

Types of Business	Successful Company Ratio	Unsuccessful Company Ratio	Number of Companies
Retailing			
Building materials	15.1	5.2	96
Department stores	7.3	3.9	202
Discount stores	7.5	4.4	180
Gasoline service stations	21.2	5.4	84
Groceries and meats	23.0	12.7	156
Tires, batteries, and accessories	8.4	3.9	69
Variety stores	6.0	3.5	63
Women's specialty shops	9.4	4.8	208
Wholesaling			
Chemicals and allied products	16.2	7.3	55
Drugs and sundries	10.2	5.6	110
Electrical parts, supplies	10.2	5.6	156
Electronics equipment	5.6	3.3	56
Household appliances	10.6	4.8	111
Machinery and equipment	10.9	5.0	211
Metals and minerals	11.4	4.1	68
Paper	9.7	5.5	157
Petroleum products	41.1	13.0	75

Source: Burr W. Hupp, Managing Director, Chicago Office, Drake Sheahan/Stewart Dougall, Inc., "Inventory Policy is a Top Management Responsibility," *Handling and Shipping*, Aug. 1967, p. 48. Reprinted from *Handling and Shipping*, August, and copyright, 1967, by Industrial Publishing Company, a division of Pittway Corporation.

States. It is obvious that one of the major purposes of this warehouse system is to maintain a constant supply of basic stock for a firm's distribution system.

A warehouse system, however, does not have as its sole purpose the maintenance of basic stocks. Many firms maintain warehouses for many other reasons. Some firms find that warehouses are important to guard against transportation slowdowns during periods of peak demand. A manufacturer of toys may find that he has to maintain warehouses simply because at the peak Christmas season trucking firms are operating at near capacity and are generally slower to deliver than at other months of the year.

Warehouses are also used in many industries for the purposes of speculative buying or the availability of price discounts during the off season. A manufacturer of a product using cocoa may find that purchasing the product at certain times of the year when a glut occurs can guarantee him a low price, particularly if cocoa is an important ingredient in his finished product. Buying during off seasons can also result in receiving substantial price discounts from manufacturers. Many manufacturers find, for instance, that if they purchase raw materials or finished products (such as electrical motors) during an off-season period, they can qualify for discounts, particularly if they are willing to take immediate delivery. This same policy prevails throughout the channel of distribution. Thus the wholesaler of boats, motors, and boating supplies can obtain substantial discounts from boating

375

manufacturers if he is willing to place orders and accept delivery of the merchandise well before the boating season starts in the spring.

In some agricultural markets, warehouses are used to ripen and condition products. In the liquor industry, warehouses are used to age the product.

Finally, the manufacturer is well aware of the fact that warehousing allows him the privilege of gaining favorable transportation rate savings. It is relatively cheaper to ship or accept shipment of a full truckload or carload of merchandise than a less-than-carload delivery. The rate is not only less, but the handling of a full shipment is more efficient.

Warehouse Location

Although more will be said about transportation later, it should be pointed out that transportation costs are among the highest costs in a physical distribution system (refer to Table 18-1). The size of this cost is directly related to the firm's location of warehouses.

By adding warehouses, the manufacturer finds that he lowers the distance that must be traveled between his factories and his customers. Costs tend to decrease as distance decreases. As a balancing factor, one must remember that as the manufacturer's number of warehouses tends to increase, the opportunities to deliver a truckload lot to each warehouse decrease. In some cases, the manufacturer may find that he is unable to ship carload or truckload lots to his distribution system. As a result, he conceivably could end up with higher transportation costs. Thus the decision to build warehouses must be based primarily on its impact on full-truckload transportation costs balanced against less-than-truckload shipping costs, plus the additional costs of maintaining a warehouse.

Many firms, therefore, maintain a rather centralized warehouse system in contrast to a decentralized arrangement. Yet some firms prefer a decentralized warehouse system in order to better service their customers. This factor, of course, is major in the decision to open up many warehouses throughout the country. Many considerations enter into this decision. The following factors are important in choosing a decentralized warehouse system:[6]

1. When a firm is distributing products of high substitutability, or products of an essential nature.

2. When a firm has products of high marketability and low dollar value, but is unable to support the high costs of premium transportation from a centralized storage point and yet of low enough value so that inventory carrying charges are not excessive.

3. Products that are typically purchased by consumers in less-than-carload quantities.

4. The ease with which a product can be warehoused without the need for specialized storing facilities.

5. The tendency of the firm's customers to allow insufficient lead time in ordering and reordering merchandise can be a decisive factor.

When most of these characteristics are not present, the firm must decide to centrally warehouse its products.

---

[6]*Ibid.*, p. 198.

How do firms decide on the location of a warehouse in terms of a city? Table 18-4 indicates the savings that would accrue to a Pittsburgh manufacturing firm with a choice of a warehouse location in either Chicago or Detroit. Several facts should be noted in this illustration. First, locating the warehouse in Chicago would result in an estimated deficit of $3,127 over establishing the same warehouse at the plant in Pittsburgh. The Detroit location would result in a substantial $37,950 saving. Close study of the table seems to indicate that the major savings in inbound transportation costs occur because Detroit handles more merchandise than Chicago.

Determination of Net Savings Resulting from Location of Decentralized Warehouses   **TABLE 18-4**
at Chicago and Detroit (Comelean Corporation)

	Chicago	*Detroit*
Savings		
Transportation (inbound)	$36,000	$104,400
Increased sales	1,470	3,750
Cost reduction at Pittsburgh		
Fixed warehouse costs	864	6,000
Variable warehouse costs	8,437	20,000
Inventory carrying costs	432	3,000
In-transit inventory costs	150	400
Gross savings	$47,353	$137,550
Added costs		
Local delivery	$31,550	$ 60,000
Decentralized warehousing		
Fixed warehouse costs	5,760	10,800
Variable warehouse costs	11,250	24,000
Inventory carrying costs	1,920	4,800
Gross added costs	$50,480	$ 99,600
Net savings from decentralization	($ 3,127)	$ 37,950

Source: J. L. Heskett, R. M. Ivie, and N. A. Glaskowsky, Jr., *Business Logistics* (New York: The Ronald Press Company, 1965), p. 202.

To make this decision, a firm must analyze each warehouse possibility individually, since it is unlikely that any two locations will involve the same costs.

Public and Private Warehouses

Firms need not build their own warehouses in all markets. In fact, they may avail themselves of public warehouses. Public warehouses are warehouses, as the name implies, available for use by the general public. Many firms prefer using public warehouses for their needs, since they do not require the firm to make an investment in land and building or in personnel necessary to maintain the warehouse. Public warehouses charge manufacturers storage rates and any incurred handling charges. They are of particular interest to manufacturers who have seasonal warehousing problems. They are also of value to manufacturers who find that shifts in their markets occur, so that any permanent warehouse might become obsolete within a few years. Most of all, manufacturers who use public warehouses find them to be an excellent alternative to investing in their own building and land.

The alternative to public warehouses is private warehouses, that is, warehouses operated and owned by a private firm for its own goods. Although the same elements go into the decision to build private warehouses as in our discussion of decentralized warehouses, it should be noted that no firm involves itself in such a long-range commitment unless it can maintain production to keep the warehouse operating at near capacity. Should they not be able to, their option is to rent space in a public warehouse.

Modes of Transportation

Table 18-5 lists the major modes of transportation and the service characteristics of each. It is useful to discuss each of these modes and determine their relative costs, which is perhaps the major factor in making a decision as to what mode a manufacturer chooses to use.

TABLE 18-5   **General Relationships of Service Characteristics of the Five Modes of Transportation**

Speed	Air	>	Highway	>	Rail	>	Water	>	Pipeline
Frequency	Pipeline	>	Highway	>	Air	>	Rail	>	Water
Dependability . .	Pipeline	>	Highway	>	Rail	>	Water	>	Air
Capability.	Water	>	Rail	>	Highway	>	Air	>	Pipeline
Availability	Highway	>	Rail	>	Air	>	Water	>	Pipeline

Source: J. L. Heskett, R. M. Ivie, and N. A. Glaskowsky, Jr., *Business Logistics* (New York: The Ronald Press Company, 1964), p. 71.

Highway (usually trucks).   Trucks are usually the cheapest form of transportation for many reasons. One is that the truck operator has low fixed costs simply because he does not have to maintain costly terminals. In addition, he can use the public-owned highways. More importantly, the manufacturer knows that the truck can make door-to-door deliveries without having to transfer the goods to another carrier. As a result, truck transportation is second in terms of speed to only the airplane.

In practically all service aspects, the truck ranks high, particularly in terms of the frequency of service, dependability, and availability. In terms of its capability of carrying all kinds of cargo, however, the truck ranks behind railroads and water due to equipment limitations and federal regulations governing the weight and capacities of trucks.

Rail.   The railroad has the highest fixed costs of any form of transportation except the pipeline. This is because of the high terminal costs and the need for buying the right of way. Rail also ranks high in terms of most service factors, but in all but one case it ranks below trucking. It has been established that railroads have a higher capability in terms of carrying heavier and more diversified shipments than trucks. A railroad car may carry huge steel beams, coal, or other difficult cargos long distances at a reasonable cost. In recent years the frequency and thus the dependability of rail service has declined due to the declining profits of the industry, attributable to the burden of handling commuter passenger travel. It is expected, however, that this drag on the revenue of railroads will be somewhat lifted by pending government legislation.

Air. Air provides the speediest service by far, particularly over long distances. Although airplanes are costly, their fixed costs are less than railroads due to the fact that many communities incur the costs of many airline facilities. Much of this local support is subsidized by the federal government.

One major drawback to air transportation is its limitation in terms of the type of cargo that can be handled. Due to limitations in the size of aircraft and federal regulations regarding weight capacity, airplanes are restricted in the kinds of goods they can carry. In addition, the weight capacity forces aircraft to delay shipments until a less than capacity plane enters the terminal. The development of the huge Boeing 747 should provide the airline industry with more flexibility in freight service in the future. From a manufacturer's point of view, the airplane is also the least dependable form of transportation, since it is obviously affected by poor weather conditions and the fact that once mechanical failure occurs the plane's cargo cannot be detached as readily as that borne by a train or even a truck. In addition, the cargo may have to be sent with the plane to a faraway city where repairs can be made.

Water. Most manufacturers have little use for water transportation. Water is somewhat like airlines in that many of the facilities and terminals for water transportation are subsidized by the federal government.

Water transportation ranks very low in terms of speed, frequency of service (large boats carry a great deal and load up infrequently), dependability (water currents affect both travel and loading of boats), and availability (depends on availability of water nearby). Only in terms of its capability to carry most any cargo is the water form of transportation superior to others.

Pipelines. Pipelines are limited to the carrying of liquids. Due to the need to purchase rights of way, pipelines rank lowest in terms of speed, capability, and availability. Thus they are of little value to most manufacturers in terms of an alternative system of transportation. On the other hand, where applicable, pipelines, by their very nature, are more dependable than any form of transportation.

Coordinated Systems of Transportation

Although previously we have spoken of individual transportation modes, it is not correct to look at these systems as entities unto themselves. Obviously, many rail deliveries are made in combination with trucking firms, as are most air deliveries. In recent years, many of these transportation systems have developed coordinated systems that make it easy to overcome some of the problems inherent in transferring merchandise and goods from one vehicle to the other. Some of the newer and more interesting systems are discussed next.

Piggyback. This is one of the newer and better-known types of systems; the truck is fitted on a railroad flat car and transported to the major terminal area.

From there, the truck is then driven to its ultimate destination. This system avoids the problem of reloading the truck after it arrives at its destination.

Fishyback. Where trucks and water carriers coordinate shipments, it is referred to as "fishyback" services. Much of this service is offered in the Great Lakes and West Coast ports. Two systems seem to be used; driving the truck on the ship and driving off at the destination is the first type. In the other the container part of the truck is shipped and coordinated with the cab of the truck at the port of destination.

Rail-water. This service has been available for many years. It involves the use of specially constructed rail cars that can be easily transferred aboard ship for further transportation. It obviously eliminates the cargo changes necessary in shipments of great distances.

Transportation Expenditures

In view of our discussion, Table 18-6 indicates the proportion of revenues generated by all forms of freight transportation in the United States. As expected, the most important means of transportation is the truck, which is the most likely carrier of goods heading to the market. The truck has increased its share of the market steadily in the past 20 years. This is due to its flexibility, aided by the government policy of developing huge highway systems to all areas of the country. The growth of the highway programs has encouraged the development of industries serviced by these roads and has resulted in the growth of trucking firms servicing many of these newer easy-to-reach areas.

The increase in truck traffic has been at the expense of the railroads, which have grown at a rate of about 1 percent per year since 1950. Since 1950 truck revenues have grown 7 times, railroads by 20 percent, and pipelines and waterways have tripled. Air was not a factor in 1950. However, since 1955 air carriers have increased their operating revenue by 6 times.

Furthermore, indications are that air will increase at a faster rate in years to come due to the emergence of the large air-cargo-type planes and the availability of the equally large Boeing 747.

SUMMARY

Distribution is concerned with moving goods from the factory to the ultimate consumer at a cost of approximately 22 percent. This system may involve a full, partial, or one-step distribution arrangement.

Since the purpose of the system is to service the customer, the manufacturer must at some point determine the level of service that is necessary to compromise between the demands of the customer and the costs involved in meeting these requirements. The compromise is usually based on the type of product being sold and what the competition is offering.

TABLE 18-6 Operating Revenues by Type of Transport

Transport Agency	1950	1955	1960	1965	1967	1968	1969 (prel.)
Revenues (mil. dol.)							
Electric railways	79	60	23	13	12	12	13
Railway Express	223	241	248	316	323	299	270
Railroads	9,924	10,590	9,955	10,738	10,875	11,357	11,955
Waterlines	330	452	427	426	426	435	450
Pipelines (oil)	442	678	770	904	995	1,023	1,103
Domestic scheduled air carriers	558	1,215	2,129	3,609	4,887	5,606	6,439
Motor carriers of property	3,737	5,535	7,214	10,068	11,308	12,400	13,500
Motor carriers of passengers	539	552	667	885	945	991	1,007
Index (1957 to 1959 = 100, except as noted)							
Railroads	95	101	96	103	105	110	116
Pipelines (oil)	60	92	104	122	135	139	149
Domestic scheduled air carriers	(NA)	25	44	74	100	115	132
Motor carriers of property	58	85	111	155	175	191	208
Motor carriers of passengers	88	91	109	145	155	163	165

NA — Not available.
Source: *Statistical Abstract of the United States* (Washington, D.C.: Government Printing Office, 1971), p. 524.

Physical distribution is particularly concerned with making decisions in three major areas:

1. Inventory decisions, which include ordering and handling costs measured against the cost of losing a sale.

2. Warehousing costs, which include the proper spacing and selection of warehousing sites.

3. Mode of transportation costs, which include the choice of the mode of transportation in terms of costs and type of service offered.

QUESTIONS

1. The physical distribution system and its cost are greatest among companies with a full distribution system policy. True or false? Explain.

*2. What demands on the part of his customers must a manufacturer selling toys to small retailers take into consideration to guide his building of a total physical distribution system?

3. Aside from the actual cash outlay for an inventory, what other costs does a manufacturer usually incur?

4. How does the type of product being sold govern the type of physical distribution system necessary?

5. What are coordinated transportation systems? Do they represent an entirely new concept?

6. Why are trucks considered to be the most practical and efficient means of transportation for most manufacturers?

7. Railroads and airplanes can never be complete transportation systems for most manufacturers. Why?

8. Under what conditions would a firm build a decentralized warehouse?

9. Under what conditions would a firm use a public warehouse?

*10. Under what conditions would a major manufacturer of frozen orange juice establish a decentralized warehouse system?

*11. What new developments could increase the use of airlines as a transportation alternative in the apparel industry?

12. On one major railroad route it was determined that merchandise could be delivered from city to city in 1 hour. Yet most manufacturers of housewares preferred to use trucks, which took $1\frac{1}{2}$ hours from terminal to terminal. Why?

*In-depth questions.

Appendix

To make decisions a marketing executive must be familiar with the fundamentals of business accounting. Assuming most business students have had a course in basic accounting, this section will point out several important sources of marketing data that relate to (1) the profit and loss statement and (2) operating ratios.

Marketing
Arithmetic

Profit and Loss Statement

The profit and loss statement is the key document in the determination of how well the firm is progressing. A statement is presented in Table A-1. Here one sees that the profit and loss statement contains four major items of interest to management — sales, expenses, gross margin, and net profit.

It should be noted that the profit and loss statement can cover most any period a firm designates. Typically, however, most firms draw up an annual profit and loss statement for the owners and stockholders. During the year a firm is also likely to compute a monthly, quarterly, or semiannual statement in order to determine if the firm is meeting the financial and marketing plans.

Basically, the profit and loss statement is a rather simple device for determining how well the company is doing. Forgetting the details of the statement for the moment, one can compute the net profits from the operation in the following way:

Net sales	$188,000
Less cost of goods sold	121,150
Gross margin	66,850
Less total expenses	48,920
Net profit or loss	$ 17,930

In effect what this summary statement says is that in the year ending December 31, 1973, the firm had net sales of $188,000. During that year the firm

TABLE A-1   Profit and Loss Statement for the Year Ending December 31, 1973

			Operating Ratios (%)
Gross sales	$200,000		
Less returns and allowances	12,000		
Net sales		$188,000	100.0
Cost of goods sold:			
Inventory Jan. 1, 1973	$ 25,200		
Purchases	$122,400		
Less cash discount	450		
	121,950		
	$147,150		
Less inventory Dec. 31, 1973	26,000		
Cost of goods sold		121,150	64.4
Gross profit		$ 66,850	35.6
Operating expenses:			
Accounting and legal	1,000		0.5
Advertising	5,200		2.8
Bad debts	1,500		0.8
Delivery costs	1,500		0.8
Depreciation	1,440		0.8
Wages	21,550		11.5
Entertainment and travel	750		0.4
Insurance	650		0.3
Interest	400		0.2
Maintenance and repair	800		0.4
Miscellaneous	4,530		2.4
Rent	8,000		4.3
Supplies	600		0.3
Taxes and licenses	250		0.1
Utilities and telephone	750		0.4
Total expenses		$ 48,920	26.0
Net profit before income taxes		$ 17,930	9.5

made purchases and sold from inventory goods costing $121,150. The difference between the cost of the goods that were sold and selling price amounted to $66,850. Now from this figure the firm must pay all their expenses. Since the total expenses for the year were $48,920, the firm had earnings of just under $18,000.

Description of Profit and Loss Items

Net sales. During a typical year, firms find that customers return merchandise that was originally recorded as sales for credit. Thus not all sales during the year are final. In addition, in most retail firms the customer is charged a state or local sales tax that is turned over directly to the government body involved.

To account for these two events, it is necessary to calculate the net sales by recording the gross amount of sales made during the period under study, exclude the sales tax, and deduct any returns or allowances granted to customers. The resulting figure is referred to as net sales. Thus, as illustrated in Table A-1,

Gross sales	$200,000
Less returns and allowances	12,000
Net Sales	$188,000

Cost of goods sold.   As noted, the cost of goods sold is a calculation that has as its goal the determination of the cost value of the net sales. In the construction of the cost of goods section the retailer and manufacturer differ in their approach. This section incidentally represents the only major area in the profit and loss statement where the approach differs between manufacturers and retailers. The reason is quite simple to understand in that the retailer is a buyer of merchandise, whereas the manufacturer produces merchandise. Manufacturers refer to this section in their statement as the cost of goods manufactured.

In the retail firm the cost of goods sold is computed by adding the beginning inventory to the merchandise purchased during the year (which usually includes freight costs), less discounts received from the suppliers of merchandise, minus the ending physical inventory on December 31 in this case.

The cost of goods section in a manufacturing statement includes direct labor and other production costs that go into the cost of producing finished goods. Otherwise, the statement is similar to that of the retailer.

Gross margin.   Gross margin (or gross profit) is the difference between the net sales and the cost of goods sold. The gross margin is a key figure in that the total expenses of the firm and the net profit must not exceed this figure. Thus any increase in gross margin by the firm gives the firm more leeway in meeting its expense obligations and profit goals.

Operating expenses.   Operating expenses, as noted, are deducted from the gross margin in order to determine the net profit or loss. Operating expenses include salaries, advertising, accounting, bad debts, supplies, and numerous other categories.

Markup calculations.   After one examines the operating statement, it seems fairly obvious that the markup in the retail store must cover the total expenses and estimated profits of the firm. Thus, to determine the selling price in a store, one should assume that the markup covers the expenses (26 percent) and the net profit (9.5 percent). Combining these two figures, a 36 percent markup seems to be in order. Note that these figures equal the gross margin.

However, closer examination of the retailer's operation reveals that the initial price of goods is subject to certain reductions. For instance, some merchandise is marked down; that is, the firm finds that it cannot sell it at the original selling price. In addition, the firm may give discounts to employees or some merchandise may be stolen. To make allowances for these happenings, it is usual for the retail firm to estimate retail reductions and include them in the initial markup. Suppose that this same firm determined that reductions would amount to 4 percent of sales. The question of what should be the initial markup is answered by the following formula:

$$\text{initial markup percentage} = \frac{\text{gross margin} + \text{retail reductions}}{100 \text{ percent} + \text{retail reductions}}$$

$$\frac{36 \text{ percent} + 4 \text{ percent}}{100 \text{ percent} + 4 \text{ percent}} = 38.46 \text{ percent}$$

Thus a firm needing a gross margin of 36 percent and allowing for retail reductions of 4 percent would mark up merchandise an average of 38.46 percent, or 39 percent.

Let us suppose then that a buyer desires to mark up an individual item costing 92 cents by 39 percent (of retail). What retail price will give us the desired markup? The formula is

$$\text{retail price} = \frac{\text{cost}}{100 - \text{desired markup percentage}} \times 100$$

$$= \frac{0.92}{61} \times 100 = \$1.50$$

In some cases retailers and many wholesalers prefer to convert the goal markup of 39 percent on retail to a markup on cost. To accomplish this, they use the following formula:

$$\text{markup on cost} = \frac{\text{markup on retail}}{100 - \text{markup on retail}} \times 100$$

$$= \frac{39}{100 - 39} \times 100 = 63.39 \text{ percent}$$

63.39 percent of 92 cents = 58.32

0.91 + 58.32 = \$1.4932 = \$1.50 retail price

Although in both cases the retail price ended up the same, it should be noted that in the formula using cost percentages extra steps were necessary to arrive at the correct figure.

Stock turnover.   Stock turnover is used ordinarily as a guide for determining how much stock a firm should carry and in measuring the efficiency of the firm's operation to other similar firms. It is particularly useful in wholesaling and retailing firms.

The formulas that are most widely used are the following:

$$(1) \text{ rate of stock turnover} = \frac{\text{number of units sold}}{\text{average stock in units}}$$

$$(2) \text{ rate of stock turnover} = \frac{\text{net sales (in dollars)}}{\text{average retail stock (in dollars)}}$$

$$(3) \text{ rate of stock turnover} = \frac{\text{cost of goods sold}}{\text{average cost inventory}}$$

Formula (1) is used in cases when the firm has an inventory of the units by each merchandise category. Thus a firm that sells 500 television sets during a period and maintains an average inventory during the same period of 100 sets has a turnover rate of 5.

Formula (2) is used when the inventory figure is taken at retail prices. Formula (3) is used in cases when the inventory is available at cost prices. To obtain the average inventory, one may add the beginning inventory during the period under study to the ending inventory and divide by 2. Over a 1-year period, when monthly inventories are available, by adding all the beginning of the month inventories plus the ending inventory, one can divide by 13 and obtain the annual inventory average.

The inventory turnover figure is usually compared against some industry standard. For instance, the average appliance dealer turns over his merchandise about 4 times a year, florists 25 times, and large department stores 4 times.

Markdowns

In the retail firm the merchant fully intends to sell a product at the stipulated price. However, in many cases he finds that the consumer will not pay that price, or he has purchased too many and finds that part of his order can only be sold at a lower price. The difference between the original price and the price it is finally sold at is referred to as a markdown.

Although markdowns do not appear on the profit and loss statement, they are nevertheless considered to be important in that they help management to determine what price lines and products are subject to such reductions and perhaps get at the causal factors. Thus, should a firm find that a particular supplier's products are subject to heavy markdowns, they can then determine whether they should continue buying the product or not. In addition, retail firms can set markdown budgets for buyers and make allowances in the original markup of the merchandise for anticipated markdowns. All this can only be done if the firm is aware of past markdowns.

In most retail firms markdowns are computed as a percentage of the net selling price. Thus a buyer who originally puts a retail price of $10 on an item and later reduces the price to $7.50 has incurred a $33\frac{1}{3}$ percent markdown ($2.50 ÷ $7.50).

Operating Ratios

Operating ratios are derived from a study of the firm's profit and loss statement and the balance sheet. The most common profit and loss ratios are the expense items found in all statements.

In Table A-1 one can see that the expenses of $48,920 represent 26 percent of net sales ($48,920 ÷ $188,000). Expenses are always measured against net sales. In addition to the overall expenses of the firm, the individual expenses are measured against net sales. For instance, in the same figure advertising expenses are 2.8 percent of sales. The expense ratios can be measured against either national averages or against similar firms when the data are available.

Return on Investment

An important measurement of the operating efficiency of the firm is the return on investment. To make this computation, one has to use data from both the profit and loss statement and the balance sheet.

The appropriate formula is as follows:

$$\text{return on investment} = \frac{\text{net profits}}{\text{investment}}$$

Net profits are derived from the profit and loss statement, as in Table A-1. Investment is derived from the balance sheet of the firm and is computed as follows:

Balance Sheet

Assets	$200,000	Liabilities		$100,000
			Net worth	
		Capital stock	$60,000	
		Retained earnings	$40,000	$100,000
	$200,000			$200,000

Investment is usually referred to as the amount of money the firm has available over the assets minus the liabilities. This figure represents the net worth of the firm or the investment. In this case the net worth or the investment of the firm is $100,000. Substituting in the formula,

$$\text{return on investment} = \frac{\$17,930}{\$100,000} = 17.9 \text{ percent}$$

Thus the return on investment of this firm is slightly under 18 percent.

QUESTIONS

1. Compute the net profit of a firm from the following data:

Beginning inventory	$ 15,000
Purchases	35,000
Gross sales	180,000
Returns and allowances	30,000
Advertising	10,000
Ending inventory	25,000
Rent	25,000
Salaries	40,000
Other expenses	12,000

2. Net worth in this same firm is $300,000. Compute the return on net worth or investment. Is it high or low?

3. Relate gross margin to markdowns.

4. A firm is planning expenses at 28 percent of sales and profits of 7 percent. Retail reductions are estimated at 5 percent. What initial markup is necessary to maintain a gross margin of 35 percent?

5. Determine the stock turnover from the data found in Table A-1.

6. What is the selling price of an item purchased for $3.28 and marked up at 36 percent of retail?

7. A firm has a stock turnover of four times a year, a sales volume of $300,000, and a gross margin of 28 percent. What is the average inventory at cost?

8. What is the equivalent markup on cost if the percentage of markup on retail is
   a. 40
   b. 25
   c. 55
   d. 10

*9. Discuss the significance of a firm earning a return on investment of 24 percent before taxes and at the same time showing a profit to sales ratio of less than 1 percent.

10. Relate gross margin, expenses, and profits.

*In-depth question.

Cases

I would like to thank Stanley E. Hecht, a former student at Bernard M. Baruch College, and my friend A. Hochner, a member of the adjunct faculty at the same school, for their help on a number of these cases.

391

1

Allied Shoe Company, Inc.

Carl May is the president of the Allied Shoe Company, Inc. In recent years he has been considering the importance of coordinating marketing with the production, financial, and personnel departments.

His reasoning is brought about by the growing interest in producing products that are more closely allied with consumer preferences. To bring this about, he has held several conferences with other corporate presidents and the executive director of a shoe trade association. It is his view, as well as others', that the mortality rate of shoe products is high simply because the products are produced by one part of the firm and sold by another, with only the barest coordination among these divisions.

At the first meeting held with his staff, the production manager objected, noting that the product produced must meet certain production costs; otherwise, they cannot sell it. In addition, he observed that the shoes sold were practically all copied from more expensive competitive lines from the previous years. He was also careful to note that the company was doing well financially, in spite of the high product failure rate.

1. Do you agree? Explain.
2. What arguments should the president offer to refute the view?
3. How would this change affect production, personnel, marketing, and the financial sections of the firm?

2

Advertising Age

The following editorial appeared in *Advertising Age* (Jan. 25, 1971).

WE ARE WHAT WE ARE

We think it's pretty unrealistic to expect a marketer to say in ads that his product is just the same as the other guy's, as was proposed to the Federal Trade Commission by a group of law students and seconded by Rep. Fred B. Rooney (D., Pa.) the other day.

The suggestion probably wouldn't have merited much of a story — or much of a response — except for the fact that another seemingly far out remedy to offset the effects of misleading advertising currently is being tried out by the FTC. That's the commission's case against Standard Oil of California, in which FTC wants the company to run "corrective" ads to make up for allegedly fraudulent anti-pollution advertising in behalf of its new gasoline.

The law students — who call themselves Students Against Misleading Enterprises (SAME) — contend that chemically identical products such as aspirin and liquid bleach should be required to carry a statement in their ads that their product is chemically the same as their competitors. This would save consumers a lot of money, the SAME group asserted, because once assured that all aspirins and bleaches were alike they would go out and buy a much cheaper bottle of aspirin or bottle of bleach.

Furthermore, SAME said, affirmative disclosure would make costly ad campaigns "wasteful" and would thus "encourage competition among a large number of manufacturers for the national market. This competition would encourage manufacturers to produce their product at the lowest cost possible," the SAME students maintained.

We don't think either of these premises is soundly based. First of all, we think that the SAME group — and many others — don't understand that the product and the advertising are all rolled up into one entity in most people's minds. Even if Bayer and St. Joseph aspirins were forced to say that they contained the same ingredients as all other aspirins, this wouldn't make much difference to most consumers.

It appears to us that people are buying Bayer and St. Joseph for all kinds of reasons unrelated to the fact that aspirin is pretty much aspirin (although Sterling Drug and Plough would dispute even this, saying that they put their products through all kinds of quality control exercises that their lower-price competitors don't use).

The Bayer advertising is carefully built around the theme that we consumers can place our complete confidence in the product; what we're really buying is confidence in a product and in the company that makes it, not just aspirin. To our way of thinking, this approach is perfectly valid and justified.

In the same vein we don't think that Bayer's advertising dollars, designed to generate such confidence, can be considered "wasteful." If it enables us to buy the product with the assurance that it has a little more going for it than the next guy's product, the dollars are well spent.

And for this reason we don't think the Sterling people would cut down on their expenditures even if they had to carry a disclaimer that their product was chemically the same as everyone else's. Most Bayer users, we submit, would go right on buying Bayer because they feel that they are buying more than just aspirin; they are buying an attitude about the product — much as women don't just buy cosmetics; they buy hope.

The mistake that most of the consumerists continue to make is their assumption that by reducing products to a common denominator people will automatically perceive them in the same way and buy on price alone. This is just not true. We buy products for a host of intangible reasons, as well as for good, sound dollars-and-cents reasons. All the equalizing in the world can't change that fact.

1. Do you agree with the view expressed in the editorial?
2. How valid are the motives as indicated in this editorial?

Brewster Medicines had been a leading producer of ethical drugs for a number of years. Recently the firm developed a full line of nonprescription products through its York Division.

At a recent meeting of the firm's advertising agency and the company's legal department, the legal department indicated that a television commercial that was being considered for national broadcasting was questionable and in their opinion should be dropped.

The commercial itself promoted the firm's newest product, Rolar Cough Syrup. The commercial tried to indicate that the effects of Rolar

3

**Brewster
Medicines**

lasted for many hours. The commercial opened with a person coughing badly. Within a few seconds the mate presents a spoonful of Rolar to the obviously distressed person. After taking Rolar, the party goes to sleep and is shown in the next scene awaking, looking cheerful again, and heading off to work, obviously in good spirits.

The legal department's objection to the commercial was based on the knowledge that the product's effects last only 4 hours. The implication of the commercial according to the legal department is that the product lasts 8 hours, since most people sleep 8 hours. Thus they felt that the Federal Trade Commission might issue a cease and desist order against such advertising.

It was the view of the advertising agency that the commercial did *not* imply that the product worked 8 hours. It simply demonstrated that the product worked, and a person going to sleep with a bad cough would be able to fall asleep comfortably after taking a spoonful of Rolar. It was also their view that the FTC would not relate the sleeptime to the 4-hour potency of the product.

1. Do you agree with the agency?

4

**Lee Epstein
For Netter
Lewy Dowd
Fox Ness
& Stream.**

September 18, 1968

Professor David J. Rachman
Bernard M. Baruch College
New York, N.Y. 10010

Dear Professor Rachman:

Mr. H. Gregory Thomas, President of Chanel, Inc., has asked me to answer your letter of September 12th, since the operation about which you ask falls within the ambit of my concern.

In most states, as well as in the federal courts, rebottling of the sort you mention is permitted. Historically, the earlier cases concerned such practices as buying FRUIT OF THE LOOM fabric, making shirts from it, and advertising the shirts as "made from FRUIT OF THE LOOM cloth." The courts held that this practice was permitted. Later cases involved replacement parts. If your razor blades fit a Gillette razor, you were allowed to advertise such fact, if you made it clear that your blades were not made by Gillette. You could, therefore, use the Gillette mark in your advertising, and even on your product, in a purely descriptive sense.

Later cases allowed the sale of reconditioned and secondhand parts, still bearing the original trademark, if the vendor made it clear (a) that the goods were secondhand, and (b) that the reconditioning was not done by the original manufacturer. You can, thus, sell CHAMPION sparkplugs, bearing the CHAMPION label, and the original trademark, if you make it clear that these are secondhand plugs, not reconditioned by (or guaranteed by) the original maker.

These holdings say, essentially, that if you sell CHAMPION plugs, you can call them CHAMPION plugs, whether or not they are secondhand or reconditioned, if you label them so that the purchaser knows they are secondhand and reconditioned by someone other than the original manufacturer.

At first blush, this does not seem novel. Clearly, if you sell your used FORD, you can sell it as a FORD, without removing the name FORD from the car, so long as you make it clear that it is a secondhand car, and that it has not been overhauled by and is not guaranteed by FORD.

However, on examination, the parallel is not so obvious. A 1965 FORD is obviously not a new FORD and a prospective purchaser is not likely to mistake it for a 1969 model or to believe that it carries the original FORD guarantee. On the other hand, reconditioned spark plugs are not, on their face, identifiable as old models, and, if put into the hands of unscrupulous dealers, may be sold as new ones or as old ones overhauled, reconditioned or guaranteed by the original manufacturer.

For this reason, cases which allow the practice usually insist on having the packages bear a clear statement as to the fact that the goods are reconditioned and that this was not done by the original manufacturer.

As to rebottling: an enterprising entrepreneur thought of rebottling fragrances in small quantities and selling them at a much lower unit price (but a much higher price per ounce) than the original package, selling the product under its original trademark. The original case involved very small phials of COTY perfume, in containers shaped like a clinical thermometer, which contained only a few drops of fragrance. The case went up to the Supreme Court, and the decision (Prestonettes v. Coty, 264 U.S. 359, 68 L. Ed. 731, 44 Sup. Ct. 350 (1924)) was that this practice was not an infringement of the original manufacturer's trademark rights. The decision placed certain limitations on the operation, such as requiring the package in which the final sale was made to bear a legend in type as large as the original trademark, stating, "Bottled independently of Coty by Prestonettes," etc.

This case has been severely criticized by many scholars and in many law journals, but is still the law. When the question was raised in a recent federal case in Texas, Judge Sarah Hughes asked, "You don't expect me to overrule the Supreme Court, do you?" The decision is by Mr. Justice Holmes, and most lawyers feel that if he had been the son of a storekeeper instead of a doctor and author, he would not have decided the case the way he did.

The package you ask about (with which we are familiar) contains 1 dram and sells for 98¢ to $1. At this rate, it would sell for $8 an ounce. The product is sold by the original manufacturer for $1.75 an ounce retail, but the smallest size sold is 2 ounces, at $3.50 per package. Moreover, the repackaged product is often sold as perfume, which regularly retails at $25.00 an ounce, when, in fact, it is cologne which has a regular retail price of $1.75 per ounce.

Further, most manufacturers select their retail outlets with care, spend a great deal of money on packaging and advertising, in order to project the proper image from a marketing point of view; the rebottled packages, on the other hand are sold in "schlock" stores, in tinsely packages, and under circumstances which hurt the image which the manufacturer has built up at great trouble and expense.

In New York, there is a special law which forbids the rebottling or repackaging of merchandise and the sale of such merchandise. In a case which went to the U.S. Supreme Court, this statute was upheld. Rebottling and the sale of rebottled merchandise is now illegal in New York. However, it is still permitted in most other states, which have no such laws.

Finally, the owner of the original mark has no control over the quality and genuineness of the allegedly rebottled merchandise. If he licensed someone to use his mark, he would (under penalty of losing his mark) be required to exercise quality controls, etc. When a volunteer rebottles his merchandise, the trademark owner has no such control. The fragrance may be genuine for a while and then counterfeit. Even if it is genuine, foreign matter creeps in and essential parts are evaporated and lost in the very rebottling process. A product is sold bearing his mark under conditions which are not under his control, and this practice may seriously hurt his goodwill.

I'm afraid I have let my enthusiasm carry me away in this reply; if you have any further questions on this subject, I will try to answer them.

Yours very truly,

Lee Epstein

For the Firm

LE/ms

cc: Chanel, Inc.

1. Discuss the pros and cons of the court's decision.

5

Zagor Baby Products

Zagor Baby Products has been in business for over 40 years. For the past 10 years the firm has become the third ranking among companies selling products for the baby markets. Its two divisions sell major product lines in supermarkets and department stores, as well as drugstores. Its largest-volume line is the Zagor's baby food sold in practically all major supermarkets in the United States. This line accounts for 70 percent of the firm's sales volume.

The balance of the sales volume is accounted for by the lines sold in department and drugstores, which include baby toiletries such as powder, creams, and various baby oils.

At a meeting of the long-range planning committee of the firm, the president called to the attention of the firm a recent forecast by the government that by 1980 the United States could possibly reach a zero growth rate. That is, births would merely replace deaths, and there would be no total increase in population except from immigration. The declining birth rate he noted was due to several factors. The most obvious are the increased use of the pill as a contraceptive, the liberalized abortion laws throughout the country, and the decreasing percentage of married females over the age of 18. Since there is little indication that this trend will reverse itself, the implications for the firm are obvious. They will be competing against several other firms for a market that has little growth potential.

To offset this turn of events, the president suggested that two viable alternatives were available to the company. The first was to consider moving into other areas of product development where the marketing team the firm had created could be used. This did not seem too promising for the present, since the research and development group had spent the past 5 years looking precisely in this direction. Their efforts to date have offered the firm little hope. It is hoped that over the long run the firm will benefit from this work.

The second alternative seemed much more promising and was actually being promoted by Johnson & Johnson, the leading firm in the baby toiletries field, who are engaging in repositioning their present baby products. That is, they are attempting to sell them to adults. For example, some commercials by the firm now stress that mothers are discovering the benefits of baby powders on their own skin. Word also has it that they are seriously considering dropping the word "baby" from their product names so that they can reach a wider market. Within the next few weeks they plan to launch a major campaign to promote the firm's best-selling baby shampoo to this market.

The president was also aware of the efforts of the Gerber baby food firm's effort to reposition its products to reach the senior citizen's market. Presently, this approach is being tried in the state of Florida, and if successful it should be expanded into other areas.

1. Should Zagor reposition its products?

William Small,[1] a product merchandising manager of television sets for the Magnavox Company, a major producer of television sets, was looking at two different studies that had recently crossed his desk.

The first was an in-house study of the characteristics of consumers of Magnavox television sets. It indicated that the buyers of such sets were generally older than the buyers of other major brands.

In fact, most of the buyers seemed to fall into the 35 to 44 age group. Since Magnavox emphasizes the quality of their product and sells their sets through department stores and high-quality music outlets, it was not surprising that this group was their major customer.

The second study was in the form of a report received from the Conference Board and consisted of an analysis of income groups in the United States in a most recent year. The data that particularly caught Mr. Small's eye can be found on p. 398.

Although the data on upper income families were impressive, Mr. Small was concerned by the fact that one of the largest age groups, the 25 to 34, although comprising 18.4 percent of all families, comprised less than 8 percent of all Magnavox buyers according to the previous in-house study.

6

Magnavox
Company I

---

[1] Fictitious name and study.

Characteristics of Upper Income Households (All data 1970, unless otherwise indicated)

	All Households (%)	Under $15,000 (%)	Annual Household Income		$15,000 and Over (%)	
			Total	$15,000 to 25,000	$25,000 to 50,000	$50,000 and Over
Households, millions	64.4	52.1	12.3	9.7	2.3	0.3
Distribution of households	100.0	80.9	19.1	15.1	3.5	0.5
Distribution all income	100.0	57.6	42.3	27.9	11.0	3.4
Age of Head	100.0	100.0	100.0	100.0	100.0	100.0
Under 25	7.3	8.7	1.5	1.6	0.6	1.6
25 to 34	18.4	19.1	15.3	16.9	9.4	8.0
35 to 44	18.2	16.5	25.8	26.2	24.9	19.6
45 to 54	19.4	16.4	32.2	31.4	35.9	33.2
55 to 64	17.1	16.5	19.2	18.5	21.3	29.2
65 and over	19.6	22.8	6.0	5.4	7.8	8.3

Source: *The Expanding Upper Income Brackets* (New York: The Conference Board, November 1971).

He also noted that the Conference Board study clearly indicated that over 15 percent of these families had incomes exceeding $15,000 annually.

Mr. Small realized that the reason the younger market was not buying Magnavox was because the sets were not sold in discount stores, but instead in the more traditional outlets. Discount stores by their very nature attracted younger families who were attracted by their pricing policies.

1. What should Mr. Small do?
2. Do you agree with his interpretation of the statistics?

7

Dent-All

Charles Corrigan was a salesman for the Dent-All company, a firm that has been supplying dental supplies to dentists for several years. Mr. Corrigan was the most successful salesman with the firm and was awaiting a major promotion to a divisional or territorial management position.

During the past summer he was asked, as the firm's top salesman, to discuss his selling techniques before a new group of salesmen who were in the process of being trained. At that talk he told the salesmen that the most important part of a salesman's job in selling to dentists was an ability to determine who were the "influencers." By influencers he meant the dentists who are respected by other dentists in their particular city. He pointed out that once you have convinced the influencer to buy you can pretty much expect most of the others to follow suit.

He cautioned, however, that the influencer was not easy to find and most of all you had to eventually distinguish between the influencer and the innovator. The innovator he defined as the dentist who wants to always have the latest product in his office. However, since he is not an influencer, making a sale with him will add few customers. However, once an influencer is sold, by simply passing the word to most of the other dentists the sale of the product will increase substantially.

The problem again as he saw it was to locate the influencer. This required special study, but he could give the salesmen some useful tips as to the general characteristics of this person. He noted that the influencer was ordinarily associated with a dental school as a part-time faculty member. In some cases he was involved to some extent with significant research being done at this school. In most cases he had either published papers or was always presenting papers at the major meetings of the dental association.

Another interesting characteristic he noted was that this person was unlikely to be the dentist with the most lucrative or for that matter the busiest practice in town. He ordinarily found that this dentist scheduled his appointments 1 hour apart and was likely to spend a substantial part of his week at the university or engaged in preparing papers.

1. Do you agree with his analysis?

2. Describe the innovators and explain why they may not influence other dentists.

8

Station WRZ

Station WRZ is a major radio station in Detroit. For several years, however, the listeners to its popular music format have been declining, according to the ratings released by Pulse, Inc., the firm that rates radio stations throughout the country.

In July of the past year the firm hired Ross Manning Research, a New York based research firm, to explore the possibility of converting the station to a country-music format. Since Detroit did not have a country-music radio station, the general manager felt that a market opportunity existed. His own problem, he believed, was to determine whether people would appreciate this type of music.

To make this determination, the research firm sampled 1,500 Detroit households during a 5-month period. Each householder listened to several cassette tapes with recordings of country music and were asked for their opinions. To the surprise of management, a large portion of the listeners reported a favorable attitude toward this form of music. They also clearly identified Johnny Cash and Glen Campbell as two well-known celebrities who made the move from country music to popular. This indicated to management that the conversion from popular to country music could be made gradually by playing the better-known country recording artists.

The study also seemed to indicate that there are a lot of country music fans who do not know they like that type of music. The manager reasoned that the interest in this type of music of the dwellers in large cities stems from a desire for a return to the simple life. This is reflected in the music's concern with ecology and the simpler concepts of love, death, loneliness, and even going to jail. These are the themes of country music and should appeal to this large segment of the market.

1. Do you agree with this approach?
2. Do you agree with the interpretation of the study?

9

Munson Jacket Company

In January 1972, William Douglas, Research Director of the Munson Jacket Company, presented the findings of a study he had just completed for his company in the past year and a half. In this study he had interviewed 500 people in Cleveland, Ohio, concerning the prices they planned to pay and eventually paid for tailored jackets and slacks.

His purpose in conducting this survey was to determine the best selling price points in the sale of this merchandise and also to determine if any important trends were taking place. Since sales of these two items in his firm exceed 60 percent of total sales, the study was of considerable interest. The tables show his findings.

Price Points Comparison – Tailored Jackets

	May 1970	*Fall 1970*	*January 1971*	*Fall 1971*
Less than $25	12%	4%	4%	1%
$25 to $35	8	6	10	3
$35 to $50	19	18	23	17
$50 to $75	41	45	36	43
$75 to $100	15	19	18	25
More than $100	5	8	9	11
	100%	100%	100%	100%

Price Points Comparison – Tailored Slacks

	May 1970	*Fall 1970*	*January 1971*	*Fall 1971*
Under $10	23%	10%	7%	7%
$10 to $12	21	12	11	6
$12 to $14	15	10	11	6
$14 to $17	18	20	20	19
$17 to $20	3	5	5	5
$20 to $25	11	20	25	25
Over $25	9	23	21	32
	100%	100%	100%	100%

1. What useful information could the company get from these findings?

Packaging Research Company has been making plastic shopping bags for several years. PRC is owned by a large conglomerate that has indicated its displeasure with the latest profit report.

The plastic shopping bag has been sold by PRC to major department and specialty stores for years. The firm has a patent on their best-selling bag by virtue of its special handle and fold. This special handle and fold give the bag a custom look that makes it particularly attractive. It has proved to be especially attractive to fashion stores in most major cities.

In recent years sales of the bag have declined considerably, and the president commissioned a research study to determine why. The study reported that the bag had several major advantages over competitive products. The first, of course, was its look, which all surveyed store purchasing agents agreed was superior to any bag now on the market. In addition, most purchasing agents agreed that the bag had a long life, and they noted that several shoppers reused the bag again and again, no doubt due to its favorable

10

Packaging Research Company (PRC)

image. In addition, the agents commented that the particular handle was well received by shoppers during rainy weather since, because of the particular shape of the bag, it kept the bag tightly closed and protected the bag's contents.

On the negative side most agents noted that the bag cost 17 cents, about 5 cents more than other competing plastic shopping bags. In spite of all the advantages, most purchasing agents indicated that they usually bought competing bags. Their major rationale seemed to be that management was constantly pressuring them to lower the cost of packaging in their stores. Most felt there was little pressure to design a fashionable-looking bag.

1. What should PRC do?

11

Carter Cosmetics

Carter Cosmetics is the producer of the Beauty-Maid cosmetics lines sold in major department stores throughout the world. As with all major cosmetic companies, the firm has under consideration new lines of products practically every year. It was noted by the president at a recent meeting that 70 percent of the firm's sales this past year were derived from products that did not exist in their line 10 years ago.

The firm has noted, however, in the past several years an increasing resistance on the part of major stores to take on new lines of products. This resistance is felt most strongly by the medium-sized firms, such as Carter, since they cannot back up their new product introductions with the advertising engaged in by larger firms, such as Revlon. In addition, the large stores know that whenever a medium-sized firm introduces a new product without the aid of large advertising expenditures, if it looks promising, the larger firm will soon copy the product and insert it into their product mix. For example, in the past year a modest-sized cosmetic firm, Michele, introduced pale lipsticks with some success. Within a short period of time, however, one of the large firms picked up the idea and advertised it heavily, and to the public it appeared to be a new idea.

To offset these problems, the marketing department was charged with the task of not only coming up with new product ideas, but of also developing a new approach that would blunt the power of the large firms and lessen the resistance of the department stores to new products.

To help guide the direction of the new products, a group of planners within the firm came up with several ideas that could guide the product development people in creating new products:

Characteristics
of the
New Line

1. Age and income factors will not be exploited, but rather the outlook of the potential consumer. The line will not be directed to either the older woman or the teenager, but to "everyone who wants to be more attractive."

2. No giveaways will be offered. Although this has been a common practice in the industry for many years, it has been found that neither the

stores nor the customers really like the idea. The plan will be to produce only large sizes with accompanying complementary small purse sizes.

3. Disposables will be an important part of the product line; that is, makeup will be packaged in tubes or envelopes which will be used once and then thrown away.

4. There will be an interchangeability between men's and women's products.

5. Films will be developed to be used at the point of sale to provide instruction on the use of the products.

6. The mail-order club will be used. Consumers will join the club at a cost of $25 a year. This will enable each member to purchase $25 of merchandise and also receive samples of new products as they appear.

1. Comment on the program as outlined by the planners.

The Palmer Suit Company has been a major manufacturer of men's suits for 40 years. Their major success has been in the manufacturing of lightweight summer suits. As a matter of fact, the name "Palmer" has become almost synonymous with summer wear. In the past 5 years the firm has developed a line of sportswear to take advantage of this image. The sportswear is sold in the same shops with the regular line of men's suits.

In recent years the company has become aware of a weakness in their product line. They have noted, for instance, that the Palmer Suit Company has a product distribution pattern of 60 percent summer wear and 40 percent winter wear. Most firms in the industry have the opposite ratio.

Although at first glance this may be an advantage, the firm has noted several severe drawbacks. The first is that the summer suit usually sells for less than the winter garment. Thus the company is likely to end up getting less dollars from its suit customers than its competitors. Second, there is a distinct turn in the direction away from summer suits. That is, more buyers are leaning toward substituting sport coat and slacks combinations in preference to a suit. Third, the trend in winter suits has been toward using synthetic and lighter fabrics. As a result, the firm has learned from a research study that many customers are using their winter suits during the summer season.

In view of these problems, the firm's president, Carl Benson, called a meeting of his marketing staff to discuss the two major thoughts he had. The first was, should the company place more emphasis on the sale of the winter suits? The second was, if not, what else can the firm do to overcome this problem?

12

Palmer Suit Company

1. How would you answer these questions?

13

The Jackson Company

The Jackson Company is one of New York's largest importers of men's gloves. In recent weeks it was faced with a competitive problem. An important customer wanted to place a sizable order but clearly indicated they expected a particularly low price. Otherwise, they would place their order with a domestic source. They also pointed out that vinyl gloves were available from domestic sources at $16.50 a dozen.

In considering the pricing of its product the Jackson Company first determines its landed cost, that is, the cost of purchasing the goods from a foreign resource and the actual transportation costs involved in delivering the goods to the firm's warehouse.

To determine this landed cost, the firm has to make the following calculation:

Step 1. The importer is provided with an F.O.B. country of origin price from the manufacturer. $10.00/dozen

Step 2. On merchandise being imported, the U.S. government determines the duty for goods coming into the country. In the case of a vinyl glove it is 15 percent of the F.O.B. cost.   1.50

Step 3. Freight cost is determined by the cost of footage a particular carton has; for example, if it costs $40 for 40 cubic feet and the carton holds 5 dozen and it is 5 cubic feet, the freight rate is $1 per dozen.

$$\frac{\$40}{40 \text{ ft}} = \$1/\text{ft}, \qquad \frac{5 \text{ dozen}}{5 \text{ ft}} = 1 \text{ dozen/ft}$$

$$\$1 \times 1 \text{ dozen} = \$1.00 \qquad\qquad 1.00$$

Step 4. Cartage is the cost of transferring the carton from the pier to the warehouse; usually it is an average cost. If 1 carton costs $0.60 and there is a 5-dozen pack,

$$\frac{0.60}{5 \text{ dozen}} = \$0.12/\text{dozen} \qquad\qquad 0.12$$

Step 5. Insurance is placed on all merchandise, and it is usually 1 percent of the F.O.B. cost.   0.10

Step 6. The total of steps 1 to 5 determines the landed cost. $12.72/dozen

---

It is Jackson's policy to add a 20 percent markup to the "landed cost" of an item to determine its selling price per dozen to the retailer. In this case the price to the retailer would amount to $15.25 per dozen.

It is the firm's feeling that the retailer can sell these gloves at $2.50 each or $30 per dozen.

1. Does this approach seem reasonable?

2. What comments do you think the Jackson Company can make regarding the competition of the domestic glove company?

During a recent season, Shalimar Vanity Gloves offered their department store customers the following terms on purchases of imported gloves:

Shalimar Glove Offering for 1971

While the accompanying price list is self-explanatory, the following factors should be included in your consideration of our offering.

1. *Prices:* Prices are calculated on the lowest possible first cost, plus a minimum profit after duty and expenses are paid. Please note that all prices include 6/10 EOM terms.

2. *Commitment Price:* This price holds for all orders placed, regardless of delivery date. Styles, colors, and sizes must be specified, in addition to definite delivery dates. However, you may stagger your deliveries so that you bring in your initial Fall inventory in August, and then bring in additional quantities for October, November, and December.

3. *Backup Price:* We will back you up for a dollar value equal to your total initial orders. In other words, should your initial orders add up to $5,000, you may use an additional $5,000 worth of goods at the backup price. The fill-in can consist of any styles, sizes, or colors which are designated on the price lists. This privilege is yours until December 1, 1971. Should you need goods over and above the 100 percent backup, our regular list prices will prevail (and these are always lower than our competitors'). Incidentally, you have no obligation as to the backup quantities; this is our risk entirely.

4. *Markup:* Please note our suggested retail prices, which are very realistic and which permit you to go after additional business aggressively. At these suggested retail prices we have indicated the markup which can be obtained at both the commitment and backup costs. The average markup is obtained by assuming that you will reorder a quantity in a style equal to your initial orders. Obviously, the greater the percentage of your requirements that you commit for, the higher your markup.

5. *Quality:* Quality is guaranteed to be as per sample. We will further guarantee gloves after you have them in your stock to the extent that we will exchange gloves which have manufacturing defects. Worn gloves returned by customers will be credited at 50 percent of the commitment prices. All gloves are fully P.K. sewn, with both Bolton thumbs and quirks, and will be made from first-quality skins with first-quality workmanship.

6. *Packaging:* Should you want any gloves packaged or labelled specially for your store, we will be happy to do this on your commitment quantities, provided that labels or other packaging materials are provided by your store. We cannot provide this service on backup quantities, and these gloves will be packed neutrally.

7. *Colors:* The price lists indicate the colors that we are running for the year, but you may order any special colors that you wish on your initial orders. However, our backup stock will consist only of those colors designated on the price lists.

8. *Time Limit:*
a) Spring 1971: Stores wishing to start this program for the Spring season must have their orders in by December 1, 1970, for delivery starting February 1, 1971. Backup stock prices will be available until April 1, 1971.
b) Fall 1971: Stores adopting the program for Fall 1971 must submit their commitment orders by March 15, 1971, for deliveries starting July 1971. Backup prices will be in effect until December 1, 1971.

We feel that the proposed program has much to offer you, that the advantages are many. For example,

1. Since you will receive your deliveries at the time *you* desire, your rate of turnover must improve.

2. Our backup policy permits you to fill in missing styles, sizes, and colors at any time, and this helps maintain your stock in a saleable condition.

3. Minimization of problems inherent in importing: no losses due to pilferage or lost shipments, since we would be able to replace lost goods. Also, there is the assurance of getting correct colors and sizes. The only charges that should be charged to you by the store should be the freight charges from New York, if you are outside the metropolitan area.

4. Because you are buying from a domestic source, you will be able to get accurate information more quickly, and should it be necessary, there will be someone to complain to about adjustments.

5. Improved profits are possible because the store does not pay for any merchandise until after the goods have been received and approved. In addition, our prices include a 6 percent discount.

6. *Promotions:* The proposed program allows you to have planned promotions at your discretion. You will not have to buy job lots, or odd sizes and colors, which create markdown problems. Our prices permit you to select any items in the program, and for a short period of time during a season, offer them to your customers at 20 to 25 percent below the regular price, and still maintain an average markup on the sale goods of better than 45 percent. After the sale there will be no odds and ends, and any goods left can be marked up to the regular price for the same goods already in your inventory.

1. What is the strategy of the glove company as indicated by the offering?
2. What should the retail buyer concern himself with in evaluating this offer?

15

Magnavox Company II

In 1970 the Magnavox Company decided to drop their present advertising agency and do their own advertising. By having their own in-house agency, the firm estimated that they could operate at about half the 15 percent commission presently paid to their outside agency. Based on commissionable billings of $4 million, the firm estimated they would save $300,000.

In reviewing the operation 1 year later, the firm concluded that from the point of view of the savings the changeover was a complete success. In reality the firm saved $275,000 and gained a year of experience. Not everyone was happy, however. It was the opinion of the marketing manager for their electronic products that the executives in the firm were spending too much time on the planning of advertising, something that was handled before by their outside agency. He observed that since this time was not charged into the cost of advertising, it was difficult to measure. He believed, however, that since it was executive time, it could possibly wipe out the savings.

More importantly, however, it was his view that the quality of the advertising had declined. The quality he noted was not in the graphics but mainly in the lack of ideas that used to make Magnavox's advertising the most admired in the industry.

1. Do you believe Magnavox should return to its previous policy?

16

Arlow
Cosmetic
Company

The Arlow Cosmetic Company is one of the largest manufacturers of ladies cosmetics sold through retail department stores. In recent years the firm has developed a new product that seems to have a decided edge on its competitors. The product is an eye makeup that on the surface seems to be similar to several competitive products. It is sold with a brush at competitive prices. However, it differs from competitive products because of its ingredients.

Most eye makeup products contain an ingredient that is found in turpentine. This product tends to burn the eyelid and cause tearing, particularly when the user either cries or splashes water on the makeup. The Arlow laboratories came up with an ingredient that was an excellent substitute for this turpentine-based product, but would not cause tearing. With this distinct advantage the marketing manager of Arlow suggested that the Arlow ads should point out this clear difference to the buying public and hence gain a decided edge on their competitors. He felt that this should be done immediately.

The sales promotion manager of Arlow received the suggestion and arranged a meeting with the marketing manager. At the meeting he made several points for the manager's consideration. His main point was that the Arlow Cosmetic Company in its ads and sales promotion work never placed a great emphasis on the technicalities of the product. Their approach was emotional in that it appealed to a woman's desire to be loved and to please her loved ones. In fact, many of the appeals, particularly at Christmas time and other gift-giving holidays, were aimed at males who were major buyers of gifts for women. He noted their most recent campaign emphasized the youthful fragrances and alluring names that were part of the firm's line of products. In essence, he noted that the appeal of their products was on a purely emotional level.

As a corollary of this thought, he was convinced that any attempt to point out a distinct product difference was doomed to failure. Furthermore, he held the strong belief that most cosmetic products were in reality the same and the only differences were in their approach to meeting the emotional needs of the buyer.

1. Do you agree?
2. Do cosmetics differ completely in their approach to promotion from most other products that you know?

The Channing Company is a large producer of stationery items sold to department and stationery stores. In recent years the firm has developed a best-selling line of ball-point pens priced from $2.95 up. Although the firm sells other stationery items, the pens have been a major profit item for two reasons:

1. The sales of the pen are enhanced by a point-of-purchase display stand exclusively designed for the firm. The impact of the display is enhanced by the fact that it shows the pens in four different shapes, eight different price lines, and seven different colors on the side facing the customer, while the back of the display carries a 2-week supply of pens. Although the major competitive pens are advertised heavily on television, the Channing pens are not. It is management's view that the display makes advertising unnecessary.

2. By relying on displays, the firm found it necessary to rely on their salesmen to make sure the displays were adequately stocked. This was accomplished at little additional cost, since the salesmen called on the stores to sell other items in the line. It was important in the firm's view that the display stock be checked regularly, since the wide assortment of pens offered could develop serious stockouts.

In recent weeks the firm sent a group of young executives in training to check around and see the stock condition of the pen displays. The report they turned in was startling to management. It indicated that all displays were missing at least five of the major price lines. This was particularly crucial because these lines represented most of the best-selling low-priced pens. In some cases the executives learned that over 50 percent of the pens were out of stock.

It was management's view that the stockout condition was due to two main factors: (1) the general disinterest on the part of salespeople in filling in stocks as needed, and (2) the evident failure of Channing Company salesmen to train and urge store salespeople to maintain stocks by filling in the displays as needed and to particularly alert the buyer as to the need to reorder.

The first factor the firm felt was beyond their means to remedy. On the other hand, the second factor seemed to indicate a failure on the part of the Channing sales force.

Channing salesmen were, in the opinion of the firm, well paid. All salesmen were assigned territories and paid a 5 percent commission on all sales. This commission was received even when the home office received the order. In the past year the average salesman earned a commission of slightly over $17,000. When working, all traveling expenses were paid for by the firm. It was well recognized in the industry that Channing had a superior sales force. Although the earnings of Channing salesmen were about on a par with the rest of the industry, their superiority seemed to be in the areas of training and recruitment.

Channing was one of the few companies in the industry that attracted college graduates as sales trainees on a regular basis. The firm felt that this came about because the firm promoted from within and that the training program of the firm appealed to college students. Promotion from within had been a long-standing policy of the firm, and it was not unusual for a recruiter for Channing to point out on the company organization chart that the top 25 executives were all formerly salesmen and stock helpers.

1. What should Channing do?

The Donald Fraser Handbag Company has been in business for 10 years. During the past 5 years the firm has developed a substantial business selling its product to major chains and department stores. Although the business started by selling to small specialty stores, the firm found that its New York City location afforded it an opportunity to visit the large buying organizations of the chains and department stores regularly and thus develop opportunities with these firms.

By 1972 the firm noted that about 80 percent of their business came from 10 large firms. Harold Gorning, the president of the firm, was presented with a dilemma at his weekly meeting held with the top managers of his firm. The sales manager Cal Hubbard pointed out that the firm was concentrating too much of its efforts on the large firms and not enough on the thousands of small store owners throughout the country. He felt that by expanding the firm's sales force he could gain greater coverage of this market and surely increase sales.

Irvin Unger, the controller, took a different position. He suggested that the firm not only increase its sales to the large operators, but more importantly drop most of the small accounts. To support this view, he noted that it costs the firm practically the same to deliver a large order as a small order. In addition, small orders require a great deal of credit checking, whereas a large firm does not require any. More importantly, he noted that a recent analysis he made of returns seemed to indicate that most returns came from the small accounts. He reasoned that large firms did not find it profitable to return a few small handbags.

1. Who do you agree with? Why?
2. What are some of the drawbacks to Mr. Unger's position?

18

Donald
Fraser
Handbag
Company

The Hardware Corporation has been in the business of producing and selling housewares and gift items to wholesalers for many years. The firm maintains a sales force in the New England area that calls on wholesalers who sell mainly to small housewares stores and the more specialized gift stores.

The company produces some of its housewares items in a factory it maintains in Lowell, Massachusetts; however, all gift items are imported from Italy, France, and in some cases the Orient. About 40 percent of the housewares are bought from other companies.

19

Hardware
Corporation

Recently the firm was approached by a major discount chain concerning the possibility of getting the Hardware Corporation to operate a lease department in the firm's 18 stores located in New England. This would be a new venture for the Hardware Corporation and would propel them into the retail field for the first time.

To convince the Hardware Corporation of the potential profits involved in running a lease department in their discount stores, the discount chain presented the following analysis of the profits they could expect from a typical 4,000-square-foot department.

Department Operating Expenses

Expenses in a typical lease department include rental, advertising charges, payroll, allowances for markdowns and shortages, and sundry charges. The latter consists of telephone charges, depreciation on fixtures, wrapping, taxes (local), union costs, and in some departments a charge for using stockrooms. A typical profit and loss statement for a 4,000-square-foot department with a sales volume of $350,000 could look like this:

Net sales	$350,000	100%
Gross margin	126,000	36
Expenses		
Payroll	$31,500	9
Rent	35,000	10
Shortages and markdowns	17,500	5
Sundries	10,500	3
Total expenses	94,500	27
Before tax profit	$ 31,500	9

Obviously, a great deal of variance can occur depending upon the sales volume of the department. However, some expenses can be adjusted more easily to the realities of the department's sales volume than others.

Payroll costs are difficult to reduce since most discount stores are open six nights a week. In addition, Boston stores must remain open on Sunday. Rental costs are fixed in most outlets. A typical rental contract requires a 9 percent (7 + 2) or 10 percent (8 + 2) payment by the lessee. Typically, the addition of the 2 percent represents a pooled payment for cooperative advertising on the part of the lease operators. Here again much of the cost is fixed. Although sundry expenses do fluctuate somewhat, as the smallest part of the expenses of the department any changes in these amounts have only a slight impact on the profitability of the department.

Shortages And Markdowns

The last expense figure represents a key item in the operation of most stores. It is particularly important in discount stores because of three factors:

1. The lack of inventory control results in high pilferage rates.
2. The lack of controls mean that shortages and markdowns can only be estimated.

3. The lack of control means that there is a long delay in thwarting professional theft.

Markdowns and shortages are estimated by the organization at 5 percent. There is little basis for this figure except to note that the amount of the shortage is considered to be average for the industry.

The gross margin in the department indicates that it is maintained at 36 percent during the year. Gross margin, of course, is a direct function of the department's merchandise mix. Housewares usually carry a gross margin of 33 percent. To offset this lower-than-average markup the firm receives an average gross margin of 42 percent on all gifts sold in the department.

Gross Margin

1. Should the Hardware Corporation accept the offer?

W. K. Hoffman, Inc., is located in Baltimore, Maryland. The firm for many years was one of the major paper manufacturers in the United States. In recent years the firm ran into a severe decline in earnings and it was agreed that the company survival depended on the firm's ability to diversify into other industries.

To accomplish this the firm set up a purchasing and planning division, whose sole purpose was to identify industries that have a promising growth record and ultimately to locate firms that might be for sale in these industries.

Over the past 5 years the company has purchased several firms in the electronic industry, two manufacturers of boats, and one large chemical company. In the past 2 years the firm has moved into the retailing field and purchased a major sporting goods chain and two women's apparel chains in two separate regions.

It was the view of the planning people that retailing offered the firm an opportunity to add stability to the earnings of the main company. In addition, the retailing fields that were selected seemed to have a better-than-average growth record.

In the past week the firm was approached by the American Shoe outlets, offering to sell their 115 unit chain. American Shoe sells medium-priced women's shoes in most major cities east of the Mississippi River. Typically, the store, located in the downtown area of a large city, contains about 10,000 square feet of selling space, and appeals to the lower middle class and lower income shopper. The typical store attains a sales volume of $300,000 and requires a manager and assistant manager to operate. A typical unit contains four full-time salespeople and uses part timers during the busy seasons.

To service its stores, the firm maintains a modest-sized buying staff in New York City. In addition, one of the buyers spends several months of the year combing European markets for suitable imports. To coordinate the receiving

20

American Shoe

and distribution of the shoes to each store, the firm maintains a warehouse and computer facility to help ease the flow of thousands of shoes to the various stores.

Over the past 5 years the sales of American Shoe have increased at a modest rate. The profits, however, have managed to stay on an even level. Profits in the past 5 years have averaged about 6 percent of sales.

The planning and purchasing group in W. K. Hoffman visited several of the American Shoe outlets and were particularly interested in the centralized warehouse operation. In general they felt that American Shoe had a good reputation among consumers, but were at a loss to explain the lack of growth in terms of sales and profits over the past 5 years. They did note that several other publicly held national shoe chains had done relatively well over this same period.

In order to get an outside view of the situation, the firm hired E. Thomas Killoran, a consultant from Stamford, Connecticut. Mr. Killoran had extensive consulting experience with several large chains and was nationally recognized as a retailing expert. Killoran studied the situation for several days and reported back to the committee.

Although he felt that the American Shoe outlets were well run and constituted an efficient organization, he did not recommend that W. K. Hoffman enter into a purchase agreement. It was his view that the reason the company had seemed to have reached a profit plateau was due to the fact that most of their outlets were situated in the downtown areas rather than the superior locations of suburban business districts or shopping centers. He calculated that almost 100 of the 115 outlets were in the downtown areas. In his view the firm was entering a period that would require several millions of dollars of investment in order to move outlets into these new areas. Since most of the suburban shopping centers have been established, it was his view that American Shoe will be forced to pay a premium price for this movement. Had they made this move years before, the price would have been much less. Therefore, he suggested that it would be several years before American Shoe would become profitable.

1. Do you agree with consultant Killoran?

Index

413